REPUBLIC

Plato

Introduction and Notes by
Elizabeth Watson Scharffenberger
Translated by Benjamin Jowett

B
RNES
OBLE
SSICS

urroughs Adam Smith John Adams Voltaire Booker T. Washington Sinclair Lewis L. Frank Baum Jane Austen H. G. Wells Jules Verne James Joyce Wilhelr

s More Thomas Hardy Henry James Sir Arthur Conan Doyle Theodore Dreiser ℬ Owen Wister Virgil Joseph Conrad Karl Marx Anne Brontë Dante A

g Washington Irving W. Somerset Maugham T. S. Eliot Thomas Jefferson O. Henry Nikolai Gogol Emily Brontë Barnes & Noble Classics Sophocles Freder

Weldon Johnson Bram Stoker Miguel de Cervantes Pierre Choderlos de Laclos Henry David Thoreau Giovanni Boccaccio John Bunyan Elizabeth Gaskell Gu

Leroux Emily Dickinson Robert Louis Stevenson ℬ Niccolò Machiavelli Henrik Ibsen Hermann Hesse Geoffrey Chaucer Saint Augustine Sarah Orne

acob Grimm Richard Henry Dana Friedrich Nietzsche Wilkie Collins Barnes & Noble Classics Alexander Hamilton Louisa May Alcott James Fenimore Co

Guy de Maupassant Rafael Sabatini Edith Wharton Edith Nesbit Sir Walter Scott Hans Christian Andersen Ivan Turgenev Edgar Allan Poe ℬ Aesop

n Harriet Jacobs Euripides Barnes & Noble Classics Benjamin Franklin Marcel Proust Sigmund Freud Aristotle William Makepeace Thackeray Booth Tarkin

e Victor Hugo Thomas Bulfinch H. Rider Haggard George Bernard Shaw Sojourner Truth ℬ Henry Fielding William James John Jay Honoré de Balz

Barnes & Noble Classics Kenneth Grahame Ford Madox Ford Anthony Trollope Edmond Rostand George Eliot Ralph Waldo Emerson A. E. W. Mason

s & Noble Classics Walt Whitman F. Scott Fitzgerald Herodotus Barnes & Noble Classics Plato Mark Twain William Dean Howells Charles Dickens Cha

Milton Frances Hodgson Burnett Baroness Orczy ℬ Robert Frost Homer Kate Chopin Émile Zola Fyodor Dostoevsky Nathaniel Hawthorne Daniel De

Sinclair Charlotte Brontë Joshua Slocum Stephen Crane W. E. B. Du Bois Willa Cather Barnes & Noble Classics Oscar Wilde Sun Tzu Stendhal ℬ

nce Thomas Paine Thucydides Franz Kafka Virginia Woolf J. M. Barrie Leo Tolstoy Lao Tzu Harriet Beecher Stowe Anton Chekhov Ovid Edgar Rice Burro

John Adams Voltaire Booker T. Washington Sinclair Lewis L. Frank Baum Barnes & Noble Classics Jane Austen H. G. Wells Jules Verne James Joyce Wil

s More Thomas Hardy Henry James Sir Arthur Conan Doyle Theodore Dreiser Owen Wister ℬ Virgil Joseph Conrad Karl Marx Anne Brontë Dante A

g Washington Irving W. Somerset Maugham T. S. Eliot Thomas Jefferson O. Henry Nikolai Gogol Barnes & Noble Classics Emily Brontë Sophocles Frede

Weldon Johnson Bram Stoker Miguel de Cervantes Pierre Choderlos de Laclos Henry David Thoreau Giovanni Boccaccio John Bunyan Elizabeth Gaskell G

n Leroux Emily Dickinson Robert Louis Stevenson Niccolò Machiavelli Barnes & Noble Classics Henrik Ibsen Hermann Hesse Barnes & Noble Classics G

Saint Augustine Sarah Orne Jewett Jonathan Swift Jacob Grimm Richard Henry Dana Friedrich Nietzsche Wilkie Collins Alexander Hamilton Louisa May

ore Cooper E. M. Forster Guy de Maupassant Rafael Sabatini Edith Wharton ℬ Edith Nesbit Sir Walter Scott Barnes & Noble Classics Hans Christ

Turgenev Edgar Allan Poe Aesop James Madison Harriet Jacobs Euripides Benjamin Franklin Marcel Proust Sigmund Freud Aristotle William Makepeace Tha

agton Herman Melville Victor Hugo Thomas Bulfinch H. Rider Haggard George Bernard Shaw Sojourner Truth Henry Fielding Barnes & Noble Classics V

ay Honoré de Balzac Alexandre Dumas Kenneth Grahame Ford Madox Ford Anthony Trollope Edmond Rostand George Eliot ℬ Ralph Waldo Emers

n Lewis Carroll Barnes & Noble Classics Walt Whitman F. Scott Fitzgerald Herodotus Plato Mark Twain William Dean Howells Barnes & Noble Classic

ns Charles Darwin John Milton Frances Hodgson Burnett Baroness Orczy Robert Frost Homer Kate Chopin Émile Zola Fyodor Dostoevsky Nathaniel Hawt

Classics Daniel Defoe Jack London Upton Sinclair Charlotte Brontë Joshua Slocum Stephen Crane W. E. B. Du Bois Willa Cather Oscar Wilde Sun Tzu

awrence Thomas Paine Thucydides Franz Kafka Virginia Woolf J. M. Barrie Leo Tolstoy Lao Tzu Harriet Beecher Stowe Anton Chekhov Ovid ℬ Edga

Smith John Adams Voltaire Booker T. Washington Barnes & Noble Classics Sinclair Lewis L. Frank Baum Jane Austen H. G. Wells Barnes & Noble Clas

Joyce Wilhelm Grimm Thomas More Thomas Hardy Henry James Sir Arthur Conan Doyle Theodore Dreiser Owen Wister Virgil Joseph Conrad Karl Marx

Alighieri Rudyard Kipling Washington Irving W. Somerset Maugham T. S. Eliot Thomas Jefferson O. Henry Nikolai Gogol Emily Brontë Sophocles Frederi

Weldon Johnson Bram Barnes & Noble Classics Stoker Miguel de Cervantes Pierre Choderlos de Laclos Henry David Thoreau Giovanni Boccaccio John B

ll Gustave Flaubert Gaston Leroux Emily Dickinson Robert Louis Stevenson Niccolò Machiavelli Henrik Ibsen ℬ Hermann Hesse Geoffrey Chaucer S

Orne Jewett Jonathan Swift Jacob Grimm Richard Henry Dana Friedrich Nietzsche Wilkie Collins Alexander Hamilton Louisa May Alcott James Fenimore

r Guy de Maupassant Rafael Sabatini Edith Wharton Edith Nesbit Sir Walter Scott Barnes & Noble Classics Hans Christian Andersen Ivan Turgenev Edg

FROM THE PAGES OF *REPUBLIC*

. . . but as concerning justice, what is it?—to speak the truth and pay your debts—no more than this? And even to this are there not exceptions? (1.331c)

Is the attempt to determine the way of man's life so small a matter in your eyes—to determine how life may be passed by each one of us to the greatest advantage? (1.344d)

For my own part I openly declare that I am not convinced, and that I do not believe injustice to be more gainful than justice, even if uncontrolled and allowed to have free play. (1.345a)

I propose therefore that we inquire into the nature of justice and injustice, first as they appear in the State, and secondly in the individual, proceeding from the greater to the lesser and comparing them. (2.368e–369a)

. . . I am myself reminded that we are not all alike; there are diversities of nature among us which are adapted to different occupations. (2.370a–b)

Then it will be our duty to select, if we can, natures which are fitted for the task of guarding the city? (2.374e)

But in reality justice was such as we were describing, being concerned, however, not with the outward man, but with the inward, which is the true self and concernment of man: for the just man does not permit the several elements within him to interfere with one another, or any of them to do the work of the others—he sets in order his own inner life, and is his own master and his own law, and at peace within himself . . . (4.443c–d)

"Until philosophers are kings, or the kings and princes of this world have the spirit and power of philosophy, and political greatness and wisdom meet in one, and those commoner natures who pursue either to the exclusion of the other are compelled to stand aside, cities will never have rest from their evils—no, nor the human race, as I believe—and then only will this our State have a possibility of life and behold the light of day." (5.473d–e)

. . . for you have often been told that the idea of good is the highest knowledge, and that all other things become useful and advantageous only by their use of this. (6.505a)

—You have shown me a strange image, and they are strange prisoners.—Like ourselves, I replied; and they see only their own shadows, or the shadows of one another, which the fire throws on the opposite wall of the cave. (7.515a)

He who is the real tyrant, whatever men may think, is the real slave, and is obliged to practise the greatest adulation and servility, and to be the flatterer of the vilest of mankind. He has desires which he is utterly unable to satisfy, and has more wants than anyone, and is truly poor, if you know how to inspect the whole soul of him: all his life long he is beset with fear and is full of convulsions and distractions, even as the State he resembles: and surely the resemblance holds . . . (9.579d–e)

These, then, are the prizes and rewards and gifts which are bestowed upon the just by gods and men in this present life, in addition to the other good things which justice of herself provides . . . And yet, I said, all these are as nothing either in number or greatness in comparison with those other recompenses which await both just and unjust after death. (10.613e–614a)

PLATO

REPUBLIC

*With an Introduction and Notes
by Elizabeth Watson Scharffenberger*

George Stade

Consulting Editorial Director

ℬ

BARNES & NOBLE CLASSICS

NEW YORK

ℬ
BARNES & NOBLE CLASSICS
NEW YORK

Published by Barnes & Noble Books
122 Fifth Avenue
New York, NY 10011

www.barnesandnoble.com/classics

Plato is generally thought to have composed *Republic* sometime
during the 380s to the 350s B.C.E.
Benjamin Jowett's translation first appeared in 1871.

Published in 2004 by Barnes & Noble Classics with new Introduction,
Notes, Biography, Chronology, Appendix, Inspired By, Comments & Questions,
and For Further Reading.

Republic
ISBN 1-59308-097-2
LC Control Number 2003116604

Produced and published in conjunction with:
Fine Creative Media, Inc.
322 Eighth Avenue
New York, NY 10001
Michael J. Fine, President & Publisher

Printed in the United States of America
QM
5 7 9 10 8 6

PLATO

Plato was born into a wealthy, aristocratic Athenian family in 428 or 427 B.C.E., and he lived until 348 or 347. He had kinship ties on both sides of his family with many prominent men in Athens. His father, Ariston, died when he was a child, and his mother, Perictione, was subsequently married to Pyrilampes. Plato was raised in Pyrilampes' household along with his older brothers (Glaucon and Adeimantus), a stepbrother (Demos), and a half-brother (Antiphon). As young men, Plato and his brothers were close to Socrates.

Plato's familial connections and wealth would have made it easy for him to embark on a political career in Athens. But he did not become politically active, perhaps because he became disillusioned with politics after witnessing, first, the brutal oligarchic regime of the Thirty Tyrants, who seized control of Athens at the end of the Peloponnesian War in 404 B.C.E., and then the execution of Socrates, who was condemned to die in 399 under the restored democratic government for "not recognizing the gods recognized by the city and corrupting the youth."

Plato traveled in the years after Socrates' death, and he almost certainly spent time in Megara (near Corinth) and Syracuse (on Sicily). He became close friends with Dion, a kinsman of the tyrant of Syracuse, Dionysius I. Plato probably traveled to Syracuse three times during the period from the early 380s to the late 360s. He and Dion evidently planned to educate the tyrant's son, Dionysius II, in the hopes that, upon succeeding his father, he would put into practice the political ideals they cherished. But these hopes were never fulfilled. Upon taking power in the early 360s, Dionysius II broke with both his kinsman and his tutor.

In the early 380s, Plato began teaching what he called "philosophy" at a place near the grove of the hero Academus on the outskirts of Athens. The school came to be called the "Academy" because of its location, and Plato remained at its head until his death, when his nephew Speusippus took over its administration. After Plato's death, the Academy continued to be an important center of research and study for many centuries, attracting students from all over the Mediterranean world.

Plato probably started to compose dialogues before he established the Academy. All but a few of his dialogues feature Socrates as the main interlocutor, and most are peopled with figures who would have been well known, especially in Athens' elite circles, during the fifth century. A large body of writing attributed to Plato survives from antiquity, including *Apology* (a recreation of Socrates' defense speech), numerous dialogues, and a series of letters. Most of these works are considered to be truly by Plato, although the authenticity of some texts (including some of the letters and a handful of dialogues) has been doubted at various points in the last 2,400 years.

TABLE OF CONTENTS

THE WORLD OF PLATO
AND *REPUBLIC*

508 B.C.E.
Cleisthenes, son of Megacles, introduced sweeping political reforms to the Athenian constitution, marking the beginning of democratic government in Athens.

490
At the battle of Marathon (26.3 miles from Athens in Attica), Greek land forces, under the command of the Athenian Miltiades, son of Cimon, defeated an invading army of Persians. Most of the Greek troops who fought at Marathon came from Athens.

480
At the battle of Thermopylae (a mountain pass in northeastern Greece), Persian land forces fought against elite Spartan soldiers under the command of Leonidas, one of the Spartan kings. The entire Spartan force was killed in the battle.

480
At the battle of Salamis (an island near the port city Piraeus in Attica), Greek naval forces, under the leadership of the Athenian Themistocles, son of Neocles, defeated the Persian navy.

479
In the battle of Plataea (in Boeotia), Greek land forces decisively defeated the Persian army, which subsequently withdrew from Greece. Under the leadership of the Spartans and then the Athenians, city-states in Greece banded together in the fight to free Hellenic city-states on the coast of Asia Minor from Persian dominion. This alliance was soon called the Delian League, because its treasury was kept on the sacred island of Delos; it eventually came under the total control of the Athenians.

c.469
Socrates, son of Sophroniscus, was born.

462
Ephialtes, son of Sophronides, and Pericles, son of Xanthippus, introduced reforms to the democratic constitution, which expanded the franchise of Athenian citizens and provided more opportunities for political involvement to greater numbers of men, regardless of economic class.

458   Aeschylus of Eleusis (in Attica) produced his *Oresteia*
       tetralogy (the tragedies *Agamemnon, Libation Bearers*,
       and *Eumenides*, and the satyr-drama *Proteus*) in the annual
       theatrical competition held at the Greater Dionysia festival
       in the Theater of Dionysus on the southern slope of the
       Athenian Acropolis.

454   The treasury of the Delian League was transferred from
       the island of Delos to Athens. Under the leadership of
       Pericles, funds from the treasury were used to finance the
       construction of buildings on the Acropolis, including the
       Parthenon, which had been destroyed by the Persian inva-
       sion of 480.

450s– The relationships between Athens and other prominent
440s   city-states (notably Sparta, Corinth, and Thebes) dete-
       riorated as Athens expanded its influence throughout the
       Aegean area.

c.450 The astronomer and natural scientist Anaxagoras (from
       Clazomenae), who was closely associated with Pericles, is
       said to be prosecuted on the charge of impiety. Sources
       reporting this event claim that Anaxagoras fled Athens
       with Pericles's assistance and went to Lampsacus (on the
       eastern entrance to the Hellespont).

c.432 Protagoras of Abdera (in Thrace), a "sophist" and profes-
       sional teacher of rhetoric, visited Athens.

431   Full-scale hostilities broke out between the Pelopon-
       nesian alliance, led by Sparta, and Athens and its allies,
       marking the beginning of the Peloponnesian War. Euripi-
       des, son of Mnesarchides (or Mnesarchos), produced
       Medea in a tetralogy with two other tragedies (*Philoctetes*
       and *Dictys*) and a satyr-drama (*Theristai*) at the Greater
       Dionysia festival in Athens.

c.429? Sophocles, son of Sophilus, produced *Oedipus Tyrannus*
       (*Oedipus the King*) in a tragic tetralogy at the Greater
       Dionysia festival in Athens.

429   Pericles dies during the plague that falls upon Athens in
       the first years of the Peloponnesian War. Cleon, son of
       Cleaenetus, became the leading politician in Athens until
       his death in battle at Amphipolis in 422.

428   Plato was born into a wealthy and influential family. His
or 427 father, Ariston, died when Plato was a boy; his mother,
        Perictione, was subsequently married to her uncle Pyril-
        ampes, who was politically prominent and closely associ-
        ated with Pericles.

427   Gorgias (from Leontini on Sicily), a professional teacher of
        rhetoric, visited Athens.

423   At the Greater Dionysia festival, Aristophanes, son of
        Philippus, produced his comedy *Clouds*, in which Socrates
        is portrayed as a professional teacher of rhetoric and natu-
        ral science who runs a "Think Factory." The comedy was
        awarded third prize (out of three).

415–   Under the leadership of Alcibiades, son of Clinias and
413   former ward of Pericles, Athens sent an armada to attack
        the city of Syracuse on Sicily. After Alcibiades' defection to
        Sparta and other major setbacks, the Athenian forces were
        defeated and the Sicilian expedition ends with many lives
        lost and almost all ships in the armada destroyed.

411–   During an oligarchic coup in Athens, democratic political in-
410   stitutions were temporarily dissolved. Resistance by loyalists
        led to the restoration of the democratic constitution in 410.

405   The Spartans defeated the Athenian navy at Aegospotami
        off the coast of Asia Minor.

404   The Peloponnesian War ended as Athens surrendered to
        the Spartans. The Spartans imposed strict terms of surren-
        der upon the Athenians, including the destruction of the
        Long Walls connecting Athens to the port city Piraeus.
        They also fomented another oligarchic coup and installed
        in power a group of men, led by Plato's kinsman Critias,
        who came to be known as the Thirty Tyrants.

403   Democratic loyalists, who took refuge in Piraeus, defeated
        the Thirty Tyrants and their supporters, and the demo-
        cratic constitution was once again restored. To reduce lin-
        gering factional strife between loyal "democrats" and
        those who supported the second coup, a general amnesty
        was declared in 403. Only those deemed directly involved
        with the Thirty Tyrants were liable for prosecution for
        crimes against the *demos* (people).

399   Socrates, who had been closely associated with Alcibiades
        and other men known for their hostility to the democratic
        constitution, was charged with impiety and corrupting
        youth. He was convicted of both charges and ordered to
        commit suicide by drinking hemlock.

390s   Plato, along with other members of the Socratic circle (An-
        tisthenes, Phaedo, Eucleides, Aristippus, Aeschines, and
        Xenophon) began to write "Socratic dialogues." Athens
        reemerged as an important naval power in the Aegean
        area.

early   Plato traveled to Syracuse in or around 387, when he be-
380s   friended Dion, a kinsman of Dionysius I, the tyrant of Syra-
        cuse. It was probably upon his return to Athens from this
        trip that he began teaching "philosophy" near the grove of
        the hero Academus on the outskirts of Athens, in a school
        that came to be known as the Academy.

384   Aristotle, son of Nicomachus, was born at Stageira (in
        Chalcidice). He studied at the Academy from 367 until
        Plato's death.

378   In Thebes, the general Gorgidas formed an elite force of
        300 men that legendarily comprised pairs of lovers. The
        corps, known as the Sacred Band, reportedly remained un-
        defeated until the battle at Chaeronea in 338.

360s   After the death of Dionysius I of Syracuse (in 367), Plato
        is said to have made two trips to Sicily in order to facili-
        tate the restoration of Dion, who had been exiled by
        Dionysius I. He and Dion apparently hoped to exert po-
        litical influence on Dionysius II, the tyrant's son and suc-
        cessor. Plato probably visited Syracuse for the last time in
        361 or 360.

354   Dion was assassinated.

348   Death of Plato. Speusippus (the son of Plato's sister Potone)
or 347 became head of the Academy, and Aristotle left Athens,
        eventually arriving at the court of King Philip II of Mace-
        don, where he served for a few years as the tutor to Philip's
        son, Alexander.

344   Dionysius II was exiled to Corinth.

339   Speusippus died.

338   In the battle of Chaeronea (in Boeotia), the Macedonians under the leadership of Philip II defeated the combined forces of the Athenians and Thebans. The defeat brought Athens, Thebes, and other Greek city-states under the sway of Macedon.

335   Aristotle returned to Athens and founded a school near a grove outside the city that was sacred to Apollo Lyceius. The school will come to be known as the Lyceum.

323   Alexander the Great died in Babylon. Anti-Macedonian feeling ran high in Athens after Alexander's death, causing Aristotle to leave the city and take up residence in Chalcis (on Euboea). Upon his departure, his pupil Theophrastus took over leadership of the Lyceum.

322   Aristotle died in Chalcis.

INTRODUCTION

Plato's *Republic* has long been recognized as a timeless philosophical masterpiece. Its timelessness results from many factors: its artful composition, its vivid characterizations, its thematic sophistication, and—perhaps most important—the breadth of its interests. As it seeks a definition of "justice" and inquires into the relationship between "right behavior" and "happiness," the work delves into basic questions of ethics and psychology. In the course of this inquiry, it offers up a striking blueprint for an ideal city-state and thus makes a significant contribution to political philosophy. While making the case for the rule of "philosopher-kings," it presents influential arguments concerning the very nature of reality and the means by which we human beings might apprehend what is real and distinguish it from what we see and experience in the world around us; with compelling logic and arresting images, it encourages our interest in the fields of metaphysics and epistemology.

It also explores the psychological and social impact of popular forms of cultural discourse and, as part of its delineation of the ideal state, makes a strong—and controversial—case for the censorship of the arts and the tight control of entertainments. Lastly, it paints an awe-inspiring picture of what happens to the soul after the body's death.

Plato himself was well aware of the fundamental importance of the subjects in his dialogue. He has its interlocutors assert more than once that their conversation, whatever its shortcomings, deals with the most significant issues that human beings can discuss. Yet, timeless as *Republic*'s concerns are, it is nonetheless the product of a particular era and a particular place. The era is the fourth century B.C.E., and the place is the city-state (polis) of Athens, where Plato was born (most likely in 428 or 427 B.C.E.) and lived most of his life, and also where he founded his philosophical school, the Academy. To appreciate the scope and contours of the far-ranging conversation represented in *Republic*, it helps to know something about the city in which Plato lived and the cultural milieu in which he composed his dialogues.

Athens in the Fifth and Fourth Centuries B.C.E.: A Political Overview

Until 338 B.C.E. (about ten years after Plato's death), Athens was an independent city-state, as were the other major cities of Greece (or Hellas, as it was known in antiquity), such as Sparta, Thebes, Corinth, and Argos. For centuries, each community issued its own currency, used its own calendar, and developed its own system of government and social institutions. Territorial disputes and similar grievances frequently caused wars between city-states and their neighbors; the history of such wars and alliances is long and complicated. Yet, despite their differences, Greeks (Hellenes) throughout the Mediterranean were united by a common language and culture and system of religious beliefs and practices that, they felt, made them distinct from other peoples, whom they commonly called "barbarians."

Athens resembled other Greek city-states in that it had a predominantly agricultural economy. As in most communities in the ancient world, the work force in Athens and its surrounding territory (Attica) consisted largely of slaves who were either prisoners of war, captives bought from pirates, or their descendants. Political enfranchisement in Athens, as in all other Greek city-states, was limited to sons of enfranchised men. Participation in the government and legal system was completely closed to women. It was virtually impossible for foreigners to become naturalized citizens of Athens, although resident aliens, who were called *metics* and were almost always from other Greek city-states, were liable for military service and were generally expected to contribute, financially and otherwise, to the community. Women (that is, the wives, daughters, and sisters of citizens) and slaves, both male and female, lived totally under the control of the male head of the household.

Moreover, many of the public institutions that we take for granted, such as hospitals and law enforcement agencies, did not exist in the ancient world generally or in Athens particularly. The cultivation of homoerotic attachments between men (as "lovers," or *erastai*) and youths (as "beloveds," or *erômenoi*) in the upper echelons of Athenian society—an important backdrop to several Platonic dialogues (notably *Symposium* and *Phaedrus*)—further indicates the cultural differences between Athens and contemporary Western civilizations.

Athens differed from other Hellenic city-states in certain important social and political institutions. Unique policies implemented in the sixth century B.C.E. had far-reaching consequences for the development of the city's famous democratic form of government. Unlike in many Greek communities, the rules determining citizenship in Athens did not require a free-born native man to own land in order to be considered a citizen with some political rights. All citizens, no matter how modest their means, were eligible to attend meetings of the Assembly and scrutinize the performance of magistrates.

In 508 B.C.E., after a difficult period in the late sixth century when men who held power illegitimately (the "tyrant" Peisistratus and his sons Hippias and Hipparchus) controlled Athens, the democratic government was officially established. Its constitution was liberalized during the fifth century so that opportunities to participate directly in the political system were gradually made available to larger numbers of men. Citizens were still divided, as they were in the early sixth century, into four economic classes determined by the amount of property they owned, and they were also divided into ten "tribes."

Every year men from the highest economic classes were chosen as magistrates, some by lot and some by election. The ten elected magistrates (called *strategoi*, or "generals") exercised authority in military as well as civic matters and assumed the political leadership of the polis; most of Athens' famous statesmen—Pericles, Themistocles, Miltiades, Aristides, Cimon, Cleon, and Alcibiades—were *strategoi*. The Assembly retained the power to hear debates and vote on all domestic and foreign policies, and it scrutinized magistrates at the end of their terms in office. In addition, fifty men were chosen from each tribe every year by lot to form the Council of 500, the body that prepared business for the Assembly and in essence ran the government on a daily basis.

The average Athenian citizen, especially in the later years of the fifth century, could also exercise political power through the system of courts that tried cases ranging from murder to treason to private suits. These courts always had large juries (a minimum of 250 men, again chosen by lot), and all citizens were eligible for service. Jury duty became especially attractive to many poorer citizens after payment for such service was instituted. Since prominent men were often embroiled in legal disputes, sitting in the courts became an effective way for average people to influence the fortunes of the powerful.

As its democracy developed in the fifth century, Athens was also becoming powerful and cosmopolitan. Indeed, the development of its democracy was inextricably linked to the growth of its military influence in the Aegean Sea. This brought great wealth to the city and empowered its lower economic classes, since they furnished the majority of rowers and soldiers on warships.

Success in the Persian Wars (at the battle of Marathon in 490 B.C.E. and the battle of Salamis in 480) put Athens at the head of the Delian League, an alliance of Greek city-states that was formed to further weaken the influence of the Persians in the Mediterranean. The Athenians, however, gradually monopolized power in the League and used it to advance their own commercial and strategic interests. In the 460s, to protect the maritime trade routes vital to the growing city, Athens began to treat allies on the islands and coasts of the Aegean Sea as if they were subjects, not partners, and interfered in their affairs.

In 454, the League's treasury was transferred from the island of Delos to Athens, and allies were subsequently required to bring tribute directly to the city. In the 440s, the Athenians, led by Pericles, began using this treasury to finance buildings and extensive public works, including the Parthenon and other edifices on the Athenian Acropolis that are still standing today.

Other leading city-states in Greece, particularly Sparta, Corinth, and Thebes, became alarmed by the development of the Athenian "empire" in the Aegean Sea. Throughout the mid-fifth century, the Athenians clashed with those who opposed their maritime hegemony. In 431, the Spartans and their allies from the Peloponnese (the southern portion of Greece, then dominated by Sparta) declared war on Athens to end its control over the island city-states and coastal areas in northern Greece and Asia Minor. In the series of wars that came to be known as the Peloponnesian War, both sides gained and lost ground over several years, until the defeat of Athens in 404. As a consequence of its defeat by the Peloponnesian alliance, Athens permanently lost its exclusive influence over the Aegean islands. It had to contend for power with other city-states, particularly Thebes and Corinth, throughout the fourth century. Nonetheless, Athens remained the preeminent cultural center of Greece, and when Plato founded his Academy in the 380s, he was able to attract students from all over the Aegean area.

Democracy in Athens also survived the Peloponnesian War, but not without serious challenges. Most Athenians doubtless looked on the wealth and power of their city-state as great assets and saw themselves as the liberators and protectors, and not the oppressors, of their allies. They were also proud of their city's culture, especially of the freedom of speech and opportunities for political involvement that their constitution notionally afforded to every citizen. Even so, a small but significant percentage of men from Athens' wealthy aristocratic families considered themselves wrongly dispossessed of political power that, in their view, ought to have been their exclusive prerogative. They felt the democratic constitution left them vulnerable to exploitation and extortion, especially in the courts, where informers ("sycophants") seeking to get rich constantly threatened to bring them to trial. They also resented the prominence of politicians such as Cleon, who did not use the established "old boy" network of connections and appealed directly to the *demos*, or common people, for his power.

Wealthy Athenians also tended to disagree with the aggressive military policies that the democratic government pursued, especially the disastrous Sicilian expedition of 415–413 B.C.E., in which a good part of the Athenian navy was destroyed. While many disaffected aristocrats sought to withdraw as much as possible and live quiet lives of "noninvolvement" (*apragmosyne*), the conflict between oligarchic and populist ideologies caused increasing friction as the Peloponnesian War continued, and the disaster in Sicily galvanized some malcontents and set the stage for radical action.

In 411 a short-lived oligarchic coup suspended the constitution and dissolved the Council of 500 and the Assembly. Resistance by loyalists led to the relatively quick and bloodless restoration of both institutions in 410.

After the Athenians surrendered to the Peloponnesian alliance in 404, the Spartans helped the surviving leaders of the coup of 411 overthrow the democracy once again and install another oligarchic government. This new regime suspended the constitution once again, dissolved democratic political institutions, and severely limited political franchise. It also gained renown for its brutality, and, like the government that came into power in 411, lasted only a year. Many men loyal to the democratic constitution took refuge in the port city of Piraeus, which was only a few miles from Athens and a populist stronghold. After a series of battles with supporters of the coup, the loyalists restored democracy to Athens in 403.

To reduce lingering factional strife between loyal "democrats" and those who had supported the second coup, a general amnesty was declared in 403. Only those deemed directly involved with the Thirty Tyrants, as the leaders of the coup of 404 came to be called, were liable for prosecution. Tensions and suspicions remained elevated for many years afterward, however. Although there were no further coup attempts in the fourth century, Athenian democracy continued to generate and, to its credit, tolerate critics. Among these critics, Plato is often counted as the most forceful and articulate.

Religion and Religious Traditions

Athenians were fully invested in the established traditions of Hellenic culture. Religion, and therefore religious rituals and celebrations, were central to this culture. Like other Greeks, the Athenians believed in an array of divinities, from the Olympian gods and goddesses who had Zeus as their king, to the chthonic powers of the underworld, such as the Furies, to local deities, such as river gods. They also deified phenomena that we would consider abstractions, such as Justice, Persuasion, Fear, Madness, and Necessity. The sustained welfare of the community was thought to reside in divine favor, which could be withdrawn if the gods were slighted

in any way. Accordingly, every resident was expected to participate in rituals and celebrations in honor of the gods.

In addition to the festivals of individual city-states, Greeks also
participated in major biennial and quadrennial religious festivals,
such as those at Delphi (the oracular shrine of Apollo) and Olympia
(the shrine of Zeus). Even in times of war, men from all over the
Hellenic world attended these festivals and competed in their
well-known athletic contests. Mystery cults whose members worshiped particular deities—such as the cults devoted to the grain-
goddess Demeter and her daughter Persephone at Eleusis in
Attica—required their participants to undertake special rites of
initiation and keep cultic rituals secret from non-initiates.

The Greeks envisioned the principal Olympian gods and goddesses as members of an extended family who were virtually
omnipotent and, although capable of disguise, looked like human
beings and were frequently influenced by jealousy and other
strong passions. Overall, the gods were thought of as guarantors
of justice, rewarding those who uphold laws and customs and
punishing those who transgress. But they were also considered capable of adversely affecting human lives in what might strike us as
capricious, cruel, and unfair ways. This ambivalent understanding
of divine behavior is reflected in Greek poetry and literature, beginning with the Homeric epics (*Iliad* and *Odyssey*). In these,
deities interfere freely in human affairs and regularly assist their
favorite mortal men and women while wreaking havoc upon their
"enemies" and competing with their fellow deities.

Religious life was centered on the proper fulfillment of rites in
the home and in official public ceremonies. The Greeks put com-
paratively little emphasis on orthodoxy beyond the very basics of
belief, and they had no sacred scriptures equivalent to the Bible
or Qur'an. This lack of orthodoxy accounts in part for the variety
in the myths about the gods that have been handed down, often
with contradictory details. In the absence of orthodoxy, the Greeks
were generally tolerant of special religious sects and schools, such
as those of the Pythagoreans and Orphics, and sometimes of foreign religious rites, as long as these could be accommodated to existing beliefs and practices. Because of such tolerance, the poet
Xenophanes was able in the late sixth century B.C.E. to question

with impunity the accuracy of the representation of the gods in the Homeric epics, and to suggest that popular anthropomorphized conceptions of the gods were mere projections of the human imagination.

As Athens grew in power and prominence during the fifth century, the city attracted intellectually active individuals who sometimes entertained skeptical attitudes toward traditional understandings of the gods. But such attitudes never became popular. Even as Athenians grew more sophisticated and self-conscious about the constructs of their society and culture, most seem to have remained attached to the beliefs and practices of their ancestors. Throughout the classical period (that is, the fifth and fourth centuries B.C.E.), it remained possible to prosecute individuals for "impiety" and "not recognizing the gods recognized by the city." Such was one of the charges faced in 399 B.C.E. by Socrates, Plato's friend and mentor and the chief interlocutor of most of the Platonic dialogues.

Poetry and Poetic Traditions

By the fifth century, several poetic works enjoyed enormous popularity and achieved quasi-canonical status. Foremost among these were *Iliad* and *Odyssey*, two of the epic poems that the Greeks attributed to Homer, although most modern scholars view them as results of centuries of oral storytelling and poetic improvisation rather than as the work of one person. The epics *Cypria*, *Iliupersis* ("The Destruction of Troy"), and a series of poems collectively referred to as *Returns* (*Nostoi*), which all dealt with the Trojan War and its aftermath and which survive only in fragments, were widely known as well, as were *Theogony*, an epic dealing with the origins of the gods, and the didactic poem *Works and Days*, both composed by Hesiod in the late eighth century B.C.E. Memorizing extensive passages of poetry was a standard educational practice in the classical period. Most Athenians would have thus been well acquainted not only with the works of Homer and Hesiod, but also with those by such lyric poets as Sappho, Simonides, Pindar, and Stesichorus, and they would have known other poems in a variety of styles.

Choruses performed hymns and songs at familial rites, such as marriages, and at public festivals throughout the Hellenic world. In Athens, choral performances in honor of Dionysus gave rise during the sixth century to more sophisticated presentations featuring solo respondents. These were the precursors to the tragedies and comedies performed during the classical period at festivals in the Theatre of Dionysus on the southern slope of the Acropolis. The Dionysian festivals were "high holidays" when public and private business was suspended, and the dramas produced in them were of enormous cultural importance in democratic Athens. Although modern scholars debate whether playwrights attempted directly to influence decision-making by their fellow citizens, there is no doubt that these festivals, which intertwined civic and religious functions, helped create a sense of political identity for the Athenians.

Dramas were composed for a single performance. Nonetheless, many were circulated and memorized, and some quickly achieved quasi-canonical status in their own right. It is not surprising, then, that Plato liberally quotes passages from tragedies by Aeschylus, Sophocles, and Euripides as well as other poetic works, most notably *Iliad* and *Odyssey*. He cites comedies far less often, but this does not mean that they did not interest him. Plato was particularly concerned with Aristophanes' *Clouds*, which was performed in 423 B.C.E. and featured Socrates as a main character; even though *Clouds* was not the only comedy in which a "Socrates" appeared, *Apology* 18d–19d indicates that, in Plato's view, it fostered particularly insidious prejudices against his mentor.

As readers of *Republic* and other dialogues discover, Plato has Socrates express deep reservations about relying on poetry to educate children and to foster senses of community and social identity among adults. In *Republic* especially, Socrates repeatedly professes his fondness for the Homeric poems while voicing serious criticism of their contents and ethical and social effects. His refrain concerning tragedy and lyric poetry is similar; they are said to be "charming" and "pleasing" but also dangerous. Comedy, as might be expected, receives almost no compliments in the Platonic dialogues. Yet *Republic*'s critique of poetry—especially dramatic poetry—is not free of ironies, since Plato is himself something of a dramatist whose dialogues are masterfully constructed "plays" in prose. Moreover, as Jacob Howland observes (The Republic: *The Odyssey of Philosophy*, pp. 28–29), he is also something of a comedian who delights, just as Aristophanes does, in exposing the foibles of prominent and self-important men.

Intellectual Innovations: "Scientists," "Sophists," and Rhetoricians

The most self-important person we meet in *Republic* is Thrasymachus, a diplomat and professional rhetorician from the Greek city-state of Chalcedon on the Bosporus near the Black Sea. He does not play much of a role in the dialogue beyond its first book, but his activities as a rhetorician and, as some would say, a "sophist" lead us to consider another set of cultural, intellectual, and political phenomena that are significant in Plato's work. The systematic study of effective public speaking, and the teaching of the theory as well as the practice of rhetoric, were innovations of the fifth century; they were impelled in part by the demands that democratic institutions such as public assemblies and courts, first in Athens and then elsewhere in the Hellenic world, created. To attain political prominence and power in a democratic setting, men had to be able to persuade large crowds and hold their own in heated debates. Even those who had more modest ambitions could find themselves needing the services of a teacher of rhetoric or a professional speechwriter when they went to court, whether as plaintiffs or defendants. Thus Athenian men—especially young and wealthy ones—began to study rhetoric and techniques of argumentation in ad hoc arrangements with professional and at times highly paid instructors.

The formal study of rhetoric and argumentation was also linked to a broader set of intellectual trends that originated in the Greek city-states of Ionia (the coastal area of Asia Minor) during the seventh and sixth centuries B.C.E. The driving force behind these trends was the desire to comprehend the workings of the cosmos and all its constituent parts in systematic terms, which was fueled by a spirit of inquiry and skepticism about received truths. Xenophanes, an Ionian émigré to the Greek colonies in Italy, challenged

Homer's and Hesiod's conceptions of the gods, and Pythagoras, another Ionian émigré to Italy, studied the mathematical bases of music and theorized about the reincarnation of the human soul. Others in Ionia and elsewhere became interested in studying the movements of celestial bodies and explaining astronomical phenomena such as eclipses, in discovering the causes for change and movement in physical objects, and in speculating about the nature of matter. By the fifth century, there were many "pre-Socratic philosophers," as they are known today, active throughout the Greek world. Among them were Heraclitus, Empedocles, Zeno, Anaxagoras, Democritus, Leucippus, and—especially important to the development of Plato's thought—Parmenides of Elea (in the northwest Peloponnese). In the early fifth century, Parmenides posited proto-metaphysical concepts of "Being" (or "That Which Is"—*to on* in Greek) that challenged the assumption that any physical object in the phenomenal world "is" in the absolute sense of the verb.

Although these sorts of speculation never became popular among ordinary people, they were nonetheless culturally influential in the fifth century. This was especially true in Athens, because the city's prosperity and relative openness to foreign visitors and residents attracted itinerant teachers and intellectuals. Theorizing about natural phenomena gave rise to speculation in other fields, and human society, human behavior, and human nature were among the subjects of such observation and speculation. The development of social institutions, laws, customs, belief systems, and other cultural practices was of particular interest; the Athenian experiment with democracy arguably contributed to an increasing self-consciousness about the roles that human perception and choice, on both individual and communal levels, played in shaping society. In addition to theories about the development of civilization and the degrees of its success in molding human nature, there arose ideas about how the model society should be formed, as well as formulations concerning the correct responses by individuals to the pressures and demands of their societies.

Some of these theories seem quite bold. At the end of the fifth century, a rhetorician named Antiphon wrote a treatise titled "On Truth," in which he asserts that the laws and customs of society are

by nature's standards "unjust," and that it is consequently "just"—
by nature's standards—to disregard them, provided one is able to
do so without being punished. Rational theories concerning the organization of the cosmos inevitably challenged traditional understanding of the roles played by the gods in ordering the world.
These theories gave rise to speculation about the role of the gods in
human affairs and, in turn, led some individuals to ponder whether
the truth about the gods can be apprehended by the human mind.
Less daring but still important were experiments with city planning
undertaken in communities such as Thurii, the Athenian colony
in southern Italy founded under the leadership of Pericles in
444 B.C.E., which drew on the skills of geometers (literally, "earth-
measurers") as well as experts on law and social relationships.

Most of the itinerant intellectuals who gravitated to Athens
during and after Pericles' day—including famous figures such
as Protagoras, Hippias, Prodicus, and Gorgias—integrated their
study and instruction of rhetoric with broader interests in fields
that we today might label psychology, sociology, social theory, an-
thropology, linguistics, language theory, epistemology, music theory, theology, and cosmology. Many of them also investigated
astronomy, physics, and the other sciences, as well as mathematics
and medicine. These men and their homegrown Athenian counterparts became known as "sophists" (that is, "men who profess wisdom"), although it is not clear that the term was commonly used
in the fifth century.

In some regards, the sophists were not wholly unlike the travel-
ing poets and professional performers of Homeric epic ("rhapsodes") who had been received in Greek city-states for generations.
Many of them performed official services for their home cities
and, like Thrasymachus and the Sicilian rhetorician Gorgias (from
Leontini in Sicily), served as ambassadors to Athens. Yet the presence of these intellectually adventurous and personally ambitious
men would have inevitably struck many Athenians as an alarming
sign that times were changing, and not necessarily for the better.
Indeed, the activities of the sophists seem to have compounded
anxieties about economic and social changes that the developments
of democracy and "empire" had brought about. The sophists' fees
were typically so high that only wealthy men could afford to hire

them to instruct their sons, and their direct influence was thus limited. Their ideas and modi operandi were generally if vaguely known, however, and the public tended to see their activities, not always fairly, as threats to the traditional norms and practices that were thought to guarantee stability and prosperity in Athenian society.

The fact that the sophists appropriated the family's role in preparing young men for adult life and, moreover, charged fees for their efforts, very likely made them appear all the more suspect in the eyes of average Athenians. If Aristophanes' comedy *Clouds* can be trusted for this kind of information, the lightning rod for popular misgivings about the sophists' activities was the teaching of rhetoric. Rhetorical education, in the worst-case scenario presented by *Clouds*, could supply the means for young men to "make the weaker argument stronger" and justify their antisocial behavior; it could enable them to cast out all the received wisdom they had absorbed about the gods, society, and family.

Nonetheless, for all this apparent controversy and anxiety concerning the sophists' newfangled ideas, the changes and upheavals of Athenian society in the late fifth century had less to do with their influence than we might suppose. These upheavals, leading up to the oligarchic coups of 411–410 and 404–403, are better understood as consequences of the Peloponnesian War and the ongoing transformation of the institutions and practices of democracy. Modern scholars are in a position to see how various theories expounded by intellectuals valorized the positions taken by both proponents and detractors of Athenian democracy, but it is unclear how frequently or how keenly average Athenians concerned themselves with the ideological implications, per se, of the sophists' ideas. In addition, even though sophists were not popular in fifth-century Athens, there was relatively little backlash against them. It is true that the astronomer Anaxagoras was prosecuted on the charge of impiety in, perhaps, 450 B.C.E., and that Socrates was convicted on the charges of impiety and "corrupting the youth" in 399. Anaxagoras, however, was likely attacked because of his closeness to Pericles, and, as we shall soon discuss, there were probably political motivations behind the charges brought against Socrates as well.

The market for the higher education of young men with wealth and aspirations to political prominence did not abate in the fourth century. Various individuals, some of them native Athenians like Isocrates (436–338 B.C.E.), established schools in which rhetoric and other subjects were taught. Thus, after only a generation or so, the novel and at times controversial educational offerings of the fifth-century sophists and rhetoricians were well on their way to becoming institutionalized and mainstreamed. Plato was a direct beneficiary of this process of institutionalization and, in something of a paradox, he was indirectly beholden to the sophists. To be sure, Plato's portrayals of men like Protagoras, Hippias, and Prodicus (in *Protagoras*), Polus and Gorgias (in *Gorgias*), Euthydemus and Dionysodorus (in *Euthydemus*), and Thrasymachus (in *Republic*) are not flattering. He dismisses the claims to knowledge and expertise and educational proficiency that such "professors of wisdom" had staked for themselves, and discredits the ways in which these men and their successors—notably Isocrates—taught rhetoric and the "art" of public persuasion. Nonetheless, Plato's Academy capitalized upon the desire and demand for higher education that Protagoras, Gorgias, and others had cultivated during the preceding decades. Without the fertile field the sophists planted, Plato might never have had the opportunity to found his Academy—or write his dialogues.

Socrates

It is impossible to conceive of Plato apart from Socrates. A native Athenian who lived from approximately 470 B.C.E. until his execution in 399, Socrates committed nothing to writing. What we know of his activities comes largely from the dialogues of Plato and Xenophon, in which Socrates is very often the primary interlocutor. The other intact source—and the sole one dating to Socrates' lifetime—is Aristophanes' *Clouds*, which antedates Plato's and Xenophon's works by twenty-five years at the minimum and was composed when Socrates was not yet fifty years old. There are fragments of other comedies from the 420s that mention Socrates, and a very few fragments of works by other "Socratics" who, like Plato and Xenophon, took to writing about the man after his death and using him as a figure in dialogues.

Aristophanes presents an image of Socrates very different from those of Plato and Xenophon. In *Clouds*, Socrates is portrayed as a professional sophist running a "Think Factory." His students pay to learn rhetoric (that is, how to "make the weaker argument the stronger") and other language arts, as well as absurd "scientific" techniques (for example, how to measure the leaps of fleas) and a novel cosmology positing that Zeus "is not." This Socrates has no scruple about taking on a pupil who wants to cheat his creditors in court, and he is indirectly responsible for a young man's beating of his aged father.

According to Plato and Xenophon, however, Socrates was in no way a professional; he had no pupils and took no fees. Plato takes particular pains to distance Socrates from Aristophanes' caricature and from the sophists. He has him disavow all interest in rhetoric and admit to only a youthful and unsatisfying flirtation with the cosmological theories of Anaxagoras (for example, in *Phaedo* 96a–100a). The Socrates of Plato's works professes an exclusive commitment to making his fellow Athenians "better" by urging them to examine their values and actions systematically, on the grounds that "the unexamined life is not worth living" (*Apology* 38a). He exhorts them to think and act in consistently virtuous, just, temperate, and courageous ways, even if such behavior endangers material prosperity and life itself (for example, *Apology* 29c–30b); he argues that the welfare and health of the soul are more important than any consideration of material comfort. The Platonic Socrates is depicted, moreover, as a paragon of this consistently virtuous way of life, always electing to do what is truly beneficial over what is immediately convenient and gratifying. So consistent is his devotion to the pursuit of the "good life," for himself and others, that he is willing to permit himself to be killed for its sake (*Apology* 35c; *Gorgias* 522d–c).

Plato may well have crafted his representations of Socrates to suit his own purposes, just as Aristophanes doubtless shaped the portrayal in *Clouds* in accordance with his comic agenda. If we prefer to believe that Plato's depiction is the more accurate, it is still possible to understand how Aristophanes could have proffered such a disparate perspective on Socrates' activities. According to Plato, Socrates' self-appointed mission of spurring his fellow citizens toward self-examination—he describes himself as a gadfly sent to "rouse" Athens, as if it were a large and lazy horse, in *Apology* 30e—necessitated challenges to their most cherished values and assumptions—including their own presumptions to wisdom. As a result, he may well have irritated, infuriated, and at times humiliated them. For all the distance that Plato strives to create between his mentor and the sophists, we may imagine that, to the average Athenian, the differences between the challenges to traditional conceptions of just behavior offered by Socrates and someone like Antiphon might not have seemed so great. Socrates could have come across as just another sophist who was relentlessly critical of the traditional and the time-honored.

If Plato's depiction is reliable, Socrates was also highly critical of Athens' democratic government. We know that he traveled in the elite circles of Athenian society and was closely linked to prominent men from aristocratic families. He was particularly friendly with Pericles' ward, the charismatic and ambitious Alcibiades (450–404 B.C.E.), whose extravagant behavior and defection to the Peloponnesian alliance in 415 left his associates under a cloud of suspicion. He also knew Critias, the infamous leader of the Thirty Tyrants of 404–403, and other men who harbored open hostilities to democracy. Socrates was almost certainly not actively involved with the Thirty, but his past associations with Critias and Alcibiades may have caused unease in the tense years immediately after the democratic government was restored in 403. The general amnesty obviated his prosecution on political charges, and it is likely that the charges of impiety and corrupting youth that were officially laid against him in 399 were efforts to drive him into exile because of his political associations and views.

Socrates, however, did not go into exile, even though he could have done so after his conviction. On orders from the court that convicted him, he committed suicide by drinking hemlock. He left behind a band of friends and followers who, because of their dedication to preserving Socrates' legacy, came to be known as "Socratics." By the late 390s B.C.E., several texts purporting to contain the speeches of prosecution and defense given at Socrates' trial were in circulation; two texts by Plato and Xenophon, both titled *Apology* (which literally means "Defense"), are the only extant examples of the latter, and none of the former survives. Dialogues featuring Socrates as an interlocutor remained popular throughout the fourth century, so much so that Aristotle's *Poetics* identifies Socratic dialogues as "examples of imitation." How scrupulously any of these works—including those of Plato—aimed to represent the actual views and activities of Socrates remains an open question.

Plato

We know the names of several Socratics active during the fourth century B.C.E. in Athens and elsewhere: Antisthenes, Phaedo, Eucleides, Aristippus, Aeschines, as well as Plato and Xenophon. Only works by Plato and Xenophon survive intact, and, of these two authors, Plato is by far the more philosophically significant.

Plato was born into a wealthy, aristocratic Athenian family in 428 or 427 B.C.E., and he lived until 348 or 347. (A note in passing: "Plato" was a nickname according to one tradition, but it is now generally accepted as his given name.) He had kinship ties with many prominent men, including the notorious Critias. A large body of writing attributed to Plato survives from antiquity, including *Apology* (a recreation of Socrates' defense speech), *Republic* and a number of other dialogues, and a series of letters. Most of these works are considered genuinely Platonic, although the authenticity of some texts (including some of the letters and a handful of dialogues) has been doubted at various points in the past 2400 years.

The Seventh Letter, which many scholars today view as authentic, offers an autobiographical account explaining how the vicious abuse of power by the Thirty Tyrants and the subsequent trial and execution of Socrates under the restored democracy persuaded Plato to eschew a political career in Athens. It also details his association with the rulers of the Sicilian city of Syracuse, Dionysius I and his son Dionysius II, and their kinsman Dion, who was Plato's close friend and student. Plato visited Sicily three times during the period from the early 380s to the late 360s. He and Dion evidently planned to educate the younger Dionysius in the hopes that, upon succeeding his father, he would put into practice the political ideals they cherished. Several scholars have speculated that these political ideals were something like the proposals for the ideal state and the government of philosopher-rulers that Socrates advances in *Republic*. Whatever their aspirations were, Plato and Dion were disappointed when Dionysius II took power in the early 360s and quickly broke with his kinsman and his tutor.

Soon after Plato returned to Athens from his first visit to Syracuse in the early 380s, he began teaching at a place near the grove of the hero Academus on the city's outskirts. The school came to be called the "Academy" because of its location, and its original mission, like that of Isocrates' school, may have been to train young men for civic leadership. Plato taught what he called "philosophy" (*philosophia*) and subjects he deemed essential to its study, notably mathematical sciences.

Plato probably started to compose dialogues before he established the Academy. In all but a few of his dialogues Socrates is the main interlocutor, and most are peopled with figures who would have been well known in Athens' elite circles during the fifth century. Plato's older brothers, Glaucon and Adeimantus, play prominent parts in *Republic* and figure briefly in *Parmenides'* introduction. Several dialogues have identifiable "dramatic dates," at least in approximate terms. The gathering of sophists and their followers at Callias' house in *Protagoras*, for example, is set sometime around 432 B.C.E., and the party at Agathon's house described in *Symposium* would have taken place in the spring of 416. Most of these works also contain anachronistic details, which seem deliberately planted in order to underscore their inherent fictionality. It is important for readers to keep in mind that the dialogues are not historically accurate accounts of actual conversations, although they may aim to suggest the kinds of conversations that Socrates *could* have had with Protagoras, Agathon, Plato's brothers, and other men. Interestingly and importantly, Plato never represents himself as a speaker, although he is mentioned by Socrates in *Apology* and by Phaedo in *Phaedo*.

Many scholars have speculated about the dating of Plato's works, and at times the speculation has inspired heated controversy. Relative dating of the dialogues is complicated by the fact that there is little external evidence corroborating when any of them was composed. One long-popular approach has been to classify the texts as "early," "middle," and "late," on the grounds that there is a development in styles and concerns that reflects the maturation of Plato's thought. *Apology* and the "Socratic" dialogues, which feature Socrates in conversation with various men about basic ethical questions and tend to end "aporetically" (without reaching satisfactory resolutions), are thus thought to date to the early years of Plato's career, when he was still more or less a "Socratic." "Middle" dialogues in which Socrates is made to advance positive theories, most importantly the theory of the metaphysical "ideas," are viewed as reflecting the fruition of Plato's own philosophical inquiries. Those dialogues that reflect less interest in the theory of the ideas and deal instead with other concerns and analyses (for example, the method of "collection and division") are grouped together as "late."

According to this interpretation, *Republic* is categorized among the "middle" dialogues because, among other things, it contains one of the most detailed expositions of the theory of the ideas, which Plato almost certainly derived independently of Socrates from Parmenides' theory of "Being." Some critics accordingly estimate that it was composed during the 370s B.C.E. Yet, once again, readers should be aware that such dating is purely speculative, since it depends upon subjective estimations of the developmental stages in Plato's thought and style.

The past few decades have witnessed an explosion of interest in Plato's reliance on the dialogue format, and readers can find overviews of the topic in John M. Cooper's introduction to *Plato: Complete Works* (pp. xviii–xxi) and Ruby Blondell's *The Play of Character in Plato's Dialogues* (pp. 1–52). The fact that he chose to write not treatises, but dialogues in which different points of view compete, coupled with the fact that he never presents himself as an interlocutor, raises important questions about the relationships among written texts, Plato's actual thoughts, and his teachings at the Academy. Passages such as *Phaedrus* 274e–278b, in which Socrates asserts that a sensible and noble man treats written discourse as a mere "amusement," further complicate interpretation of all the dialogues, including *Republic*. Readers of *Republic* will note that, at a crucial moment (7.536b–c), Socrates reminds Glaucon that they are "not serious." And, although Socrates remarks more than once on the importance of the issues he and his companions are discussing, he repeatedly draws attention to their conversation's incomplete and provisional qualities.

These factors lead some scholars to argue that the dialogues cannot provide reliable guides to what Plato thought. According to this school of interpretation, *Republic* and its counterparts showcase the Socratic method of inquiry; they are intended to stimulate readers' interest in asking their own questions, but do not aim to guide them toward specific points of view, or "theories," on any given topic. Yet there is a definite set of concerns—about the unreliability of opinions held by "the many," for example, and their heedless pursuit of pleasure and gratification—that is explored and substantiated in several dialogues. The recurrence of these concerns, and the consistent manner in which they are addressed from dialogue to dialogue, suggest that Plato's written works are not only advertisements for the Socratic method of inquiry, but also vehicles for a complex agenda that is at once ethical and intellectual, cultural and political.

Succinct summary of this complex agenda is impossible. Readers interested in exploring what scholars have deduced about Plato's interests and aims are encouraged to consult one or more of the excellent studies available today, including Andrea Wilson Nightingale's *Genres in Dialogue: Plato and the Construct of Philosophy*, Angela Hobbs's *Plato and the Hero: Courage, Manliness, and the Impersonal Good*, Charles H. Kahn's *Plato and the Socratic Dialogue: The Philosophical Use of a Literary Form*, Terence Irwin's *Plato's Ethics*, Debra Nails's *Agora, Academy, and the Conduct of Philosophy*, and Josiah Ober's *Political Dissent in Democratic Athens: Intellectual Critics of Popular Rule*. This introduction to *Republic* merits discussion of just a few basic points.

First, the recurrent exposé of the unreliability of "what most people think" functions as a weapon that permits a simultaneous attack on traditional ethical understandings (for example, the identification of "justice" with retribution and vengeance) and on the particular ideological assumptions of democracy. (The most important of these assumptions was that, regardless of social position or experience, free-born male citizens were qualified to participate to some extent in political processes.) The critique that *Republic* and other Platonic texts offer concerning the pervasive materialist tendencies in Greek culture, which are repeatedly said to prioritize appearances and "external" goods (such as wealth, looks, social status, and political power) over "internal" goods and actual conditions, thus complements their more narrowly focused challenge to the soundness of Athenian democracy's presumptions and practices.

At the heart of this double-sided critique lies the concern that Hellenic culture encouraged a fundamentally childish attachment to pleasure—not just physical and sensual pleasures, but to the psychological pleasures gained through the exercise of power, or through the indulgence of ambition, pride, grief, anger, and other strong emotions. Athenian democracy is represented as exacerbating these childish tendencies, because it maximizes the number of individuals who are permitted to indulge themselves with little real restraint. The ultimate effect of democracy is to render political leaders helplessly incapable of true governance, since they are inevitably forced to gratify and flatter the common people, who can turn on them with impunity as soon as they fail to please (see, for example, *Gorgias* 500a–519c; *Republic* 6.492a–493d).

These criticisms run counter to the self-images that most Athenians—and most Greeks—would have nurtured, although the negative assessment of Athenian democracy echoes points made by other upper-class Athenians writing in the fifth and fourth centuries, such as Thucydides, Xenophon, and Isocrates. Plato distinguishes himself, however, by positioning his critique of Athens' democratic culture within a far broader interrogation of time-honored values and practices that were not specific to Athens. In so doing, he takes aim at the traditional aristocratic ideology cherished by his own social group, which assumed that the well-born and elite few—purportedly endowed with superior intelligence, skill, resources, and "excellence" (*aretē*)—possessed a natural and god-given right to power. As Andrea Wilson Nightingale argues (*Genres in Dialogue*, pp. 55–59), the dialogues time and again expose the ignorance and powerlessness of well-born men who presume and are presumed to be "superior." Even the gifted and privileged Alcibiades is made to concede the "slavishness" of his desire to "please the crowd" in *Symposium* 215e–216b.

Yet the repeated exposés of how elite individuals like Alcibiades fail to be morally and intellectually "superior" do not overturn the basic presumption that, in a given community, only a few individuals are sufficiently gifted to wield political power. Critical as they are of the conduct and attitudes of contemporary elites, the dialogues ultimately validate the principle of elitism. Against the claims of democracy's pluralist ideology, Plato's works seek to reenergize traditional aristocratic views of political power as a special responsibility and privilege reserved for the very few. In the process, however, they completely redefine who the "best men" (*hoi aristoi*) are, and completely reconfigure the meaning of traditional terms for the qualities of those best men—that is, excellence (*aretê*), wisdom (*sophia*), courage (*andreia*), temperance (*sophrosynê*), and justice (*dikaiosynê*).

At its most basic level, *Republic* is an effort to forge a consistent and meaningful redefinition of "justice" that goes against the grain of much traditional teaching. Readers will see for themselves how its reconfiguration of what is signified by the term goes hand in hand with its argument for an "aristocracy" of men called "philosophers," whose apprehension of the metaphysical ideas leads them to disdain appearances of all sorts. Their *aretê* lies in nothing outward, but rests solely in their mature reason and regard for what is beneficial to the soul.

These thoughts could have been conveyed in any number of ways, and in themselves they do not tell us why Plato chose to write dialogues as opposed to treatises. His choice must have been motivated to some extent by the fact that other members of the Socratic circle were composing dialogues, but there might have been additional reasons for his gravitation toward this versatile form. Certainly the dialogue afforded him great flexibility of expression, and with it he was able to craft attractive alternatives to the very forms of discourse (including poetic genres such as tragedy and epic) that *Republic* and other works expose as the principal carriers of problematic cultural values.

Moreover, even though the dialogues are not philosophical discourses in their own right—since such can never take place in writing (compare *Phaedrus* 274e–278b)—they are plainly models of the kinds of conversations that thoughtful men can have. They are, in some regards, advertisements for philosophy, and they might have been composed to engage the interest of young Athenian men in the philosophical studies of the Academy.

We should observe here that Isocrates, too, claimed to teach *philosophia*, using the term to express the dominant cultural values that Socrates and other Platonic interlocutors vigorously criticize. In a work titled *Antidosis* (354 or 353 B.C.E.), Isocrates explicitly casts doubt on the relevance of the kinds of studies pursued at the Academy—that is, mathematical sciences that aim at the discovery of absolute truths. Isocrates' skepticism doubtless reflects the long-running competition between his school and the Academy, and it seems likely, as Nightingale maintains (*Genres in Dialogue*, pp. 21–59), that the dialogues had the additional function of advancing Plato's far more exclusive definitions of philosophy and the philosopher. Not only do they counter Isocrates' definition of philosophy, but they also repeatedly strive to demonstrate how Plato's "brand" of philosophy is useful to both the individuals who practice it and their communities.

At times, as in books 5–10 of *Republic*, Plato has his interlocutors directly define *philosophia* and expound on its usefulness. Yet the dialogue form has the additional virtue of permitting Plato to define *philosophia* indirectly as well as directly, through the very drama of his "plays" in prose. In the dialogues he is able to show—and not merely describe—what philosophy is, and the benefits it brings as well as the challenges it imposes. On the latter score, the give-and-take of the conversations, especially those in which Socrates and his interlocutors reach neither satisfactory conclusion nor mutual understanding, highlight how emotional factors such as ambition, pride, anger, and fear affect the cognitive abilities and powers of reason in even the most intelligent people. These con versations seem designed to bear out what is claimed in book 7 of *Republic*, that the "whole soul" must be moved in order for the mind to "know," just as the whole body must be turned from darkness toward light for the eyes to see (7.518c). The rewards, however, are made to seem worth the trouble of this arduous psychological reorientation. Readers have only to contemplate the ease and grace of Socrates, even as he faces death in *Crito* and

Phaedo, to find compelling "advertisements" for the supreme value of Plato's distinctive brand of philosophy.

The dialogues present Socrates as a paragon of the philosopher's *aretê*. They simultaneously permit Plato and his readers to look back at Socrates in a nuanced manner and mark his shortcomings as well as his fine and admirable traits. Socrates may have seen it as his duty to talk to "anyone, young or old" (so *Apology* 33a), but Plato's many representations of Socrates' conversations subtly bring out how such an indiscriminate approach, however commendable in intention, is unrealistic and ultimately self-defeating. Plato himself, we should note, was considerably more selective than Socrates in his contacts; at the Academy he worked only with people eager to study with him, whom he could vet as a condition of their "admission." In Plato's hands, then, the Socratic dialogue becomes both homage to a beloved mentor and declaration of intellectual independence.

Republic

In the manuscripts and ancient citations, the title of *Republic* is given as *Politeia* ("Constitution") or *Politeiai* ("Constitutions"); *Peri dikaiou* (literally, "concerning that which is just") is sometimes listed as an alternative title. The book divisions, as those in *Laws*, are probably not Platonic, but rather the work of scholars in the third and second centuries B.C.E. The sectional numbers (for example, *Republic* 327b) found in most modern editions refer to the page and section numbers used in one of the first printed texts of Plato's dialogues, which was published in the late sixteenth century; like the book divisions, they are retained for the sake of convenience.

Again, the date of *Republic*'s composition is a matter of conjecture. Some scholars argue that it was actually composed in stages, on the grounds that the current text imperfectly marries two (or more) "dramatic" conceptions. Although the physical setting is certain (the house of the metic Polemarchus in Piraeus), there is much disagreement over the dramatic date. Debra Nails (*The People of Plato*, pp. 324–326) compellingly summarizes the evidence for viewing the current text of *Republic* as a combination of and expansion upon two earlier works: first, an inconclusive ("aporetic") *Thrasymachus* or *On Justice*, similar to *Gorgias* and *Protagoras* and set in the 420s B.C.E., which would have supplied the basis for what is now called book 1, and second, an *Ideal State*, which would have been the foundation for what is currently in books 2–5. If the latter composition featured Plato's older brothers Glaucon and Adeimantus as interlocutors, it would have been set in or after 411. This analysis comfortably accounts for the many anachronisms that arise if one attempts, as some critics do, to fix the dramatic date of *Republic* in a particular year such as 411 or 410, and it also permits some reconciliation with the apparent reference to the discussion of *Republic* as "yesterday's" conversation in *Timaeus* 17a–19e, which seems to be set in the 420s.

The text that we now possess surely could have been composed in more than one stage. Yet, since anachronisms are present in dialogues that have readily identifiable dramatic dates, the obligation to explain away *Republic*'s anachronisms by means of theories concerning its composition is less than pressing. Awkward anachronisms and all, *Republic* is a unified work with a logical and elegant organization, to which we will now direct our attention.

Socrates himself is the narrator of *Republic*, in which he tells an unknown audience about a conversation that took place "yesterday." His main interlocutors, from book 2 on, are Glaucon and Adeimantus. His host Polemarchus and Polemarchus' aged father, Cephalus, are instrumental in getting the conversation going, and the aggressive challenge posed by the rhetorician Thrasymachus in the second part of book 1 is what determines the dialogue's main interests.

Other men are present in the dialogue: Polemarchus' half-brother Lysias, a professional speech writer who is discussed in *Phaedrus* and whose works still survive; another half brother, Euthydemus; a man named Charmantides, who could be either an elderly man from the rural Attic deme of Paeania or his grandson; and Niceratus, the son of the well-respected political leader and *strategos* Nicias. These four men are silent witnesses to the conversation, as are the nameless "others" mentioned in 1.327c. Aside from the slave who calls upon Socrates and Glaucon in the first paragraph of book 1, the only other speaker is Cleitophon, an

Athenian politician who briefly comes to Thrasymachus' aid at 1.340b–c.

We do not know much about Glaucon and Adeimantus aside from what Plato shows us. They participated in a battle at Megara, to which Socrates refers at 2.368a. If this was the battle of 409 B.C.E., they could have been only a few years older than Plato, which is the estimate of most scholars; if it was an earlier battle in 424, they would have been much older. Adeimantus, along with Plato, apparently attended Socrates' trial (_Apology_ 34a), and both he and Glaucon appear on close terms with Socrates in _Republic_. Cephalus hailed originally from Syracuse on Sicily, and he and his sons were wealthy, well-established foreign residents in Athens. Represented by Plato as an old man, Cephalus was almost certainly dead by 411. _Republic_'s original readers would have also known that the Thirty Tyrants had Polemarchus executed in 404 so as to seize his property, and this fact puts Thrasymachus' passionate glamorization of the tyrant's self-aggrandizing ways (1.344a–c) in an especially ironic light. Thrasymachus, as we have already discussed, served as a diplomat in Athens for his native Chalcedon and was also a professional rhetorician, and Plato has Socrates link him to Lysias in _Phaedrus_. Cleitophon, who is associated with Lysias and Thrasymachus in the pseudo-Platonic dialogue _Cleitophon_, had become notorious for his political fickleness by the time Aristophanes produced his comedy _Frogs_ in 405 B.C.E.

The conversation in _Republic_ begins simply enough. Socrates, who has plainly been on familiar terms with Polemarchus' family for a long time, forthrightly asks Cephalus about old age. His response, that aging is not as difficult as it is often reported to be, prompts Socrates to wonder out loud whether Cephalus' easygoing attitude is in part facilitated by his wealth. The old man's response is affirmative. The wealthy, he asserts, face death without fear; their resources enable them to satisfy their debts to gods and men and also to avoid lying and cheating, and thus they can die with the confidence that they will not be punished in the afterlife. These remarks are what precipitate the discussion of just behavior and moral conduct, which Socrates introduces as he asks his elderly friend whether "justice" (_dikaiosynê_) simply consists of paying debts and telling the truth. Cephalus politely bows out of the conversation, leaving his son Polemarchus to argue that justice—meaning "right behavior" in general—does indeed consist of paying debts and giving "what is due," as poets such as Simonides claim. Socrates, however, quickly leads Polemarchus to realize that there are serious logical problems with this traditional conception of justice, in which "what is due" is defined in terms of "help" to "friends" and "harm" to "enemies," and the young man is left perplexed.

At this point, Thrasymachus leaps into the discussion, asserting that justice is simply "the advantage of the stronger," by which he clearly means that "justice" is relative—that is, "right behavior" is whatever those in power determine it to be. With a series of questions that recall those he just posed to Polemarchus, Socrates uncovers logical problems in Thrasymachus' definition as well. Thrasymachus, however, does not give up. Exploding in frustration at Socrates' naive assumptions about the responsibilities that the powerful bear to those who are under their control, he reformulates his ideas with a bold new emphasis evocative of Antiphon's thinking in "On Truth." "Justice"—that is, the circumspect avoidance of doing "wrong" to others and obedience to social rules—is doing what is advantageous to another, who is stronger and more powerful than oneself. "Injustice," on the other hand, is doing what is to one's own advantage by taking what one wants regardless of social rules and by aggrandizing oneself at the expense of others. It is what leads to "happiness," provided that one is not penalized for one's exploitations. Tyrants who kill and confiscate and rape at will, according to Thrasymachus, are the happiest men of all.

Although Socrates is able to poke holes through the logic of this new formulation with questions that hark back once again to those he has already posed, Thrasymachus' sulky concessions leave him unconvinced that he has made an effective case for the connection between justice, which through all has not been adequately defined, and "happiness." Nor are Glaucon and Adeimantus convinced, and it is their persistence at the beginning of book 2 that launches the more systematic and extensive inquiry into the nature of justice and its relationship to happiness that occupies the rest of *Republic*. In particular, the brothers ask Socrates to explain how justice is *in itself* the source of happiness, regardless of whether it is recognized and rewarded, and how the just man can be happy, regardless of his material circumstances.

The challenges of defining justice and understanding its effects on long-term happiness, fulfillment, and well-being—all of which are conveyed by the Greek word *eudaimonia*—lead to the discussion of the ideal city-state, which is posited as a large-scale vehicle for apprehending the operations of justice in the individual. Socrates, Glaucon, and Adeimantus spend a good deal of time and energy discussing how the ideal state will be organized, and how its classes of warriors and leaders will be selected, educated, and provided for; they are especially concerned in books 2 and 3 with the training and acculturation of guardian children, whose exposure to poetry (*Iliad* and *Odyssey* in particular) is to be severely curtailed lest they learn harmful values and patterns of behavior.

Yet the three never lose sight of the goals of their examination. By the end of book 4, they arrive at a working (and, in several regards, striking) definition of justice as the condition, or state of being, in which each person in the community—and each element of the individual human soul (*psyche*)—minds his/her/its own business and does his/her/its own "work." Since it has been determined that there is in the human soul, as in human society, a natural ruling element, justice is thus equated with the unencumbered rule of these elements: the "gold" class of guardians in the ideal state, which holds sway over the silver and bronze/iron classes, and, in the individual, the rational part of the soul that ought to be master of both "spirit" and appetites.

The demonstration of how the rule of the superior element generates happiness in community and individual alike, however, is postponed until books 8 and 9. At the beginning of book 5, the brothers join Polemarchus, Thrasymachus, and the others in pressing Socrates to explain some of the extraordinary provisions he has stipulated for the lifestyle of the ideal state's guardian classes. The group is most keenly interested in the proposed abolition of individual families. Socrates' explanation of the "community" of wives and children among the guardians leads to exploration of a series of related topics: (1) the near-equality of female guardians, who would be warriors and leaders; (2) the abolition of private property in the guardian classes; and (3) the overall possibility of the ideal state as it has been heretofore envisioned.

In response to Glaucon's query about this last issue, Socrates presents his bold thesis: The ideal state will come into being when "philosophers are kings, [and] the kings and philosophers of this world have the spirit and power of philosophy . . ." (5.473d–e). This statement drives the rest of the discussion in books 5–7, in which Socrates seeks with Glaucon's and Adeimantus' help to define philosophers, delineate the ultimate goal of their practice of philosophy as well as its utility, and outline the educational curriculum that would prepare philosophers, who are identified with the gold class of the ideal state, for their political responsibilities. In the course of this discussion, Socrates introduces the concept of metaphysical entities possessing true "being"; he calls them "ideas" (*ideai* and also *eidê* in Greek, terms that are sometimes translated as "forms"), and he presumes Plato's brothers know something about them. He also argues, using the image of the "divided line," that there are four distinct cognitive faculties whereby different types of objects are apprehended, ranging from the ideas themselves to entities in the phenomenal world to mere "reflections" and "imitations."

To facilitate his audience's appreciation of these abstract concepts, he develops two more striking images: the simile of the sun, which conveys the supreme importance of the idea of the good, and the allegory of the cave, which describes the difficult path of enlightenment undertaken by the philosopher. As the allegory explains, the ultimate goal of philosophy is in fact apprehension of the idea of the good, which is the source of "goodness" in all other things. Yet philosophy's arduous "upward" journey to the apprehension of "true being" is not for everyone. Only those few with the talent, training, and discipline that permit "knowledge" of the idea of the good will correctly estimate what is good in the phenomenal world. They alone, according to Socrates, should be allowed to have political power.

The alternatives to the rule of philosophers are four dysfunctional constitutions, which Socrates describes and ranks in book 8, moving from the least problematic ("timarchy," oligarchy) to the most defective (democracy, tyranny). These constitutions supply bases for identifying and analyzing the personalities of four types of individuals, who yield to the lesser elements in the soul. Their yielding to the inferior elements is contrasted with the rule of reason in the soul of the "kingly" or "aristocratic" just man, and is accordingly found to be the source of psychic dysfunction and misery. Thus Socrates, Glaucon, and Adeimantus not only establish the inviolable happiness of the just man, who is all but explicitly identified with the philosopher, but they also bring into full view (in book 9) the utterly wretched and enslaved condition of the tyrant, whose freedom and happiness Thrasymachus had celebrated in book 1. Moreover, the close association of democracy with tyranny at the end of book 8 caps the dialogue's exposé of democracy's errors and inadequacies.

With Glaucon's and Adeimantus' challenge thus met, Socrates reaffirms in book 10 the propriety of the ideal state's careful censorship of poetic texts and, adding to the arguments presented in books 2 and 3, he suggests that adults as well as children should be shielded from poetry's seductive yet dangerous charms. As Glaucon and Adeimantus rescind the cynical vision they had conjured for the sake of argument at the beginning of book 2, Socrates details how justice does in fact bear rewards in life. He thereupon draws the discussion to a close by relating a myth that describes the even greater rewards for the just—and the extreme punishments of the unjust—in the afterlife. The myth also reasserts the abiding importance of reason and philosophy for souls who, after a thousand-year absence, are about to choose their next lives in this world.

Republic covers many topics, as Socrates concedes at the beginning of book 6, (6.484a), and its exploration of justice's relationship to happiness takes a circuitous route. The dialogue's composition, however, is hardly haphazard. The preliminary conversation in book 1, though unsatisfactory, not only raises the issues that will be addressed in the rest of the work, but it also anticipates, through a variety of means, key formulations and points that Socrates will make in later books. Indeed, almost every detail in book 1 looks ahead to later developments; let us note here just a few examples of how this is so.

In his exchanges with Polemarchus and Thrasymachus, Socrates repeatedly compares the just individual/ruler to professionals with technical expertise and knowledge, such as doctors, musicians, and ships' pilots. These analogies may strike readers as bizarre if not nonsensical; they pave the way, however, for the definition of justice as the rule of the soul's rational element, and thus for the crucial associations of justice with expert knowledge—and of the philosopher with the just man. So, too, does the simple observation that each thing has a particular function (1.352e–353a) presage the definition of justice as "doing one's own work."

In addition, Socrates ultimately affirms that it is fair to conceive of justice as "giving what is due" and also as "the interest (or advantage) of the stronger," although he does so by assigning meanings to these phrases that are wholly different from those intended by Polemarchus at 1.332a–c and Thrasymachus at 1.338c. On the other hand, Thrasymachus' assumption that happiness resides in the satisfaction of appetites and desires (for example, in 1.344a–c) is completely overturned, insofar as justice is equated with the submission of the appetitive element of the soul to reason, its natural ruler. His corollary assumption that rulers willingly hold power (1.345e) is challenged in equally forceful terms by the allegory of the cave in book 7.

The ignorance in Cephalus' declaration that wealth and property are facilitators of just behavior and moral excellence (1.331a–b) is likewise exposed during the analysis of degenerate constitutions in books 8 and 9, which posits private property as the principal catalyst for personal interests that will conflict with those of the community. Cephalus' concerns for rewards and punishments in the afterlife are borne out, though, by the Myth of Er in book 10. The fact that Polemarchus immediately relies on the authority of the poet Simonides to support his problematic definition of justice (1.331d) sets the stage for Socrates' arguments in books 2, 3, and 10 concerning the need to censor poetry.

Even the small details concerning Socrates' and Glaucon's visit to Piraeus—they are spectators who wish to view (*theâsthai*) the festival of Bendis—foreshadow the emphases placed in books 5–7 on philosophical contemplation (*theôria*) of "that which is" and in book 10 on Er's vision (*thea*) of the afterlife (Nightingale, "On Wandering . . . ," pp. 33–39). The very first word of the dialogue, *katebên* ("I went down"), arguably looks ahead to the obligation that the ideal state would impose upon philosophers, who must descend (*katabainein*) from the sunlit world of "being" into the cave-prison of phenomenal experience, where they are to serve as unwilling rulers (7.519d; 7.539e).

The fact that book 10, which is something of a coda to the rest of the text, explores in depth topics of concern at the very beginning of book 1—that is, poetry's "truthfulness" and pretense to moral authority, and the afterlife's rewards for justice and punishment of wrongdoing—suggests that *Republic*'s "narrative" is structured in an almost circular pattern. This circular pattern is complex, but it has important symmetries. Most basically, the dialogue's two main concerns (defining justice and ascertaining its relationship to happiness) are treated in two corresponding sections (books 2–4 and books 8–9) that are interrupted by what is nominally a series of digressions in books 5–7.

These nominal digressions, however, create the dialogue's centerpiece, a tour de force exposition of philosophical concepts that happens to be, at the same time, a literary masterwork. The definition of the philosopher offered in books 5–7, in conjunction with the metaphysical and epistemological concepts it introduces, provides the foundation not only for the "proofs" of the just man's happiness and the tyrant's misery in book 9, but also for the renewed critique of poetic mimesis in book 10.

Moreover, the passage makes a vivid and compelling case for what were arguably Plato's own conceptions of how philosophy should be defined and pursued, and of how it could be used. The sustained distinction made in books 5–7 between the philosopher and mere "lovers of sights" (*philotheamones*), culminating in the allegory of the cave, seems fundamental to Plato's work as a whole and to the political, ethical, and cultural agenda advanced in his dialogues. As such, it is appropriately showcased at the very center of *Republic*, which is one of his most ambitiously comprehensive texts.

The complex "circular" structure of *Republic* has the additional virtue of evoking the narrative patterns of epic poems such as *Iliad* and *Odyssey*. Critics as far back as Friedrich Nietzsche have commented on Plato's rivalry with "Homer," whose works attract

particular scrutiny throughout *Republic*, and we might join Jacob
Howland (The Republic: *The Odyssey of Philosophy*, pp. 30–31)
and others in viewing the dialogue as a "philosophical epic." *Republic*'s aim, then, is perhaps not only to critique the Homeric
epics and the entire poetic tradition they head, but also to provide
a fitting alternative to them, as it reworks their narrative patterns
while revising their themes and concerns.

Republic derives coherence from its thematic focuses as well as
its "plot" development. As is natural in a conversation about justice and "right conduct," the concern for human excellence (*aretê*)
pervades the text. Its treatment of *aretê* plainly responds to works
like *Iliad* and *Odyssey* and the general values of Hellenic culture.
Against their "lessons," it seeks to redefine and limit what is meant
by *aretê*, so as to exclude from its definition all notions of material
success and identify it solely with what we would call "moral excellence" or "virtue."

Like many other Platonic texts, *Republic* advances its argument
about *aretê* by scrutinizing the role that the desire for pleasure
and the fear of pain play in determining the attitudes and values
that most people entertain about "virtue." This is not to say, as the
discussion of book 9 makes plain, that the philosopher has no regard nor desire for pleasure. Rather, the philosopher's estimation
of what constitutes the greatest pleasure differs radically from
common views, and this is why he (or she) lives more happily than
the majority of people. Like many other Platonic texts (notably
Symposium and *Phaedrus*), *Republic* is profoundly concerned with
eros—that is, "erotic" desire that can find purely spiritual and intellectual as well as physical outlets. Book 9, by no accident, represents the tyrant as overwhelmed and enslaved by sexual desire
more than any other appetite, and it thus positions him as polar
opposite to the philosopher who, as a "lover of the vision of truth"
(5.475e), achieves liberation to the fullest extent.

As the opposition of the tyrant and the philosopher indicates,
servitude and enslavement, freedom and liberation also figure
prominently in *Republic*'s nexus of thematic concerns. Thrasymachus' initial conception of the tyrant as supremely free and
happy, for all its arresting frankness, in fact reflects what most
people think—at least if we trust Glaucon and Adeimantus in

book 2—but the discussion in book 9 betrays the egregious error of this view. Much of *Republic*'s energies, then, are directed at challenging common understandings of "slavery," "enslavement," and "freedom," as well as "justice" and "excellence," and at reconfiguring what these terms mean. At the same time, the dialogue aims to demonstrate how the seemingly outrageous, "amoral" opinions espoused by a sophist like Thrasymachus do little more than reflect the thinking of the many.

The characterizations of the interlocutors are also crucial to the sense of unity and coherence in *Republic*, and they reinforce its key concerns and themes in subtle yet significant ways. Plato's representations of Thrasymachus, Polemarchus, Cephalus, Glaucon, and Adeimantus doubtless combine fact with dramatic expedience, and they are as vivid and pointed as those in any other dialogue. Readers interested in detailed and sophisticated analysis of *Republic*'s handling of "character" should consult Ruby Blondell's *The Play of Character in Plato's Dialogues* (pp. 165–250).

By way of a few simple observations, we may note the immediate contrast presented in book 1 between the aggressive and contemptuous Thrasymachus and the more easygoing Polemarchus and Cephalus. These three are to be contrasted with Glaucon and Adeimantus who, though cooperative and on excellent terms with Socrates, can be persistent questioners. In his confidence and self-importance, Thrasymachus resembles the prominent rhetoricians, sophists, and politicians familiar from other dialogues such as *Protagoras*, *Gorgias*, and *Euthydemus*; his aggressiveness also holds up a mirror to the ideology of "might makes right" that he so enthusiastically embraces. He is out of place, however, in the friendly and almost homey atmosphere of Polemarchus' house, since he is outnumbered by others keen to participate in a cooperative investigation, rather than witness a verbal competition.

Yet, as much as it owes to Polemarchus' enthusiasm and the relaxed atmosphere of his home, *Republic*'s investigation of justice gets under way only because of Glaucon and Adeimantus. Most crucially, the brothers lack Thrasymachus' egotism, and they are also plainly meant to seem sharper, better educated, and more intellectually gifted than Polemarchus. At 2.367e Socrates explicitly admires Glaucon's and Adeimantus' natural talent and ability (*physis*). The brothers' conduct and conversation are doubtless intended to reinforce his oft-repeated insistence that both political leadership and philosophy—the two are ideally identical—can be practiced only by a naturally talented, well-trained, and disciplined few.

The good-natured Cephalus lacks the youthful energy and self-discipline to exercise his mind; Polemarchus, though willing, is clearly not able to "philosophize." In contrast, Thrasymachus may have sufficient natural intelligence to engage in the kind of conversation undertaken by Socrates and Plato's brothers, but his competitive habits of self-promotion stand in his way. Modern readers may find Glaucon and Adeimantus too compliant and not sufficiently persistent in their interrogations of Socrates' formulations and assessments. It is not clear, however, that *Republic*'s original readers would have so judged them, and it may well be that the two are offered up to readers as youthful models of the philosophical temperament who have benefited from proper education and training.

As we noted above, the importance of *Republic*'s concerns is affirmed on several occasions by its own interlocutors. It is, of course, Socrates who first asserts this importance, as he incredulously asks Thrasymachus at 1.344e, "Is the attempt to determine the way of man's life so small a matter in your eyes?"

As we also remarked, *Republic*'s interlocutors draw attention to the incomplete, provisional, and at times unsatisfactory nature of their treatment of justice, happiness, the ideal political community, the theory of the ideas, the cognitive faculties of human beings, etc. The inadequacy of "the method we are employing" is acknowledged at 4.435c–d, and referring to this acknowledgment, Socrates cautions at 6.504b–d that the philosopher's examination of justice, wisdom, temperance, and courage "must take a longer and more circuitous way." His refusal to describe the idea of the good except by means of a simile, on the grounds that the task of delineating the good-in-itself is beyond the present conversation (6.506d–e), is matched by his admission in book 7 that dialectic "is not a theme to be treated of in passing only, but will have to be discussed again and again" (7.532d). *Republic*, we may conclude, is not meant to offer a definitive "last word" on any of the subjects it broaches. By no means does it tell readers everything that they need to know about justice, about the formation of functional political communities, about the practices and aims of philosophy, about the method of dialectic, about the ideas, even about poetry.

Readers familiar with Plato know well that other dialogues, notably *Statesman and Laws*, offer perspectives on these very same topics that complement, but also at times differ from, what is presented in *Republic*, and these differences further underscore the lack of definitiveness in *Republic*. Nonetheless, *Republic* is strongly suggestive, and, like its companion dialogues, it is full of "good ideas." It offers up an enjoyable and—by its own standards—wholesome mimesis of a philosophical discussion, and it grants what was surely meant to be an enticing glimpse into the actual practice of Platonic philosophy.

Republic's dialogue form encourages us to come forth with our own questions. Socrates' defense of his conception of the ideal city-state *qua* ideal (5.472d–e), for example, may prompt us to wonder whether Plato actually thought this theoretical model for a political community was practicable. The gradual identification of the just man with the philosopher in books 6–9 invites speculation as to whether, on the logic of *Republic*, anyone *but* the philosopher can be "just" and "happy."

If we approach the text from an analytic and conceptual standpoint, we find that Socrates and his companions make innumerable assumptions and countless leaps of logic. Each of these can be fairly scrutinized and contested. On a different score, we may raise any number of questions about the insights the dialogue might offer us into our world, and also about its relevance to our experiences and value systems. Much of *Republic*, especially its political philosophy and argument for censorship, is at odds with modern ideals; some readers will doubtless be dissatisfied with, among other things, its unapologetic elitism and naïve confidence in the integrity of "philosopher-rulers." Some, however, may find that its critique of ancient Athenian society opens the door to meaningful questions about contemporary cultural practices and priorities.

Whatever questions we ask, and whatever kind of "dialogue" we undertake with this text, we will do well to keep in mind that countless individuals from antiquity to the present have shared *Republic*'s concerns and been influenced by its conceptions—on matters ethical, political, metaphysical, epistemological, eschatological, or aesthetic. Various elements of Plato's thought also find important parallels in the philosophical and religious traditions of other ancient cultures, such as Confucianism and Buddhism. *Republic*, then, might have been composed by a single individual in response to a particular set of cultural circumstances in fourth-century B.C.E. Athens, but the questions it raises and the approaches it takes to dealing with these questions are not wholly unique to Plato or even to ancient Athens. The spirit of Socratic—and Platonic—inquiry thus bids each of us to ask our own questions of *Republic* and let it help us, in turn, examine ourselves and our world.

Elizabeth Watson Scharffenberger received her A.B. in Classical Languages and Literatures from the University of Chicago and her M.A., M.Phil., and Ph.D. in Classics from Columbia University. A specialist in the culture and literature of Athens during the fifth and fourth centuries B.C.E., she currently teaches at Columbia University.

Sources and Acknowledgments

For assistance in composing the introduction and notes to this volume, I have drawn on a variety of sources. James Adams' commentary on *Republic*, though more than a century old and controversial in places, has been a great asset, as have been the more recent commentaries by Stephen Halliwell and Penelope Murray. The critical studies of Plato and *Republic* listed in the bibliography have contributed much to my understanding of the dialogue and its significance; of these, I am most indebted to Andrea Wilson Nightingale's *Genres in Dialogue: Plato and the Construct of Philosophy*. Meriting special mention among the more general works is M. L. West's *Ancient Greek Music*, which supplies a wealth of important information about ancient instruments and musical tastes and is a particularly welcome companion to the study of book 3's critique of music and song.

My colleagues and students are owed my boundless gratitude, since they have enriched my appreciation of Plato and *Republic* in the good old-fashioned Socratic way. My utmost thanks go to Professor Leonardo Tarán and Professor James Coulter at Columbia University. Their graduate-level courses on Plato first sparked my enthusiasm for ancient philosophy, and their thoughtful suggestions regarding this edition of *Republic* have proven invaluable.

Many thanks are also due to the editor of this series, Jeffrey Broesche, and his staff for their patient effort in improving my work and bringing the volume to publication.

Note on the Translation

Benjamin Jowett (1818–1893) was appointed the Regius Professor of Greek at Oxford University's Balliol College in 1855. He became master of Balliol in 1870 and vice-chancellor of the University in 1882. He was a prolific translator of ancient Greek texts as well as author of many scholarly works on the classics. His translation of Plato's *Republic*, which was first published in 1871, enjoyed wide popularity for decades in English-speaking countries around the world.

In his review of the third edition of Jowett's *The Dialogues of Plato*,* the eminent American classicist Paul Shorey states the following: "Ingenious, fluent, easy are epithets we apply to Professor Jowett's renderings; we should never, I think, call them inevitable" (p. 351). Shorey thus tactfully calls our attention to the fact that Jowett's translation of Plato is not as literal as it could be. As Shorey observes throughout his review, Jowett strove not merely to translate Plato but to interpret him—and to transform his Greek into something that would appeal to English-speaking readers in Great Britain and elsewhere during the Victorian era. The diction of his translation of *Republic* is accordingly stylized in a way that is at times alien to Plato's nuanced and precise idiom, and in places its style may strike some modern readers as flowery, if not florid. To enhance its appeal to an audience familiar with English-language classics, Jowett embellished his version of *Republic* with language evocative of famous literary works dating from the Renaissance on, and readers of this edition should not be surprised if Socrates and his companions occasionally sound as if they were quoting from Shakespeare or the King James version of the Bible.

Nonetheless, Jowett's translation of *Republic* remains eminently readable, and I have introduced into it a minimum number of

---

* *American Journal of Philology* 13 (1892), pp. 349—372.

changes. Most important are the corrections called for by Paul Shorey, who spotted several places in which Jowett mistranslated the Greek text. A list of the sections in which I have incorporated the corrections recommended by Shorey is given at the end of this note. In addition, I have occasionally replaced obsolete vocabulary with words more commonly used today. Some of Jowett's choices, such as the rendering of the Greek word *theos* by "God" (with a capital G), appear so often as to make their alteration difficult; in these cases, I have left his text intact and discuss his choices—and why I disagree with them—in the endnotes. I also discuss in the endnotes a few instances in which I prefer a different reading of the Greek text but have not altered Jowett's translation.

Jowett sometimes let the Greek usage, in which nouns designating inanimate as well as animate objects have gender (that is, masculine, feminine, or neuter), guide his choice of pronouns. Thus "soul" (*psychê*), which is feminine in Greek, is referred to by feminine pronouns such as "she"; "sun," which is masculine (*helios*), is "he," and so forth. I have changed Jowett's renderings of these pronouns in only a few instances, since readers, once aware of his practice, will be able to make good sense of the passages in question.

Passages in this edition that incorporate corrections recommended by Paul Shorey:

1.341c, 1.344e, 4.437d, 4.439e, 5.464e, 5.473a, 6.490d, 6.493c–d, 6.498a, 7.523c, 7.525b, 7.526c, 7.534a, 7.540b, 8.553d, 9.575c, 9.576d, 9.579c, 9.581c, 9.581d–e, 10.607a, 10.611b.

REPUBLIC

BOOK 1

SPEAKERS*

SOCRATES   CEPHALUS

GLAUCON   THRASYMACHUS

ADEIMANTUS   CLEITOPHON

POLEMARCHUS

I WENT DOWN YESTERDAY to the Piræus† with Glaucon, the son
of Ariston, that I might offer up my prayers to the goddess;‡ and
also because I wanted to see in what manner they would celebrate
the festival, which was a new thing. I was delighted with the procession of the inhabitants; but that of the Thracians was equally,
if not more, beautiful. When we had finished our prayers and   b
viewed the spectacle, we turned in the direction of the city; and at
that instant Polemarchus, the son of Cephalus, chanced to catch
sight of us from a distance as we were starting on our way home,
and told his slave to run and bid us wait for him. The slave took
hold of me by the cloak behind, and said, Polemarchus desires
you to wait.

I turned round, and asked him where his master was.

There he is, said the slave, coming after you, if you will only wait.

Certainly we will, said Glaucon; and in a few minutes Polemarchus appeared, and with him Adeimantus, Glaucon's brother,   c
Niceratus, the son of Nicias, and several others who had been at
the procession.

---

*Information about Socrates, Thrasymachus, and other interlocutors in *Republic*
is given in the introduction.
†The major port city of Attica, about 4 miles from Athens.
‡The Thracian deity Bendis, identified by Greeks with the goddess Artemis. The
cult of Bendis was officially accepted in Piraeus in 430 or 429 B.C.E.

Polemarchus said to me, I perceive, Socrates, that you and your companion are already on your way to the city.

You are not far wrong, I said.

But do you see, he rejoined, how many we are?

Of course.

And are you stronger than all these? for if not, you will have to remain where you are.

May there not be the alternative, I said, that we may persuade you to let us go?

But can you persuade us, if we refuse to listen to you? he said.

Certainly not, replied Glaucon.

Then we are not going to listen; of that you may be assured.

328   Adeimantus added: Has no one told you of the torch-race on horseback in honor of the goddess which will take place in the evening?

With horses! I replied. That is a novelty. Will horsemen carry torches and pass them one to another during the race?

Yes, said Polemarchus; and not only so, but a festival will be celebrated at night, which you certainly ought to see. Let us rise soon after supper and see this festival; there will be a gathering of
b   young men, and we will have a good talk. Stay then, and do not be perverse.

Glaucon said, I suppose, since you insist, that we must.

Very good, I replied.

Accordingly we went with Polemarchus to his house; and there we found his brothers Lysias and Euthydemus, and with them Thrasymachus the Chalcedonian, Charmantides the Pæanian, and Cleitophon, the son of Aristonymus. There too was Cephalus, the father of Polemarchus, whom I had not seen for a long time, and I
c   thought him very much aged. He was seated on a cushioned chair, and had a garland on his head, for he had been sacrificing in the court; and there were some other chairs in the room arranged in a semicircle, upon which we sat down by him. He saluted me eagerly, and then he said:

You don't come to see me, Socrates, as often as you ought: If I were still able to go and see you I would not ask you to come to me. But at my age I can hardly get to the city, and therefore you
d   should come oftener to the Piræus. For, let me tell you that the

more the pleasures of the body fade away, the greater to me are the pleasure and charm of conversation. Do not, then, deny my request, but make our house your resort and keep company with these young men; we are old friends, and you will be quite at home with us.

I replied: There is nothing which for my part I like better, Cephalus, than conversing with aged men; for I regard them as travellers who have gone a journey which I too may have to go, and of whom I ought to inquire whether the way is smooth and easy or rugged and difficult. And this is a question which I should like to ask of you, who have arrived at that time which the poets call the "threshold of old age":* Is life harder toward the end, or what report do you give of it?

I will tell you, Socrates, he said, what my own feeling is. Men of my age flock together; we are birds of a feather, as the old proverb says;† and at our meetings the tale of my acquaintance commonly is: I cannot eat, I cannot drink; the pleasures of youth and love are fled away; there was a good time once, but now that is gone, and life is no longer life. Some complain of the slights which are put upon them by relations, and they will tell you sadly of how many evils their old age is the cause. But to me, Socrates, these complainers seem to blame that which is not really in fault. For if old age were the cause, I too, being old, and every other old man would have felt as they do. But this is not my own experience, nor that of others whom I have known. How well I remember the aged poet Sophocles,‡ when in answer to the question, How does love suit with age, Sophocles—are you still the man you were? Peace, he replied; most gladly have I escaped the thing of which you speak; I feel as if I had escaped from a mad and furious master. His words have often occurred to my mind since, and they seem as good to me now as at the time when he uttered them. For certainly old age has a great sense of calm and freedom; when the

e

329

b

c

---

*The phrase evokes the Homeric poems; compare *Iliad* 22.60 and 24.487, and *Odyssey* 15.246.
†Literally, "we who are approximately the same age often come to the same place."
‡Athenian tragedian (c.496–406 B.C.E.), active as a playwright until his death.

passions relax their hold, then, as Sophocles says, we are freed from the grasp not of one mad master only, but of many. The truth is, Socrates, that these regrets, and also the complaints about relations, are to be attributed to the same cause, which is not old age, but men's characters and tempers; for he who is of a calm and happy nature will hardly feel the pressure of age, but to him who is of an opposite disposition youth and age are equally a burden.

I listened in admiration, and wanting to draw him out, that he might go on—Yes, Cephalus, I said; but I rather suspect that people in general are not convinced by you when you speak thus; they think that old age sits lightly upon you, not because of your happy disposition, but because you are rich, and wealth is well known to be a great comforter.

You are right, he replied; they are not convinced: and there is something in what they say; not, however, so much as they imagine. I might answer them as Themistocles° answered the Seriphian† who was abusing him and saying that he was famous, not for his own merits but because he was an Athenian: "If you had been a native of my country or I of yours, neither of us would have been famous." And to those who are not rich and are impatient of old age, the same reply may be made; for to the good poor man old age cannot be a light burden, nor can a bad rich man ever have peace with himself.

May I ask, Cephalus, whether your fortune was for the most part inherited or acquired by you?

Acquired! Socrates; do you want to know how much I acquired? In the art of making money I have been midway between my father and grandfather: for my grandfather, whose name I bear, doubled and trebled the value of his patrimony, that which he inherited being much what I possess now; but my father, Lysanias, reduced the property below what it is at present; and I shall be satisfied if I leave to these my sons not less, but a little more, than I received.

°Athenian general (c.528–462 B.C.E.) who masterminded the defeat of the Persian navy at the battle of Salamis in 480 B.C.E.
†Seriphos is a small island in the Aegean Sea.

That was why I asked you the question, I replied, because I see that you are indifferent about money, which is a characteristic c rather of those who have inherited their fortunes than of those who have acquired them; the makers of fortunes have a second love of money as a creation of their own, resembling the affection of authors for their own poems, or of parents for their children, besides that natural love of it for the sake of use and profit which is common to them and all men. And hence they are very bad company, for they can talk about nothing but the praises of wealth.

That is true, he said.

Yes, that is very true, but may I ask another question?—What d do you consider to be the greatest blessing which you have reaped from your wealth?

One, he said, of which I could not expect easily to convince others. For let me tell you, Socrates, that when a man thinks himself to be near death, fears and cares enter into his mind which he never had before; the tales of a world below and the punishment which is exacted there of deeds done here were once a laughing matter to him, but now he is tormented with the thought that they may be e true: either from the weakness of age, or because he is now drawing nearer to that other place, he has a clearer view of these things; suspicions and alarms crowd thickly upon him, and he begins to reflect and consider what wrongs he has done to others. And when he finds that the sum of his transgressions is great he will many a time like a child start up in his sleep for fear, and he is filled with dark forebod- 331 ings. But to him who is conscious of no sin, sweet hope, as Pindar* charmingly says, is the kind nurse of his age:

> "Hope," he says, "cherishes the soul of him who lives in justice
> and holiness, and is the nurse of his age and the companion of his
> journey—hope which is mightiest to sway the restless soul of man.

How admirable are his words! And the great blessing of riches, I do not say to every man, but to a good man, is, that he has had no b

---

*Lyric poet (c.518–438 B.C.E.) whose work is cited again at 2.365b. The poem from which Cephalus quotes does not survive.

occasion to deceive or to defraud others, either intentionally or unintentionally; and when he departs to the world below he is not in any apprehension about offerings due to the gods or debts which he owes to men. Now to this peace of mind the possession of wealth greatly contributes; and therefore I say, that, setting one thing against another, of the many advantages which wealth has to give, to a man of sense this is in my opinion the greatest.

c   Well said, Cephalus, I replied; but as concerning justice, what is it?—to speak the truth and to pay your debts—no more than this? And even to this are there not exceptions? Suppose that a friend when in his right mind has deposited arms with me and he asks for them when he is not in his right mind, ought I to give them back to him? No one would say that I ought or that I should be right in doing so, any more than they would say that I ought always to speak the truth to one who is in his condition.

You are quite right, he replied.

d   But then, I said, speaking the truth and paying your debts is not a correct definition of justice.

Quite correct, Socrates, if Simonides* is to be believed,[1] said Polemarchus, interposing.

I fear, said Cephalus, that I must go now, for I have to look after the sacrifices, and I hand over the argument to Polemarchus and the company.

Is not Polemarchus your heir? I said.

To be sure, he answered, and went away laughing to the sacrifices.

e   Tell me then, O thou heir of the argument, what did Simonides say, and according to you, truly say, about justice?

He said that the repayment of a debt is just, and in saying so he appears to me to be right.

I shall be sorry to doubt the word of such a wise and inspired man, but his meaning, though probably clear to you, is the reverse of clear to me. For he certainly does not mean, as we were just now saying, that I ought to return a deposit of arms or of anything

---

*Lyric and elegiac poet (c.548–468 B.C.E.) from the island Ceos, whose work is also alluded to at 2.365c. The saying attributed to Simonides here does not match anything in the extant fragments of his poetry.

else to one who asks for it when he is not in his right senses; and yet   332
a deposit cannot be denied to be a debt.

True.

Then when the person who asks me is not in his right mind I
am by no means to make the return?

Certainly not.

When Simonides said that the repayment of a debt was justice,
he did not mean to include that case?

Certainly not; for he thinks that a friend ought always to do
good to a friend, and never evil.

You mean that the return of a deposit of gold which is to the injury of the receiver, if the two parties are friends, is not the re-   b
payment of a debt—that is what you would imagine him to say?

Yes.

And are enemies also to receive what we owe to them?[2]

To be sure, he said, they are to receive what we owe them; and
an enemy, as I take it, owes to an enemy that which is due or
proper to him—that is to say, evil.[3]

Simonides, then, after the manner of poets, would seem to
have spoken darkly of the nature of justice; for he really meant to   c
say that justice is the giving to each man what is proper to him,
and this he termed a debt.

That must have been his meaning, he said.

By heaven! I replied; and if we asked him what due or proper
thing is given by medicine, and to whom, what answer do you
think that he would make to us?[4]

He would surely reply that medicine gives drugs and meat and
drink to human bodies.

And what due or proper thing is given by cookery, and to what?

Seasoning to food.   d

And what is that which justice gives, and to whom?

If, Socrates, we are to be guided at all by the analogy of the
preceding instances, then justice is the art which gives good to
friends and evil to enemies.

That is his meaning, then?

I think so.

And who is best able to do good to his friends and evil to his
enemies in time of sickness?

The physician.

Or when they are on a voyage, amid the perils of the sea?

The pilot.

And in what sort of actions or with a view to what result is the just man most able to do harm to his enemy and good to his friend?

In going to war against the one and in making alliances with the other.

But when a man is well, my dear Polemarchus, there is no need of a physician?

No.

And he who is not on a voyage has no need of a pilot?

No.

Then in time of peace justice will be of no use?

I am very far from thinking so.

You think that justice may be of use in peace as well as in war?

Yes.

Like husbandry for the acquisition of corn?

Yes.

Or like shoemaking for the acquisition of shoes—that is what you mean?

Yes.

And what similar use or power of acquisition has justice in time of peace?

In contracts, Socrates, justice is of use.

And by contracts you mean partnerships?

Exactly.

But is the just man or the skilful player a more useful and better partner at a game of draughts?

The skilful player.

And in the laying of bricks and stones is the just man a more useful or better partner than the builder?

Quite the reverse.

Then in what sort of partnership is the just man a better partner than the harp-player, as in playing the harp the harp-player is certainly a better partner than the just man?

In a money partnership.

Yes, Polemarchus, but surely not in the use of money; for you do not want a just man to be your counsellor in the purchase or sale of a horse; a man who is knowing about horses would be better for that, would he not?

Certainly.

And when you want to buy a ship, the shipwright or the pilot would be better?

True.

Then what is that joint use of silver or gold in which the just man is to be preferred?

When you want a deposit to be kept safely.

You mean when money is not wanted, but allowed to lie?

Precisely.

That is to say, justice is useful when money is useless?

That is the inference.

And when you want to keep a pruning-hook safe, then justice is useful to the individual and to the State; but when you want to use it, then the art of the vine-dresser?

Clearly.

And when you want to keep a shield or a lyre, and not to use them, you would say that justice is useful; but when you want to use them, then the art of the soldier or of the musician?

Certainly.

And so of all other things—justice is useful when they are useless, and useless when they are useful?

That is the inference.

Then justice is not good for much. But let us consider this further point: Is not he who can best strike a blow in a boxing match or in any kind of fighting best able to ward off a blow?

Certainly.

And he who is most skilful in preventing or escaping from a disease is best able to create one?

True.

And he is the best guard of a camp who is best able to steal a march upon the enemy?

Certainly.

Then he who is a good keeper of anything is also a good thief?

That, I suppose, is to be inferred.

Then if the just man is good at keeping money, he is good at stealing it.

That is implied in the argument.

Then after all, the just man has turned out to be a thief. And this is a lesson which I suspect you must have learnt out of Homer,[5] for he, speaking of Autolycus,* the maternal grandfather of Odysseus, who is a favorite of his, affirms that

"He was excellent above all men in theft and perjury."

And so, you and Homer and Simonides are agreed that justice is an art of theft; to be practised, however, "for the good of friends and for the harm of enemies"—that was what you were saying?

No, certainly not that, though I do not now know what I did say; but I still stand by the latter words.

Well, there is another question: By friends and enemies do we mean those who are so really, or only in seeming?

Surely, he said, a man may be expected to love those whom he thinks good, and to hate those whom he thinks evil.

Yes, but do not persons often err about good and evil: many who are not good seem to be so, and conversely?

That is true.

Then to them the good will be enemies and the evil will be their friends?

True.

And in that case they will be right in doing good to the evil and evil to the good?

Clearly.

But the good are just and would not do an injustice?

True.

Then according to your argument it is just to injure those who do no wrong?

Nay, Socrates; the doctrine is immoral.

Then I suppose that we ought to do good to the just and harm to the unjust?

I like that better.

---

*The grandfather of Odysseus (the hero of *Odyssey*), who is described in *Odyssey* 19.392–398.

But see the consequence: Many a man who is ignorant of human nature has friends who are bad friends, and in that case he ought   e
to do harm to them; and he has good enemies whom he ought to benefit; but, if so, we shall be saying the very opposite of that which we affirmed to be the meaning of Simonides.

Very true, he said; and I think that we had better correct an error into which we seem to have fallen in the use of the words "friend" and "enemy."

What was the error, Polemarchus? I asked.

We assumed that he is a friend who seems to be or who is thought good.

And how is the error to be corrected?

We should rather say that he is a friend who is, as well as seems, good; and that he who seems only and is not good, only seems to be and is not a friend; and of an enemy the same may be said.   335

You would argue that the good are our friends and the bad our enemies?

Yes.

And instead of saying simply as we did at first, that it is just to do good to our friends and harm to our enemies, we should further say: It is just to do good to our friends when they are good, and harm to our enemies when they are evil?

Yes, that appears to me to be the truth.   b

But ought the just to injure anyone at all?

Undoubtedly he ought to injure those who are both wicked and his enemies.

When horses are injured, are they improved or deteriorated?

The latter.

Deteriorated, that is to say, in the good qualities of horses, not of dogs?[26]

Yes, of horses.

And dogs are deteriorated in the good qualities of dogs, and not of horses?

Of course.

And will not men who are injured be deteriorated in that which   c
is the proper virtue of man?

Certainly.

And that human virtue is justice?

To be sure.

Then men who are injured are of necessity made unjust?

That is the result.

But can the musician by his art make men unmusical?

Certainly not.

Or the horseman by his art make them bad horsemen?

Impossible.

d   And can the just by justice make men unjust, or speaking generally, can the good by virtue make them bad?

Assuredly not.

Any more than heat can produce cold?

It cannot.

Or drought moisture?

Clearly not.

Nor can the good harm anyone?

Impossible.

And the just is the good?

Certainly.

Then to injure a friend or anyone else is not the act of a just man, but of the opposite, who is the unjust?

I think that what you say is quite true, Socrates.

e   Then if a man says that justice consists in the repayment of debts, and that good is the debt which a just man owes to his friends, and evil the debt which he owes to his enemies—to say this is not wise; for it is not true, if, as has been clearly shown, the injuring of another can be in no case just.

I agree with you, said Polemarchus.

Then you and I are prepared to take up arms against anyone who attributes such a saying to Simonides or Bias or Pittacus,* or any other wise man or seer?

I am quite ready to do battle at your side, he said.

Shall I tell you whose I believe the saying to be?

336   Whose?

I believe that Periander or Perdiccas or Xerxes or Ismenias the

---

*Bias and Pittacus were legendary wise men ("sages") who lived in the sixth century B.C.E. Bias was from Priene (in Ionia), Pittacus from Mytilene (on the island Lesbos in the Aegean).

Theban,[7] or some other rich and mighty man, who had a great opinion of his own power, was the first to say that justice is "doing good to your friends and harm to your enemies."

Most true, he said.

Yes, I said; but if this definition of justice also breaks down, what other can be offered?

Several times in the course of the discussion Thrasymachus had made an attempt to get the argument into his own hands, and had been put down by the rest of the company, who wanted to hear the end. But when Polemarchus and I had done speaking and there was a pause, he could no longer hold his peace; and, gathering himself up, he came at us like a wild beast, seeking to devour us. We were quite panic-stricken at the sight of him.

He roared out to the whole company: What folly, Socrates, has taken possession of you all? And why do you knock under to one another? I say that if you want really to know what justice is, you should not only ask but answer, and you should not seek honor to yourself from the refutation of an opponent, but have your own answer; for there is many a one who can ask and cannot answer. And now I will not have you say that justice is duty or advantage or profit or gain or interest, for this sort of nonsense will not do for me; I must have clearness and accuracy.

I was panic-stricken at his words, and could not look at him without trembling. Indeed I believe that if I had not fixed my eye upon him, I should have been struck dumb: but when I saw his fury rising, I looked at him first, and was therefore able to reply to him.

Thrasymachus, I said, with a quiver, don't be hard upon us. Polemarchus and I may have been guilty of a little mistake in the argument, but I can assure you that the error was not intentional. If we were seeking for a piece of gold, you would not imagine that we were "knocking under to one another," and so losing our chance of finding it. And why, when we are seeking for justice, a thing more precious than many pieces of gold, do you say that we are weakly yielding to one another and not doing our utmost to get at the truth? Nay, my good friend, we are most willing and anxious to do so, but the fact is that we cannot. And if so, you people who know all things should pity us and not be angry with us.

How characteristic of Socrates! he replied, with a bitter laugh;

that's your ironical style! Did I not foresee—have I not already told you, that whatever he was asked he would refuse to answer, and try irony or any other shuffle, in order that he might avoid answering?

You are a clever man, Thrasymachus, I replied, and well know that if you ask a person what numbers make up twelve, taking care to prohibit him whom you ask from answering twice six, or

b three times four, or six times two, or four times three, "for this sort of nonsense will not do for me"—then obviously, if that is your way of putting the question, no one can answer you. But suppose that he were to retort: "Thrasymachus, what do you mean? If one of these numbers which you interdict be the true answer to the question, am I falsely to say some other number which is not the right

c one?—is that your meaning?"—How would you answer him?

Just as if the two cases were at all alike! he said.

Why should they not be? I replied; and even if they are not, but only appear to be so to the person who is asked, ought he not to say what he thinks, whether you and I forbid him or not?

I presume then that you are going to make one of the interdicted answers?

I dare say that I may, notwithstanding the danger, if upon reflection I approve of any of them.

d But what if I give you an answer about justice other and better, he said, than any of these? What do you deserve to have done to you?

Done to me!—as becomes the ignorant, I must learn from the wise—that is what I deserve to have done to me.

What, and no payment! A pleasant notion!

I will pay when I have the money, I replied.

But you have, Socrates, said Glaucon: and you, Thrasymachus, need be under no anxiety about money, for we will all make a contribution for Socrates.

e Yes, he replied, and then Socrates will do as he always does—refuse to answer himself, but take and pull to pieces the answer of someone else.

Why, my good friend, I said, how can anyone answer who knows, and says that he knows, just nothing; and who, even if he has some faint notions of his own, is told by a man of authority not to utter them? The natural thing is, that the speaker should be someone

338 like yourself who professes to know and can tell what he knows.

Will you then kindly answer, for the edification of the company and of myself?

Glaucon and the rest of the company joined in my request, and Thrasymachus, as anyone might see, was in reality eager to speak; for he thought that he had an excellent answer, and would distinguish himself. But at first he affected to insist on my answering; at length he consented to begin. Behold, he said, the wisdom of Socrates; he refuses to teach himself, and goes about learning of others, to whom he never even says, Thank you.

That I learn of others, I replied, is quite true; but that I am ungrateful I wholly deny. Money I have none, and therefore I pay in praise, which is all I have; and how ready I am to praise anyone who appears to me to speak well you will very soon find out when you answer; for I expect that you will answer well.

Listen, then, he said; I proclaim that justice is nothing else than the interest of the stronger.[8] And now why do you not praise me? But of course you won't.

Let me first understand you, I replied. Justice, as you say, is the interest of the stronger. What, Thrasymachus, is the meaning of this? You cannot mean to say that because Polydamas, the pancratiast, is stronger than we are, and finds the eating of beef conducive to his bodily strength, that to eat beef is therefore equally for our good who are weaker than he is, and right and just for us?

That's abominable of you, Socrates; you take the words in the sense which is most damaging to the argument.

Not at all, my good sir, I said; I am trying to understand them; and I wish that you would be a little clearer.

Well, he said, have you never heard that forms of government differ—there are tyrannies, and there are democracies, and there are aristocracies?[9]

Yes, I know.

And the government is the ruling power in each State?

Certainly.

And the different forms of government make laws democratical, aristocratical, tyrannical, with a view to their several interests; and these laws, which are made by them for their own interests, are the justice which they deliver to their subjects, and him who transgresses them they punish as a breaker of the law, and unjust. And that is what I mean when I say that in all States there is the same principle of justice, which is the interest of the government; and as the government must be supposed to have power, the only reasonable conclusion is that everywhere there is one principle of justice, which is the interest of the stronger.

Now I understand you, I said; and whether you are right or not I will try to discover. But let me remark that in defining justice you have yourself used the word "interest," which you forbade me to use. It is true, however, that in your definition the words "of the stronger" are added.

A small addition, you must allow, he said.

Great or small, never mind about that: we must first inquire whether what you are saying is the truth. Now we are both agreed that justice is interest of some sort, but you go on to say "of the stronger"; about this addition I am not so sure, and must therefore consider further.

Proceed.

I will; and first tell me, Do you admit that it is just for subjects to obey their rulers?

I do.

But are the rulers of States absolutely infallible, or are they sometimes liable to err?

To be sure, he replied, they are liable to err.

Then in making their laws they may sometimes make them rightly, and sometimes not?

True.

When they make them rightly, they make them agreeably to their interest; when they are mistaken, contrary to their interest; you admit that?

Yes.

And the laws which they make must be obeyed by their subjects—and that is what you call justice?

Doubtless.

Then justice, according to your argument, is not only obedience to the interest of the stronger, but the reverse?

What is that you are saying? he asked.

I am only repeating what you are saying, I believe. But let us consider: Have we not admitted that the rulers may be mistaken about their own interest in what they command, and also that to obey them is justice? Has not that been admitted?

Yes.

Then you must also have acknowledged justice not to be for the interest of the stronger, when the rulers unintentionally command things to be done which are to their own injury. For if, as you say, justice is the obedience which the subject renders to their commands, in that case, O wisest of men, is there any escape from the conclusion that the weaker are commanded to do, not what is for the interest, but what is for the injury of the stronger?

Nothing can be clearer, Socrates, said Polemarchus.

Yes, said Cleitophon, interposing, if you are allowed to be his witness.

But there is no need of any witness, said Polemarchus, for Thrasymachus himself acknowledges that rulers may sometime command what is not for their own interest, and that for subjects to obey them is justice.

Yes, Polemarchus—Thrasymachus said that for subjects to do what was commanded by their rulers is just.

Yes, Cleitophon, but he also said that justice is the interest of the stronger, and, while admitting both these propositions, he further acknowledged that the stronger may command the weaker who are his subjects to do what is not for his own interest; whence follows that justice is the injury quite as much as the interest of the stronger.

But, said Cleitophon, he meant by the interest of the stronger what the stronger thought to be his interest—this was what the weaker had to do; and this was affirmed by him to be justice.

Those were not his words, rejoined Polemarchus.

Never mind, I replied, if he now says that they are, let us accept his statement. Tell me, Thrasymachus, I said, did you mean by justice what the stronger thought to be his interest, whether really so or not?

Certainly not, he said. Do you suppose that I call him who is mistaken the stronger at the time when he is mistaken?

Yes, I said, my impression was that you did so, when you admitted that the ruler was not infallible, but might be sometimes mistaken.

d   You argue like an informer,* Socrates. Do you mean, for example, that he who is mistaken about the sick is a physician in that he
is mistaken? or that he who errs in arithmetic or grammar is an
arithmetician or grammarian at the time when he is making the
mistake, in respect of the mistake? True, we say that the physician
or arithmetician or grammarian has made a mistake, but this is
only a way of speaking; for the fact is that neither the grammarian
e   nor any other person of skill ever makes a mistake in so far as he
is what his name implies; they none of them err unless their skill
fails them, and then they cease to be skilled artists. No artist or
sage or ruler errs at the time when he is what his name implies;
though he is commonly said to err, and I adopted the common
mode of speaking. But to be perfectly accurate, since you are such
341   a lover of accuracy, we should say that the ruler, in so far as he is a
ruler, is unerring, and, being unerring, always commands that
which is for his own interest; and the subject is required to execute his commands; and therefore, as I said at first and now repeat, justice is the interest of the stronger.

        Indeed, Thrasymachus, and do I really appear to you to argue
like an informer?

        Certainly, he replied.

        And do you suppose that I ask these questions with any design
of injuring you in the argument?

        Nay, he replied, "suppose" is not the word—I know it; but you
b   will be found out, and by sheer force of argument you will never
prevail.

        I shall not make the attempt, my dear man; but to avoid any mis-
understanding occurring between us in future, let me ask, in what
sense do you speak of a ruler or stronger whose interest, as you were
saying, he being the superior, it is just that the inferior should execute—is he a ruler in the popular or in the strict sense of the term?

        In the strictest of all senses, he said. And now cheat and play
the informer if you can; I ask no quarter at your hands. But you
never will be able, never.

---

*The expression suggests that, in Thrasymachus' view, Socrates is wrangling
unscrupulously for the sake of personal gain.

And do you imagine, I said, that I am such a madman as to try   c
and cheat Thrasymachus? I might as well shave a lion.

Why, he said, you made the attempt a minute ago, though you
proved to be a thing of naught with regard to that, too.

Enough, I said, of these civilities. It will be better that I should
ask you a question: Is the physician, taken in that strict sense of
which you are speaking, a healer of the sick or a maker of money?
And remember that I am now speaking of the true physician.

A healer of the sick, he replied.

And the pilot—that is to say, the true pilot—is he a captain of
sailors or a mere sailor?

A captain of sailors.

The circumstance that he sails in the ship is not to be taken into   d
account; neither is he to be called a sailor; the name pilot by which
he is distinguished has nothing to do with sailing, but is significant
of his skill and of his authority over the sailors.

Very true, he said.

Now, I said, every art has an interest?[10]

Certainly.

For which the art has to consider and provide?

Yes, that is the aim of art.

And the interest of any art is the perfection of it—this and
nothing else?

What do you mean?   e

I mean what I may illustrate negatively by the example of the
body. Suppose you were to ask me whether the body is self-
sufficing or has wants, I should reply: Certainly the body has
wants; for the body may be ill and require to be cured, and has
therefore interests to which the art of medicine ministers; and
this is the origin and intention of medicine, as you will acknowledge. Am I not right?

Quite right, he replied.

But is the art of medicine or any other art faulty or deficient   342
in any quality in the same way that the eye may be deficient in sight
or the ear fail of hearing, and therefore requires another art to
provide for the interests of seeing and hearing—has art in itself, I
say, any similar liability to fault or defect, and does every art require another supplementary art to provide for its interests, and

that another and another without end? Or have the arts to look only
b   after their own interests? Or have they no need either of themselves or of another?—having no faults or defects, they have no
need to correct them, either by the exercise of their own art or of
any other; they have only to consider the interest of their subject-
matter. For every art remains pure and faultless while remaining
true—that is to say, while perfect and unimpaired. Take the words
in your precise sense, and tell me whether I am not right.

Yes, clearly.

c   Then medicine does not consider the interest of medicine, but
the interest of the body?

True, he said.

Nor does the art of horsemanship consider the interests of the
art of horsemanship, but the interests of the horse; neither do any
other arts care for themselves, for they have no needs; they care
only for that which is the subject of their art?

True, he said.

But surely, Thrasymachus, the arts are the superiors and rulers
of their own subjects?

To this he assented with a good deal of reluctance.

Then, I said, no science or art considers or enjoins the interest
of the stronger or superior, but only the interest of the subject and
d   weaker?

He made an attempt to contest this proposition also, but finally
acquiesced.

Then, I continued, no physician, in so far as he is a physician, considers his own good in what he prescribes, but the good of his patient; for the true physician is also a ruler having the human body as
a subject, and is not a mere money-maker; that has been admitted?

Yes.

And the pilot likewise, in the strict sense of the term, is a ruler
of sailors, and not a mere sailor?

e   That has been admitted.

And such a pilot and ruler will provide and prescribe for the interest of the sailor who is under him, and not for his own or the
ruler's interest?

He gave a reluctant "Yes."

Then, I said, Thrasymachus, there is no one in any rule who, in

so far as he is a ruler, considers or enjoins what is for his own interest, but always what is for the interest of his subject or suitable to
his art; to that he looks, and that alone he considers in everything
which he says and does.

When we had got to this point in the argument, and everyone   343
saw that the definition of justice had been completely upset,
Thrasymachus, instead of replying to me, said, Tell me, Socrates,
have you got a nurse?

Why do you ask such a question, I said, when you ought rather
to be answering?

Because she leaves you to snivel, and never wipes your nose:
she has not even taught you to know the shepherd from the sheep.

What makes you say that? I replied.

Because you fancy that the shepherd or cowherd fattens or   b
tends the sheep or oxen with a view to their own good and not to
the good of himself or his master; and you further imagine that the
rulers of States, if they are true rulers, never think of their subjects as sheep, and that they are not studying their own advantage
day and night.[11] Oh, no; and so entirely astray are you in your   c
ideas about the just and unjust as not even to know that justice
and the just are in reality another's good; that is to say, the interest
of the ruler and stronger, and the loss of the subject and servant;
and injustice the opposite; for the unjust is lord over the truly simple and just: he is the stronger, and his subjects do what is for his
interest, and minister to his happiness, which is very far from
being their own. Consider further, most foolish Socrates, that the   d
just is always a loser in comparison with the unjust. First of all, in
private contracts: wherever the unjust is the partner of the just
you will find that, when the partnership is dissolved, the unjust
man has always more and the just less.[12] Secondly, in their dealings with the State: when there is an income-tax, the just man will
pay more and the unjust less on the same amount of income; and
when there is anything to be received the one gains nothing and
the other much. Observe also what happens when they take an of-   e
fice; there is the just man neglecting his affairs and perhaps suffering other losses, and getting nothing out of the public, because
he is just; moreover he is hated by his friends and acquaintance
for refusing to serve them in unlawful ways. But all this is reversed

in the case of the unjust man. I am speaking, as before, of injustice on a large scale in which the advantage of the unjust is most apparent; and my meaning will be most clearly seen if we turn to that highest form of injustice in which the criminal is the happiest of men,[13] and the sufferers or those who refuse to do injustice are the most miserable—that is to say tyranny, which by fraud and force takes away the property of others, not little by little but wholesale; comprehending in one, things sacred as well as profane, private and public; for which acts of wrong, if he were detected perpetrating any one of them singly, he would be punished and incur great disgrace—they who do such wrong in particular cases are called robbers of temples, and man-stealers and burglars and swindlers and thieves. But when a man besides taking away the money of the citizens has made slaves of them, then, instead of these names of reproach, he is termed happy and blessed, not only by the citizens but by all who hear of his having achieved the consummation of injustice. For mankind censure injustice, fearing that they may be the victims of it and not because they shrink from committing it. And thus, as I have shown, Socrates, injustice, when on a sufficient scale, has more strength and freedom and mastery than justice; and, as I said at first, justice is the interest of the stronger, whereas injustice is a man's own profit and interest.

Thrasymachus, when he had thus spoken, having, like a bathman,* deluged our ears with his words, had a mind to go away. But the company would not let him; they insisted that he should remain and defend his position; and I myself added my own humble request that he would not leave us. Thrasymachus, I said to him, excellent man, how suggestive are your remarks! And are you going to run away before you have fairly taught or learned whether they are true or not? Is the attempt to determine the way of man's life so small a matter in your eyes—to determine how life may be passed by each one of us to the greatest advantage?[14]

And do I differ from you, he said, as to the importance of the inquiry?

---

*That is, an attendant at a public bath. Aristophanes, *Knights* 1403 stereotypes bathmen, along with prostitutes, as disreputable individuals.

You appear to differ, I replied, or else to have no care or thought about us, Thrasymachus—whether we live better or worse from not knowing what you say you know, is to you a matter of indifference. Prithee, friend, do not keep your knowledge   345 to yourself; we are a large party; and any benefit which you confer upon us will be amply rewarded. For my own part I openly declare that I am not convinced, and that I do not believe injustice to be more gainful than justice, even if uncontrolled and allowed to have free play.[15] For, granting that there may be an unjust man who is able to commit injustice either by fraud or force, still this does not convince me of the superior advantage of injustice, and there may be others who are in the same predicament   b with myself. Perhaps we may be wrong; if so, you in your wisdom should convince us that we are mistaken in preferring justice to injustice.

And how am I to convince you, he said, if you are not already convinced by what I have just said; what more can I do for you? Would you have me put the proof bodily into your souls?

Heaven forbid! I said; I would only ask you to be consistent; or, if you change, change openly and let there be no deception. For I must remark, Thrasymachus, if you will recall what was previously   c said, that although you began by defining the true physician in an exact sense, you did not observe a like exactness when speaking of the shepherd; you thought that the shepherd as a shepherd tends the sheep not with a view to their own good, but like a mere diner or banqueter with a view to the pleasures of the table; or, again, as a trader for sale in the market, and not as a shepherd. Yet surely the   d art of the shepherd is concerned only with the good of his subjects; he has only to provide the best for them, since the perfection of the art is already insured whenever all the requirements of it are satisfied. And that was what I was saying just now about the ruler. I conceived that the art of the ruler, considered as a ruler, whether in a State or in private life, could only regard the good of his flock or subjects; whereas you seem to think that the rulers in States,   e that is to say, the true rulers, like being in authority.

Think! Nay, I am sure of it.

Then why in the case of lesser offices do men never take them willingly without payment, unless under the idea that they govern for the advantage not of themselves but of others? Let me ask you a question: Are not the several arts different, by reason of their each having a separate function? And, my dear illustrious friend, do say what you think, that we may make a little progress.

Yes, that is the difference, he replied.

And each art gives us a particular good and not merely a general one—medicine, for example, gives us health; navigation, safety at sea, and so on?

Yes, he said.

And the art of payment has the special function of giving pay: but we do not confuse this with other arts, any more than the art of the pilot is to be confused with the art of medicine, because the health of the pilot may be improved by a sea voyage. You would not be inclined to say, would you? that navigation is the art of medicine, at least if we are to adopt your exact use of language?

Certainly not.

Or because a man is in good health when he receives pay you would not say that the art of payment is medicine?

I should not.

Nor would you say that medicine is the art of receiving pay because a man takes fees when he is engaged in healing?

Certainly not.

And we have admitted, I said, that the good of each art is specially confined to the art?

Yes.

Then, if there be any good which all artists have in common, that is to be attributed to something of which they all have the common use?

True, he replied.

And when the artist is benefited by receiving pay the advantage is gained by an additional use of the art of pay, which is not the art professed by him?

He gave a reluctant assent to this.

Then the pay is not derived by the several artists from their respective arts. But the truth is, that while the art of medicine gives health, and the art of the builder builds a house, another art attends them which is the art of pay. The various arts may be doing their own business and benefiting that over which they preside, but would the artist receive any benefit from his art unless he were paid as well?

I suppose not.

But does he therefore confer no benefit when he works for nothing? e

Certainly, he confers a benefit.

Then now, Thrasymachus, there is no longer any doubt that neither arts nor governments provide for their own interests; but, as we were before saying, they rule and provide for the interests of their subjects who are the weaker and not the stronger—to their good they attend and not to the good of the superior. And this is the reason, my dear Thrasymachus, why, as I was just now saying, no one is willing to govern; because no one likes to take in hand the reformation of evils which are not his concern, without remuneration.[16] For, in the execution of his work, and in giving his 347 orders to another, the true artist does not regard his own interest, but always that of his subjects; and therefore in order that rulers may be willing to rule, they must be paid in one of three modes of payment, money, or honor, or a penalty for refusing.

What do you mean, Socrates? said Glaucon. The first two modes of payment are intelligible enough, but what the penalty is I do not understand, or how a penalty can be a payment.

You mean that you do not understand the nature of this payment which to the best men is the great inducement to rule? Of b course you know that ambition and avarice are held to be, as indeed they are, a disgrace?

Very true.

And for this reason, I said, money and honor have no attraction for them; good men do not wish to be openly demanding payment for governing and so to get the name of hirelings, nor by secretly helping themselves out of the public revenues to get the name of thieves. And not being ambitious they do not care about honor. Wherefore necessity must be laid upon them, and they must be induced to serve from the fear of punishment. And this, as I imag- c ine, is the reason why the forwardness to take office, instead of waiting to be compelled, has been deemed dishonorable. Now the worst part of the punishment is that he who refuses to rule is liable to be ruled by one who is worse than himself. And the fear of this, as I conceive, induces the good to take office, not because they would, but because they cannot help—not under the idea that they are going to have any benefit or enjoyment themselves, but as a necessity, and because they are not able to commit the task of ruling to anyone who is better than themselves, or indeed as good. For there is reason to think that if a city were composed entirely of good men, then to avoid office would be as much an object of contention as to obtain office is at present; then we should have plain proof that the true ruler is not meant by nature to regard his own interest, but that of his subjects; and everyone who knew this would choose rather to receive a benefit from another than to have the trouble of conferring one. So far am I from agreeing with Thrasymachus that justice is the interest of the stronger. This latter question need not be further discussed at present; but when Thrasymachus says that the life of the unjust is more advantageous than that of the just, his new statement appears to me to be of a far more serious character. Which of us has spoken truly? And which sort of life, Glaucon, do you prefer?

I for my part deem the life of the just to be the more advantageous, he answered.

Did you hear all the advantages of the unjust which Thrasymachus was rehearsing?

Yes, I heard him, he replied, but he has not convinced me.

Then shall we try to find some way of convincing him, if we can, that he is saying what is not true?

Most certainly, he replied.

If, I said, he makes a set speech and we make another recounting all the advantages of being just, and he answers and we rejoin, there must be a numbering and measuring of the goods which are claimed on either side, and in the end we shall want judges to decide; but if we proceed in our inquiry as we lately did, by making admissions to one another, we shall unite the offices of judge and advocate in our own persons.

Very good, he said.

And which method do I understand you to prefer? I said.

That which you propose.

Well, then, Thrasymachus, I said, suppose you begin at the

beginning and answer me. You say that perfect injustice is more gainful than perfect justice?

Yes, that is what I say, and I have given you my reasons.   c

And what is your view about them? Would you call one of them virtue and the other vice?

Certainly.

I suppose that you would call justice virtue and injustice vice?

What a charming notion! So likely too, seeing that I affirm injustice to be profitable and justice not.

What else then would you say?

The opposite, he replied.

And would you call justice vice?

No, I would rather say sublime simplicity.

Then would you call injustice malignity?[17]   d

No; I would rather say discretion.

And do the unjust appear to you to be wise and good?

Yes, he said; at any rate those of them who are able to be perfectly unjust, and who have the power of subduing States and nations; but perhaps you imagine me to be talking of cutpurses. Even this profession, if undetected, has advantages, though they are not to be compared with those of which I was just now speaking.

I do not think that I misapprehend your meaning, Thrasy-   e
machus, I replied; but still I cannot hear without amazement that you class injustice with wisdom and virtue, and justice with the opposite.

Certainly I do so class them.

Now, I said, you are on more substantial and almost unanswerable ground; for if the injustice which you were maintaining to be profitable had been admitted by you as by others to be vice and deformity, an answer might have been given to you on received principles; but now I perceive that you will call injustice honorable and strong, and to the unjust you will attribute all the quali-   349
ties which were attributed by us before to the just, seeing that you do not hesitate to rank injustice with wisdom and virtue.

You have guessed most infallibly, he replied.

Then I certainly ought not to shrink from going through with the argument so long as I have reason to think that you, Thrasymachus, are speaking your real mind; for I do believe that you are now in earnest and are not amusing yourself at our expense.

I may be in earnest or not, but what is that to you?—to refute the argument is your business.

b   Very true, I said; that is what I have to do: But will you be so good as answer yet one more question? Does the just man try to gain any advantage over the just?

Far otherwise; if he did he would not be the simple amusing creature which he is.

And would he try to go beyond just action?

He would not.

And how would he regard the attempt to gain an advantage over the unjust; would that be considered by him as just or unjust?

He would think it just, and would try to gain the advantage; but he would not be able.

Whether he would or would not be able, I said, is not to the point. My question is only whether the just man, while refusing to
c   have more than another just man, would wish and claim to have more than the unjust?

Yes, he would.

And what of the unjust—does he claim to have more than the just man and to do more than is just?

Of course, he said, for he claims to have more than all men.

And the unjust man will strive and struggle to obtain more than the just man or action, in order that he may have more than all?

True.

We may put the matter thus, I said—the just does not desire more than his like, but more than his unlike, whereas the unjust
d   desires more than both his like and his unlike?

Nothing, he said, can be better than that statement.

And the unjust is good° and wise, and the just is neither?

Good again, he said.

And is not the unjust like the wise and good, and the just unlike them?

°"Good" here is *agathos* in Greek, the positive form of the superlative adjective *aristos*.

Of course, he said, he who is of a certain nature, is like those who are of a certain nature; he who is not, not.

Each of them, I said, is such as his like is?

Certainly, he replied.

Very good, Thrasymachus, I said; and now to take the case of the arts: you would admit that one man is a musician and another not a musician?

Yes.   e

And which is wise and which is foolish?

Clearly the musician is wise, and he who is not a musician is foolish.

And he is good in as far as he is wise, and bad in as far as he is foolish?

Yes.

And you would say the same sort of thing of the physician?

Yes.

And do you think, my excellent friend, that a musician when he adjusts the lyre° would desire or claim to exceed or go beyond a musician in the tightening and loosening the strings?

I do not think that he would.

But he would claim to exceed the non-musician?

Of course.

And what would you say of the physician? In prescribing meats   350
and drinks would he wish to go beyond another physician or beyond the practice of medicine?

He would not.

But he would wish to go beyond the non-physician?

Yes.

And about knowledge and ignorance in general; see whether you think that any man who has knowledge ever would wish to have the choice of saying or doing more than another man who has knowledge. Would he not rather say or do the same as his like in the same case?

That, I suppose, can hardly be denied.

°"Lyre" (*lyra*) can refer to any number of stringed instruments commonly played in ancient Greece.

And what of the ignorant? would he not desire to have more than either the knowing or the ignorant?

I dare say.

And the knowing is wise?

Yes.

And the wise is good?

True.

Then the wise and good will not desire to gain more than his like, but more than his unlike and opposite?

I suppose so.

Whereas the bad and ignorant will desire to gain more than both?

Yes.

But did we not say, Thrasymachus, that the unjust goes beyond both his like and unlike? Were not these your words?

They were.

And you also said that the just will not go beyond his like, but his unlike?

Yes.

Then the just is like the wise and good, and the unjust like the evil and ignorant?

That is the inference.

And each of them is such as his like is?

That was admitted.

Then the just has turned out to be wise and good, and the unjust evil and ignorant.

Thrasymachus made all these admissions, not fluently, as I repeat them, but with extreme reluctance; it was a hot summer's day, and the perspiration poured from him in torrents; and then I saw what I had never seen before, Thrasymachus blushing. As we were now agreed that justice was virtue and wisdom, and injustice vice and ignorance, I proceeded to another point:

Well, I said, Thrasymachus, that matter is now settled; but were we not also saying that injustice had strength—do you remember?

Yes, I remember, he said, but do not suppose that I approve of what you are saying or have no answer; if, however, I were to answer, you would be quite certain to accuse me of haranguing; therefore either permit me to have my say out, or if you would rather ask, do so, and I will answer "Very good," as they say to story-telling old women, and will nod "Yes" and "No."

Certainly not, I said, if contrary to your real opinion.

Yes, he said, I will, to please you, since you will not let me speak. What else would you have?

Nothing in the world, I said; and if you are so disposed I will ask and you shall answer.

Proceed.

Then I will repeat the question which I asked before, in order that our examination of the relative nature of justice and injustice may be carried on regularly. A statement was made that injustice is stronger and more powerful than justice, but now justice, having been identified with wisdom and virtue, is easily shown to be stronger than injustice, if injustice is ignorance; this can no longer be questioned by anyone. But I want to view the matter, Thrasymachus, in a different way: You would not deny that a State may be unjust and may be unjustly attempting to enslave other States, or may have already enslaved them, and may be holding many of them in subjection?

True, he replied; and I will add that the best and most perfectly unjust State will be most likely to do so.

I know, I said, that such was your position; but what I would further consider is, whether this power which is possessed by the superior State can exist or be exercised without justice or only with justice.

If you are right in your view, and justice is wisdom, then only with justice; but if I am right, then without justice.

I am delighted, Thrasymachus, to see you not only nodding assent and dissent, but making answers which are quite excellent.

That is out of civility to you, he replied.

You are very kind, I said; and would you have the goodness also to inform me, whether you think that a State, or an army, or a band of robbers and thieves, or any other gang of evildoers could act at all if they injured one another?

No, indeed, he said, they could not.

But if they abstained from injuring one another, then they might act together better?

Yes.

And this is because injustice creates divisions and hatreds and fighting, and justice imparts harmony and friendship; is not that true, Thrasymachus?

I agree, he said, because I do not wish to quarrel with you.

How good of you, I said; but I should like to know also whether injustice, having this tendency to arouse hatred, wherever existing, among slaves or among freemen, will not make them hate one another and set them at variance and render them incapable of common action?

e

Certainly.

And even if injustice be found in two only, will they not quarrel and fight, and become enemies to one another and to the just?

They will.

And suppose injustice abiding in a single person, would your wisdom say that she loses or that she retains her natural power?

Let us assume that she retains her power.

Yet is not the power which injustice exercises of such a nature that wherever she takes up her abode, whether in a city, in an army, in a family, or in any other body, that body is, to begin with, rendered incapable of united action by reason of sedition and dis-

352   traction? and does it not become its own enemy and at variance with all that opposes it, and with the just? Is not this the case?

Yes, certainly.

And is not injustice equally fatal when existing in a single person—in the first place rendering him incapable of action because he is not at unity with himself, and in the second place making him an enemy to himself and the just?[18] Is not that true, Thrasymachus?

Yes.

And, O my friend, I said, surely the gods are just?

Granted that they are.

b   But, if so, the unjust will be the enemy of the gods, and the just will be their friends?

Feast away in triumph, and take your fill of the argument; I will not oppose you, lest I should displease the company.

Well, then, proceed with your answers, and let me have the remainder of my repast. For we have already shown that the just are clearly wiser and better and abler than the unjust, and that the

unjust are incapable of common action; nay, more, that to speak
as we did of men who are evil acting at any time vigorously to-   c
gether, is not strictly true, for, if they had been perfectly evil, they
would have laid hands upon one another; but it is evident that there
must have been some remnant of justice in them, which enabled
them to combine; if there had not been they would have injured
one another as well as their victims; they were but half-villains in
their enterprises; for had they been whole villains, and utterly unjust, they would have been utterly incapable of action. That, as I   d
believe, is the truth of the matter, and not what you said at first.
But whether the just have a better and happier life than the unjust
is a further question which we also proposed to consider. I think
that they have, and for the reasons which I have given; but still I
should like to examine further, for no light matter is at stake, nothing less than the rule of human life.

Proceed.

I will proceed by asking a question: Would you not say that a
horse has some end?[19]

I should.   e

And the end or use of a horse or of anything would be that
which could not be accomplished, or not so well accomplished, by
any other thing?

I do not understand, he said.

Let me explain: Can you see, except with the eye?

Certainly not.

Or hear, except with the ear?

No.

These, then, may be truly said to be the ends of these organs?

They may.

But you can cut off a vine-branch with a dagger or with a   353
chisel, and in many other ways?

Of course.

And yet not so well as with a pruning-hook made for the purpose?

True.

May we not say that this is the end of a pruning-hook?

We may.

Then now I think you will have no difficulty in understanding my meaning when I asked the question whether the end of anything would be that which could not be accomplished, or not so well accomplished, by any other thing?

I understand your meaning, he said, and assent.

And that to which an end is appointed has also an excellence? Need I ask again whether the eye has an end?

It has.

And has not the eye an excellence?[20]

Yes.

And the ear has an end and an excellence also?

True.

And the same is true of all other things; they have each of them an end and a special excellence?

That is so.

Well, and can the eyes fulfil their end if they are wanting in their own proper excellence and have a defect instead?

How can they, he said, if they are blind and cannot see?

You mean to say, if they have lost their proper excellence, which is sight; but I have not arrived at that point yet. I would rather ask the question more generally, and only inquire whether the things which fulfil their ends fulfil them by their own proper excellence, and fail of fulfilling them by their own defect?

Certainly, he replied.

I might say the same of the ears; when deprived of their own proper excellence they cannot fulfil their end?

True.

And the same observation will apply to all other things?

I agree.

Well; and has not the soul an end which nothing else can fulfil?[21] For example, to superintend and command and deliberate and the like. Are not these functions proper to the soul, and can they rightly be assigned to any other?

To no other.

And is not life to be reckoned among the ends of the soul?

Assuredly, he said.

And has not the soul an excellence also?

Yes.

And can she or can she not fulfil her own ends when deprived   e
of that excellence?

She cannot.

Then an evil soul must necessarily be an evil ruler and superin-
tendent, and the good soul a good ruler?

Yes, necessarily.

And we have admitted that justice is the excellence of the soul,
and injustice the defect of the soul?

That has been admitted.

Then the just soul and the just man will live well, and the unjust man will live ill?

That is what your argument proves.

And he who lives well is blessed and happy, and he who lives ill
the reverse of happy?

Certainly.

Then the just is happy, and the unjust miserable?   354

So be it.

But happiness, and not misery, is profitable?

Of course.

Then, my blessed Thrasymachus, injustice can never be more
profitable than justice.

Let this, Socrates, he said, be your entertainment at the Ben-
didea.°

For which I am indebted to you, I said, now that you have grown
gentle toward me and have left off scolding. Nevertheless, I have
not been well entertained; but that was my own fault and not   b
yours.[22] As an epicure snatches a taste of every dish which is successively brought to table, he not having allowed himself time to
enjoy the one before, so have I gone from one subject to another
without having discovered what I sought at first, the nature of justice. I left that inquiry and turned away to consider whether justice
is virtue and wisdom, or evil and folly; and when there arose a
further question about the comparative advantages of justice and
injustice, I could not refrain from passing on to that. And the result

---

°Festival in honor of the goddess Bendis; see the first paragraph of 1.327.

of the whole discussion has been that I know nothing at all. For I
c   know not what justice is, and therefore I am not likely to know
whether it is or is not a virtue, nor can I say whether the just man
is happy or unhappy.

BOOK 2

W<small>ITH THESE WORDS</small> I was thinking that I had made an end of the
discussion; but the end, in truth, proved to be only a beginning.
For Glaucon, who is always the most courageous of men, was dissatisfied at Thrasymachus's retirement. So he said to me: Socrates,
do you wish really to persuade us, or only to seem to have persuaded us, that to be just is always better than to be unjust?[1]

I should wish really to persuade you, I replied, if I could.

Then you certainly have not succeeded. Let me ask you now:
Are there not some good things which we welcome for their own
sakes, and independently of their consequences, as, for example,
harmless pleasures and enjoyments, which delight us at the time,
although nothing follows from them?

I agree in thinking that there is such a class, I replied.

Is there not also a second class of goods, such as knowledge,
sight, health, which are desirable not only in themselves, but also
for their results?

Certainly, I said.

And would you not recognize a third class, such as gymnastic, and
the care of the sick, and the physician's art; also the various ways of
money-making—these do us good but we regard them as disagreeable; and no one would choose them for their own sakes, but only
for the sake of some reward or result which flows from them?

There is, I said, this third class also. But why do you ask?

Because I want to know: In which of the three classes would
you place justice?

In the highest class, I replied—among those goods which he
who would be happy desires both for their own sake and for the
sake of their results.

Then the many are of another mind; they think that justice is to
be reckoned in the troublesome class, among goods which are
to be pursued for the sake of rewards and of reputation, but in
themselves are disagreeable and rather to be avoided.

I know, I said, that this is their manner of thinking, and that this was the thesis which Thrasymachus was maintaining just now, when he censured justice and praised injustice. But I am too slow-witted to be convinced by him.

b   I wish, he said, that you would hear me as well as him, and then I shall see whether you and I agree. For Thrasymachus seems to me, like a snake, to have been charmed by your voice sooner than he ought to have been; but to my mind the nature of justice and injustice has not yet been made clear. Setting aside their rewards and results, I want to know what they are in themselves, and how they inwardly work in the soul. If you please, then, I will revive the

c   argument of Thrasymachus. And first I will speak of the nature and origin of justice according to the common view of them. Secondly, I will show that all men who practise justice do so against their will, of necessity, but not as a good. And thirdly, I will argue that there is reason in this view, for the life of the unjust is after all better far than the life of the just—if what they say is true, Socrates, since I myself am not of their opinion. But still I acknowledge that I am perplexed when I hear the voices of Thrasymachus and myriads of others dinning in my ears; and, on the other hand, I have never yet heard the superiority of justice to injustice maintained

d   by anyone in a satisfactory way. I want to hear justice praised in respect of itself; then I shall be satisfied, and you are the person from whom I think that I am most likely to hear this; and therefore I will praise the unjust life to the utmost of my power, and my manner of speaking will indicate the manner in which I desire to hear you too praising justice and censuring injustice. Will you say whether you approve of my proposal?

Indeed I do; nor can I imagine any theme about which a man of sense would oftener wish to converse.

e   I am delighted, he replied, to hear you say so, and shall begin by speaking, as I proposed, of the nature and origin of justice.

They say that to do injustice is, by nature, good; to suffer injustice, evil; but that the evil is greater than the good.[2] And so when men have both done and suffered injustice and have had experience of both, not being able to avoid the one and obtain the other,

359   they think that they had better agree among themselves to have neither; hence there arise laws and mutual covenants; and that

which is ordained by law is termed by them lawful and just. This they affirm to be the origin and nature of justice; it is a mean or compromise, between the best of all, which is to do injustice and not be punished, and the worst of all, which is to suffer injustice without the power of retaliation; and justice, being at a middle point between the two, is tolerated not as a good, but as the lesser evil, and honored by reason of the inability of men to do injustice. For no man who is worthy to be called a man would ever submit to such an agreement if he were able to resist; he would be mad if he did. Such is the received account, Socrates, of the nature and origin of justice.

Now that those who practise justice do so involuntarily and because they have not the power to be unjust will best appear if we imagine something of this kind: having given both to the just and the unjust power to do what they will, let us watch and see whither desire will lead them; then we shall discover in the very act the just and unjust man to be proceeding along the same road, following their interest, which all natures deem to be their good, and are only diverted into the path of justice by the force of law. The liberty which we are supposing may be most completely given to them in the form of such a power as is said to have been possessed by Gyges, the ancestor of Crœsus the Lydian.* According to the tradition, Gyges was a shepherd in the service of the King of Lydia; there was a great storm, and an earthquake made an opening in the earth at the place where he was feeding his flock. Amazed at the sight, he descended into the opening, where, among other marvels, he beheld a hollow brazen horse, having doors, at which he, stooping and looking in, saw a dead body of stature, as appeared to him, more than human and having nothing on but a gold ring; this he took from the finger of the dead and reascended. Now the shepherds met together, according to custom, that they might send their monthly report about the flocks to the King; into their assembly he came having

b

c

d

e

---

*In book 1 of his *Histories*, Herodotus (c.490–420 B.C.E.) relates a somewhat different story about how Gyges came to be king of Lydia (in western Asia Minor) in the late eighth century B.C.E. His descendant Croesus ruled Lydia in the middle of the sixth century B.C.E.

the ring on his finger, and as he was sitting among them he chanced to turn the flange of the ring inside his hand, when instantly he became invisible to the rest of the company and they began to speak of him as if he were no longer present. He was astonished at this, and again touching the ring he turned the flange outward and reappeared; he made several trials of the ring, and always with the same result—when he turned the flange inward he became invisible, when outward he reappeared. Whereupon he contrived to be chosen one of the messengers who were sent to the court; where as soon as he arrived he seduced the Queen, and with her help conspired against the King and killed him and took the kingdom. Suppose now that there were two such magic rings, and the just put on one of them and the unjust the other; no man can be imagined to be of such an iron nature that he would stand fast in justice. No man would keep his hands off what was not his own when he could safely take what he liked out of the market, or go into houses and sleep with anyone at his pleasure, or kill or release from prison whom he would, and in all respects be like a god among men. Then the actions of the just would be as the actions of the unjust; they would both come at last to the same point. And this we may truly affirm to be a great proof that a man is just, not willingly or because he thinks that justice is any good to him individually, but of necessity, for wherever anyone thinks that he can safely be unjust, there he is unjust.[3] For all men believe in their hearts that injustice is far more profitable to the individual than justice, and he who argues as I have been supposing, will say that they are right. If you could imagine anyone obtaining this power of becoming invisible, and never doing any wrong or touching what was another's, he would be thought by the lookers-on to be a most wretched idiot, although they would praise him to one another's faces, and keep up appearances with one another from a fear that they too might suffer injustice. Enough of this.

Now, if we are to form a real judgment of the life of the just and unjust, we must isolate them; there is no other way; and how is the isolation to be effected? I answer: Let the unjust man be entirely unjust, and the just man entirely just; nothing is to be taken away from either of them, and both are to be perfectly

furnished for the work of their respective lives. First, let the unjust be like other distinguished masters of craft; like the skilful
pilot or physician, who knows intuitively his own powers and
keeps within their limits, and who, if he fails at any point, is able   361
to recover himself. So let the unjust make his unjust attempts in
the right way, and lie hidden if he means to be great in his injustice
(he who is found out is nobody): for the highest reach of injustice
is, to be deemed just when you are not. Therefore I say that in
the perfectly unjust man we must assume the most perfect injustice; there is to be no deduction, but we must allow him, while
doing the most unjust acts, to have acquired the greatest reputa-   b
tion for justice. If he have taken a false step he must be able to
recover himself; he must be one who can speak with effect, if any
of his deeds come to light, and who can force his way where force
is required by his courage and strength, and command of money
and friends. And at his side let us place the just man in his noble-
ness and simplicity, wishing, as Æschylus° says, to be and not to
seem good. There must be no seeming, for if he seem to be just
he will be honored and rewarded, and then we shall not know   c
whether he is just for the sake of justice or for the sake of honor
and rewards; therefore, let him be clothed in justice only, and
have no other covering; and he must be imagined in a state of life
the opposite of the former. Let him be the best of men, and let
him be thought the worst; then he will have been put to the
proof; and we shall see whether he will be affected by the fear of
infamy and its consequences. And let him continue thus to the   d
hour of death; being just and seeming to be unjust. When both
have reached the uttermost extreme, the one of justice and the
other of injustice, let judgment be given which of them is the
happier of the two.

Heavens! my dear Glaucon, I said, how energetically you polish
them up for the decision, first one and then the other, as if they
were two statues.

I do my best, he said. And now that we know what they are like

---

°Athenian tragedian (c.525–456 B.C.E.). The reference here is to *Seven Against
Thebes* 592–594.

there is no difficulty in tracing out the sort of life which awaits either of them. This I will proceed to describe; but as you may think e the description a little too coarse, I ask you to suppose, Socrates, that the words which follow are not mine. Let me put them into the mouths of the eulogists of injustice: They will tell you that the just man who is thought unjust will be scourged, racked, bound—will 362 have his eyes burnt out; and, at last, after suffering every kind of evil, he will be impaled. Then he will understand that he ought to seem only, and not to be, just; the words of Æschylus may be more truly spoken of the unjust than of the just. For the unjust is pursuing a reality; he does not live with a view to appearances—he wants to be really unjust and not to seem only—

> "His mind has a soil deep and fertile,
> Out of which spring his prudent counsels."*

b   In the first place, he is thought just, and therefore bears rule in the city; he can marry whom he will, and give in marriage to whom he will; also he can trade and deal where he likes, and always to his own advantage, because he has no misgivings about injustice; and at every contest, whether in public or private, he gets the better of his antagonists, and gains at their expense, and is c rich, and out of his gains he can benefit his friends, and harm his enemies;⁴ moreover, he can offer sacrifices, and dedicate gifts to the gods abundantly and magnificently, and can honor the gods or any man whom he wants to honor in a far better style than the just, and therefore he is likely to be dearer than they are to the gods. And thus, Socrates, gods and men are said to unite in making the life of the unjust better than the life of the just.

d   I was going to say something in answer to Glaucon, when Adeimantus, his brother, interposed: Socrates, he said, you do not suppose that there is nothing more to be urged?

Why, what else is there? I answered.

The strongest point of all has not been even mentioned, he replied.

---

*Aeschylus, *Seven Against Thebes* 574–575.

Well, then, according to the proverb, "Let brother help brother"*—if he fails in any part, do you assist him; although I must confess that Glaucon has already said quite enough to lay me in the dust, and take from me the power of helping justice.

Nonsense, he replied. But let me add something more: There   e
is another side to Glaucon's argument about the praise and censure of justice and injustice, which is equally required in order to
bring out what I believe to be his meaning. Parents and tutors are
always telling their sons and their wards that they are to be just;   363
but why? not for the sake of justice, but for the sake of character
and reputation; in the hope of obtaining for him who is reputed
just some of those offices, marriages, and the like which Glaucon
has enumerated among the advantages accruing to the unjust
from the reputation of justice. More, however, is made of appearances by this class of persons than by the others; for they
throw in the good opinion of the gods, and will tell you of a
shower of benefits which the heavens, as they say, rain upon the
pious; and this accords with the testimony of the noble Hesiod[†]
and Homer, the first of whom says that the gods make the oaks of
the just—   b

> "To bear acorns at their summit, and bees in the middle;
> And the sheep are bowed down with the weight of their fleeces,"[‡]

and many other blessings of a like kind are provided for them.
And Homer has a very similar strain; for he speaks of one whose
fame is

> "As the fame of some blameless king who, like a god,
> Maintains justice; to whom the black earth brings forth

---

*An ancient commentator (scholiast) states that the source of the proverb is *Odyssey* 16.97–98; compare *Iliad* 21.308–309.

†Poet from Boeotia (c. late eighth century B.C.E.), author of several major poems in dactylic hexameter, including the extant *Theogony* (about the origins of various gods and their conflicts with one another) and the didactic poem *Works and Days*. As far back as the fifth century B.C.E., Hesiod was frequently linked to (or contrasted with) Homer.

‡Hesiod, *Works and Days* 232–233.

Wheat and barley, whose trees are bowed with fruit,

c   And his sheep never fail to bear, and the sea gives him fish."°

Still grander are the gifts of heaven which Musæus and his son[†]
vouchsafe to the just; they take them down into the world below,
where they have the saints lying on couches at a feast, everlast-
ingly drunk, crowned with garlands; their idea seems to be that an
d   immortality of drunkenness is the highest meed of virtue. Some
extend their rewards yet further; the posterity, as they say, of the
faithful and just shall survive to the third and fourth generation.
This is the style in which they praise justice. But about the wicked
there is another strain; they bury them in a slough in Hades[‡] and
make them carry water in a sieve; also while they are yet living
they bring them to infamy, and inflict upon them the punishments
e   which Glaucon described as the portion of the just who are reputed to be unjust; nothing else does their invention supply. Such
is their manner of praising the one and censuring the other.

Once more, Socrates, I will ask you to consider another way of
speaking about justice and injustice, which is not confined to the po-
364   ets, but is found in prose writers. The universal voice of mankind
is always declaring that justice and virtue are honorable, but grievous and toilsome; and that the pleasures of vice and injustice are
easy of attainment, and are only censured by law and opinion. They
say also that honesty is for the most part less profitable than dishonesty; and they are quite ready to call wicked men happy, and to
honor them both in public and private when they are rich or in any
other way influential, while they despise and overlook those who
may be weak and poor, even though acknowledging them to be bet-
b   ter than the others. But most extraordinary of all is their mode of
speaking about virtue and the gods: they say that the gods apportion
calamity and misery to many good men, and good and happiness to

---

°*Odyssey* 19.109–112.

†Musaeus was a legendary singer, often associated with the singer Orpheus and
also with the god Apollo, the Muses, and the Moon (see below at 2.364e). "His
son" probably refers to Eumolpus, the legendary ancestor of the Eumolpidae clan
in Eleusis.

‡God of the underworld; by extension, the underworld itself.

the wicked. And mendicant prophets* go to rich men's doors and persuade them that they have a power committed to them by the gods of making an atonement for a man's own or his ancestor's sins by sacrifices or charms, with rejoicings and feasts; and they promise to harm an enemy, whether just or unjust, at a small cost; with magic arts and incantations binding heaven, as they say, to execute their will. And the poets are the authorities to whom they appeal, now smoothing the path of vice with the words of Hesiod:

c

> "Vice may be had in abundance without trouble; the way is smooth and her dwelling-place is near. But before virtue the gods have set toil,"[†]

d

and a tedious and uphill road: then citing Homer as a witness that the gods may be influenced by men; for he also says:

> "The gods, too, may be turned from their purpose; and men pray to them and avert their wrath by sacrifices and soothing entreaties, and by libations and the odor of fat, when they have sinned and transgressed."[‡]

e

And they produce a host of books written by Musæus and Orpheus,[§] who were children of the Moon and the muses—that is what they say—according to which they perform their ritual, and persuade not only individuals, but whole cities, that expiations and atonements for sin may be made by sacrifices and amusements which fill a vacant hour, and are equally at the service of the living and the dead; the latter sort they call mysteries, and they redeem us from the pains of hell, but if we neglect them no one knows what awaits us.

365

He proceeded: And now when the young hear all this said about virtue and vice, and the way in which gods and men regard

---

*Itinerant prophets and seers, as well as bards and musicians, would have traditionally been guests in the households of wealthy, powerful men in Greek city-states.

†Hesiod, *Works and Days* 287–289.

‡Adapted from *Iliad* 9.497–501.

§Legendary Thracian singer and founder of the religious movement called Orphism, which entertained ideas about reincarnation and transmigration of the soul. The phrase "host of books" refers to Orphic texts.

them, how are their minds likely to be affected, my dear Socrates—
those of them, I mean, who are quick-witted, and, like bees on the
wing, light on every flower, and from all that they hear are prone to
draw conclusions as to what manner of persons they should be and
in what way they should walk if they would make the best of life?
b   Probably the youth will say to himself in the words of Pindar:

> "Can I by justice or by crooked ways of deceit ascend a loftier
> tower which may be a fortress to me all my days?"°

For what men say is that, if I am really just and am not also thought
just, profit there is none, but the pain and loss on the other hand
are unmistakable. But if, though unjust, I acquire the reputation of
justice, a heavenly life is promised to me. Since then, as wise men
c   prove, appearance tyrannizes over truth† and is lord of happiness,
to appearance I must devote myself. I will describe around me a
picture and shadow of virtue to be the vestibule and exterior of my
house; behind I will trail the subtle and crafty fox, as Archilochus,‡
greatest of sages, recommends. But I hear someone exclaiming
that the concealment of wickedness is often difficult; to which I
answer, Nothing great is easy. Nevertheless, the argument indicates this, if we would be happy, to be the path along which we
d   should proceed. With a view to concealment we will establish secret brotherhoods and political clubs.⁵ And there are professors of
rhetoric⁶ who teach the art of persuading courts and assemblies;
and so, partly by persuasion and partly by force, I shall make unlawful gains and not be punished. Still I hear a voice saying that
the gods cannot be deceived, neither can they be compelled. But
what if there are no gods? or, suppose them to have no care of human things—why in either case should we mind about conceal-
e   ment? And even if there are gods, and they do care about us, yet
we know of them only from tradition and the genealogies of the

---

°From a poem by Pindar that is no longer extant.
†The allusion is to a poem by Simonides.
‡Archilochus was an iambic and elegiac poet (early seventh century B.C.E.) from
the island Paros; two extant fragments of Archilochus' poetry deal with clever
foxes.

poets; and these are the very persons who say that they may be influenced and turned by "sacrifices and soothing entreaties and by offerings."° Let us be consistent, then, and believe both or neither. If the poets speak truly, why, then, we had better be unjust, and offer of the fruits of injustice; for if we are just, although we may escape the vengeance of heaven, we shall lose the gains of injustice; but, if we are unjust, we shall keep the gains, and by our sinning and praying, and praying and sinning, the gods will be propitiated, and we shall not be punished. "But there is a world below in which either we or our posterity will suffer for our unjust deeds." Yes, my friend, will be the reflection, but there are mysteries and atoning deities, and these have great power. That is what mighty cities declare; and the children of the gods, who were their poets and prophets, bear a like testimony.

On what principle, then, shall we any longer choose justice rather than the worst injustice? when, if we only unite the latter with a deceitful regard to appearances, we shall fare to our mind both with gods and men, in life and after death, as the most numerous and the highest authorities tell us. Knowing all this, Socrates, how can a man who has any superiority of mind or person or rank or wealth, be willing to honor justice; or indeed to refrain from laughing when he hears justice praised? And even if there should be someone who is able to disprove the truth of my words, and who is satisfied that justice is best, still he is not angry with the unjust, but is very ready to forgive them, because he also knows that men are not just of their own free will;[7] unless, peradventure, there be someone whom the divinity within him may have inspired with a hatred of injustice, or who has attained knowledge of the truth— but no other man. Only he blames injustice, who, owing to cowardice or age or some weakness, has not the power of being unjust. And this is proved by the fact that when he obtains this power, he immediately becomes unjust as far as he can be.

The cause of all this, Socrates, was indicated by us at the beginning of the argument, when my brother and I told you how astonished we were to find that of all the professing panegyrists of

366

b

c

d

°From *Iliad* 9.497–501, adapted above at 2.364d–e.

e   justice—beginning with the ancient heroes of whom any memo-
rial has been preserved to us, and ending with the men of our
own time—no one has ever blamed injustice or praised justice except with a view to the glories, honors, and benefits which flow
from them. No one has ever adequately described either in verse
or prose the true essential nature of either of them abiding in the
soul, and invisible to any human or divine eye; or shown that of all
the things of a man's soul which he has within him, justice is the
greatest good, and injustice the greatest evil. Had this been the
367   universal strain, had you sought to persuade us of this from our
youth upward, we should not have been on the watch to keep one
another from doing wrong, but everyone would have been his
own watchman[8] because afraid, if he did wrong, of harboring in
himself the greatest of evils. I dare say that Thrasymachus and
others would seriously hold the language which I have been
merely repeating, and words even stronger than these about
justice and injustice, grossly, as I conceive, perverting their true
nature. But I speak in this vehement manner, as I must frankly
b   confess to you, because I want to hear from you the opposite side;
and I would ask you to show not only the superiority which justice
has over injustice, but what effect they have on the possessor of
them which makes the one to be a good and the other an evil to
him. And please, as Glaucon requested of you, to exclude reputa-
tions; for unless you take away from each of them his true reputation and add on the false, we shall say that you do not praise
justice, but the appearance of it; we shall think that you are only
c   exhorting us to keep injustice dark, and that you really agree with
Thrasymachus in thinking that justice is another's good and the interest of the stronger, and that injustice is a man's own profit and
interest, though injurious to the weaker. Now as you have admitted that justice is one of that highest class of goods which are desired, indeed, for their results, but in a far greater degree for their
own sakes—like sight or hearing or knowledge or health, or any
d   other real and natural and not merely conventional good—I would
ask you in your praise of justice to regard one point only: I mean
the essential good and evil which justice and injustice work in the
possessors of them. Let others praise justice and censure injustice, magnifying the rewards and honors of the one and abusing

the other; that is a manner of arguing which, coming from them, I am ready to tolerate, but from you who have spent your whole life in the consideration of this question, unless I hear the contrary e from your own lips, I expect something better. And therefore, I say, not only prove to us that justice is better than injustice, but show what they either of them do to the possessor of them, which makes the one to be a good and the other an evil, whether seen or unseen by gods and men.

I had always admired the natural ability of Glaucon and Adeimantus,[9] but on hearing these words I was quite delighted, and said: Sons of an illustrious father,* that was not a bad begin- 368 ning of the elegiac verses which the admirer of Glaucon† made in honor of you after you had distinguished yourselves at the battle of Megara:‡

"Sons of Ariston," he sang, "divine offspring of an illustrious hero."§

The epithet is very appropriate, for there is something truly divine in being able to argue as you have done for the superiority of injustice, and remaining unconvinced by your own arguments. And I do believe that you are not convinced—this I infer from your gen- b eral character, for had I judged only from your speeches I should have mistrusted you. But now, the greater my confidence in you, the greater is my difficulty in knowing what to say. For I am in a strait between two; on the one hand I feel that I am unequal to the task; and my inability is brought home to me by the fact that you were not satisfied with the answer which I made to Thrasymachus, proving, as I thought, the superiority which justice has over injustice. And yet I cannot refuse to help, while breath and speech

---

*Literally, "sons of that man"—that is, Thrasymachus. Glaucon and Adeimantus are Thrasymachus' "sons" insofar as they have continued the argument he began in book 1.
†Possibly Critias (460–403 B.C.E.), a distant relation of Plato and his brothers, who eventually led the oligarchic coup of 404–403 B.C.E.
‡There were battles at Megara in 424 and 409 B.C.E.; if the "dramatic date" of *Republic* is meant to be 411 or 410 B.C.E., reference to the battle in 409 would be an anachronism.
§The name Ariston evokes the adjective *aristos* ("best"); compare 9.580b.

c   remain to me; I am afraid that there would be an impiety in being present when justice is evil spoken of and not lifting up a hand in her defence. And therefore I had best give such help as I can.

Glaucon and the rest entreated me by all means not to let the question drop, but to proceed in the investigation. They wanted to arrive at the truth, first, about the nature of justice and injustice, and secondly, about their relative advantages. I told them, what I really thought, that the inquiry would be of a serious nature, and would require very good eyes. Seeing then, I said, that we are no

d   great wits, I think that we had better adopt a method which I may illustrate thus; suppose that a short-sighted person had been asked by someone to read small letters from a distance; and it occurred to someone else that they might be found in another place which was larger and in which the letters were larger—if they were the same and he could read the larger letters first, and then proceed to the lesser—this would have been thought a rare piece of good-fortune.

Very true, said Adeimantus; but how does the illustration apply

e   to our inquiry?

I will tell you, I replied; justice, which is the subject of our inquiry, is, as you know, sometimes spoken of as the virtue of an individual, and sometimes as the virtue of a State.*

True, he replied.

And is not a State larger than an individual?

It is.

Then in the larger the quantity of justice is likely to be larger and more easily discernible. I propose therefore that we inquire into the nature of justice and injustice, first as they appear in the

369   State, and secondly in the individual, proceeding from the greater to the lesser and comparing them.[10]

That, he said, is an excellent proposal.

And if we imagine the State in process of creation, we shall see the justice and injustice of the State in process of creation also.

I dare say.

When the State is completed there may be a hope that the object of our search will be more easily discovered.

---

*That is, a polis, or city-state.

Yes, far more easily.

b

But ought we to attempt to construct one? I said; for to do so, as I am inclined to think, will be a very serious task. Reflect therefore.

I have reflected, said Adeimantus, and am anxious that you should proceed.

A State, I said, arises, as I conceive, out of the needs of mankind; no one is self-sufficing, but all of us have many wants. Can any other origin of a State be imagined?[11]

There can be no other.

Then, as we have many wants, and many persons are needed to supply them, one takes a helper for one purpose and another for another; and when these partners and helpers are gathered together in one habitation the body of inhabitants is termed a State.

c

True, he said.

And they exchange with one another, and one gives, and another receives, under the idea that the exchange will be for their good.

Very true.

Then, I said, let us begin and create in idea a State; and yet the true creator is necessity, who is the mother of our invention.*

Of course, he replied.

Now the first and greatest of necessities is food, which is the condition of life and existence.

d

Certainly.

The second is a dwelling, and the third clothing and the like.

True.

And now let us see how our city will be able to supply this great demand: We may suppose that one man is a husbandman, another a builder, someone else a weaver—shall we add to them a shoemaker, or perhaps some other purveyor to our bodily wants?

Quite right.

The barest notion of a State must include four or five men

Clearly.

e

And how will they proceed? Will each bring the result of his labors into a common stock?—the individual husbandman, for example, producing for four, and laboring four times as long and

---

*The Greek means, literally, "our need will create [or determine] it."

as much as he need in the provision of food with which he supplies others as well as himself; or will he have nothing to do with
others and not be at the trouble of producing for them, but provide for himself alone a fourth of the food in a fourth of the time,
370 and in the remaining three-fourths of his time be employed in
making a house or a coat or a pair of shoes, having no partnership
with others, but supplying himself all his own wants?

Adeimantus thought that he should aim at producing food only
and not at producing everything.

Probably, I replied, that would be the better way; and when I
hear you say this, I am myself reminded that we are not all alike;
b there are diversities of natures among us which are adapted to
different occupations.[12]

Very true.

And will you have a work better done when the workman has
many occupations, or when he has only one?

When he has only one.

Further, there can be no doubt that a work is spoilt when not
done at the right time?

No doubt.

For business is not disposed to wait until the doer of the business is at leisure; but the doer must follow up what he is doing,
c and make the business his first object.

He must.

And if so, we must infer that all things are produced more plen-
tifully and easily and of a better quality when one man does one
thing which is natural to him and does it at the right time, and
leaves other things.[13]

Undoubtedly.

Then more than four citizens will be required; for the husbandman will not make his own plough or mattock, or other im-
d plements of agriculture, if they are to be good for anything.
Neither will the builder make his tools—and he, too, needs many;
and in like manner the weaver and shoemaker.

True.

Then carpenters and smiths and many other artisans will be
sharers in our little State, which is already beginning to grow?

True.

Yet even if we add cowherds, shepherds, and other herdsmen, in order that our husbandmen may have oxen to plough with, and builders as well as husbandmen may have draught cattle, and curriers and weavers fleeces and hides—still our State will not be very large.

That is true; yet neither will it be a very small State which contains all these.

Then, again, there is the situation of the city—to find a place where nothing need be imported is well-nigh impossible.

Impossible.

Then there must be another class of citizens who will bring the required supply from another city?

There must.

But if the trader goes empty-handed, having nothing which they require who would supply his need, he will come back empty-handed.

That is certain.

And therefore what they produce at home must be not only enough for themselves, but such both in quantity and quality as to accommodate those from whom their wants are supplied.

Very true.

Then more husbandmen and more artisans will be required?

They will.

Not to mention the importers and exporters, who are called merchants?

Yes.

Then we shall want merchants?

We shall.

And if merchandise is to be carried over the sea, skilful sailors will also be needed, and in considerable numbers?

Yes, in considerable numbers.

Then, again, within the city, how will they exchange their productions? To secure such an exchange was, as you will remember, one of our principal objects when we formed them into a society and constituted a State.

Clearly they will buy and sell.

Then they will need a market-place, and a money-token for purposes of exchange.

Certainly.

c   Suppose now that a husbandman or an artisan brings some production to market, and he comes at a time when there is no one to exchange with him—is he to leave his calling and sit idle in the market-place?

Not at all; he will find people there who, seeing the want, undertake the office of salesmen. In well-ordered States they are commonly those who are the weakest in bodily strength, and therefore of little use for any other purpose;[14] their duty is to be in the mar-
d   ket, and to give money in exchange for goods to those who desire to sell, and to take money from those who desire to buy.

This want, then, creates a class of retail-traders in our State. Is not "retailer" the term which is applied to those who sit in the market-place engaged in buying and selling, while those who wander from one city to another are called merchants?

Yes, he said.

e   And there is another class of servants, who are intellectually hardly on the level of companionship; still they have plenty of bodily strength for labor, which accordingly they sell, and are called, if I do not mistake, hirelings, "hire" being the name which is given to the price of their labor.

True.

Then hirelings will help to make up our population?

Yes.

And now, Adeimantus, is our State matured and perfected?

I think so.

Where, then, is justice, and where is injustice, and in what part of the State did they spring up?

372   Probably in the dealings of these citizens with one another.[15] I cannot imagine that they are more likely to be found anywhere else.

I dare say that you are right in your suggestion, I said; we had better think the matter out, and not shrink from the inquiry.

Let us then consider, first of all, what will be their way of life, now that we have thus established them. Will they not produce corn and wine and clothes and shoes, and build houses for themselves? And when they are housed, they will work, in summer, commonly, stripped and barefoot, but in winter substantially
b   clothed and shod. They will feed on barley-meal and flour of

wheat, baking and kneading them, making noble cakes and loaves; these they will serve up on a mat of reeds or on clean leaves, themselves reclining the while upon beds strewn with yew or myrtle. And they and their children will feast, drinking of the wine which they have made, wearing garlands on their heads, and hymning the praises of the gods, in happy converse with one another. And they will take care that their families do not exceed their means; having an eye to poverty or war.

But, said Glaucon, interposing, you have not given them a relish to their meal.

True, I replied, I had forgotten; of course they must have a relish—salt and olives and cheese—and they will boil roots and herbs such as country people prepare; for a dessert we shall give them figs and peas and beans; and they will roast myrtle-berries and acorns at the fire, drinking in moderation. And with such a diet they may be expected to live in peace and health to a good old age, and bequeath a similar life to their children after them.

Yes, Socrates, he said, and if you were providing for a city of pigs, how else would you feed the beasts?

But what would you have, Glaucon? I replied.

Why, he said, you should give them the ordinary conveniences of life. People who are to be comfortable are accustomed to lie on sofas, and dine off tables, and they should have sauces and sweets in the modern style.

Yes, I said, now I understand: the question which you would have me consider is, not only how a State, but how a luxurious State is created; and possibly there is no harm in this, for in such a State we shall be more likely to see how justice and injustice originate. In my opinion the true and healthy constitution of the State is the one which I have described. But if you wish also to see a State at fever-heat, I have no objection. For I suspect that many will not be satisfied with the simpler way of life. They will be for adding sofas and tables and other furniture; also dainties and perfumes and incense and courtesans° and cakes, all these not of one sort only, but

°*Hetairai* in Greek. "Courtesans and cakes" are juxtaposed in lists of luxuries in, for example, Aristophanes, *Acharnians* 1090–1092.

in every variety. We must go beyond the necessaries of which I was at first speaking, such as houses and clothes and shoes; the arts of the painter and the embroiderer will have to be set in motion, and gold and ivory and all sorts of materials must be procured.

b   True, he said.

Then we must enlarge our borders; for the original healthy State is no longer sufficient. Now will the city have to fill and swell with a multitude of callings which are not required by any natural want; such as the whole tribe of hunters and actors, of whom one large class have to do with forms and colors; another will be the votaries of music—poets and their attendant train of rhapsodists, players, dancers, contractors; also makers of diverse kinds of articles, in-

c   cluding women's dresses. And we shall want more servants. Will not tutors be also in request, and nurses wet and dry, hairdressers, and barbers, as well as confectioners and cooks; and swineherds,° too, who were not needed and therefore had no place in the former edition of our State, but are needed now? They must not be forgotten: and there will be animals of many other kinds, if people eat them.

Certainly.

d   And living in this way we shall have much greater need of physicians than before?

Much greater.

And the country which was enough to support the original inhabitants will be too small now, and not enough?

Quite true.

Then a slice of our neighbors' land will be wanted by us for pasture and tillage, and they will want a slice of ours, if, like ourselves, they exceed the limit of necessity, and give themselves up to the unlimited accumulation of wealth?

e   That, Socrates, will be inevitable.

And so we shall go to war, Glaucon. Shall we not?

Most certainly, he replied.

Then, without determining as yet whether war does good or

°That is, to raise pigs for food. Although animals in the "healthy city" would be slaughtered for their hides, the inhabitants would apparently subsist on a vegetarian diet (2.372b).

harm, thus much we may affirm, that now we have discovered war to be derived from causes which are also the causes of almost all the evils in States, private as well as public.

Undoubtedly.

And our State must once more enlarge; and this time the enlargement will be nothing short of a whole army, which will have   374 to go out and fight with the invaders for all that we have, as well as for the things and persons whom we were describing above.

Why? he said; are they not capable of defending themselves?

No, I said; not if we were right in the principle which was acknowledged by all of us when we were framing the State. The principle, as you will remember, was that one man cannot practise many arts with success.

Very true, he said.

But is not war an art?   b

Certainly.

And an art requiring as much attention as shoemaking?

Quite true.

And the shoemaker was not allowed by us to be a husbandman, or a weaver, or a builder—in order that we might have our shoes well made; but to him and to every other worker was assigned one work for which he was by nature fitted, and at that he was to continue working all his life long and at no other; he was not to let   c opportunities slip, and then he would become a good workman. Now nothing can be more important than that the work of a soldier should be well done. But is war an art so easily acquired that a man may be a warrior who is also a husbandman, or shoemaker, or other artisan;[17] although no one in the world would be a good dice or draught player who merely took up the game as a recreation, and had not from his earliest years devoted himself to this and nothing else? No tools will make a man a skilled workman or master of defence, nor be of any use to him who has not learned how to handle them, and has never bestowed any attention upon them. How, then, will he who takes up a shield or other implement   d of war become a good fighter all in a day, whether with heavy-armed or any other kind of troops?

Yes, he said, the tools which would teach men their own use would be beyond price.

e   And the higher the duties of the guardian, I said, the more
time and skill and art and application will be needed by him?

No doubt, he replied.

Will he not also require natural aptitude for his calling?

Certainly.

Then it will be our duty to select, if we can, natures which are
fitted for the task of guarding the city?

It will.

And the selection will be no easy matter, I said; but we must be
brave and do our best.

375   We must.

Is not the noble youth very like a well-bred dog in respect of
guarding and watching?

What do you mean?

I mean that both of them ought to be quick to see, and swift to
overtake the enemy when they see him; and strong too if, when
they have caught him, they have to fight with him.

All these qualities, he replied, will certainly be required by them.

Well, and your guardian must be brave if he is to fight well?

Certainly.

And is he likely to be brave who has no spirit, whether horse or
dog or any other animal? Have you never observed how invincible

b   and unconquerable is spirit and how the presence of it makes the
soul of any creature to be absolutely fearless and indomitable?

I have.

Then now we have a clear notion of the bodily qualities which
are required in the guardian.

True.

And also of the mental ones; his soul is to be full of spirit?

Yes.

But are not these spirited natures apt to be savage with one another, and with everybody else?

A difficulty by no means easy to overcome, he replied.

c   Whereas, I said, they ought to be dangerous to their enemies,
and gentle to their friends; if not, they will destroy themselves
without waiting for their enemies to destroy them.

True, he said.

What is to be done, then? I said; how shall we find a gentle nature which has also a great spirit, for the one is the contradiction of the other?[18]

True.

He will not be a good guardian who is wanting in either of these two qualities; and yet the combination of them appears to be impossible; and hence we must infer that to be a good guardian is impossible.   d

I am afraid that what you say is true, he replied.

Here feeling perplexed I began to think over what had preceded. My friend, I said, no wonder that we are in a perplexity; for we have lost sight of the image which we had before us.

What do you mean? he said.

I mean to say that there do exist natures gifted with those opposite qualities.

And where do you find them?

Many animals, I replied, furnish examples of them; our friend   e
the dog is a very good one: you know that well-bred dogs are perfectly gentle to their familiars and acquaintances, and the reverse to strangers.

Yes, I know.

Then there is nothing impossible or out of the order of nature in our finding a guardian who has a similar combination of qualities?

Certainly not.

Would not he who is fitted to be a guardian, besides the spirited nature, need to have the qualities of a philosopher?

I do not apprehend your meaning.   376

The trait of which I am speaking, I replied, may be also seen in the dog, and is remarkable in the animal.

What trait?

Why, a dog, whenever he sees a stranger, is angry; when an acquaintance, he welcomes him, although the one has never done him any harm, nor the other any good. Did this never strike you as curious?

The matter never struck me before; but I quite recognize the truth of your remark.

And surely this instinct of the dog is very charming; your dog is a true philosopher.   b

Why?

Why, because he distinguishes the face of a friend and of an enemy only by the criterion of knowing and not knowing. And must not an animal be a lover of learning who determines what he likes and dislikes by the test of knowledge and ignorance?

Most assuredly.

And is not the love of learning the love of wisdom, which is philosophy?

They are the same, he replied.

c And may we not say confidently of man also, that he who is likely to be gentle to his friends and acquaintances, must by nature be a lover of wisdom and knowledge?

That we may safely affirm.

Then he who is to be a really good and noble guardian of the State will require to unite in himself philosophy and spirit and swiftness and strength?

Undoubtedly.

Then we have found the desired natures; and now that we have found them, how are they to be reared and educated?[19] Is not this an inquiry which may be expected to throw light on the greater in-

d quiry which is our final end—How do justice and injustice grow up in States? for we do not want either to omit what is to the point or to draw out the argument to an inconvenient length.

Adeimantus thought that the inquiry would be of great service to us.

Then, I said, my dear friend, the task must not be given up, even if somewhat long.

Certainly not.

Come then, and let us pass a leisure hour in story-telling, and our story shall be the education of our heroes.

e By all means.

And what shall be their education? Can we find a better than the traditional sort?—and this has two divisions, gymnastics for the body, and music for the soul.[20]

True.

Shall we begin education with music, and go on to gymnastics afterward?

By all means.

And when you speak of music, do you include literature or not?

I do.

And literature may be either true or false?

Yes.

And the young should be trained in both kinds, and we begin   377
with the false?

I do not understand your meaning, he said.

You know, I said, that we begin by telling children stories which, though not wholly destitute of truth, are in the main fictitious; and these stories are told them when they are not of an age to learn gymnastics.

Very true.

That was my meaning when I said that we must teach music before gymnastics.

Quite right, he said.

You know also that the beginning is the most important part of any work, especially in the case of a young and tender thing; for that is the time at which the character is being formed and the de-   b
sired impression is more readily taken.

Quite true.

And shall we just carelessly allow children to hear any casual tales which may be devised by casual persons, and to receive into their minds ideas for the most part the very opposite of those which we should wish them to have when they are grown up?

We cannot.

Then the first thing will be to establish a censorship of the writers of fiction, and let the censors receive any tale of fiction which   c
is good, and reject the bad; and we will desire mothers and nurses to tell their children the authorized ones only. Let them fashion the mind with such tales, even more fondly than they mould the body with their hands; but most of those which are now in use must be discarded.

Of what tales are you speaking? he said.

You may find a model of the lesser in the greater,[21] I said; for they are necessarily of the same type, and there is the same spirit in both of them.   d

Very likely, he replied; but I do not as yet know what you would term the greater.

Those, I said, which are narrated by Homer and Hesiod, and

the rest of the poets, who have ever been the great storytellers of mankind.

But which stories do you mean, he said; and what fault do you find with them?

A fault which is most serious, I said; the fault of telling a lie, and, what is more, a bad lie.

But when is this fault committed?

e   Whenever an erroneous representation is made of the nature of gods and heroes—as when a painter paints a portrait not having the shadow of a likeness to the original.

Yes, he said, that sort of thing is certainly very blamable; but what are the stories which you mean?

First of all, I said, there was that greatest of all lies in high places, which the poet told about Uranus, and which was a bad lie 378   too—I mean what Hesiod says that Uranus did, and how Cronus retaliated on him.* The doings of Cronus, and the sufferings which in turn his son inflicted upon him, even if they were true, ought certainly not to be lightly told to young and thoughtless persons; if possible, they had better be buried in silence. But if there is an absolute necessity for their mention, a chosen few might hear them in a mystery, and they should sacrifice not a common [Eleusinian] pig,† but some huge and unprocurable victim; and then the number of the hearers will be very few indeed.

Why, yes, said he, those stories are extremely objectionable.

b   Yes, Adeimantus, they are stories not to be repeated in our State; the young man should not be told that in committing the worst of crimes he is far from doing anything outrageous;[22] and that even if he chastises his father when he does wrong, in whatever manner, he will only be following the example of the first and greatest among the gods.

I entirely agree with you, he said; in my opinion those stories are quite unfit to be repeated.

---

*Uranus (*Ouranos* in Greek), the ancient deity of the sky and mate of Gaia (Earth), was castrated by his son Cronus (Hesiod, *Theogony* 154–181); Cronus was in turn deposed by his son, Zeus, the current ruler of the cosmos (Hesiod, *Theogony* 453–506).
†Pigs were typically sacrificed in the initiatory rites for the mystery cult at Eleusis.

Neither, if we mean our future guardians to regard the habit of quarrelling among themselves as of all things the basest, should c any word be said to them of the wars in heaven, and of the plots and fightings of the gods against one another, for they are not true. No, we shall never mention the battles of the giants,* or let them be embroidered on garments; and we shall be silent about the innumerable other quarrels of gods and heroes with their friends and relatives. If they would only believe us we would tell them that quarrelling is unholy, and that never up to this time has there been any quarrel between citizens; this is what old men and old women should begin by telling children; and when they grow up, the poets d also should be told to compose them in a similar spirit. But the narrative of Hephæstus binding Here his mother,† or how on another occasion Zeus sent him flying for taking her part when she was being beaten,‡ and all the battles of the gods in Homer—these tales must not be admitted into our State, whether they are supposed to have an allegorical meaning or not. For a young person cannot judge what is allegorical and what is literal;²³ anything that he receives into his mind at that age is likely to become indelible and e unalterable; and therefore it is most important that the tales which the young first hear should be models of virtuous thoughts.

There you are right, he replied; but if anyone asks where are such models to be found and of what tales are you speaking—how shall we answer him?

I said to him, You and I, Adeimantus, at this moment are not poets, but founders of a State: now the founders of a State ought 379 to know the general forms in which poets should cast their tales, and the limits which must be observed by them, but to make the tales is not their business.

Very true, he said; but what are these forms of theology which you mean?

---

*There are several accounts of battles between the Olympian gods, led by Zeus, and the giants (created, according to Hesiod, *Theogony* 185, when the blood of the castrated Uranus fell onto Gaia).

†The story of Hephaestus' binding of his mother Here (Hera), the wife and sister of Zeus, was apparently related by Pindar. Hephaestus is the god of fire and metal-working crafts.

‡*Iliad* 1.586–594. Zeus' punishment left Hephaestus permanently lame.

Something of this kind, I replied: God is always to be represented as he truly is,[24] whatever be the sort of poetry, epic, lyric, or tragic, in which the representation is given.

Right.

b   And is he not truly good? and must he not be represented as such?

Certainly.

And no good thing is hurtful?

No, indeed.

And that which is not hurtful hurts not?

Certainly not.

And that which hurts not does no evil?

No.

And can that which does no evil be a cause of evil?

Impossible.

And the good is advantageous?

Yes.

And therefore the cause of well-being?

Yes.

It follows, therefore, that the good is not the cause of all things, but of the good only?

c   Assuredly.

Then God, if he be good, is not the author of all things, as the many assert, but he is the cause of a few things only, and not of most things that occur to men. For few are the goods of human life, and many are the evils, and the good is to be attributed to God alone; of the evils the causes are to be sought elsewhere, and not in him.

That appears to me to be most true, he said.

Then we must not listen to Homer or to any other poet who is
d   guilty of the folly of saying that two casks

"Lie at the threshold of Zeus, full of lots, one of good, the other of evil lots,"*

and that he to whom Zeus gives a mixture of the two

---

*This quotation and the two following are from *Iliad* 24.527–532.

"Sometimes meets with evil fortune, at other times with good;"

but that he to whom is given the cup of unmingled ill,

"Him wild hunger drives o'er the beauteous earth."

And again—

"Zeus, who is the dispenser of good and evil to us."* e

And if anyone asserts that the violation of oaths and treaties, which was really the work of Pandarus,† was brought about by Athene‡ and Zeus, or that the strife and contention of the gods were instigated by Themis and Zeus,§ he shall not have our approval; neither will we allow our young men to hear the words of Æschylus,[25] that 380

"God plants guilt among men when he desires utterly to destroy a house."‖

And if a poet writes of the sufferings of Niobe#—the subject of the tragedy in which these iambic verses occur—or of the house of Pelops,[26] or of the Trojan War or on any similar theme, either we must not permit him to say that these are the works of God, or if they are of God, he must devise some explanation of them such as we are seeking: he must say that God did what was just and right, and they were the better for being punished; but that those who b

---

*Source unknown.
†In *Iliad* 4, the Trojan Pandarus breaks the truce between the Greeks and the Trojans by shooting an arrow at Menelaus, the husband of Helen and the brother of Agamemnon, the leader of the Greek forces.
‡Daughter of Zeus, goddess of war, wisdom, and crafts, and patron of the Greeks at Troy. In *Iliad* 4.85–104, Athena disguises herself as a Trojan and prompts Pandarus to wound Menelaus.
§Probably a reference to *Iliad* 20.1–74, where Zeus dispatches the goddess Themis to call the gods to the council.
‖From a lost play about Niobe by Aeschylus.
#Daughter of Tantalus and wife of Amphion, Niobe boasted that her twelve children made her more blessed than the goddess Leto, mother (by Zeus) of the gods Apollo and Artemis. Apollo and Artemis killed all the children of Niobe, who subsequently turned to stone in grief.

are punished are miserable, and that God is the author of their misery—the poet is not to be permitted to say; though he may say that the wicked are miserable because they require to be punished, and are benefited by receiving punishment from God; but that God being good is the author of evil to anyone is to be strenuously denied, and not to be said or sung or heard in verse or prose by anyone whether old or young in any well-ordered commonwealth. Such a fiction is suicidal, ruinous, impious.

I agree with you, he replied, and am ready to give my assent to the law.

Let this then be one of our rules and principles concerning the gods, to which our poets and reciters will be expected to conform— that God is not the author of all things, but of good only.

That will do, he said.

And what do you think of a second principle? Shall I ask you whether God is a magician, and of a nature to appear insidiously now in one shape, and now in another—sometimes himself changing and passing into many forms, sometimes deceiving us with the semblance of such transformations; or is he one and the same immutably fixed in his own proper image?

I cannot answer you, he said, without more thought.

Well, I said; but if we suppose a change in anything, that change must be effected either by the thing itself or by some other thing?

Most certainly.

And things which are at their best are also least liable to be altered or discomposed; for example, when healthiest and strongest, the human frame is least liable to be affected by meats and drinks, and the plant which is in the fullest vigor also suffers least from winds or the heat of the sun or any similar causes.

Of course.

And will not the bravest and wisest soul be least confused or deranged by any external influence?

True.

And the same principle, as I should suppose, applies to all composite things—furniture, houses, garments: when good and well made, they are least altered by time and circumstances.

Very true.

Then everything which is good, whether made by art or nature, b
or both, is least liable to suffer change from without?

True.

But surely God and the things of God are in every way perfect?

Of course they are.

Then he can hardly be compelled by external influence to take
many shapes?

He cannot.

But may he not change and transform himself?

Clearly, he said, that must be the case if he is changed at all.

And will he then change himself for the better and fairer, or for
the worse and more unsightly?

If he change at all he can only change for the worse, for we c
cannot suppose him to be deficient either in virtue or beauty.

Very true, Adeimantus; but then, would anyone, whether God
or man, desire to make himself worse?

Impossible.

Then it is impossible that God should ever be willing to change;
being, as is supposed, the fairest and best that is conceivable,
every God remains absolutely and forever in his own form.

That necessarily follows, he said, in my judgment.

Then, I said, my dear friend, let none of the poets tell us that d

"The gods, taking the disguise of strangers from other lands, walk
up and down cities in all sorts of forms;"°

and let no one slander Proteus† and Thetis,‡ neither let anyone, either in tragedy or in any other kind of poetry, introduce Here dis-
guised in the likeness of a priestess asking an alms

"For the life-giving daughters of Inachus the river of Argos;"§

°*Odyssey* 17.485–486.
†*Odyssey* 4.455–460 describes the shape-changing of Proteus, a minor sea-god.
‡Pindar, in the fourth Nemean ode, describes how Thetis, a minor goddess who
became (by the mortal Peleus) the mother of the mortal warrior Achilles, trans-
formed herself in order to avoid marrying Peleus.
§From a lost play by Aeschylus.

e   —let us have no more lies of that sort. Neither must we have mothers under the influence of the poets scaring their children with a bad
version of these myths—telling how certain gods, as they say, "Go
about by night in the likeness of so many strangers and in diverse
forms;"* but let them take heed lest they make cowards of their
children, and at the same time speak blasphemy against the gods.

Heaven forbid, he said.

But although the gods are themselves unchangeable, still by
witchcraft and deception they may make us think that they appear
in various forms?

Perhaps, he replied.

382   Well, but can you imagine that God will be willing to lie,
whether in word or deed, or to put forth a phantom of himself?

I cannot say, he replied.

Do you not know, I said, that the true lie, if such an expression
may be allowed, is hated of gods and men?

What do you mean? he said.

I mean that no one is willingly deceived in that which is the truest
and highest part of himself, or about the truest and highest matters;
there, above all, he is most afraid of a lie having possession of him.

Still, he said, I do not comprehend you.

b   The reason is, I replied, that you attribute some profound
meaning to my words; but I am only saying that deception, or
being deceived or uninformed about the highest realities in the
highest part of themselves, which is the soul, and in that part of
them to have and to hold the lie, is what mankind least like;—that,
I say, is what they utterly detest.

There is nothing more hateful to them.

And, as I was just now remarking, this ignorance in the soul of
him who is deceived may be called the true lie; for the lie in words
is only a kind of imitation and shadowy image of a previous affec-
c   tion of the soul, not pure unadulterated falsehood. Am I not right?

Perfectly right.

The true lie is hated not only by the gods, but also by men?

---

*Indicated here are the tales about "bogey monsters," such as those mentioned in
Aristophanes, *Frogs* 293.

Yes.

Whereas the lie in words is in certain cases useful and not hateful;[27] in dealing with enemies—that would be an instance; or again, when those whom we call our friends in a fit of madness or illusion are going to do some harm, then it is useful and is a sort of medicine or preventive; also in the tales of mythology, of which we were just now speaking—because we do not know the truth about ancient times, we make falsehood as much like truth as we can, and so turn it to account.

Very true, he said.

But can any of these reasons apply to God? Can we suppose that he is ignorant of antiquity, and therefore has recourse to invention?

That would be ridiculous, he said.

Then the lying poet has no place in our idea of God?

I should say not.

Or perhaps he may tell a lie because he is afraid of enemies?

That is inconceivable.

But he may have friends who are senseless or mad?

But no mad or senseless person can be a friend of God.

Then no motive can be imagined why God should lie?

None whatever.

Then the superhuman, and divine, is absolutely incapable of falsehood?

Yes.

Then is God perfectly simple and true both in word and deed; he changes not; he deceives not, either by sign or word, by dream or waking vision.

Your thoughts, he said, are the reflection of my own.

You agree with me then, I said, that this is the second type or form in which we should write and speak about divine things. The gods are not magicians who transform themselves, neither do they deceive mankind in any way.

I grant that.

Then, although we are admirers of Homer, we do not admire the lying dream which Zeus sends to Agamemnon;* neither will

d

e

383

Iliad 2.1–34.

we praise the verses of Æschylus in which Thetis says that Apollo
at her nuptials

b   "was celebrating in song her fair progeny whose days were to be
      long, and to know no sickness. And when he had spoken of my lot
      as in all things blessed of heaven, he raised a note of triumph and
      cheered my soul. And I thought that the word of Phœbus, being
      divine and full of prophecy, would not fail. And now he himself
      who uttered the strain, he who was present at the banquet, and
      who said this—he it is who has slain my son."*

      These are the kind of sentiments about the gods which will
c   arouse our anger; and he who utters them shall be refused a chorus;
      neither shall we allow teachers to make use of them in the instruc-
      tion of the young, meaning, as we do, that our guardians, as far as
      men can be, should be true worshippers of the gods and like them.

      I entirely agree, he said, in these principles, and promise to
      make them my laws.

---

*Perhaps from Aeschylus' lost *Contest of Arms* (*Hoplon krisis*). Whatever the origin of the quotation, "her fair progeny" refers to Achilles, and "Phoebus" refers to
the god Apollo.

BOOK 3

SUCH, THEN, I SAID, are our principles concerning how the gods are to be represented—some tales are to be told, and others are not to be told to our disciples from their youth upward, if we mean them to honor the gods and their parents, and to value friendship with one another.

Yes; and I think that our principles are right, he said.

But if they are to be courageous, must they not learn other lessons beside these, and lessons of such a kind as will take away the fear of death? Can any man be courageous who has the fear of death in him?

Certainly not, he said.

And can he be fearless of death, or will he choose death in battle rather than defeat and slavery, who believes the world below to be real and terrible?

Impossible.

Then we must assume a control over the narrators of this class of tales as well as over the others, and beg them not simply to revile, but rather to commend the world below, intimating to them that their descriptions are untrue, and will do harm to our future warriors.

That will be our duty, he said.

Then, I said, we shall have to obliterate many obnoxious passages, beginning with the verses

"I would rather be a serf on the land of a poor and portionless man
than rule over all the dead who have come to naught."[*]

---

[*]*Odyssey* 11.489–491. The verses, spoken by the ghost of Achilles in the underworld, are also quoted in *Republic* at 7.516d. From this point on, the representation of Achilles' conduct (in *Iliad*) is one of the chief foci of Socrates' criticism of poetry's content.

We must also expunge the verse, which tells us how Pluto feared

d
"Lest the mansions grim and squalid which the gods abhor should be seen both of mortals and immortals."[*]

And again:

"O heavens! verily in the house of Hades there is soul and ghostly form but no mind at all!"[†]

Again of Tiresias:

"[To him even after death did Persephone grant mind,] that he alone should be wise; but the other souls are flitting shades."[‡]

Again:

387
"The soul flying from the limbs had gone to Hades, lamenting her fate, leaving manhood and youth."[§]

Again:

"And the soul, with shrilling cry, passed like smoke beneath the earth."[‖]

And,

"As bats in hollow of mystic cavern, whenever any of them has dropped out of the string and falls from the rock, fly shrilling and cling to one another, so did they with shrilling cry hold together as they moved."[#]

---

[*]*Iliad* 20.64–65. Pluto is another name for Hades, the god of the underworld.
[†]*Iliad* 23.103–104.
[‡]*Odyssey* 11.493–495. Tiresias is the legendary blind Theban prophet. In *Odyssey* 11, in order to learn about his future, Odysseus calls up the spirit of Tiresias from the underworld.
[§]*Iliad* 16.856–857.
[‖]*Iliad* 23.100.
[#]*Odyssey* 246–249.

And we must beg Homer and the other poets not to be angry if we   b
strike out these and similar passages, not because they are unpo-
etical, or unattractive to the popular ear, but because the greater
the poetical charm of them, the less are they suitable for the ears
of boys and men who are meant to be free, and who should fear
slavery more than death.

Undoubtedly.

Also we shall have to reject all the terrible and appalling names
which describe the world below—Cocytus and Styx,° ghosts under
the earth, and sapless shades, and any similar words of which the   c
very mention causes a shudder to pass through the inmost soul of
him who hears them. I do not say that these horrible stories may
not have a use of some kind; but there is a danger that the nerves
of our guardians may be rendered too excitable and effeminate by
them.

There is a real danger, he said.

Then we must have no more of them.

True.

Another and a nobler strain must be composed and sung by us.

Clearly.

And shall we proceed to get rid of the weepings and wailings of   d
famous men?

They will go with the rest.

But shall we be right in getting rid of them? Reflect: our principle is that the good man will not consider death terrible to any
other good man who is his comrade.

Yes; that is our principle.

And therefore he will not sorrow for his departed friend as
though he had suffered anything terrible?

He will not.

Such a one, as we further maintain, is sufficient for himself
and his own happiness, and therefore is least in need of other men.   e

True, he said.

And for this reason the loss of a son or brother, or the deprivation of fortune, is to him of all men least terrible.

°Two rivers in the underworld.

Assuredly.

And therefore he will be least likely to lament, and will bear with the greatest equanimity any misfortune of this sort which may befall him.

Yes, he will feel such a misfortune far less than another.

Then we shall be right in getting rid of the lamentations of famous men, and making them over to women (and not even to women who are good for anything), or to men of a baser sort, in order that those who are being educated by us to be the defenders of their country may scorn to do the like.

That will be very right.

Then we will once more entreat Homer and the other poets not to depict Achilles,* who is the son of a goddess, first lying on his side, then on his back, and then on his face; then starting up and sailing in a frenzy along the shores of the barren sea; now taking the sooty ashes in both his hands† and pouring them over his head, or weeping and wailing in the various modes which Homer has delineated. Nor should he describe Priam, the kinsman of the gods, as praying and beseeching,

"Rolling in the dirt, calling each man loudly by his name."‡

Still more earnestly will we beg of him at all events not to introduce the gods lamenting and saying,

"Alas! my misery! Alas! that I bore the bravest to my sorrow."§

But if he must introduce the gods, at any rate let him not dare so completely to misrepresent the greatest of the gods, as to make him say—

---

*Allusion to *Iliad* 24.10–12, which describes the grief of Achilles as he mourns for his recently killed companion Patroclus.

†Allusion to *Iliad* 18.23, when Achilles first learns of Patroclus' death.

‡*Iliad* 22.414–415. Priam, king of Troy, is "kinsman of the gods" because he is descended from Zeus.

§*Iliad* 18.54. Thetis, Achilles' mother, is the speaker.

> "O heavens! with my eyes verily I behold a dear friend of mine chased round and round the city, and my heart is sorrowful."*

Or again:

> "Woe is me that I am fated to have Sarpedon, dearest of men to me, subdued at the hands of Patroclus the son of Menœtius."†

d

For if, my sweet Adeimantus, our youth seriously listen to such unworthy representations of the gods, instead of laughing at them as they ought, hardly will any of them deem that he himself, being but a man, can be dishonored by similar actions; neither will he rebuke any inclination which may arise in his mind to say and do the like. And instead of having any shame or self-control, he will be always whining and lamenting on slight occasions.

Yes, he said, that is most true.

e

Yes, I replied; but that surely is what ought not to be, as the argument has just proved to us; and by that proof we must abide until it is disproved by a better.

It ought not to be.

Neither ought our guardians to be given to laughter. For a fit of laughter which has been indulged to excess almost always produces a violent reaction.

So I believe.

Then persons of worth, even if only mortal men, must not be represented as overcome by laughter, and still less must such a representation of the gods be allowed.

389

Still less of the gods, as you say, he replied.

Then we shall not suffer such an expression to be used about the gods as that of Homer when he describes how

> "Inextinguishable laughter arose among the blessed gods, when they saw Hephæstus bustling about the mansion."‡

Iliad 22.168. The speaker is Zeus.
†*Iliad* 16.433. Again, the speaker is Zeus. Sarpedon is Zeus' son by a mortal woman and is hence himself mortal. Zeus laments his pending death at the hands of Patroclus.
‡*Iliad* 1.599.

On your views, we must not admit them.

On my views, if you like to father them on me; that we must
b   not admit them is certain.

Again, truth should be highly valued; if, as we were saying, a lie
is useless to the gods, and useful only as a medicine to men, then
the use of such medicines should be restricted to physicians; private individuals have no business with them.

Clearly not, he said.

Then if anyone at all is to have the privilege of lying, the rulers
of the State should be the persons; and they, in their dealings either with enemies or with their own citizens, may be allowed to lie
for the public good. But nobody else should meddle with anything
of the kind; and although the rulers have this privilege, for a private man to lie to them in return is to be deemed a more heinous
c   fault than for the patient or the pupil of a gymnasium not to speak
the truth about his own bodily illnesses to the physician or to the
trainer, or for a sailor not to tell the captain what is happening
about the ship and the rest of the crew, and how things are going
with himself or his fellow-sailors.

Most true, he said.

If, then, the ruler catches anybody besides himself lying in the
d   State,

> "Any of the craftsmen, whether he be priest or physician or car-
> penter,"*

he will punish him for introducing a practice which is equally subversive and destructive of ship or State.[1]

Most certainly, he said, if our idea of the State is ever carried
out.

In the next place our youth must be temperate?

Certainly.

Are not the chief elements of temperance, speaking generally,
e   obedience to commanders and self-control in sensual pleasures?

True.

Odyssey 17.383–384.

Then we shall approve such language as that of Diomede in Homer,

"Friend, sit still and obey my word,"°

and the verses which follow,

"The Greeks marched breathing prowess,"
". . . in silent awe of their leaders."†

and other sentiments of the same kind.

We shall.

What of this line,

"O heavy with wine, who hast the eyes of a dog and the heart of a stag,"‡

and of the words which follow? Would you say that these, or any   390
similar impertinences which private individuals are supposed to address to their rulers, whether in verse or prose, are well or ill spoken?

They are ill spoken.

They may very possibly afford some amusement, but they do
not conduce to temperance. And therefore they are likely to do
harm to our young men— you would agree with me there?

Yes.

And then, again, to make the wisest of men say that nothing in
his opinion is more glorious than

"When the tables are full of bread and meat, and the cup-bearer   b
carries round wine which he draws from the bowl and pours into
the cups;"§

°*Iliad* 4.412. Diomedes was one of the Greek chieftains at Troy.
†These verses do not follow *Iliad* 4.412. The first is *Iliad* 3.8, the second *Iliad* 4.431.
‡*Iliad* 1.225, addressed by Achilles to Agamemnon. Although Achilles is the best
warrior in the Greek army, Agamemnon is its commander; hence the judgment
that Achilles' words are "ill spoken."
§*Odyssey* 9.8–10.

is it fit or conducive to temperance for a young man to hear such words? or the verse

"The saddest of fates is to die and meet destiny from hunger"?[°]

What would you say again to the tale of Zeus, who, while other gods and men were asleep and he the only one awake, lay devising plans, but forgot them all in a moment through his lust, and was so completely overcome at the sight of Here that he would not even go into the hut, but wanted to lie with her on the ground, declaring that he had never been in such a state of rapture before, even when they first met one another,

"Without the knowledge of their parents"[†]

or that other tale of how Hephæstus, because of similar goings on, cast a chain around Ares and Aphrodite?[‡]

Indeed, he said, I am strongly of opinion that they ought not to hear that sort of thing.

But any deeds of endurance which are done or told by famous men, these they ought to see and hear; as, for example, what is said in the verses,

"He smote his breast, and thus reproached his heart,
Endure, my heart; far worse hast thou endured!"[§]

Certainly, he said.

In the next place, we must not let them be receivers of gifts or lovers of money.

[°]*Odyssey* 12.342.
[†]*Iliad* 14.281. In *Iliad* 14, Here (Hera) seduces Zeus and thus temporarily distracts him from his supervision of the battle between the Greeks and the Trojans. The description above of Zeus lying awake "devising plans" is actually derived from *Iliad* 2.1–4.
[‡]In *Odyssey* 8.266–366, the Phaeacian bard Demodocus relates a story about how Hephaestus caught his wife, Aphrodite, the goddess of lust and sensuality, in bed with the handsome young war-god Ares.
[§]Odysseus in *Odyssey* 20.17–18.

Certainly not.
Neither must we sing to them of

"Gifts persuading gods, and persuading reverend kings."°

Neither is Phœnix, the tutor of Achilles, to be approved or deemed to have given his pupil good counsel when he told him that he should take the gifts of the Greeks and assist them;† but that without a gift he should not lay aside his anger. Neither will we believe or acknowledge Achilles himself to have been such a lover of money that he took Agamemnon's gifts,‡ or that when he had received payment he restored the dead body of Hector, but that without payment he was unwilling to do so.§

Undoubtedly, he said, these are not sentiments which can be approved.

Loving Homer as I do, I hardly like to say[2] that in attributing these feelings to Achilles, or in believing that they are truly attributed to him, he is guilty of downright impiety. As little can I believe the narrative of his insolence to Apollo, where he says,

"Thou hast wronged me, O far-darter, most abominable of deities.
Verily I would be even with thee, if I had only the power;"‖

or his insubordination to the river-god,# on whose divinity he is ready to lay hands; or his offerings to the dead Patroclus of his own hair,°° which had been previously dedicated to the other

---

°Saying attributed to Hesiod.
†In *Iliad* 9, Phoenix (along with Odysseus and Ajax) brings gifts from Agamemnon to Achilles in an effort to persuade Achilles to relent in his anger toward Agamemnon and to rejoin the fighting against the Trojans.
‡Although Achilles refuses the gifts from Agamemnon in *Iliad* 9, he accepts them in *Iliad* 19 as he prepares to go back into battle.
§Achilles kills Hector, the leading warrior of the Trojans and Priam's son, in *Iliad* 22. In *Iliad* 24, he accepts ransom for Hector's body and returns it to Priam.
‖*Iliad* 22.15 and 20.
#Achilles fights the river-god Scamander in *Iliad* 21.
°°*Iliad* 23.140–151. Achilles vowed to offer locks of his hair to the river Spercheius if he safely returned to Greece after the war; by the time he prepares Patroclus' funeral pyre in *Iliad* 23, however, he knows that he will die in Troy.

river-god Spercheius, and that he actually performed this vow; or that he dragged Hector round the tomb of Patroclus,° and slaughtered the captives at the pyre;† of all this I cannot believe that he was guilty, any more than I can allow our citizens to believe that he, the wise Cheiron's‡ pupil, the son of a goddess and of Peleus who was the gentlest of men and third in descent from Zeus, was so disordered in his wits as to be at one time the slave of two seemingly inconsistent passions, meanness, not untainted by avarice, combined with overweening contempt of gods and men.

You are quite right, he replied.

And let us equally refuse to believe, or allow to be repeated, the tale of Theseus, son of Poseidon, or of Peirithous, son of Zeus, going forth as they did to perpetrate a horrid rape;§ or of any other hero or son of a god daring to do such impious and dreadful things as they falsely ascribe to them in our day: and let us further compel the poets to declare either that these acts were not done by them, or that they were not the sons of God; both in the same breath they shall not be permitted to affirm. We will not have them trying to persuade our youth that the gods are the authors of evil, and that heroes are no better than men—sentiments which, as we were saying, are neither pious nor true, for we have already proved that evil cannot come from the gods.

Assuredly not.

And, further, they are likely to have a bad effect on those who hear them; for everybody will begin to excuse his own vices when he is convinced that similar wickednesses are always being perpetrated by

"The kindred of the gods, the relatives of Zeus, whose ancestral altar, the altar of Zeus, is aloft in air on the peak of Ida,"

°*Iliad* 24.14–17.
†*Iliad* 23.175–177.
‡Cheiron was the centaur (half-human, half-horse) who was Achilles' tutor.
§Theseus was a legendary king of Athens and descendant of Poseidon, god of the sea; he and his companion Peirithous ventured to the underworld to steal away Persephone, goddess of the underworld, from her husband, Hades.

and who have

"the blood of deities yet flowing in their veins."°

And therefore let us put an end to such tales, lest they engender laxity of morals among the young.   392

By all means, he replied.

But now that we are determining what classes of subjects are or are not to be spoken of, let us see whether any have been omitted by us. The manner in which gods and demigods and heroes and the world below should be treated has been already laid down.

Very true.

And what shall we say about men? That is clearly the remaining portion of our subject.

Clearly so.

But we are not in a condition to answer this question at present, my friend.

Why not?

Because, if I am not mistaken, we shall have to say that about men poets and story-tellers are guilty of making the gravest mis-   b statements when they tell us that wicked men are often happy, and the good miserable; and that injustice is profitable when undetected, but that justice is a man's own loss and another's gain— these things we shall forbid them to utter, and command them to sing and say the opposite.

To be sure we shall, he replied.

But if you admit that I am right in this, then I shall maintain that you have implied the principle for which we have been all along contending.

I grant the truth of your inference.

That such things are or are not to be said about men is a question   c which we cannot determine until we have discovered what justice is, and how naturally advantageous to the possessor, whether he seem to be just or not.[3]

°Both quotations are from Aeschylus' tragedy *Niobe*. Ida is the mountain near the city of Troy.

Most true, he said.

Enough of the subjects of poetry: let us now speak of the style; and when this has been considered, both matter and manner will have been completely treated.

I do not understand what you mean, said Adeimantus.

d   Then I must make you understand; and perhaps I may be more intelligible if I put the matter in this way. You are aware, I suppose, that all mythology and poetry are a narration of events, either past, present, or to come?

Certainly, he replied.

And narration may be either simple narration or imitation, or a union of the two?[4]

That, again, he said, I do not quite understand.

I fear that I must be a ridiculous teacher when I have so much difficulty in making myself apprehended. Like a bad speaker, therefore, I will not take the whole of the subject, but will break a

e   piece off in illustration of my meaning. You know the first lines of the "Iliad," in which the poet says that Chryses prayed Agamemnon to release his daughter, and that Agamemnon flew into a passion with him; whereupon Chryses, failing of his object, invoked

393 the anger of the god against the Achæans. Now as far as these lines,

"And he prayed all the Greeks, but especially the two sons of Atreus, the chiefs of the people,"[*]

the poet is speaking in his own person; he never leads us to suppose that he is anyone else. But in what follows he takes the person of

b   Chryses, and then he does all that he can to make us believe that the speaker is not Homer, but the aged priest himself. And in this double form he has cast the entire narrative of the events which occurred at Troy and in Ithaca and throughout the "Odyssey."

Yes.

---

[*]*Iliad* 1.15–16. Chryses, priest of Apollo in a town near Troy that had been plundered by the Greeks, seeks to pay ransom for his daughter Chryseis but is rebuffed by Agamemnon, who has taken her as a concubine. The god who becomes angered against the Greeks because of Chryses' prayer is Apollo.

And a narrative it remains both in the speeches which the poet recites from time to time and in the intermediate passages?

Quite true.

But when the poet speaks in the person of another, may we not   c
say that he assimilates his style to that of the person who, as he informs you, is going to speak?

Certainly.

And this assimilation of himself to another, either by the use of voice or gesture, is the imitation of the person whose character he assumes?

Of course.

Then in this case the narrative of the poet may be said to proceed by way of imitation?

Very true.

Or, if the poet everywhere appears and never conceals himself, then again the imitation is dropped, and his poetry becomes simple   d
narration. However, in order that I may make my meaning quite clear, and that you may no more say, "I don't understand," I will show how the change might be effected. If Homer had said, "The priest came, having his daughter's ransom in his hands, supplicating the Achæans, and above all the kings;" and then if, instead of speaking in the person of Chryses, he had continued in his own person, the words would have been, not imitation, but simple narration. The passage would have run as follows (I am no poet, and therefore I drop the metre): "The priest came and prayed the gods on behalf of the Greeks that they might capture Troy and re-   e
turn safely home, but begged that they would give him back his daughter, and take the ransom which he brought, and respect the god. Thus he spoke, and the other Greeks revered the priest and assented. But Agamemnon was wroth, and bade him depart and not come again, lest the staff and chaplets of the god should be of no avail to him—the daughter of Chryses should not be released, he said—she should grow old with him in Argos. And then he told him to go away and not to provoke him, if he intended to get home unscathed. And the old man went away in fear and silence, and,   394
when he had left the camp, he called upon Apollo by his many names, reminding him of everything which he had done pleasing to him, whether in building his temples, or in offering sacrifice,

and praying that his good deeds might be returned to him, and that the Achæans* might expiate his tears by the arrows of the
b   god"—and so on. In this way the whole becomes simple narrative.

I understand, he said.

Or you may suppose the opposite case—that the intermediate passages are omitted, and the dialogue only left.

That also, he said, I understand; you mean, for example, as in tragedy.

You have conceived my meaning perfectly; and if I mistake not, what you failed to apprehend before is now made clear to you, that poetry and mythology are, in some cases, wholly imitative—instances of this are supplied by tragedy and comedy; there is
c   likewise the opposite style, in which the poet is the only speaker—of this the dithyramb† affords the best example; and the combination of both is found in epic and in several other styles of poetry. Do I take you with me?

Yes, he said; I see now what you meant.

I will ask you to remember also what I began by saying, that we had done with the subject and might proceed to the style.

Yes, I remember.

d   In saying this, I intended to imply that we must come to an understanding about the mimetic art—whether the poets, in narrating their stories, are to be allowed by us to imitate, and if so, whether in whole or in part, and if the latter, in what parts; or should all imitation be prohibited?

You mean, I suspect, to ask whether tragedy and comedy shall be admitted into our State?

Yes, I said; but there may be more than this in question: I really do not know as yet, but whither the argument may blow, thither we go.

And go we will, he said.

e   Then, Adeimantus, let me ask you whether our guardians

---

*The Greeks in *Iliad* and *Odyssey* are typically called Achaeans, Danaans, and Argives.

†Dithyrambs were narrative poems performed by large choruses (some composed of men, some of boys); they were featured, along with tragedies and comedies, in festal competitions at the Theater of Dionysus in Athens.

ought to be imitators; or rather, has not this question been decided by the rule already laid down that one man can only do one thing well, and not many; and that if he attempt many, he will altogether fail of gaining much reputation in any?

Certainly.

And this is equally true of imitation; no one man can imitate many things as well as he would imitate a single one?

He cannot.

Then the same person will hardly be able to play a serious part   395
in life, and at the same time to be an imitator and imitate many other parts as well; for even when two species of imitation are nearly allied, the same persons cannot succeed in both, as, for example, the writers of tragedy and comedy—did you not just now call them imitations?

Yes, I did; and you are right in thinking that the same persons cannot succeed in both.

Any more than they can be rhapsodists and actors at once?

True.

Neither are comic and tragic actors the same; yet all these   b
things are but imitations.

They are so.

And human nature,* Adeimantus, appears to have been coined into yet smaller pieces, and to be as incapable of imitating many things well, as of performing well the actions of which the imitations are copies.

Quite true, he replied.

If then we adhere to our original notion and bear in mind that our guardians, setting aside every other business, are to dedicate themselves wholly to the maintenance of freedom in the State, making this their craft, and engaging in no work which does not   c
bear on this end, they ought not to practise or imitate anything else; if they imitate at all, they should imitate from youth upward only those characters which are suitable to their profession—the courageous, temperate, holy, free, and the like; but they should not depict or be skilful at imitating any kind of illiberality or baseness,

*Once again, *physis*; see note 9 on 2.367e, page 358.

d   lest from imitation they should come to be what they imitate. Did you never observe how imitations, beginning in early youth and continuing far into life, at length grow into habits and become a second nature, affecting body, voice, and mind?

Yes, certainly, he said.

Then, I said, we will not allow those for whom we profess a care and of whom we say that they ought to be good men, to imitate a woman, whether young or old, quarrelling with her husband, or striving and vaunting against the gods in conceit of her happiness,

e   or when she is in affliction, or sorrow, or weeping; and certainly not one who is in sickness, love, or labor.

Very right, he said.

Neither must they represent slaves, male or female, performing the offices of slaves?

They must not.

And surely not bad men, whether cowards or any others, who do the reverse of what we have just been prescribing, who scold or mock or revile one another in drink or out of drink, or who in

396 any other manner sin against themselves and their neighbors in word or deed, as the manner of such is. Neither should they be trained to imitate the action or speech of men or women who are mad or bad; for madness, like vice, is to be known but not to be practised or imitated.

Very true, he replied.

Neither may they imitate smiths or other artificers, or oarsmen, or boatswains, or the like?

b   How can they, he said, when they are not allowed to apply their minds to the callings of any of these?

Nor may they imitate the neighing of horses, the bellowing of bulls, the murmur of rivers and roll of the ocean, thunder, and all that sort of thing?

Nay, he said, if madness be forbidden, neither may they copy the behavior of madmen.

You mean, I said, if I understand you aright, that there is one

c   sort of narrative style which may be employed by a truly good man when he has anything to say, and that another sort will be used by a man of an opposite character and education.

And which are these two sorts? he asked.

Suppose, I answered, that a just and good man in the course of a narration comes on some saying or action of another good man—I should imagine that he will like to personate him, and will not be ashamed of this sort of imitation: he will be most ready to   d
play the part of the good man when he is acting firmly and wisely; in a less degree when he is overtaken by illness or love or drink, or has met with any other disaster. But when he comes to a character which is unworthy of him, he will not make a study of that; he will disdain such a person, and will assume his likeness, if at all, for a moment only when he is performing some good action; at other times he will be ashamed to play a part which he has never prac-tised, nor will he like to fashion and frame himself after the baser models; he feels the employment of such an art, unless in jest, to   e
be beneath him, and his mind revolts at it.

So I should expect, he replied.

Then he will adopt a mode of narration such as we have illus-trated out of Homer, that is to say, his style will be both imitative and narrative; but there will be very little of the former, and a great deal of the latter. Do you agree?

Certainly, he said; that is the model which such a speaker must necessarily take.

But there is another sort of character who will narrate anything,   397
and, the worse he is, the more unscrupulous he will be; nothing will be too bad for him: and he will be ready to imitate anything, not as a joke, but in right good earnest, and before a large company. As I was just now saying, he will attempt to represent the roll of thunder, the noise of wind and hail, or the creaking of wheels, and pulleys, and the various sounds of flutes, pipes, trumpets, and all sorts of instruments: he will bark like a dog, bleat like a sheep, or crow like a cock; his entire art will consist in imitation of voice and gesture,   b
and there will be very little narration.

That, he said, will be his mode of speaking.

These, then, are the two kinds of style?

Yes.

And you would agree with me in saying that one of them is simple and has but slight changes; and if the harmony and rhythm are also chosen for their simplicity, the result is that the speaker, if he speaks correctly, is always pretty much the same in style, and he will keep within the limits of a single harmony (for the changes are not great), and in like manner he will make use of nearly the same rhythm?

That is quite true, he said.

Whereas the other requires all sorts of harmonies and all sorts of rhythms, if the music and the style are to correspond, because the style has all sorts of changes.

That is also perfectly true, he replied.

And do not the two styles, or the mixture of the two, comprehend all poetry, and every form of expression in words? No one can say anything except in one or other of them or in both together.

They include all, he said.

And shall we receive into our State all the three styles, or one only of the two unmixed styles? or would you include the mixed?

I should prefer only to admit the pure imitator of virtue.

Yes, I said, Adeimantus; but the mixed style is also very charming: and indeed the pantomimic, which is the opposite of the one chosen by you, is the most popular style with children and their attendants, and with the world in general.[5]

I do not deny it.

But I suppose you would argue that such a style is unsuitable to our State, in which human nature is not twofold or manifold, for one man plays one part only?

Yes; quite unsuitable.

And this is the reason why in our State, and in our State only, we shall find a shoemaker to be a shoemaker and not a pilot also, and a husbandman to be a husbandman and not a dicast also, and a soldier a soldier and not a trader also, and the same throughout?

True, he said.

And therefore when any one of these pantomimic gentlemen, who are so clever that they can imitate anything, comes to us, and makes a proposal to exhibit himself and his poetry, we will fall down and worship him as a sweet and holy and wonderful being; but we must also inform him that in our State such as he are not permitted to exist; the law will not allow them. And so when we have anointed him with myrrh, and set a garland of wool upon his head, we shall send him away to another city. For we mean to employ for our souls' health the rougher and severer poet or story-teller, who

will imitate the style of the virtuous only, and will follow those b
models which we prescribed at first when we began the education
of our soldiers.

We certainly will, he said, if we have the power.

Then now, my friend, I said, that part of music or literary education which relates to the story or myth may be considered to be
finished; for the matter and manner have both been discussed.

I think so too, he said.

Next in order will follow melody and song. c

That is obvious.

Everyone can see already what we ought to say about them, if
we are to be consistent with ourselves.

I fear, said Glaucon, laughing, that the word "everyone" hardly
includes me, for I cannot at the moment say what they should be;
though I may guess.

At any rate you can tell that a song or ode has three parts—the
words, the melody,* and the rhythm; that degree of knowledge I d
may presuppose?

Yes, he said; so much as that you may.

And as for the words, there will surely be no difference between
words which are and which are not set to music; both will conform
to the same laws, and these have been already determined by us?

Yes.

And the melody and rhythm will depend upon the words?

Certainly.

We were saying, when we spoke of the subject-matter, that we
had no need of lamentation and strains of sorrow?

True.

And which are the harmonies expressive of sorrow? You are e
musical, and can tell me.

The harmonies which you mean are the mixed or tenor Lydian,
and the full-toned or bass Lydian, and such like.[6]

These then, I said, must be banished; they are of no use, even to
women who have a character to maintain, and much less to men.

---

*In Greek, *harmonia* ("harmony," referring literally to the "attunement" of lyre
strings); also translated as "mode."

Certainly.

In the next place, drunkenness and softness and indolence are utterly unbecoming the character of our guardians.

Utterly unbecoming.

And which are the soft or drinking harmonies?

The Ionian, he replied, and the Lydian; they are termed "relaxed."

399   Well, and are these of any military use?

Quite the reverse, he replied; and if so, the Dorian and the Phrygian are the only ones which you have left.

I answered: Of the harmonies I know nothing, but I want to have one warlike, to sound the note or accent which a brave man utters in the hour of danger and stern resolve, or when his cause is failing, and he is going to wounds or death or is overtaken by some other evil, and at every such crisis meets the blows of fortune with firm step and a determination to endure; and another to be used by him in times of peace and freedom of action, when there is no pressure of necessity, and he is seeking to persuade God by prayer, or man by instruction and admonition, or on the other hand, when he is expressing his willingness to yield to persuasion or entreaty or admonition, and which represents him when by prudent conduct he has attained his end, not carried away by his success, but acting moderately and wisely under the circumstances, and acquiescing in the event. These two harmonies I ask you to leave; the strain of necessity and the strain of freedom, the strain of the unfortunate and the strain of the fortunate, the strain of courage, and the strain of temperance; these, I say, leave.

And these, he replied, are the Dorian and Phrygian harmonies of which I was just now speaking.

Then, I said, if these and these only are to be used in our songs and melodies, we shall not want multiplicity of notes or a panharmonic scale?

I suppose not.

Then we shall not maintain the artificers of lyres with three corners and complex scales, or the makers of any other many-stringed, curiously harmonized instruments?[7]

Certainly not.

But what do you say to flute-makers and flute-players? Would you admit them into our State when you reflect that in this composite use of harmony the flute° is worse than all the stringed instruments put together; even the panharmonic music is only an imitation of the flute?

Clearly not.

There remain then only the lyre and the harp† for use in the city, and the shepherds may have a pipe in the country.

That is surely the conclusion to be drawn from the argument.

The preferring of Apollo and his instruments to Marsyas and his instruments is not at all strange, I said.[8]

Not at all, he replied.

And so, by the dog of Egypt,‡ we have been unconsciously purging the State, which not long ago we termed luxurious.

And we have done wisely, he replied.

Then let us now finish the purgation, I said. Next in order to harmonies, rhythms will naturally follow, and they should be subject to the same rules, for we ought not to seek out complex systems of metre, or metres of every kind,[9] but rather to discover what rhythms are the expressions of a courageous and harmonious life; and when we have found them, we shall adapt the foot and the melody to words having a like spirit, not the words to the foot and melody. To say what these rhythms are will be your duty—you must teach me them, as you have already taught me the harmonies.

But, indeed, he replied, I cannot tell you. I only know that there are some three principles of rhythm out of which metrical systems are framed,[10] just as in sounds there are four notes out of which all the harmonies are composed;[11] that is an observation which I have made. But of what sort of lives they are severally the imitations I am unable to say.

°Although the word *aulos* is commonly translated as "flute," the *aulos* is not, properly speaking, flute-like. "Pipe" is a more accurate rendering of *aulos*; it is a different instrument from the rustic Pan's pipe (*syrinx*) that Socrates deems appropriate for shepherds.

†The Greek actually reads "the lyre and cithara"; the cithara was the specific type of lyre used by professional musicians (citharists, who played the instrument but did not sing, and citharodes, who played and sang).

‡Anubis; compare 9.592a and *Gorgias* 428b. Plato at times represents Socrates swearing unusual oaths—for example, "by the goose."

Then, I said, we must take Damon* into our counsels; and
he will tell us what rhythms are expressive of meanness, or insolence, or fury, or other unworthiness, and what are to be reserved
for the expression of opposite feelings. And I think that I have
an indistinct recollection of his mentioning a complex Cretic
rhythm; also a dactylic or heroic, and he arranged them in some
manner which I do not quite understand, making the rhythms
equal in the rise and fall of the foot, long and short alternating;
and, unless I am mistaken, he spoke of an iambic as well as of a
trochaic rhythm, and assigned to them short and long quantities.

c   Also in some cases he appeared to praise or censure the movement of the foot quite as much as the rhythm; or perhaps a combination of the two; for I am not certain what he meant. These
matters, however, as I was saying, had better be referred to Damon himself, for the analysis of the subject would be difficult,
you know?

Rather so, I should say.

But there is no difficulty in seeing that grace or the absence of
grace is an effect of good or bad rhythm.

None at all.

d   And also that good and bad rhythm naturally assimilate to a
good and bad style; and that harmony and discord in like manner
follow style; for our principle is that rhythm and harmony are regulated by the words, and not the words by them.[12]

Just so, he said, they should follow the words.

And will not the words and the character of the style depend
on the temper of the soul?

Yes.

And everything else on the style?

Yes.

Then beauty of style and harmony and grace and good rhythm
e   depend on simplicity[13]—I mean the true simplicity of a rightly
and nobly ordered mind and character, not that other simplicity
which is only an euphemism for folly?

Very true, he replied.

---

*Influential theorist on music from Athens (fifth century B.C.E.).

And if our youth are to do their work in life, must they not make these graces and harmonies their perpetual aim?

They must.

And surely the art of the painter and every other creative and constructive art are full of them—weaving, embroidery, architecture, and every kind of manufacture; also nature, animal and vegetable—in all of them there is grace or the absence of grace. And ugliness and discord and inharmonious motion are nearly allied to ill-words and ill-nature, as grace and harmony are the twin sisters of goodness and virtue and bear their likeness.

That is quite true, he said.

But shall our superintendence go no further, and are the poets only to be required by us to express the image of the good in their works, on pain, if they do anything else, of expulsion from our State? Or is the same control to be extended to other artists, and are they also to be prohibited from exhibiting the opposite forms of vice and intemperance and meanness and indecency in sculpture and building and the other creative arts; and is he who cannot conform to this rule of ours to be prevented from practising his art in our State, lest the taste of our citizens be corrupted by him? We would not have our guardians grow up amid images of moral deformity, as in some noxious pasture, and there browse and feed upon many a baneful herb and flower day by day, little by little, until they silently gather a festering mass of corruption in their own soul. Let our artists rather be those who are gifted to discern the true nature of the beautiful and graceful; then will our youth dwell in a land of health,[14] amid fair sights and sounds, and receive the good in everything; and beauty, the effluence of fair works, shall flow into the eye and ear, like a health-giving breeze from a purer region, and insensibly draw the soul from earliest years into likeness and sympathy with the beauty of reason.

There can be no nobler training than that, he replied.

And therefore, I said, Glaucon, musical training is a more potent instrument than any other, because rhythm and harmony find their way into the inward places of the soul, on which they mightily fasten, imparting grace, and making the soul of him who is rightly educated graceful, or of him who is ill-educated ungraceful; and also because he who has received this true education of

401

b

c

d

e

the inner being will most shrewdly perceive omissions or faults in art and nature, and with a true taste, while he praises and rejoices over and receives into his soul the good, and becomes noble and
402   good, he will justly blame and hate the bad, now in the days of his youth, even before he is able to know the reason why; and when reason comes he will recognize and salute the friend with whom his education has made him long familiar.

Yes, he said, I quite agree with you in thinking that our youth should be trained in music and on the grounds which you mention.

Just as in learning to read, I said, we were satisfied when we knew the letters of the alphabet, which are very few, in all their recurring sizes and combinations; not slighting them as unimportant whether they occupy a space large or small, but everywhere
b   eager to make them out; and not thinking ourselves perfect in the art of reading until we recognize them wherever they are found:

True—

Or, as we recognize the reflection of letters in the water, or in a mirror, only when we know the letters themselves; the same art and study giving us the knowledge of both:

Exactly—

Even so, as I maintain, neither we nor our guardians, whom
c   we have to educate, can ever become musical until we and they know the essential forms of temperance, courage, liberality, magnificence, and their kindred, as well as the contrary forms, in all their combinations, and can recognize them and their images wherever they are found, not slighting them either in small things or great, but believing them all to be within the sphere of one art and study.[15]

Most assuredly.

d   And when a beautiful soul harmonizes with a beautiful form, and the two are cast in one mould, that will be the fairest of sights to him who has an eye to see it?

The fairest indeed.

And the fairest is also the loveliest?

That may be assumed.

And the man who has the spirit of harmony will be most in love with the loveliest; but he will not love him who is of an inharmo-
e   nious soul?

That is true, he replied, if the deficiency be in his soul; but if there be any merely bodily defect in another he will be patient of it, and will love all the same.

I perceive, I said, that you have or have had experiences of this sort, and I agree. But let me ask you another question: Has excess of pleasure any affinity to temperance?[16]

How can that be? he replied; pleasure deprives a man of the use of his faculties quite as much as pain.

Or any affinity to virtue in general?

None whatever.　　　　　　　　　　　　　　　　　　　　　　403

Any affinity to wantonness and intemperance?

Yes, the greatest.

And is there any greater or keener pleasure than that of sensual love?

No, nor a madder.

Whereas true love is a love of beauty and order—temperate and harmonious?

Quite true, he said.

Then no intemperance or madness should be allowed to approach true love?

Certainly not.

Then mad or intemperate pleasure must never be allowed to come near the lover and his beloved; neither of them can have any part in it if their love is of the right sort?　　　　　　b

No, indeed, Socrates, it must never come near them.

Then I suppose that in the city which we are founding you would make a law to the effect that a friend should use no other familiarity to his love than a father would use to his son, and then only for a noble purpose, and he must first have the other's consent; and this rule is to limit him in all his intercourse, and he is never to be seen going further, or, if he exceeds, he is to be deemed guilty　　c of coarseness and bad taste.

I quite agree, he said.

Thus much of music, which makes a fair ending; for what should be the end of music if not the love of beauty?

I agree, he said.

After music comes gymnastics, in which our youth are next to be trained.

Certainly.

Gymnastics as well as music should begin in early years; the training in it should be careful and should continue through life.

d   Now my belief is—and this is a matter upon which I should like to have your opinion in confirmation of my own, but my own belief is—not that the good body by any bodily excellence improves the soul, but, on the contrary, that the good soul, by her own excellence, improves the body as far as this may be possible. What do you say?

Yes, I agree.

Then, to the mind when adequately trained, we shall be right in handing over the more particular care of the body; and in order
e   to avoid prolixity we will now only give the general outlines of the subject.

Very good.

That they must abstain from intoxication has been already re-marked by us; for of all persons a guardian should be the last to get drunk and not know where in the world he is.

Yes, he said; that a guardian should require another guardian to take care of him is ridiculous indeed.

But next, what shall we say of their food; for the men are in training for the great contest of all—are they not?

Yes, he said.

404   And will the habit of body of our ordinary athletes be suited to them?

Why not?

I am afraid, I said, that a habit of body such as they have is but a sleepy sort of thing, and rather perilous to health. Do you not observe that these athletes sleep away their lives, and are liable to most dangerous illnesses if they depart, in ever so slight a degree, from their customary regimen?

Yes, I do.

Then, I said, a finer sort of training will be required for our warrior athletes, who are to be like wakeful dogs, and to see and hear with the utmost keenness; amid the many changes of water and also of food, of summer heat and winter cold, which they will
b   have to endure when on a campaign, they must not be liable to break down in health.

That is my view.

The really excellent gymnastics is twin sister of that simple music which we were just now describing.

How so?

Why, I conceive that there is a gymnastics which, like our music, is simple and good; and especially the military gymnastics.

What do you mean?

My meaning may be learned from Homer;[17] he, you know, feeds his heroes at their feasts, when they are campaigning, on soldiers' fare; they have no fish, although they are on the shores of the   c
Hellespont, and they are not allowed boiled meats, but only roast, which is the food most convenient for soldiers, requiring only that they should light a fire, and not involving the trouble of carrying about pots and pans.

True.

And I can hardly be mistaken in saying that sweet sauces are nowhere mentioned in Homer. In proscribing them, however, he is not singular; all professional athletes are well aware that a man who is to be in good condition should take nothing of the kind.

Yes, he said; and knowing this, they are quite right in not taking them.

Then you would not approve of Syracusan dinners, and the re-   d
finements of Sicilian cookery?

I think not.

Nor, if a man is to be in condition, would you allow him to have a Corinthian girl* as his fair friend?

Certainly not.

Neither would you approve of the delicacies, as they are thought, of Athenian confectionery?†

Certainly not.

All such feeding and living may be rightly compared by us to melody and song composed in the panharmonic style, and in all   e
the rhythms.

Exactly.

---

*That is, a prostitute.

†Cakes (*pemmata*); compare 2.373a for the juxtaposition of "courtesans" and cakes.

There complexity engendered license, and here disease; whereas simplicity in music was the parent of temperance in the soul; and simplicity in gymnastics of health in the body.

Most true, he said.

405   But when intemperance and diseases multiply in a State, halls of justice and medicine are always being opened; and the arts of the doctor and the lawyer give themselves airs, finding how keen is the interest which not only the slaves but the freemen of a city take about them.

Of course.

And yet what greater proof can there be of a bad and disgraceful state of education than this, that not only artisans and the meaner sort of people need the skill of first-rate physicians and judges, but also those who would profess to have had a liberal education? Is it not disgraceful, and a great sign of the want of good-breeding, that a man should have to go abroad for his law and physic because he has none of his own at home, and must therefore surrender himself into the hands of other men whom he makes lords and judges over him?

b

Of all things, he said, the most disgraceful.

Would you say "most," I replied, when you consider that there is a further stage of the evil in which a man is not only a life-long litigant, passing all his days in the courts, either as plaintiff or defendant, but is actually led by his bad taste to pride himself on his litigiousness;[18] he imagines that he is a master in dishonesty; able to take every crooked turn, and wriggle into and out of every hole, bending like a withy and getting out of the way of justice: and all for what?—in order to gain small points not worth mentioning, he not knowing that so to order his life as to be able to do without a napping judge is a far higher and nobler sort of thing. Is not that still more disgraceful?

c

Yes, he said, that is still more disgraceful.

Well, I said, and to require the help of medicine, not when a wound has to be cured, or on occasion of an epidemic, but just because, by indolence and a habit of life such as we have been describing, men fill themselves with waters and winds, as if their bodies were a marsh, compelling the ingenious sons of

d

Asclepius* to find more names for diseases, such as flatulence and catarrh; is not this, too, a disgrace?

Yes, he said, they do certainly give very strange and newfangled names to diseases.

Yes, I said, and I do not believe that there were any such diseases in the days of Asclepius; and this I infer from the circumstance that the hero Eurypylus,† after he has been wounded in Homer, drinks a cup of Pramnian wine well besprinkled with barley-meal and grated cheese, which are certainly inflammatory, and yet the sons of Asclepius who were at the Trojan war do not blame the damsel who gives him the drink, or rebuke Patroclus, who is treating his case.

e

406

Well, he said, that was surely an extraordinary drink to be given to a person in his condition.

Not so extraordinary, I replied, if you bear in mind that in former days, as is commonly said, before the time of Herodicus,‡ the guild of Asclepius did not practise our present system of medicine, which may be said to educate diseases. But Herodicus, being a trainer, and himself of a sickly constitution, by a combination of training and doctoring found out a way of torturing first and chiefly himself, and secondly the rest of the world.

b

How was that? he said.

By the invention of lingering death; for he had a mortal disease which he perpetually tended, and as recovery was out of the question, he passed his entire life as an invalid; he could do nothing but attend upon himself, and he was in constant torment whenever he departed in anything from his usual regimen, and so dying hard, by the help of science he struggled on to old age.

---

*The Asclepiadae were a group of physicians with schools in Cyrene, Rhodes, and elsewhere. Asclepius was a legendary healer and son of Apollo.

†Greek chieftain at Troy. Socrates plainly refers to *Iliad* 11.833, but it was Machaon, not Eurypylus, who was given the wine-barley-cheese drink in *Iliad* 11.614. The sons of Asclepius at the Trojan War are Machaon and Podalirius, the two doctors in the Greek army.

‡Physician (from Megara, fifth century B.C.E.) who was an expert in physical training and diet. He is not to be confused the brother of the Sicilian rhetorician Gorgias, also named Herodicus, who is mentioned in *Gorgias* 448b and was also a physician.

A rare reward of his skill!

c   Yes, I said; a reward which a man might fairly expect who never understood that, if Asclepius did not instruct his descendants in valetudinarian arts, the omission arose, not from ignorance or inexperience of such a branch of medicine, but because he knew that in all well-ordered States every individual has an occupation to which he must attend, and has therefore no leisure to spend in continually being ill. This we remark in the case of the artisan, but, ludicrously enough, do not apply the same rule to people of the richer sort.

How do you mean? he said.

d   I mean this: When a carpenter is ill he asks the physician for a rough and ready cure; an emetic or a purge or a cautery or the knife—these are his remedies. And if someone prescribes for him a course of dietetics, and tells him that he must swathe and swaddle his head, and all that sort of thing, he replies at once that he has no time to be ill, and that he sees no good in a life which is spent in nursing his disease to the neglect of his customary employment; and therefore bidding good-by to this sort of physician, he resumes
e   his ordinary habits, and either gets well and lives and does his business, or, if his constitution fails, he dies and has no more trouble.

Yes, he said, and a man in his condition of life ought to use the art of medicine thus far only.

407   Has he not, I said, an occupation; and what profit would there be in his life if he were deprived of his occupation?

Quite true, he said.

But with the rich man this is otherwise; of him we do not say that he has any specially appointed work which he must perform, if he would live.

He is generally supposed to have nothing to do.

Then you never heard of the saying of Phocylides,* that as soon as a man has a livelihood he should practise virtue?

Nay, he said, I think that he had better begin somewhat sooner.

Let us not have a dispute with him about this, I said; but rather ask ourselves: Is the practise of virtue obligatory on the rich man, or can he live without it? And if obligatory on him, then let us

---

*Poet from Miletus (sixth century B.C.E.). Plato distorts the emphases of Phocylides' verse.

raise a further question, whether this dieting of disorders, which is an impediment to the application of the mind in carpentering   b and the mechanical arts, does not equally stand in the way of the sentiment of Phocylides?

Of that, he replied, there can be no doubt; such excessive care of the body, when carried beyond the rules of gymnastics, is most inimical to the practice of virtue.

Yes, indeed, I replied, and equally incompatible with the management of a house, an army, or an office of state; and, what is most important of all, irreconcilable with any kind of study or thought or self-reflection—there is a constant suspicion that headache and   c giddiness are to be ascribed to philosophy, and hence all practising or making trial of virtue in the higher sense is absolutely stopped; for a man is always fancying that he is being made ill, and is in constant anxiety about the state of his body.

Yes, likely enough.

And therefore Asclepius may be supposed to have exhibited the power of his art only to persons who, being generally of healthy constitution and habits of life, had a definite ailment; such as these he cured by purges and operations, and bade them live as usual,   d herein consulting the interests of the State; but bodies which disease had penetrated through and through he would not have attempted to cure by gradual processes of evacuation and infusion: he did not want to lengthen out good-for-nothing lives, or to have weak fathers begetting weaker sons;—if a man was not able to live in the ordinary way he had no business to cure him; for such a   e cure would have been of no use either to himself, or to the State.

Then, he said, you regard Asclepius as a statesman.[19]

Clearly; and his character is further illustrated by his sons. Note that they were heroes in the days of old and practised the medi-   408 cines of which I am speaking at the siege of Troy: You will remember how, when Pandarus wounded Menelaus, they

"Sucked the blood out of the wound, and sprinkled soothing remedies,"°

°Adaptation of *Iliad* 4.218.

but they never prescribed what the patient was afterward to eat or drink in the case of Menelaus, any more than in the case of Eurypylus; the remedies, as they conceived, were enough to heal any

b   man who before he was wounded was healthy and regular in his habits; and even though he did happen to drink a cup of Pramnian wine, he might get well all the same. But they would have nothing to do with unhealthy and intemperate subjects, whose lives were of no use either to themselves or others; the art of medicine was not designed for their good, and though they were as rich as Midas,* the sons of Asclepius would have declined to attend them.

They were very acute persons, those sons of Asclepius.

Naturally so, I replied. Nevertheless, the tragedians and Pindar disobeying our behests,† although they acknowledge that Asclepius was the son of Apollo, say also that he was bribed into healing a rich man who was at the point of death, and for this reason he

c   was struck by lightning. But we, in accordance with the principle already affirmed by us, will not believe them when they tell us both; if he was the son of a god, we maintain that he was not avaricious; or, if he was avaricious, he was not the son of a god.

All that, Socrates, is excellent; but I should like to put a question to you: Ought there not to be good physicians in a State, and are

d   not the best those who have treated the greatest number of constitutions, good and bad? and are not the best judges in like manner those who are acquainted with all sorts of moral natures?[20]

Yes, I said, I too would have good judges and good physicians. But do you know whom I think good?

Will you tell me?

I will, if I can. Let me, however, note that in the same question you join two things which are not the same.

How so? he asked.

Why, I said, you join physicians and judges. Now the most

---

*King of Phrygia in northwestern Asia Minor (late eighth to early seventh century B.C.E.) who was proverbially wealthy. Plato perhaps alludes here to a line in a poem by Tyrtaeus (Spartan but possibly of Athenian birth, early seventh century B.C.E.). The story of Midas' "golden touch" can be found in the Roman poet Ovid's *Metamorphoses* 11.

†That is, by representing heroic figures such as Asclepius taking bribes; compare 3.390e–391a.

skilful physicians are those who, from their youth upward, have combined with the knowledge of their art the greatest experience of disease; they had better not be robust in health, and should have had all manner of diseases in their own persons. For the   e body, as I conceive, is not the instrument with which they cure the body; in that case we could not allow them ever to be or to have been sickly; but they cure the body with the mind, and the mind which has become and is sick can cure nothing.

That is very true, he said.

But with the judge it is otherwise; since he governs mind by   409 mind; he ought not therefore to have been trained among vicious minds, and to have associated with them from youth upward, and to have gone through the whole calendar of crime, only in order that he may quickly infer the crimes of others as he might their bodily diseases from his own self-consciousness; the honorable mind which is to form a healthy judgment should have had no experience or contamination of evil habits when young. And this is the reason why in youth good men often appear to be simple, and are easily practised upon by the dishonest, because they have no examples of what evil is in their own souls.   b

Yes, he said, they are far too apt to be deceived.

Therefore, I said, the judge should not be young; he should have learned to know evil, not from his own soul, but from late and long observation of the nature of evil in others; knowledge should be his guide, not personal experience.   c

Yes, he said, that is the ideal of a judge.

Yes, I replied, and he will be a good man (which is my answer to your question); for he is good who has a good soul. But the cunning and suspicious nature of which we spoke—he who has committed many crimes, and fancies himself to be a master in wickedness—when he is among his fellows, is wonderful in the precautions which he takes, because he judges of them by himself: but when he gets into the company of men of virtue, who have the experience of age, he appears to be a fool again, owing to his unseasonable suspicions; he cannot recognize an honest man, because he has no   d pattern of honesty in himself; at the same time, as the bad are more numerous than the good, and he meets with them oftener, he thinks himself, and is by others thought to be, rather wise than foolish.

Most true, he said.

Then the good and wise judge whom we are seeking is not this man, but the other; for vice cannot know virtue too, but a virtuous nature, educated by time, will acquire a knowledge both of virtue and vice: the virtuous, and not the vicious, man has wisdom—in my opinion.

And in mine also.

This is the sort of medicine, and this is the sort of law, which you will sanction in your State. They will minister to better natures, giving health both of soul and of body; but those who are diseased in their bodies they will leave to die, and the corrupt and incurable souls they will put an end to themselves.

That is clearly the best thing both for the patients and for the State.

And thus our youth, having been educated only in that simple music which, as we said, inspires temperance, will be reluctant to go to law.

Clearly.

And the musician, who, keeping to the same track, is content to practise the simple gymnastics, will have nothing to do with medicine unless in some extreme case.

That I quite believe.

The very exercises and toils which he undergoes are intended to stimulate the spirited element of his nature, and not to increase his strength; he will not, like common athletes, use exercise and regimen to develop his muscles.

Very right, he said.

Neither are the two arts of music and gymnastics really designed, as is often supposed, the one for the training of the soul, the other for the training of the body.

What then is the real object of them?

I believe, I said, that the teachers of both have in view chiefly the improvement of the soul.

How can that be? he asked.

Did you never observe, I said, the effect on the mind itself of exclusive devotion to gymnastics, or the opposite effect of an exclusive devotion to music?

In what way shown? he said.

The one producing a temper of hardness and ferocity, the other   d
of softness and effeminacy, I replied.

Yes, he said, I am quite aware that the mere athlete becomes
too much of a savage, and that the mere musician is melted and
softened beyond what is good for him.

Yet surely, I said, this ferocity only comes from spirit, which, if
rightly educated, would give courage, but, if too much intensified,
is liable to become hard and brutal.

That I quite think.

On the other hand the philosopher will have the quality of gen-   e
tleness. And this also, when too much indulged, will turn to softness, but, if educated rightly, will be gentle and moderate.

True.

And in our opinion the guardians ought to have both these
qualities?[21]

Assuredly.

And both should be in harmony?

Beyond question.

And the harmonious soul is both temperate and courageous?   411

Yes.

And the inharmonious is cowardly and boorish?

Very true.

And, when a man allows music to play upon him and to pour
into his soul through the funnel of his ears those sweet and soft
and melancholy airs of which we were just now speaking, and his
whole life is passed in warbling and the delights of song; in the first
stage of the process the passion or spirit which is in him is tempered like iron, and made useful, instead of brittle and useless. But,
if he carries on the softening and soothing process, in the next stage   b
he begins to melt and waste, until he has wasted away his spirit and
cut out the sinews of his soul, and he becomes a feeble warrior.

Very true.

If the element of spirit is naturally weak in him the change is
speedily accomplished, but if he have a good deal, then the power
of music weakening the spirit renders him excitable; on the least
provocation he flames up at once, and is speedily extinguished;
instead of having spirit he grows irritable and passionate and is   c
quite impractical.

Exactly.

And so in gymnastics, if a man takes violent exercise and is a great feeder, and the reverse of a great student of music and philosophy, at first the high condition of his body fills him with pride and spirit, and he becomes twice the man that he was.

Certainly.

And what happens? if he do nothing else, and holds no converse with the muses, does not even that intelligence which there

d may be in him, having no taste of any sort of learning or inquiry or thought or culture, grow feeble and dull and blind, his mind never waking up or receiving nourishment, and his senses not being purged of their mists?

True, he said.

And he ends by becoming a hater of philosophy, uncivilized, never using the weapon of persuasion—he is like a wild beast, all violence and fierceness, and knows no other way of dealing; and

e he lives in all ignorance and evil conditions, and has no sense of propriety and grace.

That is quite true, he said.

And as there are two principles of human nature, one the spirited and the other the philosophical, some god, as I should say, has given mankind two arts answering to them (and only indirectly to the soul and body), in order that these two principles (like the

412 strings of an instrument) may be relaxed or drawn tighter until they are duly harmonized.

That appears to be the intention.

And he who mingles music with gymnastics in the fairest proportions, and best attempers them to the soul, may be rightly called the true musician and harmonist in a far higher sense than the tuner of the strings.

You are quite right, Socrates.

And such a presiding genius will be always required in our State if the government is to last.

b Yes, he will be absolutely necessary.

Such, then, are our principles of nurture and education: Where would be the use of going into further details about the dances of our citizens, or about their hunting and coursing, their gymnastic and equestrian contests? For these all follow the general principle, and having found that, we shall have no difficulty in discovering them.

I dare say that there will be no difficulty.

Very good, I said; then what is the next question?[22] Must we not ask who are to be rulers and who subjects?

Certainly.

There can be no doubt that the elder must rule the younger.

Clearly.

And that the best of these must rule.

That is also clear.

Now, are not the best husbandmen those who are most devoted to husbandry?

Yes.

And as we are to have the best of guardians for our city, must they not be those who have most the character of guardians?

Yes.

And to this end they ought to be wise and efficient, and to have a special care of the State?

True.

And a man will be most likely to care about that which he loves?

To be sure.

And he will be most likely to love that which he regards as having the same interests with himself, and that of which the good or evil fortune is supposed by him at any time most to affect his own?

Very true, he replied.

Then there must be a selection. Let us note among the guardians those who in their whole life show the greatest eagerness to do what is for the good of their country, and the greatest repugnance to do what is against her interests.

Those are the right men.

And they will have to be watched at every age, in order that we may see whether they preserve their resolution, and never, under the influence either of force or enchantment, forget or cast off their sense of duty to the State.

How cast off? he said.

I will explain to you, he replied. A resolution may go out of a man's mind either with his will or against his will; with his will when

he gets rid of a falsehood and learns better, against his will when-
413 ever he is deprived of a truth.

I understand, he said, the willing loss of a resolution; the meaning of the unwilling I have yet to learn.

Why, I said, do you not see that men are unwillingly deprived
of good, and willingly of evil? Is not to have lost the truth an evil,
and to possess the truth a good? and you would agree that to conceive things as they are is to possess the truth?

Yes, he replied; I agree with you in thinking that mankind are
deprived of truth against their will.

b   And is not this involuntary deprivation caused either by theft,
or force, or enchantment?

Still, he replied, I do not understand you.

I fear that I must have been talking darkly, like the tragedians.
I only mean that some men are changed by persuasion and that
others forget; argument steals away the hearts of one class, and
time of the other; and this I call theft. Now you understand me?

Yes.

Those again who are forced, are those whom the violence of
some pain or grief compels to change their opinion.

I understand, he said, and you are quite right.

c   And you would also acknowledge that the enchanted are those
who change their minds either under the softer influence of pleasure, or the sterner influence of fear?

Yes, he said; everything that deceives may be said to enchant.

Therefore, as I was just now saying, we must inquire who are
the best guardians of their own conviction that what they think
the interest of the State is to be the rule of their lives.[23] We must
watch them from their youth upward, and make them perform actions in which they are most likely to forget or to be deceived, and
he who remembers and is not deceived is to be selected, and he
d   who fails in the trial is to be rejected. That will be the way?

Yes.

And there should also be toils and pains and conflicts prescribed for them, in which they will be made to give further proof
of the same qualities.

Very right, he replied.

And then, I said, we must try them with enchantments—that is the third sort of test—and see what will be their behavior: like those who take colts amid noise and tumult to see if they are of a timid nature, so must we take our youth amid terrors of some kind, and again pass them into pleasures, and prove them more thoroughly than gold is proved in the furnace, that we may discover whether they are armed against all enchantments, and of a noble bearing always, good guardians of themselves and of the music which they have learned,[24] and retaining under all circumstances a rhythmical and harmonious nature, such as will be most serviceable to the individual and to the State. And he who at every age, as boy and youth and in mature life, has come out of the trial victorious and pure, shall be appointed a ruler and guardian of the State; he shall be honored in life and death, and shall receive sepulture and other memorials of honor, the greatest that we have to give. But him who fails, we must reject. I am inclined to think that this is the sort of way in which our rulers and guardians should be chosen and appointed. I speak generally, and not with any pretension to exactness.

And, speaking generally, I agree with you, he said.

And perhaps the word "guardian" in the fullest sense ought to be applied to this higher class only who preserve us against foreign enemies and maintain peace among our citizens at home, that the one may not have the will, or the others the power, to harm us. The young men whom we before called guardians may be more properly designated auxiliaries and supporters of the principles of the rulers.

I agree with you, he said.

How then may we devise one of those needful falsehoods of which we lately spoke—just one royal lie which may deceive the rulers, if that be possible, and at any rate the rest of the city?

What sort of lie? he said.

Nothing new, I replied; only an old Phœnician tale[25] of what has often occurred before now in other places (as the poets say, and have made the world believe), though not in our time, and I do not know whether such an event could ever happen again, or could now even be made probable, if it did.

How your words seem to hesitate on your lips!

You will not wonder, I replied, at my hesitation when you have heard.

Speak, he said, and fear not.

d   Well, then, I will speak, although I really know not how to look you in the face, or in what words to utter the audacious fiction, which I propose to communicate gradually, first to the rulers, then to the soldiers, and lastly to the people. They are to be told that their youth was a dream, and the education and training which they received from us, an appearance only; in reality during all that time they were being formed and fed in the womb of the earth,* where they themselves and their arms and ap-

e   purtenances were manufactured; when they were completed, the earth, their mother, sent them up; and so, their country being their mother and also their nurse, they are bound to advise for her good, and to defend her against attacks, and her citizens they are to regard as children of the earth and their own brothers.

You had good reason, he said, to be ashamed of the lie which you were going to tell.

415   True, I replied, but there is more coming; I have only told you half. Citizens, we shall say to them in our tale, you are brothers, yet God has framed you differently.† Some of you have the power of command, and in the composition of these he has mingled gold,[26] wherefore also they have the greatest honor; others he has made of silver, to be auxiliaries; others again who are to be husbandmen and craftsmen he has composed of brass and iron; and the species will generally be preserved in the children. But as all are of the

b   same original stock, a golden parent will sometimes have a silver son, or a silver parent a golden son. And God proclaims as a first principle to the rulers, and above all else, that there is nothing which they should so anxiously guard, or of which they are to be such good guardians, as of the purity of the race. They should observe what elements mingle in their offspring; for if the son of a golden or silver parent has an admixture of brass and iron, then

c   nature orders a transposition of ranks, and the eye of the ruler

---

*The conception of the earth (Gaia) as a mother-figure is well established in ancient Greek mythology.

†For the concept that different people have different "natures," see note 9 on 2.367e and note 12 on 2.370b.

must not be pitiful toward the child because he has to descend in the scale and become a husbandman or artisan, just as there may be sons of artisans who having an admixture of gold or silver in them are raised to honor, and become guardians or auxiliaries. For an oracle says that when a man of brass or iron guards the State, it will be destroyed. Such is the tale; is there any possibility of making our citizens believe in it?

Not in the present generation,[27] he replied; there is no way of accomplishing this; but their sons may be made to believe in the tale, and their sons' sons, and posterity after them.

I see the difficulty, I replied; yet the fostering of such a belief will make them care more for the city and for one another. Enough, however, of the fiction, which may now fly abroad upon the wings of rumor, while we arm our earth-born heroes, and lead them forth under the command of their rulers. Let them look round and select a spot whence they can best suppress insurrection, if any prove refractory within, and also defend themselves against enemies, who, like wolves, may come down on the fold from without; there let them encamp, and when they have encamped, let them sacrifice to the proper gods and prepare their dwellings.

Just so, he said.

And their dwellings must be such as will shield them against the cold of winter and the heat of summer.

I suppose that you mean houses, he replied.

Yes, I said; but they must be the houses of soldiers, and not of shopkeepers.

What is the difference? he said.

That I will endeavor to explain, I replied. To keep watchdogs, who, from want of discipline or hunger, or some evil habit or other, would turn upon the sheep and worry them, and behave not like dogs, but wolves, would be a foul and monstrous thing in a shepherd?

Truly monstrous, he said.

And therefore every care must be taken that our auxiliaries, being stronger than our citizens, may not grow to be too much for them and become savage tyrants instead of friends and allies?

Yes, great care should be taken.

And would not a really good education furnish the best safe-
guard?

But they are well-educated already, he replied.

I cannot be so confident, my dear Glaucon, I said; I am much
more certain that they ought to be, and that true education, whatever that may be, will have the greatest tendency to civilize and
c humanize them in their relations to one another, and to those who
are under their protection.

Very true, he replied.

And not only their education, but their habitations, and all that
belongs to them, should be such as will neither impair their virtue
as guardians, nor tempt them to prey upon the other citizens. Any
d man of sense must acknowledge that.

He must.

Then now let us consider what will be their way of life, if they
are to realize our idea of them. In the first place, none of them
should have any property of his own beyond what is absolutely
necessary; neither should they have a private house or store closed
against anyone who has a mind to enter; their provisions should be
only such as are required by trained warriors, who are men of
e temperance and courage; they should agree to receive from the citizens a fixed rate of pay, enough to meet the expenses of the year
and no more; and they will go to mess and live together like soldiers
in a camp. Gold and silver we will tell them that they have from
God; the diviner metal is within them, and they have therefore no
need of the dross which is current among men, and ought not to
pollute the divine by any such earthly admixture; for that com-
417 moner metal has been the source of many unholy deeds, but their
own is undefiled.[28] And they alone of all the citizens may not
touch or handle silver or gold, or be under the same roof with
them, or wear them, or drink from them. And this will be their
salvation, and they will be the saviours of the State. But should
they ever acquire homes or lands or moneys of their own, they
will become good housekeepers and husbandmen instead of
b guardians, enemies and tyrants instead of allies of the other citizens; hating and being hated, plotting and being plotted against,
they will pass their whole life in much greater terror of internal
than of external enemies, and the hour of ruin, both to themselves

and to the rest of the State, will be at hand. For all which reasons may we not say that thus shall our State be ordered, and that these shall be the regulations appointed by us for our guardians concerning their houses and all other matters?

Yes, said Glaucon.

BOOK 4

419 HERE ADEIMANTUS INTERPOSED A question: How would you answer, Socrates, said he, if a person were to say that you are making
these people miserable, and that they are the cause of their own
unhappiness; the city in fact belongs to them, but they are none
the better for it; whereas other men acquire lands, and build large
and handsome houses, and have everything handsome about them,
offering sacrifices to the gods on their own account, and practising
hospitality; moreover, as you were saying just now, they have gold
and silver, and all that is usual among the favorites of fortune; but
our poor citizens are no better than mercenaries who are quar-
420 tered in the city and are always mounting guard?

Yes, I said; and you may add that they are only fed, and not paid
in addition to their food, like other men; and therefore they cannot, if they would, take a journey of pleasure; they have no money
to spend on a mistress or any other luxurious fancy, which, as the
world goes, is thought to be happiness; and many other accusations
of the same nature might be added.

But, said he, let us suppose all this to be included in the charge.

b   You mean to ask, I said, what will be our answer?

Yes.

If we proceed along the old path, my belief, I said, is that we
shall find the answer. And our answer will be that, even as they are,
our guardians may very likely be the happiest of men; but that our
aim in founding the State was not the disproportionate happiness
of any one class, but the greatest happiness of the whole; we
thought that in a State which is ordered with a view to the good of
the whole we should be most likely to find justice, and in the ill-
c   ordered State injustice: and, having found them, we might then
decide which of the two is the happier. At present, I take it, we are
fashioning the happy State, not piecemeal, or with a view of making a few happy citizens, but as a whole; and by and by we will
proceed to view the opposite kind of State. Suppose that we were

painting a statue, and someone came up to us and said: Why do you not put the most beautiful colors on the most beautiful parts of the body—the eyes ought to be purple, but you have made them black—to him we might fairly answer: Sir, you would not surely have us beautify the eyes to such a degree that they are no longer eyes; consider rather whether, by giving this and the other features their due proportion, we make the whole beautiful. And so I say to you, do not compel us to assign to the guardians a sort of happiness which will make them anything but guardians; for we too can clothe our husbandmen in royal apparel, and set crowns of gold on their heads, and bid them till the ground as much as they like, and no more. Our potters also might be allowed to repose on couches, and feast by the fireside, passing round the wine-cup, while their wheel is conveniently at hand, and working at pottery only as much as they like; in this way we might make every class happy—and then, as you imagine, the whole State would be happy. But do not put this idea into our heads; for, if we listen to you, the husbandman will be no longer a husbandman, the potter will cease to be a potter, and no one will have the character of any distinct class in the State. Now this is not of much consequence where the corruption of society, and pretension to be what you are not, are confined to cobblers; but when the guardians of the laws and of the government are only seeming and not real guardians, then see how they turn the State upside down; and on the other hand they alone have the power of giving order and happiness to the State. We mean our guardians to be true saviours and not the destroyers of the State, whereas our opponent* is thinking of peasants at a festival, who are enjoying a life of revelry, not of citizens who are doing their duty to the State. But, if so, we mean different things, and he is speaking of something which is not a State. And therefore we must consider whether in appointing our guardians we would look to their greatest happiness individually, or whether this principle of happiness does not rather reside in the State as a whole. But if the latter be the truth, then the guardians and auxiliaries, and all others equally with them, must be compelled or

d

e

421

b

c

---

*That is, the hypothetical questioner posited at 4.419a.

induced to do their own work in the best way. And thus the whole
State will grow up in a noble order, and the several classes will receive the proportion of happiness which nature assigns to them.

I think that you are quite right.

I wonder whether you will agree with another remark which
occurs to me.

What may that be?

d   There seem to be two causes of the corruption of artisans.

What are they?

Wealth, I said, and poverty.

How do they act?

The process is as follows: When a potter becomes rich, will he,
think you, any longer take the same pains with his art?

Certainly not.

He will grow more and more indolent and careless?

Very true.

And the result will be that he becomes a worse potter?

Yes; he greatly deteriorates.

But, on the other hand, if he has no money, and cannot provide
himself with tools or instruments, he will not work equally well him-

e   self, nor will he teach his sons or apprentices to work equally well.

Certainly not.

Then, under the influence either of poverty or of wealth, workmen and their work are equally liable to degenerate?

That is evident.

Here, then, is a discovery of new evils, I said, against which the
guardians will have to watch, or they will creep into the city unob-
served.

What evils?

422   Wealth, I said, and poverty; the one is the parent of luxury and
indolence, and the other of meanness and viciousness, and both
of discontent.

That is very true, he replied; but still I should like to know,
Socrates, how our city will be able to go to war, especially against an
enemy who is rich and powerful, if deprived of the sinews of war.

There would certainly be a difficulty, I replied, in going to war
with one such enemy; but there is no difficulty where there are two

b   of them.

How so? he asked.

In the first place, I said, if we have to fight, our side will be trained warriors fighting against an army of rich men.

That is true, he said.

And do you not suppose, Adeimantus, that a single boxer who was perfect in his art would easily be a match for two stout and well-to-do gentlemen who were not boxers?

Hardly, if they came upon him at once.

What, not, I said, if he were able to run away and then turn and strike at the one who first came up? And supposing he were to do   c this several times under the heat of a scorching sun, might he not, being an expert, overturn more than one stout personage?

Certainly, he said, there would be nothing wonderful in that.

And yet rich men probably have a greater superiority in the science and practise of boxing than they have in military qualities.

Likely enough.

Then we may assume that our athletes will be able to fight with two or three times their own number?

I agree with you, for I think you right.

And suppose that, before engaging, our citizens send an em-   d bassy to one of the two cities, telling them what is the truth: Silver and gold we neither have nor are permitted to have, but you may; do you therefore come and help us in war, and take the spoils of the other city: Who, on hearing these words, would choose to fight against lean wiry dogs, rather than, with the dogs on their side, against fat and tender sheep?

That is not likely; and yet there might be a danger to the poor State if the wealth of many States were to be gathered into one.   e

But how simple of you to use the term State at all of any but our own!

Why so?

You ought to speak of other States in the plural number; not one of them is a city, but many cities, as they say in the game.* For indeed any city, however small, is in fact divided into two, one the city of the poor, the other of the rich; these are at war with one   423

---

*An obscure reference. On the divided nature of all other cities, see 8.551d.

another; and in either there are many smaller divisions, and you would be altogether beside the mark if you treated them all as a single State. But if you deal with them as many, and give the wealth or power or persons of the one to the others, you will always have a great many friends and not many enemies. And your State, while the wise order which has now been prescribed continues to prevail in her, will be the greatest of States, I do not mean to say in reputation or appearance, but in deed and truth, though she number not more than 1,000 defenders. A single State which is her equal you will hardly find, either among Hellenes or barbarians,[1] though many that appear to be as great and many times greater.

That is most true, he said.

And what, I said, will be the best limit for our rulers to fix when they are considering the size of the State and the amount of territory which they are to include, and beyond which they will not go?

What limit would you propose?

I would allow the State to increase so far as is consistent with unity; that, I think, is the proper limit.

Very good, he said.

Here then, I said, is another order which will have to be conveyed to our guardians: Let our city be accounted neither large nor small, but one and self-sufficing.

And surely, said he, this is not a very severe order which we impose upon them.

And the other, said I, of which we were speaking before is lighter still—I mean the duty of degrading the offspring of the guardians when inferior, and of elevating into the rank of guardians the offspring of the lower classes, when naturally superior. The intention was, that, in the case of the citizens generally, each individual should be put to the use for which nature intended him, one to one work, and then every man would do his own business, and be one and not many; and so the whole city would be one and not many.

Yes, he said; that is not so difficult.

The regulations which we are prescribing, my good Adeimantus, are not, as might be supposed, a number of great principles, but trifles all, if care be taken, as the saying is, of the one great thing—a thing, however, which I would rather call, not great, but sufficient for our purpose.

What may that be? he asked.

Education, I said, and nurture: If our citizens are well educated, and grow into sensible men, they will easily see their way through all these, as well as other matters which I omit; such, for example, as marriage, the possession of women and the procreation of children, which will all follow the general principle that friends have all things in common,[2] as the proverb says.

424

That will be the best way of settling them.

Also, I said, the State, if once started well, moves with accumulating force like a wheel. For good nurture and education implant good constitutions, and these good constitutions taking root in a good education improve more and more, and this improvement affects the breed in man as in other animals.

b

Very possibly, he said.

Then to sum up: This is the point to which, above all, the attention of our rulers should be directed—that music and gymnastics be preserved in their original form, and no innovation made. They must do their utmost to maintain them intact. And when anyone says that mankind most regard

"The newest song which the singers have,"*

they will be afraid that he may be praising, not new songs, but a new kind of song; and this ought not to be praised, or conceived to be the meaning of the poet; for any musical innovation is full of danger to the whole State, and ought to be prohibited. So Damon tells me, and I can quite believe him; he says that when modes of music change, the fundamental laws of the State always change with them.[3]

c

Yes, said Adeimantus; and you may add my vote to Damon's and your own.

Then, I said, our guardians must lay the foundations of their fortress in music?

d

Yes, he said; the lawlessness of which you speak too easily steals in.

---

*Compare *Odyssey* 1.351–352.

Yes, I replied, in the form of amusement; and at first sight it appears harmless.[4]

Why, yes, he said, and there is no harm; were it not that little by little this spirit of license, finding a home, imperceptibly penetrates into manners and customs; whence, issuing with greater force, it invades contracts between man and man, and from contracts goes on to laws and constitutions, in utter recklessness, ending at last, Socrates, by an overthrow of all rights, private as well as public.

Is that true? I said.

That is my belief, he replied.

Then, as I was saying, our youth should be trained from the first in a stricter system, for if amusements become lawless, and the youths themselves become lawless, they can never grow up into well-conducted and virtuous citizens.

Very true, he said.

And when they have made a good beginning in play, and by the help of music have gained the habit of good order, then this habit of order, in a manner how unlike the lawless play of the others! will accompany them in all their actions and be a principle of growth to them, and if there be any fallen places in the State will raise them up again.

Very true, he said.

Thus educated, they will invent for themselves any lesser rules which their predecessors have altogether neglected.

What do you mean?

I mean such things as these:—when the young are to be silent before their elders; how they are to show respect to them by standing and making them sit; what honor is due to parents; what garments or shoes are to be worn; the mode of dressing the hair; deportment and manners in general. You would agree with me?

Yes.

But there is, I think, small wisdom in legislating about such matters—I doubt if it is ever done; nor are any precise written enactments about them likely to be lasting.

Impossible.

It would seem, Adeimantus, that the direction in which education starts a man, will determine his future life. Does not like always attract like?

To be sure.

Until some one rare and grand result is reached which may be good, and may be the reverse of good?

That is not to be denied.

And for this reason, I said, I shall not attempt to legislate further about them.

Naturally enough, he replied.

Well, and about the business of the agora, and the ordinary dealings between man and man, or again about agreements with artisans; about insult and injury, or the commencement of actions, and the appointment of juries, what would you say? there may also arise questions about any impositions and exactions of market and harbor dues which may be required, and in general about the regulations of markets, police, harbors, and the like. But, O heavens! shall we condescend to legislate on any of these particulars?

I think, he said, that there is no need to impose laws about them on good men; what regulations are necessary they will find out soon enough for themselves.

Yes, I said, my friend, if God will only preserve to them the laws which we have given them.

And without divine help, said Adeimantus, they will go on forever making and mending the laws and their lives in the hope of attaining perfection.

You would compare them, I said, to those invalids who, having no self-restraint, will not leave off their habits of intemperance?

Exactly.

Yes, I said; and what a delightful life they lead! they are always doctoring and increasing and complicating their disorders, and always fancying that they will be cured by any panacea which anybody advises them to try.

Such cases are very common, he said, with invalids of this sort.

Yes, I replied; and the charming thing is that they deem him their worst enemy who tells them the truth, which is simply that, unless they give up eating and drinking and wenching and idling, neither drug nor cautery nor spell nor amulet nor any other remedy will avail.

Charming! he replied. I see nothing in going into a passion with a man who tells you what is right.

These gentlemen, I said, do not seem to be in your good graces.

Assuredly not.

Nor would you praise the behavior of States which act like the men whom I was just now describing. For are there not ill-ordered States in which the citizens are forbidden under pain of death to alter the constitution; and yet he who most sweetly courts those who live under this régime and indulges them and fawns upon them and is skilful in anticipating and gratifying their humors is held to be a great and good statesman—do not these States resemble the persons whom I was describing?[5]

Yes, he said; the States are as bad as the men; and I am very far from praising them.

But do you not admire, I said, the coolness and dexterity of these ready ministers of political corruption?

Yes, he said, I do; but not of all of them, for there are some whom the applause of the multitude has deluded into the belief that they are really statesmen, and these are not much to be admired.

What do you mean? I said; you should have more feeling for them. When a man cannot measure, and a great many others who cannot measure declare that he is four cubits high, can he help believing what they say?

Nay, he said, certainly not in that case.

Well, then, do not be angry with them; for are they not as good as a play, trying their hand at paltry reforms such as I was describing; they are always fancying that by legislation they will make an end of frauds in contracts, and the other rascalities which I was mentioning, not knowing that they are in reality cutting off the heads of a hydra?*

Yes, he said; that is just what they are doing.

I conceive, I said, that the true legislator will not trouble himself with this class of enactments whether concerning laws or the constitution either in an ill-ordered or in a well-ordered State; for in the former they are quite useless, and in the latter there will be

---

*The Hydra was a mythical monster with multiple heads; when one head was cut off, two more grew back in its place.

no difficulty in devising them; and many of them will naturally flow out of our previous regulations.

What, then, he said, is still remaining to us of the work of legislation?

Nothing to us, I replied; but to Apollo, the god of Delphi,* there remains the ordering of the greatest and noblest and chiefest things of all.

Which are they? he said.

The institution of temples and sacrifices, and the entire service of gods, demigods,† and heroes;‡ also the ordering of the repositories of the dead, and the rites which have to be observed by him who would propitiate the inhabitants of the world below.§ These are matters of which we are ignorant ourselves, and as founders of a city we should be unwise in trusting them to any interpreter but our ancestral deity.‖ He is the god who sits in the centre, on the navel of the earth, and he is the interpreter of religion to all mankind.

You are right, and we will do as you propose.

But where, amid all this, is justice? Son of Ariston, tell me where. Now that our city has been made habitable, light a candle and search, and get your brother and Polemarchus and the rest of our friends to help, and let us see where in it we can discover justice and where injustice, and in what they differ from one another, and which of them the man who would be happy should have for his portion, whether seen or unseen by gods and men.

Nonsense, said Glaucon: did you not promise to search yourself, saying that for you not to help justice in her need would be an impiety?

---

*Site of an important pan-Hellenic sanctuary dedicated to Apollo. The oracular shrine at Delphi, where Apollo was thought to prophesy through his priestess (the Pythia), was conceived of as resting on the supposed center ("navel") of the earth.

†*Daimones* in Greek; that is, guardian spirits.

‡Figures such as Achilles, Heracles, Theseus, and Helen, as well as less well known and locally important figures, were worshiped throughout the Greek world in hero cults.

§That is, chthonic deities such as the Furies (Eumenides) and Persephone.

‖That is, Apollo.

I do not deny that I said so; and as you remind me, I will be as good as my word; but you must join.

We will, he replied.

Well, then, I hope to make the discovery in this way: I mean to begin with the assumption that our State, if rightly ordered, is perfect.

That is most certain.

And being perfect, is therefore wise and valiant and temperate and just.

That is likewise clear.

And whichever of these qualities we find in the State, the one which is not found will be the residue?

428 Very good.

If there were four things, and we were searching for one of them, wherever it might be, the one sought for might be known to us from the first, and there would be no further trouble; or we might know the other three first, and then the fourth would clearly be the one left.

Very true, he said.

And is not a similar method to be pursued about the virtues, which are also four in number?[6]

Clearly.

First among the virtues found in the State, wisdom comes into view, and in this I detect a certain peculiarity.

b

What is that?

The State which we have been describing is said to be wise as being good in counsel?

Very true.

And good counsel is clearly a kind of knowledge, for not by ignorance, but by knowledge, do men counsel well?

Clearly.

And the kinds of knowledge in a State are many and diverse?

Of course.

There is the knowledge of the carpenter; but is that the sort of knowledge which gives a city the title of wise and good in counsel?

c Certainly not; that would only give a city the reputation of skill in carpentering.

Then a city is not to be called wise because possessing a

knowledge which counsels for the best about wooden implements?

Certainly not.

Nor by reason of a knowledge which advises about brazen pots, he said, nor as possessing any other similar knowledge?

Not by reason of any of them, he said.

Nor yet by reason of a knowledge which cultivates the earth; that would give the city the name of agricultural?

Yes.

Well, I said, and is there any knowledge in our recently founded State among any of the citizens which advises, not about any particular thing in the State, but about the whole, and considers how   d
a State can best deal with itself and with other States?

There certainly is.

And what is this knowledge, and among whom is it found? I asked.

It is the knowledge of the guardians, he replied, and is found among those whom we were just now describing as perfect guardians.

And what is the name which the city derives from the possession of this sort of knowledge?

The name of good in counsel and truly wise.

And will there be in our city more of these true guardians or more smiths?   e

The smiths, he replied, will be far more numerous.

Will not the guardians be the smallest of all the classes who receive a name from the profession of some kind of knowledge?

Much the smallest.

And so by reason of the smallest part or class, and of the knowledge which resides in this presiding and ruling part of itself, the whole State, being thus constituted according to nature, will be wise; and this, which has the only knowledge worthy to be called wisdom, has been ordained by nature to be of all classes the least.   429

Most true.

Thus, then, I said, the nature and place in the State of one of the four virtues have somehow or other been discovered.

And, in my humble opinion, very satisfactorily discovered, he replied.

Again, I said, there is no difficulty in seeing the nature of courage, and in what part that quality resides which gives the name of courageous to the State.

How do you mean?

b   Why, I said, everyone who calls any State courageous or cowardly, will be thinking of the part which fights and goes out to war on the State's behalf.

No one, he replied, would ever think of any other.

The rest of the citizens may be courageous or may be cowardly, but their courage or cowardice will not, as I conceive, have the effect of making the city either the one or the other.

Certainly not.

The city will be courageous in virtue of a portion of herself which preserves under all circumstances that opinion about the
c   nature of things to be feared and not to be feared in which our legislator educated them; and this is what you term courage.

I should like to hear what you are saying once more, for I do not think that I perfectly understand you.

I mean that courage is a kind of salvation.

Salvation of what?

Of the opinion respecting things to be feared, what they are and of what nature, which the law implants through education; and I mean by the words "under all circumstances" to intimate that in pleasure or in pain, or under the influence of desire or fear, a
d   man preserves, and does not lose this opinion. Shall I give you an illustration?

If you please.

You know, I said, that dyers, when they want to dye wool for making the true sea-purple, begin by selecting their white color first; this they prepare and dress with much care and pains, in order that the white ground may take the purple hue in full perfection.
e   The dyeing then proceeds; and whatever is dyed in this manner becomes a fast color, and no washing either with lyes or without them can take away the bloom. But, when the ground has not been duly prepared, you will have noticed how poor is the look either of purple or of any other color.

Yes, he said; I know that they have a washed-out and ridiculous appearance.

Then now, I said, you will understand what our object was in selecting our soldiers, and educating them in music and gymnastics; we were contriving influences which would prepare them to take the dye of the laws in perfection, and the color of their opinion about dangers and of every other opinion was to be indelibly fixed by their nurture and training, not to be washed away by such potent lyes as pleasure—mightier agent far in washing the soul than any soda or lye; or by sorrow, fear, and desire, the mightiest of all other solvents. And this sort of universal saving power of true opinion in conformity with law about real and false dangers I call and maintain to be courage, unless you disagree.

But I agree, he replied; for I suppose that you mean to exclude mere uninstructed courage, such as that of a wild beast or of a slave—this, in your opinion, is not the courage which the law ordains, and ought to have another name.

Most certainly.

Then I may infer courage to be such as you describe?

Why, yes, said I, you may, and if you add the words "of a citizen," you will not be far wrong—hereafter, if you like, we will carry the examination further, but at present we are seeking, not for courage, but justice; and for the purpose of our inquiry we have said enough.

You are right, he replied.

Two virtues remain to be discovered in the State—first, temperance, and then justice, which is the end of our search.

Very true.

Now, can we find justice without troubling ourselves about temperance?

I do not know how that can be accomplished, he said, nor do I desire that justice should be brought to light and temperance lost sight of; and therefore I wish that you would do me the favor of considering temperance first.

Certainly, I replied, I should not be justified in refusing your request.

Then consider, he said.

Yes, I replied; I will; and as far as I can at present see, the virtue of temperance has more of the nature of harmony and symphony than the preceding.

How so? he asked.

Temperance, I replied, is the ordering or controlling of certain

pleasures and desires; this is curiously enough implied in the saying of "a man being his own master;"* and other traces of the
same notion may be found in language.

No doubt, he said.

There is something ridiculous in the expression "master of himself;" for the master is also the servant and the servant the master;
and in all these modes of speaking the same person is denoted.

Certainly.

The meaning is, I believe, that in the human soul there is a better and also a worse principle; and when the better has the worse
under control, then a man is said to be master of himself; and this
is a term of praise: but when, owing to evil education or association,
the better principle, which is also the smaller, is overwhelmed by
the greater mass of the worse—in this case he is blamed and is
called the slave of self and unprincipled.

Yes, there is reason in that.

And now, I said, look at our newly created State, and there you
will find one of these two conditions realized; for the State, as you
will acknowledge, may be justly called master of itself, if the words
"temperance" and "self-mastery" truly express the rule of the better part over the worse.

Yes, he said, I see that what you say is true.

Let me further note that the manifold and complex pleasures
and desires and pains are generally found in children and
women and servants, and in the freemen so called who are of
the lowest and more numerous class.

Certainly, he said.

Whereas the simple and moderate desires which follow reason,
and are under the guidance of mind and true opinion, are to be
found only in a few, and those the best born and best educated.

Very true.

These two, as you may perceive, have a place in our State; and
the meaner desires of the many are held down by the virtuous desires and wisdom of the few.

---

*The concept of self-mastery (literally, being "superior" to oneself) was integral
to the popular understanding of moderation (*sophrosynê*).

That I perceive, he said.

Then if there be any city which may be described as master of its own pleasures and desires, and master of itself, ours may claim such a designation?

Certainly, he replied.

It may also be called temperate, and for the same reasons?

Yes.

And if there be any State in which rulers and subjects will be agreed as to the question who are to rule, that again will be our State?   e

Undoubtedly.

And the citizens being thus agreed among themselves, in which class will temperance be found—in the rulers or in the subjects?

In both, as I should imagine, he replied.

Do you observe that we were not far wrong in our guess that temperance was a sort of harmony?

Why so?

Why, because temperance is unlike courage and wisdom, each of which resides in a part only, the one making the State wise and   432
the other valiant; not so temperance, which extends to the whole, and runs through all the notes of the scale, and produces a harmony of the weaker and the stronger and the middle class,* whether you suppose them to be stronger or weaker in wisdom, or power, or numbers, or wealth, or anything else. Most truly then may we deem temperance to be the agreement of the naturally superior and inferior, as to the right to rule of either, both in States and individuals.

I entirely agree with you.   b

And so, I said, we may consider three out of the four virtues to have been discovered in our State. The last of those qualities which make a State virtuous must be justice, if we only knew what that was.

The inference is obvious.

The time then has arrived, Glaucon, when, like huntsmen, we should surround the cover, and look sharp that justice does not

---

*The "weaker" class is the "bronze/iron" class of artisans and farmers; the "stronger" is the "gold" class of rulers, and the "middle" is the "silver" class of auxiliaries.

steal away, and pass out of sight and escape us; for beyond a doubt she is somewhere in this country: watch therefore and strive to catch a sight of her, and if you see her first, let me know.

Would that I could! but you should regard me rather as a follower who has just eyes enough to see what you show him—that is about as much as I am good for.

Offer up a prayer with me and follow.

I will, but you must show me the way.

Here is no path, I said, and the wood is dark and perplexing; still we must push on.

Let us push on.

Here I saw something: Halloo! I said, I begin to perceive a track, and I believe that the quarry will not escape.

Good news, he said.

Truly, I said, we are stupid fellows.

Why so?

Why, my good sir, at the beginning of our inquiry, ages ago, there was Justice tumbling out at our feet, and we never saw her; nothing could be more ridiculous.[7] Like people who go about looking for what they have in their hands—that was the way with us—we looked not at what we were seeking, but at what was far off in the distance; and therefore, I suppose, we missed her.

What do you mean?

I mean to say that in reality for a long time past we have been talking of Justice, and have failed to recognize her.

I grow impatient at the length of your exordium.

Well, then, tell me, I said, whether I am right or not: You remember the original principle* which we were always laying down at the foundation of the State, that one man should practise one thing only, the thing to which his nature was best adapted; now justice is this principle or a part of it.

Yes, we often said that one man should do one thing only.

Further, we affirmed that Justice was doing one's own business, and not being a busybody;[8] we said so again and again, and many others have said the same to us.

---

*Compare 2.370b; also 2.372a.

Yes, we said so.

Then to do one's own business in a certain way may be assumed to be justice. Can you tell me whence I derive this inference?

I cannot, but I should like to be told.

Because I think that this is the only virtue which remains in the State when the other virtues of temperance and courage and wisdom are abstracted; and, that this is the ultimate cause and condition of the existence of all of them, and while remaining in them is also their preservative; and we were saying that if the three   c were discovered by us, justice would be the fourth, or remaining one.

That follows of necessity.

If we are asked to determine which of these four qualities by its presence contributes most to the excellence of the State, whether the agreement of rulers and subjects, or the preservation in the soldiers of the opinion which the law ordains about the true nature of dangers, or wisdom and watchfulness in the rulers, or whether this other which I am mentioning, and which is found in children and   d women, slave and freeman, artisan, ruler, subject—the quality, I mean, of everyone doing his own work, and not being a busybody, would claim the palm—the question is not so easily answered.

Certainly, he replied, there would be a difficulty in saying which.

Then the power of each individual in the State to do his own work appears to compete with the other political virtues, wisdom, temperance, courage.

Yes, he said.

And the virtue which enters into this competition is justice?   e

Exactly.

Let us look at the question from another point of view: Are not the rulers in a State those to whom you would intrust the office of determining suits-at-law?

Certainly.

And are suits decided on any other ground but that a man may neither take what is another's, nor be deprived of what is his own?

Yes; that is their principle.

Which is a just principle?

Yes.

Then on this view also justice will be admitted to be the having
434 and doing what is a man's own, and belongs to him?

Very true.

Think, now, and say whether you agree with me or not. Suppose
a carpenter to be doing the business of a cobbler, or a cobbler of a
carpenter; and suppose them to exchange their implements or
their duties, or the same person to be doing the work of both, or
whatever be the change; do you think that any great harm would
result to the State?

Not much.

But when the cobbler or any other man whom nature designed
b to be a trader, having his heart lifted up by wealth or strength or
the number of his followers, or any like advantage, attempts to force
his way into the class of warriors, or a warrior into that of legisla-
tors and guardians, for which he is unfitted, and either to take the
implements or the duties of the other; or when one man is trader,
legislator, and warrior all in one, then I think you will agree with
me in saying that this interchange and this meddling of one with
another is the ruin of the State.

Most true.

Seeing, then, I said, that there are three distinct classes, any
meddling of one with another, or the change of one into another,
c is the greatest harm to the State, and may be most justly termed
evil-doing?

Precisely.

And the greatest degree of evil-doing to one's own city would
be termed by you injustice?

Certainly.

This, then, is injustice; and on the other hand when the trader,
the auxiliary, and the guardian each do their own business, that is
justice, and will make the city just.

d I agree with you.

We will not, I said, be over-positive as yet; but if, on trial, this conception of justice be verified in the individual as well as in the State,
there will be no longer any room for doubt; if it be not verified, we
must have a fresh inquiry. First let us complete the old investigation,
which we began, as you remember, under the impression that, if we
could previously examine justice on the larger scale, there would be

less difficulty in discerning her in the individual. That larger example appeared to be the State, and accordingly we constructed as good a one as we could, knowing well that in the good State justice would be found. Let the discovery which we made be now applied to the individual—if they agree, we shall be satisfied; or, if there be a difference in the individual, we will come back to the State and have another trial of the theory. The friction of the two when rubbed together may possibly strike a light in which justice will shine forth, and the vision which is then revealed we will fix in our souls. e

435

That will be in regular course; let us do as you say.

I proceeded to ask: When two things, a greater and less, are called by the same name, are they like or unlike in so far as they are called the same?

Like, he replied.

The just man then, if we regard the idea of justice only, will be like the just State? b

He will.

And a State was thought by us to be just when the three classes in the State severally did their own business; and also thought to be temperate and valiant and wise by reason of certain other affections and qualities of these same classes?

True, he said.

And so of the individual; we may assume that he has the same three principles in his own soul which are found in the State; and he may be rightly described in the same terms, because he is affected in the same manner?[9] c

Certainly, he said.

Once more, then, O my friend, we have alighted upon an easy question—whether the soul has these three principles or not?

An easy question! Nay, rather, Socrates, the proverb holds that hard is the good.

Very true, I said; and I do not think that the method which we are employing is at all adequate to the accurate solution of this question;[10] the true method is another and a longer one. Still we may arrive at a solution not below the level of the previous inquiry. d

May we not be satisfied with that? he said; under the circumstances, I am quite content.

I, too, I replied, shall be extremely well satisfied.

Then faint not in pursuing the speculation, he said.

e   Must we not acknowledge, I said, that in each of us there are the same principles and habits which there are in the State; and that from the individual they pass into the State?—how else can they come there? Take the quality of passion or spirit; it would be ridiculous to imagine that this quality, when found in States, is not derived from the individuals who are supposed to possess it, *e.g.,* the Thracians, Scythians, and in general the Northern nations;[11] and

436   the same may be said of the love of knowledge, which is the special characteristic of our part of the world, or of the love of money, which may, with equal truth, be attributed to the Phœnicians and Egyptians.

Exactly so, he said.

There is no difficulty in understanding this.

None whatever.

But the question is not quite so easy when we proceed to ask whether these principles are three or one; whether, that is to say, we learn with one part of our nature, are angry with another, and with a third part desire the satisfaction of our natural appetites; or

b   whether the whole soul comes into play in each sort of action—to determine that is the difficulty.

Yes, he said; there lies the difficulty.

Then let us now try and determine whether they are the same or different.

How can we? he asked.

I replied as follows: The same thing clearly cannot act or be acted upon in the same part or in relation to the same thing at the same time, in contrary ways; and therefore whenever this contradiction occurs in things apparently the same, we know that they

c   are really not the same, but different.

Good.

For example, I said, can the same thing be at rest and in motion at the same time in the same part?

Impossible.

Still, I said, let us have a more precise statement of terms, lest we should hereafter fall out by the way. Imagine the case of a man who is standing and also moving his hands and his head, and suppose a person to say that one and the same person is in motion and at rest at the same moment—to such a mode of speech we should object, and should rather say that one part of him is in motion while another is at rest.

Very true.

And suppose the objector to refine still further, and to draw the nice distinction that not only parts of tops, but whole tops, when they spin round with their pegs fixed on the spot, are at rest and in motion at the same time (and he may say the same of anything which revolves in the same spot), his objection would not be admitted by us, because in such cases things are not at rest and in motion in the same parts of themselves; we should rather say that they have both an axis and a circumference; and that the axis stands still, for there is no deviation from the perpendicular; and that the circumference goes round. But if, while revolving, the axis inclines either to the right or left, forward or backward, then in no point of view can they be at rest.

That is the correct mode of describing them, he replied.

Then none of these objections will confuse us, or incline us to believe that the same thing at the same time, in the same part or in relation to the same thing, can act or be acted upon in contrary ways.

Certainly not, according to my way of thinking.

Yet, I said, that we may not be compelled to examine all such objections, and prove at length that they are untrue, let us assume their absurdity, and go forward on the understanding that hereafter, if this assumption turn out to be untrue, all the consequences which follow shall be withdrawn.

Yes, he said, that will be the best way.

Well, I said, would you not allow that assent and dissent, desire and aversion, attraction and repulsion, are all of them opposites, whether they are regarded as active or passive (for that makes no difference in the fact of their opposition)?

Yes, he said, they are opposites.

Well, I said, and hunger and thirst, and the desires in general, and again willing and wishing—all these you would refer to the classes already mentioned. You would say—would you not?—that the soul of him who desires is seeking after the object of his desire; or that he is drawing to himself the thing which he wishes to possess: or again, when a person wants anything to be given him, his mind, longing for the realization of his desire, intimates his wish to have it by a nod of assent, as if he had been asked a question?

Very true.

And what would you say of unwillingness and dislike and the absence of desire; should not these be referred to the opposite class of repulsion and rejection?

Certainly.

Since these things are so, shall we say, then, that there is a distinct class of desires in the soul, and that the most conspicuous of these are the ones we call "hunger" and "thirst"?

Let us take that class, he said.

The object of one is food, and of the other drink?

Yes.

And here comes the point: is not thirst the desire which the soul has of drink, and of drink only; not of drink qualified by anything else;[12] for example, warm or cold, or much or little, or, in a word, drink of any particular sort: but if the thirst be accompanied by heat, then the desire is of cold drink; or, if accompanied by cold, then of warm drink; or, if the thirst be excessive, then the drink which is desired will be excessive; or, if not great, the quantity of drink will also be small: but thirst pure and simple will desire drink pure and simple, which is the natural satisfaction of thirst, as food is of hunger?

Yes, he said; the simple desire is, as you say, in every case of the simple object, and the qualified desire of the qualified object.

But here a confusion may arise; and I should wish to guard against an opponent starting up and saying that no man desires drink only, but good drink, or food only, but good food; for good is the universal object of desire, and thirst being a desire, will necessarily be thirst after good drink; and the same is true of every other desire.

Yes, he replied, the opponent might have something to say.

Nevertheless I should still maintain, that of relatives some have a quality attached to either term of the relation; others are simple and have their correlatives simple.

I do not know what you mean.

Well, you know of course that the greater is relative to the less?

Certainly.

And the much greater to the much less?

Yes.

And the sometime greater to the sometime less, and the greater that is to be to the less that is to be?

Certainly, he said.

And so of more or less, and of other correlative terms, such as the double and the half, or, again, the heavier and the lighter, the swifter and the slower; and of hot and cold, and of any other relatives; is not this true of all of them? c

Yes.

And does not the same principle hold in the sciences? The object of science is knowledge (assuming that to be the true definition), but the object of a particular science is a particular kind of knowledge; I mean, for example, that the science of house-building d is a kind of knowledge which is defined and distinguished from other kinds and is therefore termed architecture.

Certainly.

Because it has a particular quality which no other has?

Yes.

And it has this particular quality because it has an object of a particular kind; and this is true of the other arts and sciences?

Yes.

Now, then, if I have made myself clear, you will understand my original meaning in what I said about relatives. My meaning was, that if one term of a relation is taken alone, the other is taken alone; if one term is qualified, the other is also qualified. I do not mean to say that relatives may not be disparate, or that the science e of health is healthy, or of disease necessarily diseased, or that the sciences of good and evil are therefore good and evil; but only that, when the term "science" is no longer used absolutely, but has a qualified object which in this case is the nature of health and disease, it becomes defined, and is hence called not merely science, but the science of medicine.

I quite understand, and, I think, as you do.

Would you not say that thirst is one of these essentially relative terms, having clearly a relation—— 439

Yes, thirst is relative to drink.

And a certain kind of thirst is relative to a certain kind of drink; but thirst taken alone is neither of much nor little, nor of good nor bad, nor of any particular kind of drink, but of drink only?

Certainly.

b
Then the soul of the thirsty one, in so far as he is thirsty, desires only drink; for this he yearns and tries to obtain it?

That is plain.

And if you suppose something which pulls a thirsty soul away from drink, that must be different from the thirsty principle which draws him like a beast to drink; for, as we were saying, the same thing cannot at the same time with the same part of itself act in contrary ways about the same.

Impossible.

No more than you can say that the hands of the archer push and pull the bow at the same time, but what you say is that one hand pushes and the other pulls.

c
Exactly so, he replied.

And might a man be thirsty, and yet unwilling to drink?

Yes, he said, it constantly happens.

And in such a case what is one to say? Would you not say that there was something in the soul bidding a man to drink, and something else forbidding him, which is other and stronger than the principle which bids him?

I should say so.

And the forbidding principle is derived from reason, and that
d
which bids and attracts proceeds from passion and disease?

Clearly.

Then we may fairly assume that they are two, and that they differ from one another; the one with which a man reasons, we may call the rational principle of the soul; the other, with which he loves, and hungers, and thirsts, and feels the flutterings of any other desire, may be termed the irrational or appetitive, the ally of sundry pleasures and satisfactions?

e
Yes, he said, we may fairly assume them to be different.

Then let us accordingly determine that there are two principles existing in the soul. And what of passion, or spirit? Is it a third, or akin to one of the preceding?[13]

I should be inclined to say—akin to desire.

Well, I said, there is a story which I remember to have heard, and in which I put faith. The story is, that Leontius, the son of Aglaion,* coming up one day from the Piræus, under the north wall on the outside, observed some dead bodies lying on the ground at the place of execution. He felt a desire to see them, and also a dread and abhorrence of them; for a time he struggled and covered his eyes, but at length the desire got the better of him; and forcing them open, he ran up to the dead bodies, saying, Look, ye wretches,   440 take your fill of the fair sight.

I have heard the story myself, he said.

The moral of the tale is, that anger at times goes to war with desire, as though they were two distinct things.

Yes; that is the meaning, he said.

And are there not many other cases in which we observe that when a man's desires violently prevail over his reason, he reviles himself, and is angry at the violence within him, and that in this   b struggle, which is like the struggle of factions in a State, his spirit is on the side of his reason; but for the passionate or spirited element to take part with the desires when reason decides that it should not be opposed, is a sort of thing which I believe that you never observed occurring in yourself, nor, as I should imagine, in anyone else?

Certainly not.

Suppose that a man thinks he has done a wrong to another, the   c nobler he is, the less able is he to feel indignant at any suffering, such as hunger, or cold, or any other pain which the injured person may inflict upon him—these he deems to be just, and, as I say, his anger refuses to be excited by them.

True, he said.

But when he thinks that he is the sufferer of the wrong, then he boils and chafes, and is on the side of what he believes to be justice; and because he suffers hunger or cold or other pain he is only the more determined to persevere and conquer. His noble spirit

---

*In a fragment of a lost comedy, someone named Leotrophidas is said to seem as "comely as a corpse" to a certain Leontius, who is presumably the same individual as the one described in this anecdote.

will not be quelled until he either slays or is slain; or until he hears
d   the voice of the shepherd, that is, reason, bidding his dog bark no
more.

The illustration is perfect, he replied; and in our State, as we
were saying, the auxiliaries were to be dogs, and to hear the voice
of the rulers, who are their shepherds.

I perceive, I said, that you quite understand me; there is, however, a further point which I wish you to consider.

e   What point?

You remember that passion or spirit appeared at first sight to be
a kind of desire, but now we should say quite the contrary; for in
the conflict of the soul spirit is arrayed on the side of the rational
principle.

Most assuredly.

But a further question arises: Is passion different from reason
also, or only a kind of reason; in which latter case, instead of three
principles in the soul, there will only be two, the rational and
the concupiscent; or rather, as the State was composed of three
441   classes, traders, auxiliaries, counsellors, so may there not be in the
individual soul a third element which is passion or spirit, and
when not corrupted by bad education is the natural auxiliary of
reason?

Yes, he said, there must be a third.

Yes, I replied, if passion, which has already been shown to be
different from desire, turn out also to be different from reason.

But that is easily proved: We may observe even in young children that they are full of spirit almost as soon as they are born,
b   whereas some of them never seem to attain to the use of reason,
and most of them late enough.

Excellent, I said, and you may see passion equally in brute animals, which is a further proof of the truth of what you are saying.
And we may once more appeal to the words of Homer, which
have been already quoted by us,

"He smote his breast, and thus rebuked his soul;"*

Odyssey 20.17, quoted with approval above at 3.390d.

for in this verse Homer has clearly supposed the power which reasons about the better and worse to be different from the unrea-   c
soning anger which is rebuked by it.

Very true, he said.

And so, after much tossing, we have reached land, and are fairly
agreed that the same principles which exist in the State exist also
in the individual, and that they are three in number.

Exactly.

Must we not then infer that the individual is wise in the same
way, and in virtue of the same quality which makes the State wise?

Certainly.

Also that the same quality which constitutes courage in the   d
State constitutes courage in the individual, and that both the State
and the individual bear the same relation to all the other virtues?

Assuredly.

And the individual will be acknowledged by us to be just in the
same way in which the State is just?

That follows of course.

We cannot but remember that the justice of the State consisted
in each of the three classes doing the work of its own class?

We are not very likely to have forgotten, he said.

We must recollect that the individual in whom the several qualities of his nature do their own work will be just, and will do his   e
own work?

Yes, he said, we must remember that too.

And ought not the rational principle, which is wise, and has the
care of the whole soul, to rule, and the passionate or spirited principle to be the subject and ally?

Certainly.

And, as we were saying, the united influence of music and gymnastic will bring them into accord, nerving and sustaining the reason with noble words and lessons, and moderating and soothing   442
and civilizing the wildness of passion by harmony and rhythm?

Quite true, he said.

And these two, thus nurtured and educated, and having learned
truly to know their own functions, will rule over the concupiscent,
which in each of us is the largest part of the soul and by nature
most insatiable of gain;[14] over this they will keep guard, lest, waxing

great and strong with the fulness of bodily pleasures, as they are termed, the concupiscent soul, no longer confined to her own b sphere, should attempt to enslave and rule those who are not her natural-born subjects, and overturn the whole life of man?

Very true, he said.

Both together will they not be the best defenders of the whole soul and the whole body against attacks from without; the one counselling, and the other fighting under his leader, and courageously executing his commands and counsels?

True.

And he is to be deemed courageous whose spirit retains in plea-c sure and in pain the commands of reason about what he ought or ought not to fear?

Right, he replied.

And him we call wise who has in him that little part which rules, and which proclaims these commands; that part too being supposed to have a knowledge of what is for the interest of each of the three parts and of the whole?

Assuredly.

And would you not say that he is temperate who has these same elements in friendly harmony, in whom the one ruling principle of reason, and the two subject ones of spirit and desire, are equally d agreed that reason ought to rule, and do not rebel?

Certainly, he said, that is the true account of temperance whether in the State or individual.

And surely, I said, we have explained again and again how and by virtue of what quality a man will be just.

That is very certain.

And is justice dimmer in the individual, and is her form different, or is she the same which we found her to be in the State?

There is no difference, in my opinion, he said.

Because, if any doubt is still lingering in our minds, a few com-e monplace instances will satisfy us of the truth of what I am saying.

What sort of instances do you mean?

If the case is put to us, must we not admit that the just State, or the man who is trained in the principles of such a State, will be less likely than the unjust to make away with a deposit of gold or 443 silver? Would anyone deny this?

No one, he replied.

Will the just man or citizen ever be guilty of sacrilege or theft, or treachery either to his friends or to his country?

Never.

Neither will he ever break faith where there have been oaths or agreements.

Impossible.

No one will be less likely to commit adultery, or to dishonor his father and mother, or to fail in his religious duties?

No one.

And the reason is that each part of him is doing its own business, whether in ruling or being ruled?   b

Exactly so.

Are you satisfied, then, that the quality which makes such men and such States is justice, or do you hope to discover some other?

Not I, indeed.

Then our dream has been realized; and the suspicion which we entertained at the beginning of our work of construction, that some divine power must have conducted us to a primary form of justice,   c
has now been verified?

Yes, certainly.

And the division of labor which required the carpenter and the shoemaker and the rest of the citizens to be doing each his own business, and not another's, was a shadow of justice, and for that reason it was of use?

Clearly.

But in reality justice was such as we were describing, being concerned, however, not with the outward man, but with the inward, which is the true self and concernment of man:[15] for the   d
just man does not permit the several elements within him to interfere with one another, or any of them to do the work of others—he sets in order his own inner life, and is his own master and his own law, and at peace with himself; and when he has bound together the three principles within him, which may be compared to the higher, lower, and middle notes of the scale, and the intermediate intervals—when he has bound all these together, and is no   e
longer many, but has become one entirely temperate and perfectly adjusted nature, then he proceeds to act, if he has to act, whether

in a matter of property, or in the treatment of the body, or in some affair of politics or private business; always thinking and calling that which preserves and co-operates with this harmonious condition just and good action, and the knowledge which presides over it wisdom, and that which at any time impairs this condition he will call unjust action, and the opinion which presides over it ignorance.

You have said the exact truth, Socrates.

Very good; and if we were to affirm that we had discovered the just man and the just State, and the nature of justice in each of them, we should not be telling a falsehood?

Most certainly not.

May we say so, then?

Let us say so.

And now, I said, injustice has to be considered.

Clearly.

Must not injustice be a strife which arises among the three principles—a meddlesomeness, and interference,[16] and rising up of a part of the soul against the whole, an assertion of unlawful authority, which is made by a rebellious subject against a true prince, of whom he is the natural vassal—what is all this confusion and delusion but injustice, and intemperance, and cowardice, and ignorance, and every form of vice?

Exactly so.

And if the nature of justice and injustice be known, then the meaning of acting unjustly and being unjust, or, again, of acting justly, will also be perfectly clear?

What do you mean? he said.

Why, I said, they are like disease and health; being in the soul just what disease and health are in the body.[17]

How so? he said.

Why, I said, that which is healthy causes health, and that which is unhealthy causes disease.

Yes.

And just actions cause justice, and unjust actions cause injustice?

That is certain.

And the creation of health is the institution of a natural order and government of one by another in the parts of the body; and the creation of disease is the production of a state of things at variance with this natural order?

True.

And is not the creation of justice the institution of a natural order and government of one by another in the parts of the soul, and the creation of injustice the production of a state of things at variance with the natural order?

Exactly so, he said.

Then virtue is the health, and beauty, and well-being of the soul, and vice the disease, and weakness, and deformity, of the same?   e

True.

And do not good practices lead to virtue, and evil practices to vice?

Assuredly.

Still our old question of the comparative advantage of justice and injustice has not been answered: Which is the more profitable, to be just and act justly and practise virtue, whether seen or   445 unseen of gods and men, or to be unjust and act unjustly, if only unpunished and unreformed?

In my judgment, Socrates, the question has now become ridiculous. We know that, when the bodily constitution is gone, life is no longer endurable, though pampered with all kinds of meats and drinks, and having all wealth and all power; and shall we be told that when the very essence of the vital principle is under-   b mined and corrupted, life is still worth having to a man, if only he be allowed to do whatever he likes with the single exception that he is not to acquire justice and virtue, or to escape from injustice and vice; assuming them both to be such as we have described?

Yes, I said, the question is, as you say, ridiculous. Still, as we are near the spot at which we may see the truth in the clearest manner with our own eyes, let us not faint by the way.

Certainly not, he replied.

Come up hither, I said, and behold the various forms of vice,   c those of them, I mean, which are worth looking at.

I am following you, he replied: proceed.

I said: The argument seems to have reached a height from which, as from some tower of speculation, a man may look down

and see that virtue is one, but that the forms of vice are innumerable; there being four special ones which are deserving of note.

What do you mean? he said.

I mean, I replied, that there appear to be as many forms of the
soul as there are distinct forms of the State.

How many?

There are five of the State, and five of the soul, I said.

d   What are they?

The first, I said, is that which we have been describing, and
which may be said to have two names, monarchy and aristocracy,
according as rule is exercised by one distinguished man or by many.

True, he replied.

But I regard the two names as describing one form only; for
e   whether the government is in the hands of one or many, if the
governors have been trained in the manner which we have supposed, the fundamental laws of the State will be maintained.

That is true, he replied.

BOOK 5

SUCH IS THE GOOD and true City or State, and the good and true 449 man is of the same pattern; and if this is right every other is wrong; and the evil is one which affects not only the ordering of the State, but also the regulation of the individual soul, and is exhibited in four forms.

What are they? he said.

I was proceeding to tell the order in which the four evil forms appeared to me to succeed one another, when Polemarchus, who b was sitting a little way off, just beyond Adeimantus, began to whisper to him:[1] stretching forth his hand, he took hold of the upper part of his coat by the shoulder, and drew him toward him, leaning forward himself so as to be quite close and saying something in his ear, of which I only caught the words, "Shall we let him off, or what shall we do?"

Certainly not, said Adeimantus, raising his voice.

Who is it, I said, whom you are refusing to let off?

You, he said.

I repeated, Why am I especially not to be let off? c

Why, he said, we think that you are lazy, and mean to cheat us out of a whole chapter which is a very important part of the story; and you fancy that we shall not notice your airy way of proceeding; as if it were self-evident to everybody, that in the matter of women and children "friends have all things in common."*

And was I not right, Adeimantus?

Yes, he said; but what is right in this particular case, like everything else, requires to be explained; for community may be of many kinds. Please, therefore, to say what sort of community you mean. We have been long expecting that you would tell us some- d thing about the family life of your citizens—how they will bring

---

*Compare 4.424a.

149

children into the world, and rear them when they have arrived, and, in general, what is the nature of this community of women and children—for we are of opinion that the right or wrong management of such matters will have a great and paramount influence on the State for good or for evil.[2] And now, since the question is still 450 undetermined, and you are taking in hand another State, we have resolved, as you heard, not to let you go until you give an account of all this.

To that resolution, said Glaucon, you may regard me as saying: Agreed.

And without more ado, said Thrasymachus, you may consider us all to be equally agreed.

I said, You know not what you are doing in thus assailing me: What an argument are you raising about the State! Just as I thought that I had finished, and was only too glad that I had laid this question to sleep, and was reflecting how fortunate I was in your acceptance of what I then said, you ask me to begin again at b the very foundation, ignorant of what a hornet's nest of words you are stirring. Now I foresaw this gathering trouble, and avoided it.

For what purpose do you conceive that we have come here, said Thrasymachus—to look for gold, or to hear discourse?

Yes, but discourse should have a limit.

Yes, Socrates, said Glaucon, and the whole of life is the only limit which wise men assign to the hearing of such discourses. But never mind about us; take heart yourself and answer the question c in your own way: What sort of community of women and children is this which is to prevail among our guardians? and how shall we manage the period between birth and education, which seems to require the greatest care? Tell us how these things will be.

Yes, my simple friend, but the answer is the reverse of easy; many more doubts arise about this than about our previous conclusions. For the practicability of what is said may be doubted; and looked at in another point of view, whether the scheme, if ever so practicable, would be for the best, is also doubtful. Hence d I feel a reluctance to approach the subject, lest our aspiration, my dear friend, should turn out to be a dream only.

Fear not, he replied, for your audience will not be hard upon you; they are not sceptical or hostile.

I said: My good friend, I suppose that you mean to encourage me by these words.

Yes, he said.

Then let me tell you that you are doing just the reverse; the encouragement which you offer would have been all very well had I myself believed that I knew what I was talking about. To declare the truth about matters of high interest which a man honors and loves, among wise men who love him, need occasion no fear or faltering in his mind; but to carry on an argument when you are yourself only a hesitating inquirer, which is my condition, is a dangerous and slippery thing; and the danger is not that I shall be laughed at (of which the fear would be childish), but that I shall miss the truth where I have most need to be sure of my footing, and drag my friends after me in my fall.[3] And I pray Nemesis* not to visit upon me the words which I am going to utter. For I do indeed believe that to be an involuntary homicide is a less crime than to be a deceiver about beauty, or goodness, or justice, in the matter of laws. And that is a risk which I would rather run among enemies than among friends; and therefore you do well to encourage me.

Glaucon laughed and said: Well, then, Socrates, in case you and your argument do us any serious injury you shall be acquitted beforehand of the homicide, and shall not be held to be a deceiver; take courage then and speak.

Well, I said, the law says that when a man is acquitted he is free from guilt, and what holds at law may hold in argument.

Then why should you mind?

Well, I replied, I suppose that I must retrace my steps and say what I perhaps ought to have said before in the proper place. The part of the men has been played out, and now properly enough comes the turn of the women. Of them I will proceed to speak, and the more readily since I am invited by you.

For men born and educated like our citizens, the only way, in my opinion, of arriving at a right conclusion about the possession and use of women and children is to follow the path on which we

* Goddess and personification of retribution.

originally started, when we said that the men were to be the guardians and watch-dogs of the herd.

True.

d   Let us further suppose the birth and education of our women to be subject to similar or nearly similar regulations; then we shall see whether the result accords with our design.

What do you mean?

What I mean may be put into the form of a question, I said: Are dogs divided into he's and she's, or do they both share equally in hunting and in keeping watch and in the other duties of dogs? or do we intrust to the males the entire and exclusive care of the flocks, while we leave the females at home, under the idea that the bearing and the suckling of their puppies are labor enough for them?

e   No, he said, they share alike; the only difference between them is that the males are stronger and the females weaker.

But can you use different animals for the same purpose, unless they are bred and fed in the same way?

You cannot.

Then, if women are to have the same duties as men, they must have the same nurture and education?

452   Yes.

The education which was assigned to the men was music and gymnastics.

Yes.

Then women must be taught music and gymnastics and also the art of war, which they must practise like the men?

That is the inference, I suppose.

I should rather expect, I said, that several of our proposals if they are carried out, being unusual, may appear ridiculous.[4]

No doubt of it.

Yes, and the most ridiculous thing of all will be the sight of women naked in the palæstra,* exercising with the men, especially when they are no longer young; they certainly will not be a vision

---

*That is, a wrestling school. Spartan women exercised and trained in public. Athenians of the classical period found the Spartan practice distasteful and ridiculous.

of beauty, any more than the enthusiastic old men who, in spite of   b
wrinkles and ugliness, continue to frequent the gymnasia.

Yes, indeed, he said: according to present notions the proposal
would be thought ridiculous.

But then, I said, as we have determined to speak our minds, we
must not fear the jests of the wits which will be directed against
this sort of innovation; how they will talk of women's attainments,
both in music and gymnastics, and above all about their wearing
armor and riding upon horseback!   c

Very true, he replied.

Yet, having begun, we must go forward to the rough places of
the law; at the same time begging of these gentlemen* for once in
their lives to be serious. Not long ago, as we shall remind them,
the Hellenes were of the opinion, which is still generally received
among the barbarians, that the sight of a naked man was ridiculous
and improper; and when first the Cretans, and then the Lacedæ-
monians, introduced the custom,[5] the wits of that day might equally
have ridiculed the innovation.   d

No doubt.

But when experience showed that to let all things be uncovered
was far better than to cover them up, and the ludicrous effect to
the outward eye had vanished before the better principle which
reason asserted, then the man was perceived to be a fool who directs the shafts of his ridicule at any other sight but that of folly
and vice, or seriously inclines to weigh the beautiful by any other
standard but that of the good.   e

Very true, he replied.

First, then, whether the question is to be put in jest or in earnest,
let us come to an understanding about the nature of woman: Is
she capable of sharing either wholly or partially in the actions of   453
men, or not at all? And is the art of war one of those arts in which
she can or cannot share? That will be the best way of commencing
the inquiry, and will probably lead to the fairest conclusion.

That will be much the best way.

---

*That is, the hypothetical critics of Socrates' proposals concerning the training of
female guardians. See also the references to "the adversary's position" and "our
opponents" below in 453a–b.

Shall we take the other side first and begin by arguing against ourselves? in this manner the adversary's position will not be undefended.

b   Why not? he said.

Then let us put a speech into the mouths of our opponents. They will say: "Socrates and Glaucon, no adversary need convict you, for you yourselves, at the first foundation of the State, admitted the principle that everybody was to do the one work suited to his own nature." And certainly, if I am not mistaken, such an admission was made by us. "And do not the natures of men and women differ very much indeed?" And we shall reply, Of course they do. Then we shall be asked, "Whether the tasks assigned to men and to women should not be different, and such as are agree-

c   able to their different natures?" Certainly they should. "But if so, have you not fallen into a serious inconsistency in saying that men and women, whose natures are so entirely different, ought to perform the same actions?" What defence will you make for us, my good sir, against anyone who offers these objections?

That is not an easy question to answer when asked suddenly; and I shall and I do beg of you to draw out the case on our side.

These are the objections, Glaucon, and there are many others of a like kind, which I foresaw long ago; they made me afraid and

d   reluctant to take in hand any law about the possession and nurture of women and children.

By Zeus, he said, the problem to be solved is anything but easy.

Why, yes, I said, but the fact is that when a man is out of his depth, whether he has fallen into a little swimming-bath or into mid-ocean, he has to swim all the same.

Very true.

And must not we swim and try to reach the shore—we will hope that Arion's dolphin* or some other miraculous help may save us?

e   I suppose so, he said.

Well, then, let us see if any way of escape can be found. We acknowledged—did we not?—that different natures ought to have

---

*Arion (seventh century B.C.E.) was a musician from Lesbos; a dolphin supposedly rescued him after he was thrown overboard.

different pursuits, and that men's and women's natures are different. And now what are we saying?—that different natures ought to have the same pursuits—this is the inconsistency which is charged upon us.

Precisely.

Verily, Glaucon, I said, glorious is the power of the art of contradiction![6]   454

Why do you say so?

Because I think that many a man falls into the practice against his will. When he thinks that he is reasoning he is really disputing, just because he cannot define and divide, and so know that of which he is speaking; and he will pursue a merely verbal opposition in the spirit of contention and not of fair discussion.

Yes, he replied, such is very often the case; but what has that to do with us and our argument?

A great deal; for there is certainly a danger of our getting unintentionally into a verbal opposition.   b

In what way?

Why we valiantly and pugnaciously insist upon the verbal truth, that different natures ought to have different pursuits, but we never considered at all what was the meaning of sameness or difference of nature, or why we distinguished them when we assigned different pursuits to different natures and the same to the same natures.

Why, no, he said, that was never considered by us.

I said: Suppose that by way of illustration we were to ask the   c
question whether there is not an opposition in nature between bald men and hairy men; and if this is admitted by us, then, if bald men are cobblers, we should forbid the hairy men to be cobblers, and conversely?

That would be a jest, he said.

Yes, I said, a jest; and why? because we never meant when we constructed the State, that the opposition of natures should extend to every difference, but only to those differences which affected the pursuit in which the individual is engaged; we should   d
have argued, for example, that a physician and one who is in mind a physician may be said to have the same nature.[7]

True.

Whereas the physician and the carpenter have different natures?
Certainly.

And if, I said, the male and female sex appear to differ in their fitness for any art or pursuit, we should say that such pursuit or art ought to be assigned to one or the other of them; but if the difference consists only in women bearing and men begetting children, this does not amount to a proof that a woman differs from a man in respect of the sort of education she should receive;[8] and we shall therefore continue to maintain that our guardians and their wives ought to have the same pursuits.

Very true, he said.

Next, we shall ask our opponent how, in reference to any of the pursuits or arts of civic life, the nature of a woman differs from that of a man?

That will be quite fair.

And perhaps he, like yourself, will reply that to give a sufficient answer on the instant is not easy; but after a little reflection there is no difficulty.

Yes, perhaps.

Suppose then that we invite him to accompany us in the argument, and then we may hope to show him that there is nothing peculiar in the constitution of women which would affect them in the administration of the State.

By all means.

Let us say to him: Come now, and we will ask you a question: When you spoke of a nature gifted or not gifted in any respect, did you mean to say that one man will acquire a thing easily, another with difficulty; a little learning will lead the one to discover a great deal, whereas the other, after much study and application, no sooner learns than he forgets; or again, did you mean, that the one has a body which is a good servant to his mind, while the body of the other is a hinderance to him?—would not these be the sort of differences which distinguish the man gifted by nature from the one who is ungifted?

No one will deny that.

And can you mention any pursuit of mankind in which the male sex has not all these gifts and qualities in a higher degree than the female? Need I waste time in speaking of the art of weaving, and

the management of pancakes and preserves, in which womankind
does really appear to be great, and in which for her to be beaten by
a man is of all things the most absurd?   d

You are quite right, he replied, in maintaining the general inferiority of the female sex: although many women are in many things
superior to many men, yet on the whole what you say is true.

And if so, my friend, I said, there is no special faculty of administration in a State which a woman has because she is a woman, or
which a man has by virtue of his sex, but the gifts of nature are alike
diffused in both; all the pursuits of men are the pursuits of women
also, but in all of them a woman is inferior to a man.   e

Very true.

Then are we to impose all our enactments on men and none of
them on women?

That will never do.

One woman has a gift of healing, another not; one is a musician,
and another has no music in her nature?

Very true.

And one woman has a turn for gymnastic and military exer-   456
cises, and another is unwarlike and hates gymnastics?

Certainly.

And one woman is a philosopher, and another is an enemy of
philosophy; one has spirit, and another is without spirit?

That is also true.

Then one woman will have the temper of a guardian, and another not. Was not the selection of the male guardians determined by differences of this sort?

Yes.

Men and women alike possess the qualities which make a
guardian; they differ only in their comparative strength or weakness.

Obviously.

And those women who have such qualities are to be selected as   b
the companions and colleagues of men who have similar qualities
and whom they resemble in capacity and in character?

Very true.

And ought not the same natures to have the same pursuits?

They ought.

Then, as we were saying before, there is nothing unnatural in assigning music and gymnastics to the wives of the guardians—to that point we come round again.

Certainly not.

c   The law which we then enacted was agreeable to nature, and therefore not an impossibility or mere aspiration; and the contrary practice, which prevails at present, is in reality a violation of nature.

That appears to be true.

We had to consider, first, whether our proposals were possible, and secondly whether they were the most beneficial?

Yes.

And the possibility has been acknowledged?

Yes.

The very great benefit has next to be established?

Quite so.

You will admit that the same education which makes a man a good guardian will make a woman a good guardian; for their orig-
d   inal nature is the same?

Yes.

I should like to ask you a question.

What is it?

Would you say that all men are equal in excellence, or is one man better than another?

The latter.

And in the commonwealth which we were founding do you conceive the guardians who have been brought up on our model system to be more perfect men, or the cobblers whose education has been cobbling?

What a ridiculous question!

You have answered me, I replied: Well, and may we not further
e   say that our guardians are the best of our citizens?

By far the best.

And will not their wives be the best women?

Yes, by far the best.

And can there be anything better for the interests of the State than that the men and women of a State should be as good as possible?

There can be nothing better.

And this is what the arts of music and gymnastics, when present in such a manner as we have described, will accomplish? 457

Certainly.

Then we have made an enactment not only possible but in the highest degree beneficial to the State?

True.

Then let the wives of our guardians strip, for their virtue will be their robe, and let them share in the toils of war and the defence of their country; only in the distribution of labors the lighter are to be assigned to the women, who are the weaker natures, but in other respects their duties are to be the same. And as for the man who laughs at naked women exercising their bodies from the best b of motives, in his laughter he is plucking

"A fruit of unripe wisdom,"*

and he himself is ignorant of what he is laughing at, or what he is about; for that is, and ever will be, the best of sayings, "that the useful is the noble, and the hurtful is the base."

Very true.

Here, then, is one difficulty in our law about women, which we may say that we have now escaped; the wave has not swallowed us up alive for enacting that the guardians of either sex should have all their pursuits in common; to the utility and also to the possibil- c ity of this arrangement the consistency of the argument with itself bears witness.

Yes, that was a mighty wave which you have escaped.[9]

Yes, I said, but a greater is coming; you will not think much of this when you see the next.

Go on; let me see.

The law, I said, which is the sequel of this and of all that has preceded, is to the following effect, "that the wives of our guardians are to be common, and their children are to be common, and no d parent is to know his own child, nor any child his parent."

---

*From a lost poem by Pindar.

Yes, he said, that is a much greater wave than the other; and the
possibility as well as the utility of such a law are far more ques-
tionable.

I do not think, I said, that there can be any dispute about the
very great utility of having wives and children in common; the
possibility is quite another matter, and will be very much disputed.

e   I think that a good many doubts may be raised about both.

You imply that the two questions must be combined, I replied.
Now I meant that you should admit the utility; and in this way, as
I thought, I should escape from one of them, and then there would
remain only the possibility.

But that little attempt is detected, and therefore you will please
to give a defence of both.

Well, I said, I submit to my fate. Yet grant me a little favor: let
458   me feast my mind with the dream as day-dreamers are in the habit
of feasting themselves when they are walking alone; for before
they have discovered any means of effecting their wishes—that is
a matter which never troubles them—they would rather not tire
themselves by thinking about possibilities; but assuming that what
they desire is already granted to them, they proceed with their
plan, and delight in detailing what they mean to do when their
wish has come true—that is a way which they have of not doing
much good to a capacity which was never good for much. Now
b   I myself am beginning to lose heart, and I should like, with your
permission, to pass over the question of possibility at present. Assuming therefore the possibility of the proposal, I shall now proceed to inquire how the rulers will carry out these arrangements,
and I shall demonstrate that our plan, if executed, will be of the
greatest benefit to the State and to the guardians. First of all, then,
if you have no objection, I will endeavor with your help to consider
the advantages of the measure; and hereafter the question of possibility.

I have no objection; proceed.

First, I think that if our rulers and their auxiliaries are to be wor-
c   thy of the name which they bear, there must be willingness to obey
in the one and the power of command in the other; the guardians
themselves must obey the laws, and they must also imitate the
spirit of them in any details which are intrusted to their care.

That is right, he said.

You, I said, who are their legislator, having selected the men, will now select the women and give them to them; they must be as far as possible of like natures with them; and they must live in common houses and meet at common meals. None of them will have anything specially his or her own; they will be together, and d will be brought up together, and will associate at gymnastic exercises. And so they will be drawn by a necessity of their natures to have intercourse with each other—necessity is not too strong a word, I think?

Yes, he said; necessity, not geometrical, but another sort of necessity which lovers know, and which is far more convincing and constraining to the mass of mankind.[10]

True, I said; and this, Glaucon, like all the rest must proceed after an orderly fashion; in a city of the blessed,* licentiousness is an unholy thing which the rulers will forbid. e

Yes, he said, and it ought not to be permitted.

Then clearly the next thing will be to make matrimony sacred in the highest degree,[11] and what is most beneficial will be deemed sacred?

Exactly.

And how can marriages be made most beneficial? that is a question which I put to you, because I see in your house dogs for hunting, and of the nobler sort of birds not a few. Now, I beseech you, do tell me, have you ever attended to their pairing and breeding? 459

In what particulars?

Why, in the first place, although they are all of a good sort, are not some better than others?

True.

And do you breed from them all indifferently, or do you take care to breed from the best only?

From the best.

And do you take the oldest or the youngest, or only those of b ripe age?

I choose only those of ripe age.

---

*Literally, in the city of the *eudaimones*; see note 13 on 1.344a.

And if care was not taken in the breeding, your dogs and birds would greatly deteriorate?

Certainly.

And the same of horses and of animals in general?

Undoubtedly.

Good heavens! my dear friend, I said, what consummate skill will our rulers need if the same principle holds of the human species!

Certainly, the same principle holds; but why does this involve c any particular skill?

Because, I said, our rulers will often have to practise upon the body corporate with medicines. Now you know that when patients do not require medicines, but have only to be put under a regimen, the inferior sort of practitioner is deemed to be good enough; but when medicine has to be given, then the doctor should be more of a man.

That is quite true, he said; but to what are you alluding?

I mean, I replied, that our rulers will find a considerable dose of falsehood and deceit necessary for the good of their subjects: we were saying that the use of all these things regarded as medi- d cines might be of advantage.[12]

And we were very right.

And this lawful use of them seems likely to be often needed in the regulations of marriages and births.

How so?

Why, I said, the principle has been already laid down that the best of either sex should be united with the best as often, and the inferior with the inferior as seldom, as possible; and that they should rear the offspring of the one sort of union, but not of the other, if the flock is to be maintained in first-rate condi- tion. Now these goings on must be a secret which the rulers only e know, or there will be a further danger of our herd, as the guardians may be termed, breaking out into rebellion.

Very true.

Had we better not appoint certain festivals at which we will bring together the brides and bridegrooms, and sacrifices will be offered and suitable wedding songs composed by our poets: the 460   number of weddings is a matter which must be left to the discretion of the rulers, whose aim will be to preserve the average of population? There are many other things which they will have to consider, such as the effects of wars and diseases and any similar agencies, in order as far as this is possible to prevent the State from becoming either too large or too small.

Certainly, he replied.

We shall have to invent some ingenious kind of lots which the less worthy may draw on each occasion of our bringing them together, and then they will accuse their own ill-luck and not the rulers.

To be sure, he said.

And I think that our braver and better youth, besides their   b
other honors and rewards, might have greater facilities of intercourse with women given them; their bravery will be a reason, and such fathers ought to have as many sons as possible.

True.

And the proper officers, whether male or female or both, for offices are to be held by women as well as by men——

Yes——

The proper officers will take the offspring of the good parents   c
to the pen or fold, and there they will deposit them with certain nurses who dwell in a separate quarter; but the offspring of the inferior, or of the better when they chance to be deformed, will be put away in some mysterious, unknown place, as they should be.[13]

Yes, he said, that must be done if the breed of the guardians is to be kept pure.

They will provide for their nurture, and will bring the mothers to the fold when they are full of milk, taking the greatest possible   d
care that no mother recognizes her own child; and other wet-nurses may be engaged if more are required. Care will also be taken that the process of suckling shall not be protracted too long; and the mothers will have no getting up at night or other trouble, but will hand over all this sort of thing to the nurses and attendants.

You suppose the wives of our guardians to have a fine easy time of it when they are having children.

Why, said I, and so they ought. Let us, however, proceed with our scheme. We were saying that the parents should be in the prime of life?

Very true.

e   And what is the prime of life? May it not be defined as a period
of about twenty years in a woman's life, and thirty years in a
man's?

Which years do you mean to include?

A woman, I said, at twenty years of age may begin to bear children to the State, and continue to bear them until forty;[14] a man
may begin at five-and-twenty, when he has passed the point at
which the pulse of life beats quickest, and continue to beget children until he be fifty-five.

461   Certainly, he said, both in men and women those years are the
prime of physical as well as of intellectual vigor.

Anyone above or below the prescribed ages who takes part in
the public hymeneals shall be said to have done an unholy and
unrighteous thing; the child of which he is the father, if it steals
into life, will have been conceived under auspices very unlike the
sacrifices and prayers, which at each hymeneal priestesses and
priests and the whole city will offer, that the new generation may
be better and more useful than their good and useful parents,
b   whereas his child will be the offspring of darkness and strange
lust.

Very true, he replied.

And the same law will apply to any one of those within the prescribed age who forms a connection with any woman in the prime
of life without the sanction of the rulers; for we shall say that he is
raising up a bastard to the State, uncertified and unconsecrated.

Very true, he replied.

This applies, however, only to those who are within the speci-
fied age: after that we will allow them to range at will, except that
a man may not marry his daughter or his daughter's daughter, or
c   his mother or his mother's mother; and women, on the other hand,
are prohibited from marrying their sons or fathers, or son's son or
father's father, and so on in either direction. And we grant all this,
accompanying the permission with strict orders to prevent any
embryo which may come into being from seeing the light; and if
any force a way to the birth, the parents must understand that the
offspring of such a union cannot be maintained, and arrange accordingly.

That also, he said, is a reasonable proposition. But how will they know who are fathers and daughters, and so on?   d

They will never know. The way will be this: dating from the day of the hymeneal, the bridegroom who was then married will call all the male children who are born in the seventh and the tenth month° afterward his sons, and the female children his daughters, and they will call him father, and he will call their children his grandchildren, and they will call the elder generation grandfathers and grandmothers. All who were begotten at the time when their fathers and mothers came together will be called their brothers and sisters, and these, as I was saying, will be forbidden to inter-   e marry. This, however, is not to be understood as an absolute prohibition of the marriage of brothers and sisters; if the lot favors them, and they receive the sanction of the Pythian oracle,† the law will allow them.

Quite right, he replied.

Such is the scheme, Glaucon, according to which the guardians of our State are to have their wives and families in common. And now you would have the argument show that this community is consistent with the rest of our polity, and also that nothing can be better—would you not?   462

Yes, certainly.

Shall we try to find a common basis by asking of ourselves what ought to be the chief aim of the legislator in making laws and in the organization of a State—what is the greatest good, and what is the greatest evil, and then consider whether our previous description has the stamp of the good or of the evil?

By all means.

Can there be any greater evil than discord and distraction and plurality where unity ought to reign? or any greater good than the   b bond of unity?

There cannot.

°Some ancient medical writers claimed that children are not born in the eighth month of pregnancy; this perhaps explains Socrates' choice of wording.

†See 4.427b for Socrates' designation of Apollo as the patron deity of the ideal state and for Apollo's association with the Pythian oracle at Delphi; compare 7.540b–c.

And there is unity where there is community of pleasures and pains—where all the citizens are glad or grieved on the same occasions of joy and sorrow?

No doubt.

Yes; and where there is no common but only private feeling a State is disorganized—when you have one-half of the world triumphing and the other plunged in grief at the same events happening to the city or the citizens?

c

Certainly.

Such differences commonly originate in a disagreement about the use of the terms "mine" and "not mine," "his" and "not his."

Exactly so.

And is not that the best-ordered State in which the greatest number of persons apply the terms "mine" and "not mine" in the same way to the same thing?[15]

Quite true.

Or that again which most nearly approaches to the condition of the individual—as in the body, when but a finger of one of us is hurt, the whole frame, drawn toward the soul as a centre and forming one kingdom under the ruling power therein, feels the hurt and sympathizes all together with the part affected, and we say that the man has a pain in his finger; and the same expression is used about any other part of the body, which has a sensation of pain at suffering or of pleasure at the alleviation of suffering.

d

Very true, he replied; and I agree with you that in the best-ordered State there is the nearest approach to this common feeling which you describe.

Then when any one of the citizens experiences any good or evil, the whole State will make his case their own, and will either rejoice or sorrow with him?

e

Yes, he said, that is what will happen in a well-ordered State.

It will now be time, I said, for us to return to our State and see whether this or some other form is most in accordance with these fundamental principles.

Very good.

Our State, like every other, has rulers and subjects?

463

True.

All of whom will call one another citizens?

Of course.

But is there not another name which people give to their rulers in other States?

Generally they call them masters, but in democratic States they simply call them rulers.

And in our State what other name besides that of citizens do the people give the rulers?

They are called saviours and helpers, he replied.   b

And what do the rulers call the people?

Their maintainers and foster-fathers.

And what do they call them in other States?

Slaves.

And what do the rulers call one another in other States?

Fellow-rulers.

And what in ours?

Fellow-guardians.

Did you ever know an example in any other State of a ruler who would speak of one of his colleagues as his friend and of another as not being his friend?

Yes, very often.

And the friend he regards and describes as one in whom he has an interest, and the other as a stranger in whom he has no in-   c
terest?

Exactly.

But would any of your guardians think or speak of any other guardian as a stranger?

Certainly he would not; for everyone whom they meet will be regarded by them either as a brother or sister, or father or mother, or son or daughter, or as the child or parent of those who are thus connected with him.

Capital, I said; but let me ask you once more: Shall they be a family in name only; or shall they in all their actions be true to the name? For example, in the use of the word "father," would the care   d
of a father be implied and the filial reverence and duty and obedience to him which the law commands; and is the violator of these duties to be regarded as an impious and unrighteous person who is not likely to receive much good either at the hands of God or of man? Are these to be or not to be the strains which the children

will hear repeated in their ears by all the citizens about those who are intimated to them to be their parents and the rest of their kinsfolk?

These, he said, and none other; for what can be more ridiculous than for them to utter the names of family ties with the lips only and not to act in the spirit of them?

Then in our city the language of harmony and concord will be more often heard than in any other. As I was describing before, when anyone is well or ill, the universal word will be "with me it is well" or "it is ill."

Most true.

And agreeably to this mode of thinking and speaking, were we not saying that they will have their pleasures and pains in common?

Yes, and so they will.

And they will have a common interest in the same thing which they will alike call "my own," and having this common interest they will have a common feeling of pleasure and pain?

Yes, far more so than in other States.

And the reason of this, over and above the general constitution of the State, will be that the guardians will have a community of women and children?

That will be the chief reason.

And this unity of feeling we admitted to be the greatest good, as was implied in our comparison of a well-ordered State to the relation of the body and the members, when affected by pleasure or pain?

That we acknowledged, and very rightly.

Then the community of wives and children among our citizens is clearly the source of the greatest good to the State?

Certainly.

And this agrees with the other principle which we were affirming—that the guardians were not to have houses or lands or any other property; their pay was to be their food, which they were to receive from the other citizens, and they were to have no private expenses; for we intended them to preserve their true character of guardians.

Right, he replied.

Both the community of property and the community of families, as I am saying, tend to make them more truly guardians; they will not tear the city in pieces by differing about "mine" and "not mine;" each man dragging any acquisition which he has made into a separate house of his own, where he has a separate wife and d children and private pleasures and pains; but all will be affected as far as may be by the same pleasures and pains because they are all of one opinion about what is near and dear to them, and therefore they all tend toward a common end.

Certainly, he replied.

And as they have nothing but their persons which they can call their own, suits and complaints will have no existence among them; they will be delivered from all those quarrels of which money or e children or relations are the occasion.

Of course they will.

Neither will trials for assault or insult ever be likely to occur among them. For that equals should defend themselves against equals we shall maintain to be honorable and right; we shall compel them to care for their bodies.

That is good, he said.

Yes; and there is a further good in the law; viz., that if a man 465 has a quarrel with another he will satisfy his resentment then and there, and not proceed to more dangerous lengths.

Certainly.

To the elder shall be assigned the duty of ruling and chastising the younger.

Clearly.

Nor can there be a doubt that the younger will not strike or do any other violence to an elder, unless the magistrates command him; nor will he slight him in any way. For there are two guardians, shame and fear, mighty to prevent him: shame, which makes men refrain from laying hands on those who are to them in the relation b of parents; fear, that the injured one will be succored by the others who are his brothers, sons, fathers.

That is true, he replied.

Then in every way the laws will help the citizens to keep the peace with one another?

Yes, there will be no want of peace.

And as the guardians will never quarrel among themselves there will be no danger of the rest of the city being divided either against them or against one another.

None whatever.

c   I hardly like even to mention the little meannesses of which they will be rid, for they are beneath notice: such, for example, as the flattery of the rich by the poor, and all the pains and pangs which men experience in bringing up a family, and in finding money to buy necessaries for their household, borrowing and then repudiating, getting how they can, and giving the money into the hands of women and slaves to keep—the many evils of so many kinds which people suffer in this way are mean enough and obvious enough, and not worth speaking of.

d   Yes, he said, a man has no need of eyes in order to perceive that.

And from all these evils they will be delivered, and their life will be blessed as the life of Olympic victors and yet more blessed.

How so?

The Olympic victor, I said, is deemed happy in receiving a part only of the blessedness which is secured to our citizens, who have won a more glorious victory and have a more complete maintenance at the public cost.[16] For the victory which they have won is the salvation of the whole State; and the crown with which they and their children are crowned is the fulness of all that life needs; e they receive rewards from the hands of their country while living, and after death have an honorable burial.

Do you remember, I said, how in the course of the previous discussion someone who shall be nameless accused us of making 466 our guardians unhappy—they had nothing and might have possessed all things—to whom we replied that, if an occasion offered, we might perhaps hereafter consider this question, but that, as at present divided, we would make our guardians truly guardians, and that we were fashioning the State with a view to the greatest happiness, not of any particular class, but of the whole?

Yes, I remember.

And what do you say, now that the life of our protectors is made out to be far better and nobler than that of Olympic victors—is b the life of shoemakers, or any other artisans, or of husbandmen, to be compared with it?

Certainly not.

At the same time I ought here to repeat what I have said else-where, that if any of our guardians shall try to be happy in such a manner that he will cease to be a guardian, and is not content with this safe and harmonious life, which, in our judgment, is of all lives the best, but, infatuated by some youthful conceit of happiness which gets up into his head shall seek to appropriate the whole State to himself, then he will have to learn how wisely Hesiod spoke, when he said, "half is more than the whole."*

If he were to consult me, I should say to him: Stay where you are, when you have the offer of such a life.

You agree then, I said, that men and women are to have a com-mon way of life such as we have described—common education, common children; and they are to watch over the citizens in com-mon whether abiding in the city or going out to war; they are to keep watch together, and to hunt together like dogs; and always and in all things, as far as they are able, women are to share with the men? And in so doing they will do what is best, and will not vi-olate, but preserve, the natural relation of the sexes.

I agree with you, he replied.

The inquiry, I said, has yet to be made, whether such a commu-nity will be found possible—as among other animals, so also among men—and if possible, in what way possible?[17]

You have anticipated the question which I was about to suggest.

There is no difficulty, I said, in seeing how war will be carried on by them.

How?

Why, of course they will go on expeditions together; and will take with them any of their children who are strong enough, that, after the manner of the artisan's child, they may look on at the work which they will have to do when they are grown up; and be-sides looking on they will have to help and be of use in war, and to wait upon their fathers and mothers. Did you never observe in the arts how the potters' boys look on and help, long before they touch the wheel?

Works and Days 40.

Yes, I have.

And shall potters be more careful in educating their children and in giving them the opportunity of seeing and practising their duties than our guardians will be?

The idea is ridiculous, he said.

There is also the effect on the parents, with whom, as with other animals, the presence of their young ones will be the great-
b est incentive to valor.

That is quite true, Socrates; and yet if they are defeated, which may often happen in war, how great the danger is! the children will be lost as well as their parents, and the State will never re-cover.

True, I said; but would you never allow them to run any risk?

I am far from saying that.

Well, but if they are ever to run a risk should they not do so on some occasion when, if they escape disaster, they will be the bet-ter for it?

Clearly.

c Whether the future soldiers do or do not see war in the days of their youth is a very important matter, for the sake of which some risk may fairly be incurred.

Yes, very important.

This then must be our first step—to make our children specta-tors of war; but we must also contrive that they shall be secured against danger; then all will be well.

True.

Their parents may be supposed not to be blind to the risks of
d war, but to know, as far as human foresight can, what expeditions are safe and what dangerous?

That may be assumed.

And they will take them on the safe expeditions and be cautious about the dangerous ones?

True.

And they will place them under the command of experienced veterans who will be their leaders and teachers?

Very properly.

Still, the dangers of war cannot be always foreseen; there is a good deal of chance about them?

True.

Then against such chances the children must be at once furnished with wings, in order that in the hour of need they may fly away and escape.

What do you mean? he said.   e

I mean that we must mount them on horses in their earliest youth, and when they have learnt to ride, take them on horseback to see war: the horses must not be spirited and warlike, but the most tractable and yet the swiftest that can be had. In this way they will get an excellent view of what is hereafter to be their own business; and if there is danger they have only to follow their elder leaders and escape.

I believe that you are right, he said.

Next, as to war; what are to be the relations of your soldiers to   468 one another and to their enemies? I should be inclined to propose that the soldier who leaves his rank or throws away his arms, or is guilty of any other act of cowardice, should be degraded into the rank of a husbandman or artisan. What do you think?

By all means, I should say.

And he who allows himself to be taken prisoner may as well be made a present of to his enemies; he is their lawful prey, and let them do what they like with him.

Certainly.   b

But the hero who has distinguished himself, what shall be done to him? In the first place, he shall receive honor in the army from his youthful comrades; every one of them in succession shall crown him.* What do you say?

I approve.

And what do you say to his receiving the right hand of fellowship?

To that too, I agree.

But you will hardly agree to my next proposal.

What is your proposal?

That he should kiss and be kissed by them.

Most certainly, and I should be disposed to go further, and say:

---

*That is, with garlands.

c   Let no one whom he has a mind to kiss refuse to be kissed by him
while the expedition lasts. So that if there be a lover in the army,
whether his love be youth or maiden, he may be more eager to win
the prize of valor.

Capital, I said. That the brave man is to have more wives than
others has been already determined: and he is to have first choices
in such matters more than others, in order that he may have as
many children as possible?

Agreed.

Again, there is another manner in which, according to Homer,
d   brave youths should be honored; for he tells how Ajax, after he had
distinguished himself in battle, was rewarded with long chines,*
which seems to be a compliment appropriate to a hero in the
flower of his age, being not only a tribute of honor but also a very
strengthening thing.

Most true, he said.

Then in this, I said, Homer shall be our teacher; and we too, at
sacrifices and on the like occasions, will honor the brave according
to the measure of their valor, whether men or women, with hymns
and those other distinctions which we were mentioning; also with

"seats of precedence, and meats and full cups;"[†]

e   and in honoring them, we shall be at the same time training them.

That, he replied, is excellent.

Yes, I said; and when a man dies gloriously in war shall we not
say, in the first place, that he is of the golden race?

To be sure.

Nay, have we not the authority of Hesiod for affirming that
469   when they are dead

"They are holy angels upon the earth, authors of good, averters of
evil, the guardians of speech-gifted men"?[‡]

---

*Reference to *Iliad* 7.321–322.
†*Iliad* 8.162.
‡*Works and Days* 121–122. The verses describe how members of the primeval
golden race became, after their blessed lives and painless deaths, "guardians"
(*phylakes*) of the living.

Yes; and we accept his authority.

We must learn of the god* now we are to order the sepulture of divine and heroic personages, and what is to be their special distinction; and we must do as he bids?

By all means.

And in ages to come we will reverence them and kneel before their sepulchres as at the graves of heroes. And not only they, but any who are deemed pre-eminently good, whether they die from age or in any other way, shall be admitted to the same honors.

That is very right, he said.

Next, how shall our soldiers treat their enemies? What about this?

In what respect do you mean?

First of all, in regard to slavery? Do you think it right that Hellenes should enslave Hellenic States, or allow others to enslave them, if they can help?[18] Should not their custom be to spare them, considering the danger which there is that the whole race may one day fall under the yoke of the barbarians?

To spare them is infinitely better.

Then no Hellene should be owned by them as a slave; that is a rule which they will observe and advise the other Hellenes to observe.

Certainly, he said; they will in this way be united against the barbarians and will keep their hands off one another.

Next as to the slain; ought the conquerors, I said, to take anything but their armor? Does not the practice of despoiling an enemy afford an excuse for not facing the battle? Cowards skulk about the dead, pretending that they are fulfilling a duty, and many an army before now has been lost from this love of plunder.

Very true.

And is there not illiberality and avarice in robbing a corpse,[19] and also a degree of meanness and womanishness in making an enemy of the dead body when the real enemy has flown away and left only his fighting gear behind him—is not this rather like a dog

---

*That is, Apollo; compare 5.470a.

e who cannot get at his assailant, quarrelling with the stones which strike him instead?

Very like a dog, he said.

Then we must abstain from spoiling the dead or hindering their burial?

Yes, he replied, we most certainly must.

Neither shall we offer up arms at the temples of the gods, least of all the arms of Hellenes, if we care to maintain good feeling with
470 other Hellenes; and, indeed, we have reason to fear that the offering of spoils taken from kinsmen may be a pollution unless commanded by the god himself?

Very true.

Again, as to the devastation of Hellenic territory or the burning of houses, what is to be the practice?

May I have the pleasure, he said, of hearing your opinion?

Both should be forbidden, in my judgment; I would take the
b annual produce and no more. Shall I tell you why?

Pray do.

Why, you see, there is a difference in the names "discord" and "war," and I imagine that there is also a difference in their natures; the one is expressive of what is internal and domestic, the other of what is external and foreign; and the first of the two is termed discord, and only the second, war.

That is a very proper distinction, he replied.

c And may I not observe with equal propriety that the Hellenic race is all united together by ties of blood and friendship, and alien and strange to the barbarians?

Very good, he said.

And therefore when Hellenes fight with barbarians, and barbarians with Hellenes, they will be described by us as being at war when they fight, and by nature enemies, and this kind of antagonism should be called war; but when Hellenes fight with one another we shall say that Hellas is then in a state of disorder and discord,[20] they being by nature friends; and such enmity is to be
d called discord.

I agree.

Consider then, I said, when that which we have acknowledged to be discord occurs, and a city is divided, if both parties destroy the lands and burn the houses of one another, how wicked does the strife appear! No true lover of his country would bring himself to tear in pieces his own nurse and mother: There might be reason in the conqueror depriving the conquered of their harvest, but still they would have the idea of peace in their hearts, and would not mean to go on fighting forever.   e

Yes, he said, that is a better temper than the other.

And will not the city, which you are founding, be an Hellenic city?

It ought to be, he replied.

Then will not the citizens be good and civilized?

Yes, very civilized.

And will they not be lovers of Hellas, and think of Hellas as their own land, and share in the common temples?

Most certainly.

And any difference which arises among them will be regarded   471
by them as discord only—a quarrel among friends, which is not to be called a war?

Certainly not.

Then they will quarrel as those who intend some day to be reconciled?

Certainly.

They will use friendly correction, but will not enslave or destroy their opponents, they will be correctors, not enemies?

Just so.

And as they are Hellenes themselves they will not devastate Hellas, nor will they burn houses, nor ever suppose that the whole population of a city—men, women, and children—are equally their enemies, for they know that the guilt of war is always confined to a few persons and that the many are their friends. And for all these   b
reasons they will be unwilling to waste their lands and raze their houses; their enmity to them will only last until the many innocent sufferers have compelled the guilty few to give satisfaction?

I agree, he said, that our citizens should thus deal with their Hellenic enemies; and with barbarians as the Hellenes now deal with one another.

Then let us enact this law also for our guardians: that they are neither to devastate the lands of Hellenes nor to burn their houses.   c

Agreed; and we may agree also in thinking that these, like all our previous enactments, are very good.

But still I must say, Socrates, that if you are allowed to go on in this way you will entirely forget the other question which at the commencement of this discussion you thrust aside: Is such an order of things possible, and how, if at all?[21] For I am quite ready to acknowledge that the plan which you propose, if only feasible, would do all sorts of good to the State. I will add, what you have

d   omitted, that your citizens will be the bravest of warriors, and will never leave their ranks, for they will all know one another, and each will call the other father, brother, son; and if you suppose the women to join their armies, whether in the same rank or in the rear, either as a terror to the enemy, or as auxiliaries in case of need, I know that they will then be absolutely invincible; and there are many domestic advantages which might also be men-

e   tioned and which I also fully acknowledge: but, as I admit all these advantages and as many more as you please, if only this State of yours were to come into existence, we need say no more about them; assuming then the existence of the State, let us now turn to the question of possibility and ways and means—the rest may be left.

472   If I loiter for a moment, you instantly make a raid upon me, I said, and have no mercy; I have hardly escaped the first and second waves, and you seem not to be aware that you are now bringing upon me the third, which is the greatest and heaviest. When you have seen and heard the third wave, I think you will be more considerate and will acknowledge that some fear and hesitation were natural respecting a proposal so extraordinary as that which I have now to state and investigate.

The more appeals of this sort which you make, he said, the

b   more determined are we that you shall tell us how such a State is possible: speak out and at once.

Let me begin by reminding you that we found our way hither in the search after justice and injustice.

True, he replied; but what of that?

I was only going to ask whether, if we have discovered them, we are to require that the just man should in nothing fail of ab-

c   solute justice; or may we be satisfied with an approximation, and the attainment in him of a higher degree of justice than is to be found in other men?

The approximation will be enough.

We were inquiring into the nature of absolute justice and into the character of the perfectly just, and into injustice and the perfectly unjust, that we might have an ideal. We were to look at these in order that we might judge of our own happiness and unhappiness according to the standard which they exhibited and the degree in which we resembled them, but not with any view of showing that they could exist in fact.

d

True, he said.

Would a painter be any the worse because, after having delineated with consummate art an ideal of a perfectly beautiful man, he was unable to show that any such man could ever have existed?

He would be none the worse.

Well, and were we not creating an ideal of a perfect State?

To be sure.

e

And is our theory a worse theory because we are unable to prove the possibility of a city being ordered in the manner described?[22]

Surely not, he replied.

That is the truth, I said. But if, at your request, I am to try and show how and under what conditions the possibility is highest, I must ask you, having this in view, to repeat your former admissions.

What admissions?

Is it possible for anything to be accomplished in deed as it is expressed in word? Or is it inevitable that what is done falls short of what is said in attaining to the truth, even though this is not generally thought to be the case? What do you say?

473

I agree.

Then you must not insist on my proving that the actual State will in every respect coincide with the ideal: if we are only able to discover how a city may be governed nearly as we proposed, you will admit that we have discovered the possibility which you demand; and will be contented. I am sure that I should be contented—will not you?

b

Yes, I will.

Let me next endeavor to show what is that fault in States which is the cause of their present maladministration, and what is the least change which will enable a State to pass into the truer form; and let the change, if possible, be of one thing only, or, if not, of two; at any rate, let the changes be as few and slight as possible.

c   Certainly, he replied.

I think, I said, that there might be a reform of the State if only one change were made, which is not a slight or easy though still a possible one.

What is it? he said.

Now then, I said, I go to meet that which I liken to the greatest of the waves; yet shall the word be spoken, even though the wave break and drown me in laughter and dishonor; and do you mark my words.

Proceed.

I said: "Until philosophers are kings, or the kings and princes of this world have the spirit and power of philosophy, and political greatness and wisdom meet in one, and those commoner natures who pursue either to the exclusion of the other are compelled to stand aside, cities will never have rest from their evils—no, nor the human race, as I believe—and then only will this our State have a possibility of life and behold the light of day."[23] Such was the thought, my dear Glaucon, which I would fain have uttered if it had not seemed too extravagant; for to be convinced that in no other State can there be happiness private or public is indeed a hard thing.

Socrates, what do you mean? I would have you consider that the word which you have uttered is one at which numerous persons, and very respectable persons too, in a figure pulling off their coats all in a moment, and seizing any weapon that comes to hand, will run at you might and main, before you know where you are, intending to do heaven knows what; and if you don't prepare an answer, and put yourself in motion, you will be "pared by their fine wits," and no mistake.

You got me into the scrape, I said.

And I was quite right; however, I will do all I can to get you out of it; but I can only give you good-will and good advice, and, perhaps, I may be able to fit answers to your questions better than another—that is all. And now, having such an auxiliary, you must do your best to show the unbelievers that you are right.

I ought to try, I said, since you offer me such invaluable assistance. And I think that, if there is to be a chance of our escaping, we must explain to them whom we mean when we say that philosophers are to rule in the State; then we shall be able to defend ourselves: There will be discovered to be some natures who ought to study philosophy and to be leaders in the State; and others who are not born to be philosophers, and are meant to be followers rather than leaders.

Then now for a definition, he said.

Follow me, I said, and I hope that I may in some way or other be able to give you a satisfactory explanation.

Proceed.

I dare say that you remember, and therefore I need not remind you, that a lover, if he is worthy of the name, ought to show his love, not to some one part of that which he loves, but to the whole.

I really do not understand, and therefore beg of you to assist my memory.

Another person, I said, might fairly reply as you do; but a man of pleasure like yourself* ought to know that all who are in the flower of youth do somehow or other raise a pang or emotion in a lover's breast, and are thought by him to be worthy of his affectionate regards. Is not this a way which you have with the fair: one has a snub nose, and you praise his charming face; the hook-nose of another has, you say, a royal look; while he who is neither snub nor hooked has the grace of regularity: the dark visage is manly, the fair are children of the gods; and as to the sweet "honey-pale," as they are called, what is the very name but the invention of a lover who talks in diminutives, and is not averse to paleness if appearing on the cheek of youth? In a word, there is no excuse which you will not make, and nothing which you will not say, in order not to lose a single flower that blooms in the spring-time of youth.

If you make me an authority in matters of love, for the sake of the argument, I assent.

---

*Literally, an "erotic man" (*anêr erotikos*); see note 16 on 3.402e.

And what do you say of lovers of wine? Do you not see them doing the same? They are glad of any pretext of drinking any wine.

Very good.

And the same is true of ambitious men; if they cannot command an army, they are willing to command a file; and if they can-
b   not be honored by really great and important persons, they are
glad to be honored by lesser and meaner people—but honor of
some kind they must have.

Exactly.

Once more let me ask: Does he who desires any class of goods,
desire the whole class or a part only?

The whole.

And may we not say of the philosopher that he is a lover, not of
a part of wisdom only, but of the whole?

Yes, of the whole.

And he who dislikes learning, especially in youth, when he has
c   no power of judging what is good and what is not, such a one we
maintain not to be a philosopher or a lover of knowledge, just as
he who refuses his food is not hungry, and may be said to have a
bad appetite and not a good one?

Very true, he said.

Whereas he who has a taste for every sort of knowledge and
who is curious to learn and is never satisfied, may be justly termed
a philosopher? Am I not right?

d   Glaucon said: If curiosity makes a philosopher, you will find
many a strange being will have a title to the name. All the lovers of
sights have a delight in learning, and must therefore be included.
Musical amateurs, too, are a folk strangely out of place among
philosophers, for they are the last persons in the world who would
come to anything like a philosophical discussion, if they could help,
while they run about at the Dionysiac festivals as if they had let
out their ears to hear every chorus; whether the performance is in
town or country—that makes no difference—they are there. Now
are we to maintain that all these and any who have similar tastes,
e   as well as the professors of quite minor arts, are philosophers?

Certainly not, I replied; they are only an imitation.

He said: Who then are the true philosophers?

Those, I said, who are lovers of the vision of truth.

That is also good, he said; but I should like to know what you mean?

To another, I replied, I might have a difficulty in explaining; but I am sure that you will admit a proposition which I am about to make.

What is the proposition?

That since beauty is the opposite of ugliness, they are two?

Certainly.   476

And inasmuch as they are two, each of them is one?

True again.

And of just and unjust, good and evil, and of every other class, the same remark holds: taken singly, each of them is one; but from the various combinations of them with actions and things and with one another, they are seen in all sorts of lights and appear many?

Very true.

And this is the distinction which I draw between the sight-loving, art-loving, practical class and those of whom I am speaking, and who are alone worthy of the name of philosophers.   b

How do you distinguish them? he said.

The lovers of sounds and sights, I replied, are, as I conceive, fond of fine tones and colors and forms and all the artificial products that are made out of them, but their minds are incapable of seeing or loving absolute beauty.

True, he replied.   c

Few are they who are able to attain to the sight of this.

Very true.

And he who, having a sense of beautiful things has no sense of absolute beauty, or who, if another lead him to a knowledge of that beauty is unable to follow—of such a one I ask, Is he awake or in a dream only? Reflect: is not the dreamer, sleeping or waking, one who likens dissimilar things, who puts the copy in the place of the real object?

I should certainly say that such a one was dreaming.

But take the case of the other, who recognizes the existence of absolute beauty and is able to distinguish the idea from the objects which participate in the idea, neither putting the objects in the place of the idea nor the idea in the place of the objects—is he a dreamer, or is he awake?[24]   d

He is wide awake.

And may we not say that the mind of the one who knows has knowledge, and that the mind of the other, who opines only, has opinion?

Certainly.

But suppose that the latter should quarrel with us and dispute our statement,[25] can we administer any soothing cordial or advice to him, without revealing to him that there is sad disorder in his wits?

We must certainly offer him some good advice, he replied.

Come, then, and let us think of something to say to him. Shall we begin by assuring him that he is welcome to any knowledge which he may have, and that we are rejoiced at his having it? But we should like to ask him a question: Does he who has knowledge know something or nothing? (You must answer for him).

I answer that he knows something.

Something that is or is not?[26]

Something that is; for how can that which is not ever be known?[27]

And are we assured, after looking at the matter from many points of view, that absolute being is or may be absolutely known, but that the utterly non-existent is utterly unknown?

Nothing can be more certain.

Good. But if there be anything which is of such a nature as to be and not to be, that will have a place intermediate between pure being and the absolute negation of being?

Yes, between them.

And, as knowledge corresponded to being and ignorance of necessity to not-being, for that intermediate between being and not-being there has to be discovered a corresponding intermediate between ignorance and knowledge, if there be such?

Certainly.

Do we admit the existence of opinion?

Undoubtedly.

As being the same with knowledge, or another faculty?

Another faculty.

Then opinion and knowledge have to do with different kinds of matter corresponding to this difference of faculties?

Yes.

And knowledge is relative to being and knows being. But before I proceed further I will make a division.

What division?

I will begin by placing faculties in a class by themselves: they c are powers in us, and in all other things, by which we do as we do. Sight and hearing, for example, I should call faculties. Have I clearly explained the class which I mean?

Yes, I quite understand.

Then let me tell you my view about them. I do not see them, and therefore the distinctions of figure, color, and the like, which enable me to discern the differences of some things, do not apply d to them. In speaking of a faculty I think only of its sphere and its result; and that which has the same sphere and the same result I call the same faculty, but that which has another sphere and another result I call different. Would that be your way of speaking?

Yes.

And will you be so very good as to answer one more question? Would you say that knowledge is a faculty, or in what class would you place it?

Certainly knowledge is a faculty, and the mightiest of all faculties.

And is opinion also a faculty? e

Certainly, he said; for opinion is that with which we are able to form an opinion.

And yet you were acknowledging a little while ago that knowledge is not the same as opinion?

Why, yes, he said: how can any reasonable being ever identify that which is infallible with that which errs?

An excellent answer, proving, I said, that we are quite conscious of a distinction between them. 410

Yes.

Then knowledge and opinion having distinct powers have also distinct spheres or subject-matters?

That is certain.

Being is the sphere or subject-matter of knowledge, and knowledge is to know the nature of being?

Yes.

And opinion is to have an opinion?

Yes.

And do we know what we opine? or is the subject-matter of opinion the same as the subject-matter of knowledge?

Nay, he replied, that has been already disproven; if difference
b in faculty implies difference in the sphere or subject-matter, and if, as we were saying, opinion and knowledge are distinct faculties, then the sphere of knowledge and of opinion cannot be the same.

Then if being is the subject-matter of knowledge, something else must be the subject-matter of opinion?

Yes, something else.

Well, then, is not-being the subject-matter of opinion? or, rather, how can there be an opinion at all about not-being? Reflect: when a man has an opinion, has he not an opinion about something? Can he have an opinion which is an opinion about nothing?

Impossible.

He who has an opinion, has an opinion about some one thing?

Yes.

And not-being is not one thing, but, properly speaking, nothing?

True.

Of not-being, ignorance was assumed to be the necessary cor-
c relative; of being, knowledge?

True, he said.

Then opinion is not concerned either with being or with not-being?

Not with either.

And can therefore neither be ignorance nor knowledge?

That seems to be true.

But is opinion to be sought without and beyond either of them, in a greater clearness than knowledge, or in a greater darkness than ignorance?

In neither.

Then I suppose that opinion appears to you to be darker than knowledge, but lighter than ignorance?

Both; and in no small degree.
d And also to be within and between them?

Yes.

Then you would infer that opinion is intermediate?[28]

No question.

But were we not saying before, that if anything appeared to be of a sort which is and is not at the same time, that sort of thing would appear also to lie in the interval between pure being and absolute not-being; and that the corresponding faculty is neither knowledge nor ignorance, but will be found in the interval between them?

True.

And in that interval there has now been discovered something which we call opinion?

There has.

Then what remains to be discovered is the object which partakes equally of the nature of being and not-being, and cannot rightly be termed either, pure and simple; this unknown term, when discovered, we may truly call the subject of opinion, and assign each to their proper faculty—the extremes to the faculties of the extremes and the mean to the faculty of the mean.

True.

This being premised, I would ask the gentleman who is of opinion that there is no absolute or unchangeable idea of beauty—in whose opinion the beautiful is the manifold—he, I say, your lover of beautiful sights, who cannot bear to be told that the beautiful is one, and the just is one, or that anything is one—to him I would appeal, saying, Will you be so very kind, sir, as to tell us whether, of all these beautiful things, there is one which will not be found ugly; or of the just, which will not be found unjust; or of the holy, which will not also be unholy?

No, he replied; the beautiful will in some point of view be found ugly; and the same is true of the rest.

And may not the many which are doubles be also halves?—doubles, that is, of one thing, and halves of another?

Quite true.

And things great and small, heavy and light, as they are termed, will not be denoted by these any more than by the opposite names?

True; both these and the opposite names will always attach to all of them.

And can any one of those many things which are called by particular names be said to be this rather than not to be this?

He replied: They are like the punning riddles which are asked at
c   feasts or the children's puzzle about the eunuch aiming at the bat,[29]
with what he hit him, as they say in the puzzle, and upon what the
bat was sitting. The individual objects of which I am speaking are
also a riddle, and have a double sense: nor can you fix them in your
mind, either as being or not-being, or both, or neither.

Then what will you do with them? I said. Can they have a better place than between being and not-being? For they are clearly
not in greater darkness or negation than not-being, or more full of
d   light and existence than being.

That is quite true, he said.

Thus then we seem to have discovered that the many ideas
which the multitude entertain about the beautiful and about all
other things are tossing about in some region which is halfway between pure being and pure not-being?

We have.

Yes; and we had before agreed that anything of this kind which
we might find was to be described as matter of opinion, and not as
matter of knowledge; being the intermediate flux which is caught
and detained by the intermediate faculty.

e   Quite true.

Then those who see the many beautiful, and who yet neither
see absolute beauty, nor can follow any guide who points the way
thither; who see the many just, and not absolute justice, and the
like—such persons may be said to have opinion but not knowledge?

That is certain.

But those who see the absolute and eternal and immutable may
be said to know, and not to have opinion only?

Neither can that be denied.

480   The one love and embrace the subjects of knowledge, the
other those of opinion? The latter are the same, as I dare say you
will remember, who listened to sweet sounds and gazed upon fair
colors, but would not tolerate the existence of absolute beauty.

Yes, I remember.

Shall we then be guilty of any impropriety in calling them
lovers of opinion rather than lovers of wisdom, and will they be
very angry with us for thus describing them?

I shall tell them not to be angry; no man should be angry at what is true.

But those who love the truth in each thing are to be called lovers of wisdom and not lovers of opinion.

Assuredly.

BOOK 6

484 AND THUS, GLAUCON, AFTER the argument has gone a weary way, the true and the false philosophers have at length appeared in view.

I do not think, he said, that the way could have been shortened.

I suppose not, I said; and yet I believe that we might have had a better view of both of them if the discussion could have been confined to this one subject and if there were not many other questions awaiting us, which he who desires to see in what respect

b the life of the just differs from that of the unjust must consider. [1]

And what is the next question? he asked.

Surely, I said, the one which follows next in order. Inasmuch as philosophers only are able to grasp the eternal and unchangeable, and those who wander in the region of the many and variable are not philosophers, I must ask you which of the two classes should be the rulers of our State?

And how can we rightly answer that question?

Whichever of the two are best able to guard the laws and insti-

c tutions of our State—let them be our guardians.

Very good.

Neither, I said, can there be any question that the guardian who is to keep anything should have eyes rather than no eyes?

There can be no question of that.

And are not those who are verily and indeed wanting in the knowledge of the true being of each thing, and who have in their

d souls no clear pattern, and are unable as with a painter's eye to look at the absolute truth and to that original to repair, and having perfect vision of the other world to order the laws about beauty, goodness, justice in this, if not already ordered, and to guard and preserve the order of them—are not such persons, I ask, simply blind? [2]

Truly, he replied, they are much in that condition.

And shall they be our guardians when there are others who,

besides being their equals in experience and falling short of them in no particular of virtue, also know the very truth of each thing?

There can be no reason, he said, for rejecting those who have this greatest of all great qualities; they must always have the first place unless they fail in some other respect.

Suppose, then, I said, that we determine how far they can unite 485 this and the other excellences.

By all means.

In the first place, as we began by observing, the nature of the philosopher has to be ascertained.[3] We must come to an understanding about him, and, when we have done so, then, if I am not mistaken, we shall also acknowledge that such a union of qualities is possible, and that those in whom they are united, and those only, should be rulers in the State.

What do you mean?

Let us suppose that philosophical minds always love knowledge of a sort which shows them the eternal nature not varying from b generation and corruption.

Agreed.

And further, I said, let us agree that they are lovers of all true being; there is no part whether greater or less, or more or less honorable, which they are willing to renounce; as we said before of the lover and the man of ambition.

True.

And if they are to be what we were describing, is there not an- c other quality which they should also possess?

What quality?

Truthfulness: they will never intentionally receive into their minds falsehood, which is their detestation, and they will love the truth.

Yes, that may be safely affirmed of them.

"May be," my friend, I replied, is not the word; say rather, "must be affirmed:" for he whose nature is amorous of anything cannot help loving all that belongs or is akin to the object of his affections.

Right, he said.

And is there anything more akin to wisdom than truth?

How can there be?

Can the same nature be a lover of wisdom and a lover of false-
d   hood?

Never.

The true lover of learning then must from his earliest youth, as
far as in him lies, desire all truth?

Assuredly.

But then again, as we know by experience, he whose desires are
strong in one direction will have them weaker in others; they will
be like a stream which has been drawn off into another channel.

True.

He whose desires are drawn toward knowledge in every form
will be absorbed in the pleasures of the soul, and will hardly feel
bodily pleasure—I mean, if he be a true philosopher and not a
e   sham one.

That is most certain.

Such a one is sure to be temperate and the reverse of covetous;
for the motives which make another man desirous of having and
spending, have no place in his character.

Very true.

486   Another criterion of the philosophical nature has also to be
considered.

What is that?

There should be no secret corner of illiberality;[4] nothing can
be more antagonistic than meanness to a soul which is ever longing after the whole of things both divine and human.

Most true, he replied.

Then how can he who has magnificence of mind and is the
spectator of all time and all existence, think much of human life?

He cannot.

b   Or can such a one account death fearful?

No, indeed.

Then the cowardly and mean nature has no part in true philosophy?

Certainly not.

Or again: can he who is harmoniously constituted, who is not
covetous or mean, or a boaster, or a coward—can he, I say, ever be
unjust or hard in his dealings?

Impossible.

Then you will soon observe whether a man is just and gentle, or rude and unsociable; these are the signs which distinguish even in youth the philosophical nature from the unphilosophical.

True.

There is another point which should be remarked.   c

What point?

Whether he has or has not a pleasure in learning; for no one will love that which gives him pain, and in which after much toil he makes little progress.

Certainly not.

And again, if he is forgetful and retains nothing of what he learns, will he not be an empty vessel?

That is certain.

Laboring in vain, he must end in hating himself and his fruitless occupation?

Yes.

Then a soul which forgets cannot be ranked among genuine   d philosophic natures; we must insist that the philosopher should have a good memory?

Certainly.

And once more, the inharmonious and unseemly nature can only tend to disproportion?

Undoubtedly.

And do you consider truth to be akin to proportion or to disproportion?

To proportion.

Then, besides other qualities, we must try to find a naturally well-proportioned and gracious mind, which will move spontaneously toward the true being of everything.

Certainly.

Well, and do not all these qualities, which we have been enu-   e merating, go together, and are they not, in a manner, necessary to a soul, which is to have a full and perfect participation of being?

They are absolutely necessary, he replied.   487

And must not that be a blameless study which he only can pursue who has the gift of a good memory, and is quick to learn— noble, gracious, the friend of truth, justice, courage, temperance, who are his kindred?

The god of jealousy* himself, he said, could find no fault with such a study.

And to men like him, I said, when perfected by years and education, and to these only you will intrust the State.

b   Here Adeimantus interposed and said: To these statements, Socrates, no one can offer a reply; but when you talk in this way, a strange feeling passes over the minds of your hearers: They fancy that they are led astray a little at each step in the argument, owing to their own want of skill in asking and answering questions; these littles accumulate, and at the end of the discussion they are found to have sustained a mighty overthrow and all their former notions appear to be turned upside down.[5] And as unskilful players of draughts are at last shut up by their more skilful adversaries and have no piece to move, so they too find themselves shut up at last; for they have nothing to say in this new game of which words are the counters; and yet all the time they are in the right. The observation is suggested to me by what is now occurring. For any one of us might say, that although in words he is not able to meet you at each step of the argument, he sees as a fact that the votaries of philosophy, when they carry on the study, not only in youth as a part of education, but as the pursuit of their maturer years, most of them become strange monsters, not to say utter rogues, and that those who may be considered the best of them are made useless to the world by the very study which you extol.

Well, and do you think that those who say so are wrong?

I cannot tell, he replied; but I should like to know what is your opinion.

Hear my answer; I am of opinion that they are quite right.

Then how can you be justified in saying that cities will not cease from evil until philosophers rule in them, when philosophers are acknowledged by us to be of no use to them?

You ask a question, I said, to which a reply can only be given in a parable.

Yes, Socrates; and that is a way of speaking to which you are not at all accustomed, I suppose.

---

*Momus is, properly speaking, the personification of censure and faultfinding.

I perceive, I said, that you are vastly amused at having plunged me into such a hopeless discussion; but now hear the parable, and then you will be still more amused at the meagreness of my imagination: for the manner in which the best men are treated in their own States is so grievous that no single thing on earth is comparable to it; and therefore, if I am to plead their cause, I must have recourse to fiction, and put together a figure made up of many things, like the fabulous unions of goats and stags which are found in pictures. Imagine then a fleet or a ship in which there is a captain who is taller and stronger than any of the crew, but he is a little deaf and has a similar infirmity in sight, and his knowledge of navigation is not much better.[6] The sailors are quarrelling with one another about the steering—everyone is of opinion that he has a right to steer, though he has never learned the art of navigation and cannot tell who taught him or when he learned, and will further assert that it cannot be taught, and they are ready to cut in pieces anyone who says the contrary. They throng about the captain, begging and praying him to commit the helm to them; and if at any time they do not prevail, but others are preferred to them, they kill the others or throw them overboard, and having first chained up the noble captain's senses with drink or some narcotic drug, they mutiny and take possession of the ship and make free with the stores; thus, eating and drinking, they proceed on their voyage in such manner as might be expected of them. Him who is their partisan and cleverly aids them in their plot for getting the ship out of the captain's hands into their own whether by force or persuasion, they compliment with the name of sailor, pilot, able seaman, and abuse the other sort of man, whom they call a good-for-nothing; but that the true pilot must pay attention to the year and seasons and sky and stars and winds, and whatever else belongs to his art, if he intends to be really qualified for the command of a ship, and that he must and will be the steerer, whether other people like or not—the possibility of this union of authority with the steerer's art has never seriously entered into their thoughts or been made part of their calling. Now in vessels which are in a state of mutiny and by sailors who are mutineers, how will the true pilot be regarded? Will he not be called by them a prater, a stargazer, a good-for-nothing?

488

b

c

d

e

489

Of course, said Adeimantus.

Then you will hardly need, I said, to hear the interpretation of the figure, which describes the true philosopher in his relation to the State; for you understand already.

Certainly.

Then suppose you now take this parable to the gentleman° who is surprised at finding that philosophers have no honor in their cities; explain it to him and try to convince him that their having b honor would be far more extraordinary.

I will.

Say to him, that, in deeming the best votaries of philosophy to be useless to the rest of the world, he is right; but also tell him to attribute their uselessness to the fault of those who will not use them, and not to themselves. The pilot should not humbly beg the sailors to be commanded by him—that is not the order of nature; neither are "the wise to go to the doors of the rich"—the ingenious author of this saying† told a lie—but the truth is, that, when c a man is ill, whether he be rich or poor, to the physician he must go, and he who wants to be governed, to him who is able to govern. The ruler who is good for anything ought not to beg his subjects to be ruled by him; although the present governors of mankind are of a different stamp; they may be justly compared to the mutinous sailors, and the true helmsmen to those who are called by them good-for-nothings and star-gazers.

Precisely so, he said.

For these reasons, and among men like these, philosophy, the noblest pursuit of all, is not likely to be much esteemed by those d of the opposite faction;‡ not that the greatest and most lasting injury is done to her by her opponents, but by her own professing followers, the same of whom you suppose the accuser to say that the greater number of them are arrant rogues, and the best are useless; in which opinion I agreed.

°That is, the hypothetical critic posited by Adeimantus at 6.487c.
†The saying was attributed to Simonides.
‡Literally, "those who practice opposite things"—that is, politicians and their ilk who, in their bids for power, displace philosophers from political leadership, just as the mutinous sailors in the image of the ship stand in the way of the true helmsman.

Yes.

And the reason why the good are useless has now been explained?

True.

Then shall we proceed to show that the corruption of the majority is also unavoidable, and that this is not to be laid to the charge of philosophy any more than the other?

By all means.

And let us ask and answer in turn, first going back to the description of the gentle and noble nature. Truth, as you will remember, was his leader, whom he followed always and in all things; failing in this, he was an impostor, and had no part or lot in true philosophy.

Yes, that was said.

Well, and is not this one quality, to mention no others, greatly at variance with present notions of him?

Certainly, he said.

And have we not a right to say in his defence, that the true lover of knowledge is always striving after being—that is his nature; he will not rest in the multiplicity of individuals which is an appearance only, but will go on—the keen edge will not be blunted, nor the force of his desire abate until he have attained the knowledge of the true nature of every essence by a sympathetic and kindred power in the soul, and by that power drawing near and mingling and becoming incorporate with very being, having begotten mind and truth, he will have knowledge and will live and grow truly, and then, and not till then, will he cease from his travail.

Nothing, he said, can be more just than such a description of him.

And will the love of a lie be any part of a philosopher's nature? Will he not utterly hate a lie?

He will.

And when truth is the captain, we cannot suspect any evil of the band which he leads?

Impossible.

Justice and health of mind will be of the company, and temperance will follow after?

True, he replied.

Neither is there any reason why I should again set in array the philosopher's virtues, as you will doubtless remember that courage, magnificence, apprehension, memory, were his natural gifts. And you objected that, although no one could deny what I then said, still, if you leave words and look at facts, the persons who are thus described are some of them manifestly useless, and the greater number of them depraved; inquiring into the grounds of these accusations, we have come to the question of why most are bad, and because of this we have begun discussing the nature of true philosophers and have defined it as it must be.

Exactly.

And we have next to consider the corruptions of the philosophic nature, why so many are spoiled and so few escape spoiling—I am speaking of those who were said to be useless but not wicked—and, when we have done with them, we will speak of the imitators of philosophy, what manner of men are they who aspire after a profession which is above them and of which they are unworthy, and then, by their manifold inconsistencies, bring upon philosophy and upon all philosophers that universal reprobation of which we speak.

What are these corruptions? he said.

I will see if I can explain them to you. Everyone will admit that a nature having in perfection all the qualities which we required in a philosopher is a rare plant which is seldom seen among men?

Rare indeed.

And what numberless and powerful causes tend to destroy these rare natures!

What causes?

In the first place there are their own virtues, their courage, temperance, and the rest of them, every one of which praiseworthy qualities (and this is a most singular circumstance) destroys and distracts from philosophy the soul which is the possessor of them.

That is very singular, he replied.

Then there are all the ordinary goods of life—beauty, wealth, strength, rank, and great connections in the State—you understand the sort of things—these also have a corrupting and distracting effect.

I understand; but I should like to know more precisely what you mean about them.

Grasp the truth as a whole, I said, and in the right way; you will then have no difficulty in apprehending the preceding remarks, and they will no longer appear strange to you.

And how am I to do so? he asked.

Why, I said, we know that all germs or seeds, whether veg-   d
etable or animal, when they fail to meet with proper nutriment, or climate, or soil, in proportion to their vigor, are all the more sensitive to the want of a suitable environment, for evil is a greater enemy to what is good than to what is not. [7]

Very true.

There is reason in supposing that the finest natures, when under alien conditions, receive more injury than the inferior, because the contrast is greater.

Certainly.

And may we not say, Adeimantus, that the most gifted minds,   e
when they are ill-educated, become pre-eminently bad? Do not great crimes and the spirit of pure evil spring out of a fulness of nature ruined by education rather than from any inferiority, whereas weak natures are scarcely capable of any very great good or very great evil?

There I think that you are right.

And our philosopher follows the same analogy—he is like a   492
plant which, having proper nurture, must necessarily grow and mature into all virtue, but, if sown and planted in an alien soil, becomes the most noxious of all weeds, unless he be preserved by some divine power. [8] Do you really think, as people so often say, that our youth are corrupted by Sophists, or that private teachers of the art corrupt them in any degree worth speaking of? Are not the public who say these things the greatest of all Sophists? [9] And do they not educate to perfection young and old, men and women   b
alike, and fashion them after their own hearts?

When is this accomplished? he said.

When they meet together, and the world sits down at an assembly, or in a court of law, or a theatre, or a camp, or in any other popular resort, and there is a great uproar, and they praise some things which are being said or done, and blame other things, equally exaggerating both, shouting and clapping their hands, and the echo of the rocks and the place in which they are assembled redoubles   c the sound of the praise or blame—at such a time will not a young man's heart, as they say, leap within him? Will any private training enable him to stand firm against the overwhelming flood of popular opinion? or will he be carried away by the stream? Will he not have the notions of good and evil which the public in general have—he will do as they do, and as they are, such will he be?

d   Yes, Socrates; necessity will compel him.

And yet, I said, there is a still greater necessity, which has not been mentioned.

What is that?

The gentle force of loss of citizen-rights, or confiscation, or death, which, as you are aware, these new Sophists and educators, who are the public, apply when their words are powerless.

Indeed they do; and in right good earnest.

Now what opinion of any other Sophist, or of any private person, can be expected to overcome in such an unequal contest?

e   None, he replied.

No, indeed, I said, even to make the attempt is a great piece of folly; there neither is, nor has been, nor is ever likely to be, any different type of character which has had no other training in virtue but that which is supplied by public opinion—I speak, my friend, of human virtue only; what is more than human, as the proverb says, is not included: for I would not have you ignorant that, in the

493   present evil state of governments, whatever is saved and comes to good is saved by the power of God, as we may truly say.

I quite assent, he replied.

Then let me crave your assent also to a further observation.

What are you going to say?

Why, that all those mercenary individuals, whom the many call Sophists and whom they deem to be their adversaries, do, in fact, teach nothing but the opinion of the many, that is to say, the opinions of their assemblies; and this is their wisdom. I might compare them to a man who should study the tempers and desires of a mighty strong beast who is fed by him—he would learn how to ap-

b   proach and handle him, also at what times and from what causes he is dangerous or the reverse, and what is the meaning of his several cries, and by what sounds, when another utters them, he is soothed or infuriated; and you may suppose further, that when, by continually attending upon him, he has become perfect in all this, he calls his knowledge wisdom, and makes of it a system or art, which he proceeds to teach, although he has no real notion of what he means by the principles or passions of which he is speaking, but calls this honorable and that dishonorable, or good or evil, or just or unjust, all in accordance with the tastes and tempers of the great brute. Good he pronounces to be that in which the beast delights, and evil to be that which he dislikes; and he can give no other account of them but calls mere necessities "just" and "good," having never himself seen, and having no power of explaining to others, the nature of either, or the difference between them, which is immense. By heaven, would not such a one be a rare educator?

Indeed, he would.

And in what way does he who thinks that wisdom is the discernment of the tempers and tastes of the motley multitude, whether in painting or in music, or, finally, in politics, differ from him whom I have been describing? For when a man consorts with the many, and exhibits to them his poem or other work of art or the service which he has done the State, making them his judges when he is not obliged, the so-called necessity of Diomede [10] will oblige him to produce whatever they praise. To support their claim that their capitulations to popular opinion are in truth honorable and good, did you ever hear any of them put forth an argument that was not utterly ludicrous?

No, nor am I likely to hear.

You recognize the truth of what I have been saying? Then let me ask you to consider further whether the world will ever be induced to believe in the existence of absolute beauty rather than of the many beautiful, or of the absolute in each kind rather than of the many in each kind?

Certainly not.

Then the world cannot possibly be a philosopher? [11]

Impossible.

And therefore philosophers must inevitably fall under the censure of the world?

They must.

And of individuals who consort with the mob and seek to please them?

That is evident.

Then, do you see any way in which the philosopher can be preserved in his calling to the end?—and remember what we were saying of him, that he was to have quickness and memory and courage and magnificence—these were admitted by us to be the true philosopher's gifts.

Yes.

Will not such a one from his early childhood be in all things first among us all, especially if his bodily endowments are like his mental ones?

Certainly, he said.

And his friends and fellow-citizens will want to use him as he gets older for their own purposes?

No question.

Falling at his feet, they will make requests to him and do him honor and flatter him, because they want to get into their hands now the power which he will one day possess.

That often happens, he said.

And what will a man such as he is be likely to do under such circumstances, especially if he be a citizen of a great city, rich and noble, and a tall, proper youth?[12] Will he not be full of boundless aspirations, and fancy himself able to manage the affairs of Hellenes and of barbarians, and having got such notions into his head will he not dilate and elevate himself in the fulness of vain pomp and senseless pride?

To be sure he will.

Now, when he is in this state of mind, if someone gently comes to him and tells him that he is a fool and must get understanding, which can only be got by slaving for it, do you think that, under such adverse circumstances, he will be easily induced to listen?

Far otherwise.

And even if there be someone who through inherent goodness or natural reasonableness has had his eyes opened a little and is humbled and taken captive by philosophy, how will his friends behave when they think that they are likely to lose the advantage which they were hoping to reap from his companionship? Will they not do and say anything to prevent him from yielding to his better nature and to render his teacher powerless, using to this end private intrigues as well as public prosecutions?

There can be no doubt of it.   495

And how can one who is thus circumstanced ever become a philosopher?

Impossible.

Then were we not right in saying that even the very qualities which make a man a philosopher, may, if he be ill-educated, divert him from philosophy, no less than riches and their accompaniments and the other so-called goods of life?

We were quite right.

Thus, my excellent friend, is brought about all that ruin and failure which I have been describing of the natures best adapted   b
to the best of all pursuits; they are natures which we maintain to be rare at any time; this being the class out of which come the men who are the authors of the greatest evil to States and individuals; and also of the greatest good when the tide carries them in that direction; but a small man never was the doer of any great thing either to individuals or to States.

That is most true, he said.

And so philosophy is left desolate, with her marriage rite incomplete: for her own have fallen away and forsaken her, and   c
while they are leading a false and unbecoming life, other unworthy persons, seeing that she has no kinsmen to be her protectors, enter in and dishonor her; and fasten upon her the reproaches which, as you say, her reprovers utter, who affirm of her votaries that some are good for nothing, and that the greater number deserve the severest punishment.

That is certainly what people say.

Yes; and what else would you expect, I said, when you think of the puny creatures who, seeing this land open to them—a land well stocked with fair names and showy titles—like prisoners running out of prison into a sanctuary, take a leap out of their trades   d
into philosophy; those who do so being probably the cleverest hands at their own miserable crafts? For, although philosophy be in this evil case, still there remains a dignity about her which is not to be found in the arts. And many are thus attracted by her whose natures are imperfect and whose souls are maimed and disfigured

e   by their meannesses, as their bodies are by their trades and crafts. Is not this unavoidable?

Yes.

Are they not exactly like a bald little tinker who has just got out of durance and come into a fortune—he takes a bath and puts on a new coat, and is decked out as a bridegroom going to marry his master's daughter, who is left poor and desolate?

496   A most exact parallel.

What will be the issue of such marriages? Will they not be vile and bastard?

There can be no question of it.

And when persons who are unworthy of education approach philosophy and make an alliance with her who is in a rank above them, what sort of ideas and opinions are likely to be generated? Will they not be sophisms captivating to the ear, having nothing in them genuine, or worthy of or akin to true wisdom?

No doubt, he said.

Then, Adeimantus, I said, the worthy disciples of philosophy will
b   be but a small remnant: perchance some noble and well-educated person, detained by exile in her service, who in the absence of corrupting influences remains devoted to her; or some lofty soul born in a mean city, the politics of which he contemns and neglects; and there may be a gifted few who leave the arts, which they justly despise, and come to her; or peradventure there are some who are restrained by our friend Theages's bridle;* for everything
c   in the life of Theages conspired to divert him from philosophy; but ill-health kept him away from politics. My own case of the internal sign is hardly worth mentioning, for rarely, if ever, has such a monitor been given to any other man. Those who belong to this small class have tasted how sweet and blessed a possession philosophy is, and have also seen enough of the madness of the multitude; and they know that no politician is honest, nor is there any
d   champion of justice at whose side they may fight and be saved. Such a one may be compared to a man who has fallen among wild

---

*Theages was a member of Socrates' circle who predeceased Socrates; a dialogue titled *Theages* has been preserved in the Platonic corpus but is probably not by Plato.

beasts—he will not join in the wickedness of his fellows, but neither is he able singly to resist all their fierce natures, and therefore seeing that he would be of no use to the State or to his friends, and reflecting that he would have to throw away his life without doing any good either to himself or others, he holds his peace, and goes his own way.[13] He is like one who, in the storm of dust and sleet which the driving wind hurries along, retires under the shelter of a wall; and seeing the rest of mankind full of wickedness, he is content, if only he can live his own life and be pure from evil or unrighteousness, and depart in peace and good-will, with bright hopes.   e

Yes, he said, and he will have done a great work before he departs.   497

A great work—yes; but not the greatest, unless he find a State suitable to him; for in a State which is suitable to him, he will have a larger growth and be the saviour of his country, as well as of himself.

The causes why philosophy is in such an evil name have now been sufficiently explained: the injustice of the charges against her has been shown—is there anything more which you wish to say?

Nothing more on that subject, he replied; but I should like to know which of the governments now existing is in your opinion the one adapted to her.

Not any of them, I said; and that is precisely the accusation   b which I bring against them—not one of them is worthy of the philosophic nature, and hence that nature is warped and estranged; as the exotic seed which is sown in a foreign land becomes denaturalized, and is wont to be overpowered and to lose itself in the new soil, even so this growth of philosophy, instead of persisting, degenerates and receives another character. But if philosophy ever finds in the State that perfection which she herself is, then   c will be seen that she is in truth divine, and that all other things, whether natures of men or institutions, are but human; and now, I know that you are going to ask, What that State is:

No, he said; there you are wrong, for I was going to ask another question—whether it is the State of which we are the founders and inventors, or some other?

Yes, I replied, ours in most respects; but you may remember

my saying before, that some living authority would always be required in the State having the same idea of the constitution which
guided you when as legislator you were laying down the laws.[14]

That was said, he replied.

Yes, but not in a satisfactory manner; you frightened us by interposing objections, which certainly showed that the discussion
would be long and difficult; and what still remains is the reverse of
easy.

What is there remaining?

The question how the study of philosophy may be so ordered
as not to be the ruin of the State: All great attempts are attended
with risk; "hard is the good," as men say.

Still, he said, let the point be cleared up, and the inquiry will
then be complete.

I shall not be hindered, I said, by any want of will, but, if at all,
by a want of power: my zeal you may see for yourselves; and please
to remark in what I am about to say how boldly and unhesitatingly
I declare that States should pursue philosophy, not as they do now,
but in a different spirit.[15]

In what manner?

At present, I said, the students of philosophy are quite young;
beginning when they are hardly past childhood, they devote only
the time saved from money-making and housekeeping to such
pursuits; and even those of them who are reputed to have most of
the philosophic spirit, after they pursue for a time this most difficult subject—I mean dialectic—they abandon it. Later in life, when
invited by someone else, they may, perhaps, go and hear a lecture,
and about this they make much ado, for philosophy is not considered by them to be their proper business: at last, when they grow
old, in most cases they are extinguished more truly than Heracleitus's sun, inasmuch as they never light up again.*

But what ought to be their course?

Just the opposite. In childhood and youth their study, and what
philosophy they learn, should be suited to their tender years:
during this period while they are growing up toward manhood,

---

*Heracleitus (today more commonly spelled Heraclitus) posited that the sun was
extinguished every evening and rekindled every morning.

the chief and special care should be given to their bodies that they may have them to use in the service of philosophy; as life advances and the intellect begins to mature, let them increase the gymnastics of the soul; but when the strength of our citizens fails and is past civil and military duties, then let them range at will and engage in no serious labor, as we intend them to live happily here, and to crown this life with a similar happiness in another.

How truly in earnest you are, Socrates! he said; I am sure of that; and yet most of your hearers, if I am not mistaken, are likely to be still more earnest in their opposition to you, and will never be convinced; Thrasymachus least of all.

Do not make a quarrel, I said, between Thrasymachus and me, who have recently become friends, although, indeed, we were never enemies; for I shall go on striving to the utmost until I either convert him and other men, or do something which may profit them against the day when they live again, and hold the like discourse in another state of existence.[16]

You are speaking of a time which is not very near.

Rather, I replied, of a time which is as nothing in comparison with eternity. Nevertheless, I do not wonder that the many refuse to believe; for they have never seen that of which we are now speaking realized; they have seen only a conventional imitation of philosophy, consisting of words artificially brought together, not like these of ours having a natural unity. But a human being who in word and work is perfectly moulded, as far as he can be, into the proportion and likeness of virtue—such a man ruling in a city which bears the same image, they have never yet seen, neither one nor many of them—do you think that they ever did?

No indeed.

No, my friend, and they have seldom, if ever, heard free and noble sentiments; such as men utter when they are earnestly and by every means in their power seeking after truth for the sake of knowledge, while they look coldly on the subtleties of controversy, of which the end is opinion and strife, whether they meet with them in the courts of law or in society.

They are strangers, he said, to the words of which you speak.

And this was what we foresaw, and this was the reason why truth forced us to admit, not without fear and hesitation, that neither cities nor States nor individuals will ever attain perfection until the small class of philosophers whom we termed useless but not corrupt are providentially compelled, whether they will or not,[17] to take care of the State, and until a like necessity be laid on the State to obey them; or until kings, or if not kings, the sons of kings

c or princes, are divinely inspired with a true love of true philosophy. That either or both of these alternatives are impossible, I see no reason to affirm: if they were so, we might indeed be justly ridiculed as dreamers and visionaries. Am I not right?

Quite right.

If then, in the countless ages of the past, or at the present hour in some foreign clime which is far away and beyond our ken, the

d perfected philosopher is or has been or hereafter shall be compelled by a superior power to have the charge of the State, we are ready to assert to the death, that this our constitution has been, and is—yea, and will be whenever the muse of philosophy is queen. There is no impossibility in all this; that there is a difficulty, we acknowledge ourselves.[18]

My opinion agrees with yours, he said.

But do you mean to say that this is not the opinion of the multitude?

I should imagine not, he replied.

O my friends, I said, do not attack the multitude: they will

e change their minds,[19] if, not in an aggressive spirit, but gently and with the view of soothing them and removing their dislike of over-education, you show them your philosophers as they really are and describe as you were just now doing their character and profession,

500 and then mankind will see that he of whom you are speaking is not such as they supposed—if they view him in this new light, they will surely change their notion of him, and answer in another strain. Who can be at enmity with one who loves him, who that is himself gentle and free from envy will be jealous of one in whom there is no jealousy? Nay, let me answer for you, that in a few this harsh temper may be found, but not in the majority of mankind.

I quite agree with you, he said.

b And do you not also think, as I do, that the harsh feeling which the many entertain toward philosophy originates in the pretenders, who rush in uninvited, and are always abusing them, and finding fault with them, who make persons instead of things the theme of their conversation? and nothing can be more unbecoming in philosophers than this.

It is most unbecoming.

For he, Adeimantus, whose mind is fixed upon true being, has surely no time to look down upon the affairs of earth, or to be filled with malice and envy, contending against men; his eye is ever directed toward things fixed and immutable, which he sees neither injuring nor injured by one another, but all in order moving according to reason; these he imitates, and to these he will, as far as he can, conform himself. Can a man help imitating that with which he holds reverential converse?

Impossible.

And the philosopher holding converse with the divine order, becomes orderly and divine, as far as the nature of man allows; but like everyone else, he will suffer from detraction.

Of course.

And if a necessity be laid upon him of fashioning, not only himself, but human nature generally, whether in States or individuals, into that which he beholds elsewhere, will he, think you, be an unskilful artificer of justice, temperance, and every civil virtue?[20]

Anything but unskilful.

And if the world perceives that what we are saying about him is the truth, will they be angry with philosophy? Will they disbelieve us, when we tell them that no State can be happy which is not designed by artists who imitate the heavenly pattern?

They will not be angry if they understand, he said. But how will they draw out the plan of which you are speaking?

They will begin by taking the State and the manners of men, from which, as from a tablet, they will rub out the picture, and leave a clean surface.[21] This is no easy task. But whether easy or not, herein will lie the difference between them and every other legislator—they will have nothing to do either with individual or State, and will inscribe no laws, until they have either found, or themselves made, a clean surface.

They will be very right, he said.

Having effected this, they will proceed to trace an outline of the constitution?

No doubt.

b   And when they are filling in the work, as I conceive, they will often turn their eyes upward and downward: I mean that they will first look at absolute justice and beauty and temperance, and again at the human copy; and will mingle and temper the various elements of life into the image of a man; and this they will conceive according to that other image, which, when existing among men, Homer calls the form and likeness of God.*

Very true, he said.

And one feature they will erase, and another they will put in,
c   until they have made the ways of men, as far as possible, agreeable to the ways of God?

Indeed, he said, in no way could they make a fairer picture.

And now, I said, are we beginning to persuade those whom you described as rushing at us with might and main, that the painter of constitutions is such a one as we were praising; at whom they were so very indignant because to his hands we committed the State; and are they growing a little calmer at what they have just heard?

Much calmer, if there is any sense in them.

d   Why, where can they still find any ground for objection? Will they doubt that the philosopher is a lover of truth and being?

They would not be so unreasonable.

Or that his nature, being such as we have delineated, is akin to the highest good?

Neither can they doubt this.

But again, will they tell us that such a nature, placed under favorable circumstances, will not be perfectly good and wise if any ever was? Or will they prefer those whom we have rejected?

e   Surely not.

Then will they still be angry at our saying, that, until philosophers bear rule, States and individuals will have no rest from evil, nor will this our imaginary State ever be realized?

I think that they will be less angry.

Shall we assume that they are not only less angry but quite

---

*Compare *Iliad* 1.131.

gentle, and that they have been converted and for very shame, if 502
for no other reason, cannot refuse to come to terms?

By all means, he said.

Then let us suppose that the reconciliation has been effected.
Will anyone deny the other point, that there may be sons of kings
or princes who are by nature philosophers?[22]

Surely no man, he said.

And when they have come into being will anyone say that they
must of necessity be destroyed; that they can hardly be saved is
not denied even by us; but that in the whole course of ages no sin- b
gle one of them can escape—who will venture to affirm this?

Who indeed!

But, said I, one is enough; let there be one man who has a city
obedient to his will, and he might bring into existence the ideal
polity about which the world is so incredulous.

Yes, one is enough.

The ruler may impose the laws and institutions which we have
been describing, and the citizens may possibly be willing to obey
them?

Certainly.

And that others should approve, of what we approve, is no mir-
acle or impossibility?

I think not. c

But we have sufficiently shown, in what has preceded, that all
this, if only possible, is assuredly for the best.

We have.

And now we say not only that our laws, if they could be enacted, would be for the best, but also that the enactment of them,
though difficult, is not impossible.

Very good.

And so with pain and toil we have reached the end of one subject, but more remains to be discussed; how and by what studies
and pursuits will the saviours of the constitution be created, and d
at what ages are they to apply themselves to their several studies?

Certainly.

I omitted the troublesome business of the possession of women,
and the procreation of children, and the appointment of the rulers,
because I knew that the perfect State would be eyed with jealousy

and was difficult of attainment; but that piece of cleverness was not of much service to me, for I had to discuss them all the same.

e The women and children are now disposed of, but the other question of the rulers must be investigated from the very beginning. We were saying, as you will remember, that they were to be lovers

503 of their country,* tried by the test of pleasures and pains, and neither in hardships, nor in dangers, nor at any other critical moment were to lose their patriotism—he was to be rejected who failed, but he who always came forth pure, like gold tried in the refiner's fire, was to be made a ruler, and to receive honors and rewards in life and after death. This was the sort of thing which was being

b said, and then the argument turned aside and veiled its face; not liking to stir the question which has now arisen.

I perfectly remember, he said.

Yes, my friend, I said, and I then shrank from hazarding the bold word; but now let me dare to say—that the perfect guardian must be a philosopher.[23]

Yes, he said, let that be affirmed.

And do not suppose that there will be many of them;[24] for the gifts which were deemed by us to be essential rarely grow together; they are mostly found in shreds and patches.

c What do you mean? he said.

You are aware, I replied, that quick intelligence, memory, sagacity, cleverness, and similar qualities, do not often grow together, and that persons who possess them and are at the same time high-spirited and magnanimous are not so constituted by nature as to live orderly and in a peaceful and settled manner; they are driven any way by their impulses, and all solid principle goes out of them.

Very true, he said.

On the other hand, those steadfast natures which can better be

d depended upon, which in a battle are impregnable to fear and immovable, are equally immovable when there is anything to be learned; they are always in a torpid state, and are apt to yawn and go to sleep over any intellectual toil.

Quite true.

---

*That is, at 3.412c–414b.

And yet we were saying that both qualities were necessary in those to whom the higher education is to be imparted, and who are to share in any office or command.

Certainly, he said.

And will they be a class which is rarely found?

Yes, indeed.

Then the aspirant must not only be tested in those labors and e dangers and pleasures which we mentioned before, but there is another kind of probation which we did not mention—he must be exercised also in many kinds of knowledge, to see whether the soul will be able to endure the highest of all, or will faint under them, as in any other studies and exercises. 504

Yes, he said, you are quite right in testing them. But what do you mean by the highest of all knowledge?

You may remember, I said, that we divided the soul into three parts; and distinguished the several natures of justice, temperance, courage, and wisdom?

Indeed, he said, if I had forgotten, I should not deserve to hear more.

And do you remember the word of caution which preceded the discussion of them?

To what do you refer?

We were saying, if I am not mistaken, that he who wanted to see b them in their perfect beauty must take a longer and more circuitous way, at the end of which they would appear;[25] but that we could add on a popular exposition of them on a level with the discussion which had preceded. And you replied that such an exposition would be enough for you, and so the inquiry was continued in what to me seemed to be a very inaccurate manner; whether you were satisfied or not, it is for you to say.

Yes, he said, I thought and the others thought that you gave us a fair measure of truth.

But, my friend, I said, a measure of such things which in any c degree falls short of the whole truth is not fair measure; for nothing imperfect is the measure of anything, although persons are too apt to be contented and think that they need search no further.

Not an uncommon case when people are indolent.

Yes, I said; and there cannot be any worse fault in a guardian of the State and of the laws.

True.

The guardian then, I said, must be required to take the longer

d   circuit, and toil at learning as well as at gymnastics, or he will never reach the highest knowledge of all which, as we were just now saying, is his proper calling.

What, he said, is there a knowledge still higher than this—higher than justice and the other virtues?

Yes, I said, there is. And of the virtues too we must behold not the outline merely, as at present—nothing short of the most finished picture should satisfy us. When little things are elaborated

e   with an infinity of pains, in order that they may appear in their full beauty and utmost clearness, how ridiculous that we should not think the highest truths worthy of attaining the highest accuracy!

A right noble thought; but do you suppose that we shall refrain from asking you what is this highest knowledge?

Nay, I said, ask if you will; but I am certain that you have heard the answer many times, and now you either do not understand me

505   or, as I rather think, you are disposed to be troublesome; for you have often been told that the idea of good is the highest knowledge, and that all other things become useful and advantageous only by their use of this.[26] You can hardly be ignorant that of this I was about to speak, concerning which, as you have often heard me say, we know so little; and, without which, any other knowl-

b   edge or possession of any kind will profit us nothing. Do you think that the possession of all other things is of any value if we do not possess the good? or the knowledge of all other things if we have no knowledge of beauty and goodness?

Assuredly not.

You are further aware that most people affirm pleasure to be the good,[27] but the finer sort of wits say it is knowledge?

Yes.

And you are aware too that the latter cannot explain what they mean by knowledge, but are obliged after all to say knowledge of the good?

How ridiculous!

Yes, I said, that they should begin by reproaching us with our

ignorance of the good, and then presume our knowledge of it—   c
for the good they define to be knowledge of the good, just as if we
understood them when they use the term "good"—this is of course
ridiculous.

Most true, he said.

And those who make pleasure their good are in equal perplexity; for they are compelled to admit that there are bad pleasures as
well as good.

Certainly.

And therefore to acknowledge that bad and good are the same?

True.   d

There can be no doubt about the numerous difficulties in
which this question is involved.

There can be none.

Further, do we not see that many are willing to do or to have or
to seem to be what is just and honorable without the reality; but no
one is satisfied with the appearance of good—the reality is what
they seek; in the case of the good, appearance is despised by everyone.

Very true, he said.

Of this then, which every soul of man pursues and makes the
end of all his actions, having a presentiment that there is such an   e
end, and yet hesitating because neither knowing the nature nor
having the same assurance of this as of other things, and therefore losing whatever good there is in other things—of a principle
such and so great as this ought the best men in our State, to whom   506
everything is intrusted, to be in the darkness of ignorance?

Certainly not, he said.

I am sure, I said, that he who does not know how the beautiful
and the just are likewise good will be but a sorry guardian of
them; and I suspect that no one who is ignorant of the good will
have a true knowledge of them.

That, he said, is a shrewd suspicion of yours.

And if we only have a guardian who has this knowledge, our   b
State will be perfectly ordered?

Of course, he replied; but I wish that you would tell me whether
you conceive this supreme principle of the good to be knowledge
or pleasure, or different from either?

Aye, I said, I knew all along that a fastidious gentleman like you would not be contented with the thoughts of other people about these matters.

True, Socrates; but I must say that one who like you has passed a lifetime in the study of philosophy should not be always repeat-
c   ing the opinions of others, and never telling his own.

Well, but has anyone a right to say positively what he does not know?

Not, he said, with the assurance of positive certainty; he has no right to do that: but he may say what he thinks, as a matter of opinion.

And do you not know, I said, that all mere opinions are bad, and the best of them blind? You would not deny that those who have any true notion without intelligence are only like blind men who feel their way along the road?

Very true.

And do you wish to behold what is blind and crooked and base,
d   when others will tell you of brightness and beauty?

Still, I must implore you, Socrates, said Glaucon, not to turn away just as you are reaching the goal; if you will only give such an explanation of the good as you have already given of justice and temperance and the other virtues, we shall be satisfied.

Yes, my friend, and I shall be at least equally satisfied, but I cannot help fearing that I shall fail, and that my indiscreet zeal will bring ridicule upon me. No, sweet sirs, let us not at present
e   ask what is the actual nature of the good, for to reach what is now in my thoughts would be an effort too great for me. But of the child of the good who is likest him, I would fain speak, if I could be sure that you wished to hear—otherwise, not.

By all means, he said, tell us about the child, and you shall re-main in our debt for the account of the parent.

507   I do indeed wish, I replied, that I could pay, and you receive, the account of the parent, and not, as now, of the offspring only; take, however, this latter by way of interest,* and at the same time

---

*A pun on the word *tokos*, which means both "offspring" and "interest owed on a debt."

have a care that I do not render a false account, although I have no intention of deceiving you.

Yes, we will take all the care that we can: proceed.

Yes, I said, but I must first come to an understanding with you, and remind you of what I have mentioned in the course of this discussion, and at many other times.

What? b

The old story, that there is many a beautiful and many a good, and so of other things which we describe and define; to all of them the term "many" is implied.

True, he said.

And there is an absolute beauty and an absolute good, and of other things to which the term "many" is applied there is an absolute; for they may be brought under a single idea, which is called the essence of each.

Very true.

The many, as we say, are seen but not known, and the ideas are known but not seen.

Exactly.

And what is the organ with which we see the visible things? c

The sight, he said.

And with the hearing, I said, we hear, and with the other senses perceive the other objects of sense?

True.

But have you remarked that sight is by far the most costly and complex piece of workmanship which the artificer of the senses ever contrived?[28]

No, I never have, he said.

Then reflect: has the ear or voice need of any third or additional nature in order that the one may be able to hear and the other to be heard?

Nothing of the sort.

No, indeed, I replied; and the same is true of most, if not all, the other senses—you would not say that any of them requires such an addition?

Certainly not.

But you see that without the addition of some other nature there is no seeing or being seen?

How do you mean?

Sight being, as I conceive, in the eyes, and he who has eyes wanting to see; color being also present in them, still unless there be a third nature specially adapted to the purpose, the owner of the eyes will see nothing and the colors will be invisible.

Of what nature are you speaking?

Of that which you term light, I replied.

True, he said.

Noble, then, is the bond which links together sight and visibility, and great beyond other bonds by no small difference of nature; for light is their bond, and light is no ignoble thing?

Nay, he said, the reverse of ignoble.

And which, I said, of the gods in heaven would you say was the lord of this element? Whose is that light which makes the eye to see perfectly and the visible to appear?

You mean the sun, as you and all mankind say.

May not the relation of sight to this deity* be described as follows?

How?

Neither sight nor the eye in which sight resides is the sun?

No.

Yet of all the organs of sense the eye is the most like the sun?

By far the most like.

And the power which the eye possesses is a sort of effluence which is dispensed from the sun?[29]

Exactly.

Then the sun is not sight, but the author of sight who is recognized by sight?

True, he said.

And this is he whom I call the child of the good, whom the good begat in his own likeness,† to be in the visible world, in relation to

---

*The sun (Helios) was traditionally conceived of as a deity; in later times, Apollo (Phoebus) came to be thought of as the god of the sun. *Helios* in Greek is a masculine noun; in this passage and again in book 7, Jowett uses masculine pronouns to refer to it.

†Jowett uses the masculine possessive adjective to refer to the idea of the good, although it is a neuter entity (*to agathon*), presumably because Socrates here conceives of "the good" as the "parent" or "father" of the sun.

sight and the things of sight, what the good is in the intellectual   c
world in relation to mind and the things of mind.[30]

Will you be a little more explicit? he said.

Why, you know, I said, that the eyes, when a person directs
them toward objects on which the light of day is no longer shin-
ing, but the moon and stars only, see dimly, and are nearly blind;
they seem to have no clearness of vision in them?

Very true.

But when they are directed toward objects on which the sun   d
shines, they see clearly and there is sight in them?

Certainly.

And the soul is like the eye: when resting upon that on which
truth and being shine, the soul perceives and understands, and
is radiant with intelligence; but when turned toward the twilight
of becoming and perishing, then she has opinion only, and goes
blinking about, and is first of one opinion and then of another, and
seems to have no intelligence?

Just so.

Now, that which imparts truth to the known and the power of   e
knowing to the knower is what I would have you term the idea of
good, and this you will deem to be the cause of science, and of truth
in so far as the latter becomes the subject of knowledge; beautiful
too, as are both truth and knowledge, you will be right in esteeming
this other nature as more beautiful than either; and, as in the previous instance, light and sight may be truly said to be like the sun, and   509
yet not to be the sun, so in this other sphere, science and truth may
be deemed to be like the good, but not the good; the good has a
place of honor yet higher.

What a wonder of beauty that must be, he said, which is the author of science* and truth, and yet surpasses them in beauty; for
you surely cannot mean to say that pleasure is the good?

God forbid, I replied; but may I ask you to consider the image
in another point of view?

In what point of view?   b

---

*That is, *epistemê* (also translated as "knowledge"), the cognitive faculty whereby
intelligible objects (the ideas, as opposed to objects in the phenomenal realm) are
known; see note 24 on 5.476d.

You would say, would you not? that the sun is not only the author of visibility in all visible things, but of generation and nourishment and growth, though he himself is not generation?

Certainly.

In like manner the good may be said to be not only the author of knowledge to all things known, but of their being and essence, and yet the good is not essence, but far exceeds essence in dignity and power.

c   Glaucon said, with a ludicrous earnestness: By the light of heaven, how amazing![31]

Yes, I said, and the exaggeration may be set down to you; for you made me utter my fancies.

And pray continue to utter them; at any rate let us hear if there is anything more to be said about the similitude of the sun.

Yes, I said, there is a great deal more.

Then omit nothing, however slight.

I will do my best, I said; but I should think that a great deal will have to be omitted.

I hope not, he said.

d   You have to imagine, then, that there are two ruling powers, and that one of them is set over the intellectual world, the other over the visible. I do not say heaven, lest you should fancy that I am playing upon the name (ούρανός, ορατός).* May I suppose that you have this distinction of the visible and intelligible fixed in your mind?

I have.

Now take a line which has been cut into two unequal parts, and divide each of them again in the same proportion, and suppose the two main divisions to answer, one to the visible and the other to the intelligible, and then compare the subdivisions in respect of their clearness and want of clearness, and you will find that the

e   first section in the sphere of the visible consists of images.[32] And

510   by images I mean, in the first place, shadows, and in the second place, reflections in water and in solid, smooth and polished bodies and the like: Do you understand?

Ouranos (also transliterated as "Uranus") refers to the sky (or "heavens") and to the primeval god of the sky. *Horatos* is a verbal adjective meaning "that which is seen."

Yes, I understand.

Imagine, now, the other section, of which this is only the resemblance, to include the animals which we see, and everything that grows or is made.

Very good.

Would you not admit that both the sections of this division have different degrees of truth, and that the copy is to the original as the sphere of opinion is to the sphere of knowledge?

Most undoubtedly.   b

Next proceed to consider the manner in which the sphere of the intellectual is to be divided.

In what manner?

Thus: There are two subdivisions, in the lower of which the soul uses the figures given by the former division as images; the inquiry can only be hypothetical, and instead of going upward to a principle descends to the other end; in the higher of the two, the soul passes out of hypotheses, and goes up to a principle which is above hypotheses, making no use of images as in the former case, but proceeding only in and through the ideas themselves.[33]

I do not quite understand your meaning, he said.

Then I will try again; you will understand me better when I have   c
made some preliminary remarks. You are aware that students of geometry, arithmetic, and the kindred sciences assume the odd, and the even, and the figures, and three kinds of angles, and the like, in their several branches of science; these are their hypotheses, which they and everybody are supposed to know, and therefore they do not deign to give any account of them either to themselves or others; but they begin with them, and go on until they arrive at   d
last, and in a consistent manner, at their conclusion?

Yes, he said, I know.

And do you not know also that although they make use of the visible forms and reason about them, they are thinking not of these, but of the ideals which they resemble; not of the figures which they draw, but of the absolute square and the absolute diameter, and so on—the forms which they draw or make, and which have shadows   e
and reflections in water of their own, are converted by them into images, but they are really seeking to behold the things themselves, which can only be seen with the eye of the mind?   511

That is true.

And of this kind I spoke as the intelligible, although in the search after it the soul is compelled to use hypotheses; not ascending to a first principle, because she is unable to rise above the region of hypothesis, but employing the objects of which the shadows below are resemblances in their turn as images, they having in relation to the shadows and reflections of them a greater distinctness, and therefore a higher value.

b   I understand, he said, that you are speaking of the province of geometry and the sister arts.

And when I speak of the other division of the intelligible, you will understand me to speak of that other sort of knowledge which reason itself attains by the power of dialectic,[34] using the hypotheses not as first principles, but only as hypotheses—that is to say, as steps and points of departure into a world which is above hypotheses, in order that she may soar beyond them to the first principle of the whole; and clinging to this and then to that which depends on this, by successive steps she descends again without c   the aid of any sensible object, from ideas, through ideas, and in ideas she ends.

I understand you, he replied; not perfectly, for you seem to me to be describing a task which is really tremendous; but, at any rate, I understand you to say that knowledge and being, which the science of dialectic contemplates, are clearer than the notions of the arts, as they are termed, which proceed from hypotheses only: these are also contemplated by the understanding, and not by the senses: yet, because they start from hypotheses and do not ascend d   to a principle, those who contemplate them appear to you not to exercise the higher reason upon them, although when a first principle is added to them they are cognizable by the higher reason. And the habit which is concerned with geometry and the cognate sciences I suppose that you would term understanding, and not reason, as being intermediate between opinion and reason.

You have quite conceived my meaning, I said; and now, corresponding to these four divisions, let there be four faculties in the soul—reason answering to the highest, understanding to the sec- e   ond, faith (or conviction) to the third, and perception of shadows to the last—and let there be a scale of them, and let us suppose that the several faculties have clearness in the same degree that their objects have truth.[35]

I understand, he replied, and give my assent, and accept your arrangement.

BOOK 7

514   AND NOW, I SAID, let me show in a figure how far our nature is en-
lightened or unenlightened: Behold! human beings living in an
underground den,¹ which has a mouth open toward the light and
reaching all along the den; here they have been from their childhood, and have their legs and necks chained so that they cannot
b   move, and can only see before them, being prevented by the
chains from turning round their heads. Above and behind them a
fire is blazing at a distance, and between the fire and the prisoners
there is a raised way; and you will see, if you look, a low wall built
along the way, like the screen which marionette-players have in
front of them, over which they show the puppets.

I see.

And do you see, I said, men passing along the wall carrying all
c   sorts of vessels, and statues and figures of animals made of wood
515   and stone and various materials, which appear over the wall? Some
of them are talking, others silent.

You have shown me a strange image, and they are strange prisoners.

Like ourselves, I replied; and they see only their own shadows,
or the shadows of one another, which the fire throws on the opposite wall of the cave?

True, he said; how could they see anything but the shadows if
b   they were never allowed to move their heads?

And of the objects which are being carried in like manner they
would only see the shadows?

Yes, he said.

And if they were able to converse with one another, would they
not suppose that they were naming what was actually before
them?

Very true.

And suppose further that the prison had an echo which came
from the other side, would they not be sure to fancy when one of

the passers-by spoke that the voice which they heard came from the passing shadow?

No question, he replied.

To them, I said, the truth would be literally nothing but the shadows of the images.

That is certain.

And now look again, and see what will naturally follow if the prisoners are released and disabused of their error. At first, when any of them is liberated and compelled suddenly to stand up and turn his neck round and walk and look toward the light, he will suffer sharp pains; the glare will distress him, and he will be unable to see the realities of which in his former state he had seen the shadows; and then conceive someone saying to him, that what he saw before was an illusion, but that now, when he is approaching nearer to being and his eye is turned toward more real existence, he has a clearer vision—what will be his reply? And you may further imagine that his instructor is pointing to the objects as they pass and requiring him to name them—will he not be perplexed? Will he not fancy that the shadows which he formerly saw are truer than the objects which are now shown to him?

Far truer.

And if he is compelled to look straight at the light, will he not have a pain in his eyes which will make him turn away to take refuge in the objects of vision which he can see, and which he will conceive to be in reality clearer than the things which are now being shown to him?

True, he said.

And suppose once more, that he is reluctantly dragged up a steep and rugged ascent,[2] and held fast until he is forced into the presence of the sun himself, is he not likely to be pained and irritated? When he approaches the light his eyes will be dazzled, and he will not be able to see anything at all of what are now called realities.

Not all in a moment, he said.

He will require to grow accustomed to the sight of the upper world. And first he will see the shadows best, next the reflections of men and other objects in the water, and then the objects themselves; then he will gaze upon the light of the moon and the stars

and the spangled heaven; and he will see the sky and the stars by
b   night better than the sun or the light of the sun by day?

Certainly.

Last of all he will be able to see the sun, and not mere reflections
of him in the water, but he will see him in his own proper place, and
not in another; and he will contemplate him as he is.[*]

Certainly.

He will then proceed to argue that this is he who gives the season and the years, and is the guardian of all that is in the visible
c   world, and in a certain way the cause of all things which he and his
fellows have been accustomed to behold?

Clearly, he said, he would first see the sun and then reason
about him.

And when he remembered his old habitation, and the wisdom
of the den and his fellow-prisoners, do you not suppose that he
would felicitate himself on the change, and pity them?

Certainly, he would.

And if they were in the habit of conferring honors among themselves on those who were quickest to observe the passing shadows
and to remark which of them went before, and which followed af-
d   ter, and which were together; and who were therefore best able to
draw conclusions as to the future, do you think that he would care
for such honors and glories, or envy the possessors of them?
Would he not say with Homer,

"Better to be the poor servant of a poor master,"[†]

and to endure anything, rather than think as they do and live after
their manner?

e   Yes, he said, I think that he would rather suffer anything than
entertain these false notions and live in this miserable manner.

Imagine once more, I said, such a one coming suddenly out of
the sun to be replaced in his old situation; would he not be certain
to have his eyes full of darkness?

---

[*]Once again, the word for sun in Greek (*helios*) is masculine—hence the masculine pronouns in Jowett's translation.
[†]*Odyssey* 11.489. Socrates criticizes the verse at 3.386c.

To be sure, he said.

And if there were a contest, and he had to compete in measuring the shadows with the prisoners who had never moved out of the den, while his sight was still weak, and before his eyes had become steady (and the time which would be needed to acquire this new habit of sight might be very considerable), would he not be ridiculous? Men would say of him that up he went and down he came without his eyes; and that it was better not even to think of ascending; and if anyone tried to loose another and lead him up to the light, let them only catch the offender, and they would put him to death.

No question, he said.

This entire allegory, I said, you may now append, dear Glaucon, to the previous argument; the prison-house is the world of sight, the light of the fire is the sun, and you will not misapprehend me if you interpret the journey upward to be the ascent of the soul into the intellectual world, in my view, at least, which, at your desire, I have expressed—whether rightly or wrongly, God knows.[3] But, whether true or false, my opinion is that in the world of knowledge the idea of good appears last of all, and is seen only with an effort; and, when seen, is also inferred to be the universal author of all things beautiful and right, parent of light and of the lord of light in this visible world, and the immediate source of reason and truth in the intellectual; and that this is the power upon which he who would act rationally either in public or private life must have his eye fixed.

I agree, he said, as far as I am able to understand you.

Moreover, I said, you must not wonder that those who attain to this beatific vision are unwilling to descend to human affairs; for their souls are ever hastening into the upper world where they desire to dwell; which desire of theirs is very natural, if our allegory may be trusted.

Yes, very natural.

And is there anything surprising in one who passes from divine contemplations to the degraded state of man, behaving himself in a ridiculous manner; if, while his eyes are blinking and before he has become accustomed to the surrounding darkness, he is compelled to fight in courts of law, or in other places, about the

images or the shadows of images of justice, and is endeavoring to
e meet the conceptions of those who have never yet seen absolute
justice?

Anything but surprising, he replied.

518 Anyone who has common sense will remember that the be-
wilderments of the eyes are of two kinds, and arise from two
causes, either from coming out of the light or from going into the
light, which is true of the mind's eye, quite as much as of the bodily eye; and he who remembers this when he sees anyone whose
vision is perplexed and weak, will not be too ready to laugh; he will
first ask whether that soul of man has come out of the brighter
life, and is unable to see because unaccustomed to the dark, or
having turned from darkness to the day is dazzled by excess of
b light. And he will count the one happy in his condition and state
of being, and he will pity the other; or, if he have a mind to laugh
at the soul which comes from below into the light, there will be
more reason in this than in the laugh which greets him who returns from above out of the light into the den.

That, he said, is a very just distinction.

But then, if I am right, certain professors of education[4] must
c be wrong when they say that they can put a knowledge into the
soul which was not there before, like sight into blind eyes.

They undoubtedly say this, he replied.

Whereas, our argument shows that the power and capacity
of learning exists in the soul already; and that just as the eye
was unable to turn from darkness to light without the whole
body, so too the instrument of knowledge can only by the movement of the whole soul be turned from the world of becoming
into that of being, and learn by degrees to endure the sight of
being, and of the brightest and best of being, or, in other words,
d of the good.

Very true.

And must there not be some art which will effect conversion in
the easiest and quickest manner; not implanting the faculty of
sight, for that exists already, but has been turned in the wrong direction, and is looking away from the truth?

Yes, he said, such an art may be presumed.

And whereas the other so-called virtues of the soul seem to be

akin to bodily qualities, for even when they are not originally innate they can be implanted later by habit and exercise, the virtue   e
of wisdom more than anything else contains a divine element
which always remains, and by this conversion is rendered useful
and profitable; or, on the other hand, hurtful and useless. Did you
never observe the narrow intelligence flashing from the keen eye   519
of a clever rogue—how eager he is, how clearly his paltry soul sees
the way to his end; he is the reverse of blind, but his keen eyesight
is forced into the service of evil, and he is mischievous in proportion to his cleverness?

Very true, he said.

But what if there had been a circumcision of such natures in
the days of their youth;° and they had been severed from those
sensual pleasures, such as eating and drinking, which, like leaden
weights, were attached to them at their birth, and which drag   b
them down and turn the vision of their souls upon the things that
are below—if, I say, they had been released from these impedi-
ments and turned in the opposite direction, the very same faculty
in them would have seen the truth as keenly as they see what their
eyes are turned to now.

Very likely.

Yes, I said; and there is another thing which is likely, or rather a
necessary inference from what has preceded, that neither the un-
educated and uninformed of the truth, nor yet those who never
make an end of their education, will be able ministers of the State;   c
not the former, because they have no single aim of duty which is
the rule of all their actions, private as well as public; nor the latter,
because they will not act at all except upon compulsion, fancying
that they are already dwelling apart in the islands of the blessed.†

Very true, he replied.

Then, I said, the business of us who are the founders of the
State will be to compel the best minds to attain that knowledge
which we have already shown to be the greatest of all—they must

---

°That is, as would happen in the rigorous training of future guardians that is described in books 2 and 3.
†The place where those who have led virtuous or exemplary lives were typically
thought to be ensconced after death; see also 7.540b.

continue to ascend until they arrive at the good; but when they
d   have ascended and seen enough we must not allow them to do as
they do now.

What do you mean?

I mean that they remain in the upper world: but this must not
be allowed; they must be made to descend again among the prisoners in the den, and partake of their labors and honors, whether
they are worth having or not.

But is not this unjust? he said; ought we to give them a worse
life, when they might have a better?

e   You have again forgotten, my friend, I said, the intention of the
law,* which did not aim at making any one class in the State happy
520 above the rest; the happiness was to be in the whole State, and he
held the citizens together by persuasion and necessity, making them
benefactors of the State, and therefore benefactors of one another;
to this end he created them, not to please themselves, but to be
his instruments in binding up the State.

True, he said, I had forgotten.

Observe, Glaucon, that there will be no injustice in compelling
our philosophers to have a care and providence of others; we shall
explain to them that in other States, men of their class are not
obliged to share in the toils of politics: and this is reasonable, for
b   they grow up at their own sweet will, and the government would
rather not have them. Being self-taught, they cannot be expected
to show any gratitude for a culture which they have never received.
But we have brought you into the world to be rulers of the hive,
kings of yourselves and of the other citizens, and have educated
you far better and more perfectly than they have been educated,
c   and you are better able to share in the double duty. Wherefore
each of you, when his turn comes, must go down to the general
underground abode, and get the habit of seeing in the dark.[5] When
you have acquired the habit, you will see ten thousand times better than the inhabitants of the den, and you will know what the
several images are, and what they represent, because you have

---

*The references in this paragraph are to 4.419a–421c and 3.414b–415d.

seen the beautiful and just and good in their truth. And thus our State, which is also yours, will be a reality, and not a dream only, and will be administered in a spirit unlike that of other States, in which men fight with one another about shadows only and are distracted in the struggle for power, which in their eyes is a great good. Whereas the truth is that the State in which the rulers are most reluctant to govern is always the best and most quietly governed, and the State in which they are most eager, the worst.

Quite true, he replied.

And will our pupils, when they hear this, refuse to take their turn at the toils of State, when they are allowed to spend the greater part of their time with one another in the heavenly light?

Impossible, he answered; for they are just men, and the commands which we impose upon them are just; there can be no doubt that every one of them will take office as a stern necessity, and not after the fashion of our present rulers of State.

Yes, my friend, I said; and there lies the point. You must contrive for your future rulers another and a better life than that of a ruler, and then you may have a well-ordered State; for only in the State which offers this, will they rule who are truly rich, not in silver and gold, but in virtue and wisdom, which are the true blessings of life. Whereas, if they go to the administration of public affairs, poor and hungering after their own private advantage, thinking that hence they are to snatch the chief good, order there can never be; for they will be fighting about office, and the civil and domestic broils which thus arise will be the ruin of the rulers themselves and of the whole State.

Most true, he replied.

And the only life which looks down upon the life of political ambition is that of true philosophy. Do you know of any other?

Indeed, I do not, he said.

And those who govern ought not to be lovers of the task? For, if they are, there will be rival lovers, and they will fight.

No question.

Who, then, are those whom we shall compel to be guardians? Surely they will be the men who are wisest about affairs of State, and by whom the State is best administered, and who at the same time have other honors and another and a better life than that of politics?

They are the men, and I will choose them, he replied.

c And now shall we consider in what way such guardians will be produced, and how they are to be brought from darkness to light— as some are said to have ascended from the world below to the gods?[6]

By all means, he replied.

The process, I said, is not the turning over of an oyster-shell,[7] but the turning round of a soul passing from a day which is little better than night to the true day of being, that is, the ascent from below, which we affirm to be true philosophy?

Quite so.

And should we not inquire what sort of knowledge has the d power of effecting such a change?

Certainly.

What sort of knowledge is there which would draw the soul from becoming to being? And another consideration has just oc- curred to me: You will remember that our young men are to be warrior athletes?

Yes, that was said.

Then this new kind of knowledge must have an additional quality?

What quality?

Usefulness in war.[8]

Yes, if possible.

There were two parts in our former scheme of education, were e there not?

Just so.

There was gymnastics, which presided over the growth and decay of the body, and may therefore be regarded as having to do with generation and corruption?

True.

Then that is not the knowledge which we are seeking to dis- cover?

522 No.

But what do you say of music, what also entered to a certain extent into our former scheme?

Music,* he said, as you will remember, was the counterpart of gymnastics, and trained the guardians by the influences of habit, by harmony making them harmonious, by rhythm rhythmical, but not giving them science; and the words, whether fabulous or possibly true, had kindred elements of rhythm and harmony in them. But in music there was nothing which tended to that good which you are now seeking.

b

You are most accurate, I said, in your recollection; in music there certainly was nothing of the kind. But what branch of knowledge is there, my dear Glaucon, which is of the desired nature; since all the useful arts were reckoned mean by us?

Undoubtedly; and yet if music and gymnastics are excluded, and the arts are also excluded, what remains?

Well, I said, there may be nothing left of our special subjects; and then we shall have to take something which is not special, but of the universal application.

What may that be?

A something which all arts and sciences and intelligences use in common, and which everyone first has to learn among the elements of education.

c

What is that?

The little matter of distinguishing one, two, and three—in a word, number and calculation: do not all arts and sciences necessarily partake of them?[9]

Yes.

Then the art of war partakes of them?

To be sure.

Then Palamedes,† whenever he appears in tragedy, proves Agamemnon ridiculously unfit to be a general. Did you never remark how he declares that he had invented number, and had numbered the ships and set in array the ranks of the army at Troy;

d

---

*See note 20 on 2.376e for the broad semantic range of *mousikê*, the word translated here as "music."

†Aeschylus, Sophocles, and Euripides all composed tragedies about Palamedes, a Greek chieftain at Troy, who was traditionally credited with the invention of numbers and also writing; in other sources, the god Prometheus is credited with the invention of numbers.

which implies that they had never been numbered before, and Agamemnon must be supposed literally to have been incapable of counting his own fleet—how could he if he was ignorant of number? And if that is true, what sort of general must he have been?

I should say a very strange one, if this was as you say.

e   Can we deny that a warrior should have a knowledge of arithmetic?

Certainly he should, if he is to have the smallest understanding of military tactics, or indeed, I should rather say, if he is to be a man at all.

I should like to know whether you have the same notion which I have of this study?

What is your notion?

523   It appears to me to be a study of the kind which we are seeking, and which leads naturally to reflection, but never to have been rightly used; for the true use of it is simply to draw the soul toward being.[10]

Will you explain your meaning? he said.

I will try, I said; and I wish you would share the inquiry with me, and say "yes" or "no" when I attempt to distinguish in my own mind what branches of knowledge have this attracting power, in order that we may have clearer proof that arithmetic is, as I suspect, one of them.

Explain, he said.

I mean to say that objects of sense are of two kinds; some of b   them do not invite thought because the sense is an adequate judge of them; while in the case of other objects sense is so untrustworthy that further inquiry is imperatively demanded.

You are clearly referring, he said, to the manner in which the senses are imposed upon by distance, and by painting in light and shade.

No, I said, that is not at all my meaning.

Then what is your meaning?

When speaking of uninviting objects, I mean those which do c   not pass from one sensation to the opposite; inviting objects are those which do; in this latter case the sense coming upon the object, whether at a distance or near, does not reveal any particular attribute more clearly than its opposite. An illustration will make my meaning clearer: here are three fingers—a little finger, a second finger, and a middle finger.

Very good.

You may suppose that they are seen quite close: And here comes the point.

What is it?

Each of them equally appears a finger, whether seen in the middle or at the extremity, whether white or black, or thick or thin— d it makes no difference; a finger is a finger all the same. In these cases a man is not compelled to ask of thought the question, What is a finger? for the sight never intimates to the mind that a finger is other than a finger.

True.

And therefore, I said, as we might expect, there is nothing here which invites or excites intelligence. e

There is not, he said.

But is this equally true of the greatness and smallness of the fingers? Can sight adequately perceive them? and is no difference made by the circumstance that one of the fingers is in the middle and the other at the extremity? And in like manner does the touch adequately perceive the qualities of thickness or thinness, of softness or hardness? And so of the other senses; do they give perfect intimations of such matters? Is not their mode of operation on this wise—the sense which is concerned with the quality of hardness is 524 necessarily concerned also with the quality of softness, and only intimates to the soul that the same thing is felt to be both hard and soft?

You are quite right, he said.

And must not the soul be perplexed at this intimation which the sense gives of a hard which is also soft? What, again, is the meaning of light and heavy, if that which is light is also heavy, and that which is heavy, light?

Yes, he said, these intimations which the soul receives are very b curious and require to be explained.

Yes, I said, and in these perplexities the soul naturally summons to her aid calculation and intelligence, that she may see whether the several objects announced to her are one or two.

True.

And if they turn out to be two, is not each of them one and different?

Certainly.

And if each is one, and both are two, she will conceive the two
c   as in a state of division, for if they were undivided they could only
be conceived of as one?

True.

The eye certainly did see both small and great, but only in a
confused manner; they were not distinguished.

Yes.

Whereas the thinking mind, intending to light up the chaos,
was compelled to reverse the process, and look at small and great
as separate and not confused.

Very true.

Was not this the beginning of the inquiry, "What is great?" and
"What is small?"

Exactly so.

And thus arose the distinction of the visible and the intelligible.

d   Most true.

This was what I meant when I spoke of impressions which invited the intellect, or the reverse—those which are simultaneous
with opposite impressions, invite thought; those which are not simultaneous do not.

I understand, he said, and agree with you.

And to which class do unity and number belong?[11]

I do not know, he replied.

Think a little and you will see that what has preceded will supply the answer; for if simple unity could be adequately perceived
e   by the sight or by any other sense, then, as we were saying in the
case of the finger, there would be nothing to attract toward being;
but when there is some contradiction always present, and one is
the reverse of one and involves the conception of plurality, then
thought begins to be aroused within us, and the soul perplexed
and wanting to arrive at a decision asks, "What is absolute
525 unity?"[12] This is the way in which the study of the one has a power
of drawing and converting the mind to the contemplation of true
being.

And surely, he said, this occurs notably in the case of one; for we see the same thing to be both one and infinite in multitude?

Yes, I said; and this being true of one must be equally true of all number?

Certainly.

And all arithmetic° and calculation have to do with number?

Yes.

And they appear to lead the mind toward truth?   b

Yes, in a very remarkable manner.

Then this is knowledge of the kind for which we are seeking, having a double use, military and philosophical; for the man of war must learn the art of number or he will not know how to array his troops, and the philosopher also must learn it, because he has to rise out of the sea of change and lay hold of true being, or else he will never become a true reckoner.

That is true.

And our guardian is both warrior and philosopher?

Certainly.

Then this is a kind of knowledge which legislation may fitly prescribe; and we must endeavor to persuade those who are to be the principal men of our State to go and learn arithmetic, not as   c amateurs, but they must carry on the study until they see the nature of numbers with the mind only; nor again, like merchants or retail-traders, with a view to buying or selling, but for the sake of their military use, and of the soul herself; and because this will be the easiest way for her to pass from becoming to truth and being.

That is excellent, he said.

Yes, I said, and now having spoken of it, I must add how charming the science is! and in how many ways it conduces to our de-   d sired end, if pursued in the spirit of a philosopher, and not of a shopkeeper!

How do you mean?

I mean, as I was saying, that arithmetic has a very great and elevating effect, compelling the soul to reason about abstract

---

°The term *arithmetikê*, here translated as "arithmetic," has more to do with the "science of number"—that is, the study of the characteristics of certain types of numbers (for example, even and odd)—than with simple addition, subtraction, etc.

number, and rebelling against the introduction of visible or tangible objects into the argument. You know how steadily the masters

e of the art repel and ridicule anyone who attempts to divide absolute unity[13] when he is calculating, and if you divide, they multiply, taking care that one shall continue one and not become lost in fractions.

That is very true.

526   Now, suppose a person were to say to them: O my friends, what are these wonderful numbers about which you are reasoning, in which, as you say, there is a unity such as you demand, and each unit is equal, invariable, indivisible—what would they answer?

They would answer, as I should conceive, that they were speaking of those numbers which can only be realized in thought.

Then you see that this knowledge may be truly called neces-

b sary, necessitating as it clearly does the use of the pure intelligence in the attainment of pure truth?

Yes; that is a marked characteristic of it.

And have you further observed that those who have a natural talent for calculation are generally quick at every other kind of knowledge; and even the dull, if they have had an arithmetical training, although they may derive no other advantage from it, always become much quicker than they would otherwise have been?

Very true, he said.

c And indeed, you will not find many studies more difficult, nor will you find them easily.

You will not.

And, for all these reasons, arithmetic is a kind of knowledge in which the best natures should be trained, and which must not be given up.

I agree.

Let this then be made one of our subjects of education. And next, shall we inquire whether the kindred science also concerns us?

You mean geometry?*

Exactly so.

---

*That is, plane geometry.

Clearly, he said, we are concerned with that part of geometry d
which relates to war; for in pitching a camp or taking up a position
or closing or extending the lines of an army, or any other military
manœuvre, whether in actual battle or on a march, it will make all
the difference whether a general is or is not a geometrician.

Yes, I said, but for that purpose a very little of either geometry
or calculation will be enough; the question relates rather to the
greater and more advanced part of geometry—whether that tends
in any degree to make more easy the vision of the idea of good;
and thither, as I was saying, all things tend which compel the soul e
to turn her gaze toward that place, where is the full perfection of
being, which she ought, by all means, to behold.

True, he said.

Then if geometry compels us to view being, it concerns us; if
becoming only, it does not concern us?

Yes, that is what we assert.

Yet anybody who has the least acquaintance with geometry will 527
not deny that such a conception of the science is in flat contradiction to the ordinary language of geometricians.

How so?

They have in view practice only, and are always speaking, in a
narrow and ridiculous manner, of squaring and extending and
applying and the like—they confuse the necessities of geometry
with those of daily life, whereas knowledge is the real object of
the whole science.[14] b

Certainly, he said.

Then must not a further admission be made?

What admission?

That the knowledge at which geometry aims is knowledge of
the eternal, and not of aught perishing and transient.

That, he replied, may be readily allowed, and is true.

Then, my noble friend, geometry will draw the soul toward
truth, and create the spirit of philosophy, and raise up that which
is now unhappily allowed to fall down.

Nothing will be more likely to have such an effect.

Then nothing should be more sternly laid down than that the c
inhabitants of your fair city should by all means learn geometry.
Moreover, the science has indirect effects, which are not small.

Of what kind? he said.

There are the military advantages of which you spoke, I said; and in all departments of knowledge, as experience proves, anyone who has studied geometry is infinitely quicker of apprehension than one who has not.

Yes, indeed, he said, there is an infinite difference between them.

Then shall we propose this as a second branch of knowledge which our youth will study?

Let us do so, he replied.

d   And suppose we make astronomy the third—what do you say?

I am strongly inclined to it, he said; the observation of the seasons and of months and years is as essential to the general as it is to the farmer or sailor.

I am amused, I said, at your fear of the world, which makes you guard against the appearance of insisting upon useless studies;[15] and I quite admit the difficulty of believing that in every man there is an eye of the soul which, when by other pursuits lost and

e   dimmed, is by these purified and reillumined; and is more precious far than ten thousand bodily eyes, for by it alone is truth seen. Now there are two classes of persons: one class of those who will agree with you and will take your words as a revelation; another class to whom they will be utterly unmeaning, and who will naturally deem them to be idle tales, for they see no sort of profit which is to be obtained from them. And therefore you had better decide at once

528   with which of the two you are proposing to argue. You will very likely say with neither, and that your chief aim in carrying on the argument is your own improvement; at the same time you do not grudge to others any benefit which they may receive.

I think that I should prefer to carry on the argument mainly on my own behalf.

Then take a step backward, for we have gone wrong in the order of the sciences.[16]

What was the mistake? he said.

After plane geometry, I said, we proceeded at once to solids in

b   revolution, instead of taking solids in themselves; whereas after the second dimension, the third, which is concerned with cubes and dimensions of depth, ought to have followed.

That is true, Socrates; but so little seems to be known as yet about these subjects.[17]

Why, yes, I said, and for two reasons: in the first place, no government patronizes them; this leads to a want of energy in the pursuit of them, and they are difficult; in the second place, students cannot learn them unless they have a director. But then a director can hardly be found, and, even if he could, as matters now stand, the students, who are very conceited, would not attend to c him. That, however, would be otherwise if the whole State became the director of these studies and gave honor to them; then disciples would want to come, and there would be continuous and earnest search, and discoveries would be made; since even now, disregarded as they are by the world, and maimed of their fair proportions, and although none of their votaries can tell the use of them, still these studies force their way by their natural charm, and very likely, if they had the help of the State, they would some day emerge into light.

Yes, he said, there is a remarkable charm in them. But I do not d clearly understand the change in the order. First you began with a geometry of plane surfaces?

Yes, I said.

And you placed astronomy next, and then you made a step backward?

Yes, and I have delayed you by my hurry; the ludicrous state of solid geometry, which, in natural order, should have followed, made me pass over this branch and go on to astronomy, or motion e of solids.

True, he said.

Then assuming that the science now omitted would come into existence if encouraged by the State, let us go on to astronomy, which will be fourth.

The right order, he replied. And now, Socrates, as you rebuked the vulgar manner in which I praised astronomy before, my praise shall be given in your own spirit. For everyone, as I think, must 529 see that astronomy compels the soul to look upward and leads us from this world to another.

Everyone but myself, I said; to everyone else this may be clear, but not to me.

And what, then, would you say?

I should rather say that those who elevate astronomy into philosophy appear to me to make us look downward, and not upward.

What do you mean? he asked.

You, I replied, have in your mind a truly sublime conception of our knowledge of the things above. And I dare say that if a person were to throw his head back and study the fretted ceiling, you would still think that his mind was the percipient, and not his eyes. And you are very likely right, and I may be a simpleton: but, in my opinion, that knowledge only which is of being and of the unseen can make the soul look upward, and whether a man gapes at the heavens or blinks on the ground, seeking to learn some particular of sense, I would deny that he can learn, for nothing of that sort is matter of science;[18] his soul is looking downward, not upward, whether his way to knowledge is by water or by land, whether he floats or only lies on his back.

I acknowledge, he said, the justice of your rebuke. Still, I should like to ascertain how astronomy can be learned in any manner more conducive to that knowledge of which we are speaking?

I will tell you, I said: The starry heaven which we behold is wrought upon a visible ground, and therefore, although the fairest and most perfect of visible things, must necessarily be deemed inferior far to the true motions of absolute swiftness and absolute slowness, which are relative to each other, and carry with them that which is contained in them, in the true number and in every true figure. Now, these are to be apprehended by reason and intelligence, but not by sight.

True, he replied.

The spangled heavens should be used as a pattern and with a view to that higher knowledge; their beauty is like the beauty of figures or pictures excellently wrought by the hand of Dædalus,* or some other great artist, which we may chance to behold; any geometrician who saw them would appreciate the exquisiteness

*Legendary artist and craftsman. Among other achievements, he constructed the labyrinth on Crete to contain the Minotaur.

of their workmanship, but he would never dream of thinking that in them he could find the true equal or the true double, or the truth of any other proportion.

530

No, he replied, such an idea would be ridiculous.

And will not a true astronomer have the same feeling when he looks at the movements of the stars? Will he not think that heaven and the things in heaven are framed by the Creator° of them in the most perfect manner? But he will never imagine that the proportions of night and day, or of both to the month, or of the month to the year, or of the stars to these and to one another, and any other things that are material and visible can also be eternal and subject to no deviation—that would be absurd; and it is equally absurd to take so much pains in investigating their exact truth.

b

I quite agree, though I never thought of this before.

Then, I said, in astronomy, as in geometry, we should employ problems, and let the heavens alone if we would approach the subject in the right way and so make the natural gift of reason to be of any real use.

c

That, he said, is a work infinitely beyond our present astronomers.

Yes, I said; and there are many other things which must also have a similar extension given to them, if our legislation is to be of any value. But can you tell me of any other suitable study?

No, he said, not without thinking.

Motion, I said, has many forms, and not one only; two of them are obvious enough even to wits no better than ours; and there are others, as I imagine, which may be left to wiser persons.

d

But where are the two?

There is a second, I said, which is the counterpart of the one already named.[19]

And what may that be?

The second, I said, would seem relatively to the ears to be what the first is to the eyes; for I conceive that as the eyes are designed to look up at the stars, so are the ears to hear harmonious motions;

°Literally, "the craftsman (*demiourgos*) of heaven." Compare "the artificer (*demiourgos*) of the senses" at 6.507c.

and these are sister sciences—as the Pythagoreans say,[20] and we, Glaucon, agree with them?

Yes, he replied.

e   But this, I said, is a laborious study, and therefore we had better go and learn of them; and they will tell us whether there are any other applications of these sciences. At the same time, we must not lose sight of our own higher object.

What is that?

There is a perfection which all knowledge ought to reach, and which our pupils ought also to attain, and not to fall short of, as I was saying that they did in astronomy. For in the science of har-
531   mony, as you probably know, the same thing happens. The teachers of harmony compare the sounds and consonances which are heard only, and their labor, like that of the astronomers, is in vain.[21]

Yes, by heaven! he said; and 'tis as good as a play to hear them talking about their condensed notes, as they call them;[22] they put their ears close alongside of the strings like persons catching a sound from their neighbor's wall—one set of them declaring that they distinguish an intermediate note and have found the least interval which should be the unit of measurement;[23] the others in-
b   sisting that the two sounds have passed into the same—either party setting their ears before their understanding.

You mean, I said, those gentlemen who tease and torture the strings and rack them on the pegs of the instrument: I might carry on the metaphor and speak after their manner of the blows which the plectrum[24] gives, and make accusations against the strings, both of backwardness and forwardness to sound; but this would be tedious, and therefore I will only say that these are not the men, and that I am referring to the Pythagoreans, of whom I was just now proposing to inquire about harmony. For they too are in error, like the astronomers; they investigate the numbers of the
c   harmonies which are heard, but they never attain to problems—
that is to say, they never reach the natural harmonies of number, or reflect why some numbers are harmonious and others not.

That, he said, is a thing of more than mortal knowledge.

A thing, I replied, which I would rather call useful; that is, if sought after with a view to the beautiful and good; but if pursued in any other spirit, useless.

Very true, he said.

Now, when all these studies reach the point of intercommunion and connection with one another, and come to be considered in their mutual affinities, then, I think, but not till then, will the pursuit of them have a value for our objects; otherwise there is no profit in them.

d

I suspect so; but you are speaking, Socrates, of a vast work.

What do you mean? I said; the prelude, or what?[25] Do you not know that all this is but the prelude to the actual strain which we have to learn? For you surely would not regard the skilled mathematician as a dialectician?[26]

e

Assuredly not, he said; I have hardly ever known a mathematician who was capable of reasoning.

But do you imagine that men who are unable to give and take a reason will have the knowledge which we require of them?

Neither can this be supposed.

And so, Glaucon, I said, we have at last arrived at the hymn of dialectic. This is that strain which is of the intellect only, but which the faculty of sight will nevertheless be found to imitate; for sight, as you may remember, was imagined by us after a while to behold the real animals and stars, and last of all the sun himself. And so with dialectic; when a person starts on the discovery of the absolute by the light of reason only, and without any assistance of sense, and perseveres until by pure intelligence he arrives at the perception of the absolute good, he at last finds himself at the end of the intellectual world, as in the case of sight at the end of the visible.

532

b

Exactly, he said.

Then this is the progress which you call dialectic?

True.

But the release of the prisoners from chains, and their translation from the shadows to the images and to the light, and the ascent from the underground den to the sun, while in his presence they are vainly trying to look on animals and plants and the light of the sun, but are able to perceive even with their weak eyes the images in the water (which are divine), and are the shadows of true existence (not shadows of images cast by a light of fire, which compared with the sun is only an image)—this power of elevating the highest principle in the soul to the contemplation of that

c

which is best in existence, with which we may compare the raising
of that faculty which is the very light of the body to the sight of
that which is brightest in the material and visible world—this
power is given, as I was saying, by all that study and pursuit of the
d   arts which have been described.

I agree in what you are saying, he replied, which may be hard to
believe, yet, from another point of view, is harder still to deny.
This, however, is not a theme to be treated of in passing only, but
will have to be discussed again and again. And so, whether our
conclusion be true or false, let us assume all this, and proceed at
once from the prelude or preamble to the chief strain, and describe that in like manner.[27] Say, then, what is the nature and what
are the divisions of dialectic, and what are the paths which lead
thither; for these paths will also lead to our final rest.

e   Dear Glaucon, I said, you will not be able to follow me here,
though I would do my best, and you should behold not an image
533 only, but the absolute truth, according to my notion. Whether
what I told you would or would not have been a reality I cannot
venture to say; but you would have seen something like reality; of
that I am confident.

Doubtless, he replied.

But I must also remind you that the power of dialectic alone
can reveal this, and only to one who is a disciple of the previous
sciences.

Of that assertion you may be as confident as of the last.

And assuredly no one will argue that there is any other method
of comprehending by any regular process all true existence, or of
b   ascertaining what each thing is in its own nature; for the arts in
general are concerned with the desires or opinions of men, or
are cultivated with a view to production and construction, or for
the preservation of such productions and constructions; and as
to the mathematical sciences which, as we were saying, have some
apprehension of true being—geometry and the like—they only
dream about being, but never can they behold the waking reality so
long as they leave the hypotheses which they use unexamined, and
c   are unable to give an account of them. For when a man knows not
his own first principle, and when the conclusion and intermediate
steps are also constructed out of he knows not what, how can he

imagine that such a fabric of convention can ever become science?

Impossible, he said.

Then dialectic, and dialectic alone, goes directly to the first principle and is the only science which does away with hypotheses in order to make her ground secure; the eye of the soul, which is   d
literally buried in an outlandish slough, is by her gentle aid lifted upward; and she uses as handmaids and helpers in the work of conversion, the sciences which we have been discussing. Custom terms them sciences,[28] but they ought to have some other name, implying greater clearness than opinion and less clearness than science: and this, in our previous sketch, was called understand-   e
ing. But why should we dispute about names when we have realities of such importance to consider?

Why, indeed, he said, when any name will do which expresses the thought of the mind with clearness?

At any rate, we are satisfied, as before, to have four divisions; two for intellect and two for opinion, and to call the first division science, the second understanding, the third belief, and the fourth perception of shadows, opinion being concerned with becoming,   534
and intellect with being; and so to make a proportion:

"As being is to becoming, so is pure intellect to opinion.

And as intellect is to opinion, so is science to belief, and understanding to the perception of shadows."*

But let us pass over the correlations of the objects that each faculty apprehends and their respective subdivisions, for it will be a long inquiry, many times longer than this has been.

As far as I understand, he said, I agree.   b

And do you also agree, I said, in describing the dialectician as one who attains a conception of the essence of each thing? And he who does not possess and is therefore unable to impart this conception, in whatever degree he is unable, may in that degree also be said to fail in intelligence? Will you admit so much?

Yes, he said; how can I deny it?

---

*See notes 32 on 6.509d and 33 on 510b.

And you would say the same of the conception of the good?
Until the person is able to abstract and define rationally the idea
c   of good, and unless he can run the gauntlet of all objections, and
is ready to disprove them, not by appeals to opinion, but to absolute truth, never faltering at any step of the argument—unless
he can do all this, you would say that he knows neither the idea of
good nor any other good; he apprehends only a shadow, if anything at all, which is given by opinion, and not by science;° dream-
d   ing and slumbering in this life, before he is well awake here, he
arrives at the world below, and has his final quietus.

In all that I should most certainly agree with you.

And surely you would not have the children of your ideal State,
whom you are nurturing and educating—if the ideal ever becomes a reality—you would not allow the future rulers to be like
posts, having no reason in them, and yet to be set in authority over
the highest matters?[29]

Certainly not.

Then you will make a law that they shall have such an education as will enable them to attain the greatest skill in asking and
answering questions?

e   Yes, he said, you and I together will make it.

Dialectic, then, as you will agree, is the coping-stone of the
sciences, and is set over them; no other science can be placed
535   higher—the nature of knowledge can no further go?

I agree, he said.

But to whom we are to assign these studies, and in what way they
are to be assigned, are questions which remain to be considered.

Yes, clearly.

You remember, I said, how the rulers were chosen before?†

Certainly, he said.

The same natures must still be chosen, and the preference
again given to the surest and the bravest, and, if possible, to the
b   fairest; and, having noble and generous tempers, they should also
have the natural gifts which will facilitate their education.

°The distinction is between *doxa* and *epistemê*, as at 5.476d–480a.
†Compare 3.412c–414b; also 6.494a–495b.

And what are these?

Such gifts as keenness and ready powers of acquisition; for the mind more often faints from the severity of study than from the severity of gymnastics: the toil is more entirely the mind's own, and is not shared with the body.

Very true, he replied.

Further, he of whom we are in search should have a good   c
memory, and be an unwearied solid man who is a lover of labor in any line; or he will never be able to endure the great amount of bodily exercise and to go through all the intellectual discipline and study which we require of him.

Certainly, he said; he must have natural gifts.

The mistake at present is that those who study philosophy have no vocation, and this, as I was before saying, is the reason why she has fallen into disrepute: her true sons should take her by the hand, and not bastards.

What do you mean?

In the first place, her votary should not have a lame or halting   d
industry—I mean, that he should not be half industrious and half idle: as, for example, when a man is a lover of gymnastics and hunting, and all other bodily exercises, but a hater rather than a lover of the labor of learning or listening or inquiring. Or the occupation to which he devotes himself may be of an opposite kind, and he may have the other sort of lameness.

Certainly, he said.

And as to truth, I said, is not a soul equally to be deemed halt and lame which hates voluntary falsehood and is extremely indig-   e
nant at herself and others when they tell lies, but is patient of involuntary falsehood, and does not mind wallowing like a swinish beast in the mire of ignorance, and has no shame at being detected?

To be sure.

And, again, in respect of temperance, courage, magnificence,*   536
and every other virtue, should we not carefully distinguish between the true son and the bastard? for where there is no discernment of

---

*That is, *megaloprepeia* (high-mindedness); compare 6.486a.

such qualities, States and individuals unconsciously err; and the State makes a ruler, and the individual a friend, of one who, being defective in some part of virtue, is in a figure lame or a bastard.

That is very true, he said.

b All these things, then, will have to be carefully considered by us; and if only those whom we introduce to this vast system of education and training are sound in body and mind, justice herself will have nothing to say against us, and we shall be the saviours of the constitution and of the State; but, if our pupils are men of another stamp, the reverse will happen, and we shall pour a still greater flood of ridicule on philosophy than she has to endure at present.

That would not be creditable.

Certainly not, I said; and yet perhaps, in thus turning jest into earnest I am equally ridiculous.

In what respect?

c I had forgotten, I said, that we were not serious, and spoke with too much excitement. For when I saw philosophy so undeservedly trampled under foot of men[30] I could not help feeling a sort of indignation at the authors of her disgrace: and my anger made me too vehement.

Indeed! I was listening, and did not think so.

But I, who am the speaker, felt that I was. And now let me remind you that, although in our former selection* we chose old d men, we must not do so in this. Solon† was under a delusion when he said that a man when he grows old may learn many things—for he can no more learn much than he can run much; youth is the time for any extraordinary toil.

Of course.

And, therefore, calculation and geometry and all the other elements of instruction, which are a preparation for dialectic, should be presented to the mind in childhood; not, however, under any notion of forcing our system of education.

Why not?

e Because a freeman ought not to be a slave in the acquisition of

---

*That is, at 3.412c; compare 6.498b–c.
†Athenian statesman and poet (late seventh to early sixth centuries B.C.E.).

knowledge of any kind. Bodily exercise, when compulsory, does no harm to the body; but knowledge which is acquired under compulsion obtains no hold on the mind.

Very true.

Then, my good friend, I said, do not use compulsion, but let early education be a sort of amusement; you will then be better able to find out the natural bent.   537

That is a very rational notion, he said.

Do you remember that the children, too, were to be taken to see the battle on horseback;* and that if there were no danger they were to be brought close up and, like young hounds, have a taste of blood given them?

Yes, I remember.

The same practice may be followed, I said, in all these things— labors, lessons, dangers—and he who is most at home in all of them ought to be enrolled in a select number.

At what age?   b

At the age when the necessary gymnastics are over: the period, whether of two or three years, which passes in this sort of training is useless for any other purpose; for sleep and exercise are unpropitious to learning; and the trial of who is first in gymnastic exercises is one of the most important tests to which our youth are subjected.

Certainly, he replied.

After that time those who are selected from the class of twenty years old will be promoted to higher honor, and the sciences which they learned without any order in their early education will now be brought together, and they will be able to see the natural c relationship of them to one another and to true being.

Yes, he said, that is the only kind of knowledge which takes lasting root.

Yes, I said; and the capacity for such knowledge is the great criterion of dialectical talent: the comprehensive mind is always the dialectical.

I agree with you, he said.

---

*Compare 5.467a–e.

These, I said, are the points which you must consider; and those
d   who have most of this comprehension, and who are most steadfast
in their learning, and in their military and other appointed duties,
when they have arrived at the age of thirty will have to be chosen
by you out of the select class, and elevated to higher honor; and
you will have to prove them by the help of dialectic, in order to
learn which of them is able to give up the use of sight and the
other senses, and in company with truth to attain absolute being:
And here, my friend, great caution is required.

Why great caution?

e   Do you not remark, I said, how great is the evil which dialectic
has introduced?[31]

What evil? he said.

The students of the art are filled with lawlessness.

Quite true, he said.

Do you think that there is anything so very unnatural or inex-
cusable in their case? or will you make allowance for them?

In what way make allowance?

I want you, I said, by way of parallel, to imagine a suppositi-
538   tious son who is brought up in great wealth; he is one of a great
and numerous family, and has many flatterers. When he grows up
to manhood, he learns that his alleged are not his real parents; but
who the real are he is unable to discover. Can you guess how he
will be likely to behave toward his flatterers and his supposed parents, first of all during the period when he is ignorant of the false
relation, and then again when he knows? Or shall I guess for you?

If you please.

Then I should say that while he is ignorant of the truth he will
b   be likely to honor his father and his mother and his supposed relations more than the flatterers; he will be less inclined to neglect
them when in need, or to do or say anything against them; and he
will be less willing to disobey them in any important matter.

He will.

But when he has made the discovery, I should imagine that he
would diminish his honor and regard for them, and would become
more devoted to the flatterers; their influence over him would
greatly increase; he would now live after their ways, and openly
c   associate with them, and, unless he were of an unusually good

disposition, he would trouble himself no more about his supposed parents or other relations.

Well, all that is very probable. But how is the image applicable to the disciples of philosophy?

In this way: you know that there are certain principles about justice and honor, which were taught us in childhood, and under their parental authority we have been brought up, obeying and honoring them.

That is true.

There are also opposite maxims and habits of pleasure which d
flatter and attract the soul, but do not influence those of us who have any sense of right, and they continue to obey and honor the maxims of their fathers.

True.

Now, when a man is in this state, and the questioning spirit asks what is fair or honorable, and he answers as the legislator has taught him, and then arguments many and diverse refute his words, until he is driven into believing that nothing is honorable any more than dishonorable, or just and good any more than the reverse, e
and so of all the notions which he most valued, do you think that he will still honor and obey them as before?

Impossible.

And when he ceases to think them honorable and natural as heretofore, and he fails to discover the true, can he be expected to pursue any life other than that which flatters his desires? 539

He cannot.

And from being a keeper of the law he is converted into a breaker of it?

Unquestionably.

Now all this is very natural in students of philosophy such as I have described, and also, as I was just now saying, most excusable.

Yes, he said; and, I may add, pitiable.

Therefore, that your feelings may not be moved to pity about our citizens who are now thirty years of age, every care must be taken in introducing them to dialectic.

Certainly.

There is a danger lest they should taste the dear delight too b
early; for youngsters, as you may have observed, when they first

get the taste in their mouths, argue for amusement, and are always contradicting and refuting others in imitation of those who refute them; like puppy-dogs, they rejoice in pulling and tearing at all who come near them.

Yes, he said, there is nothing which they like better.

c   And when they have made many conquests and received defeats at the hands of many, they violently and speedily get into a way of not believing anything which they believed before, and hence, not only they, but philosophy and all that relates to it is apt to have a bad name with the rest of the world.

Too true, he said.

But when a man begins to get older, he will no longer be guilty of such insanity; he will imitate the dialectician who is seeking for truth, and not the eristic,° who is contradicting for the sake of
d   amusement; and the greater moderation of his character will increase instead of diminishing the honor of the pursuit.

Very true, he said.

And did we not make special provision for this, when we said that the disciples of philosophy were to be orderly and steadfast, not, as now, any chance aspirant or intruder?

Very true.

Suppose, I said, the study of philosophy to take the place of gymnastics and to be continued diligently and earnestly and exclusively for twice the number of years which were passed in bodily exercise—will that be enough?

e   Would you say six or four years? he asked.

Say five years, I replied; at the end of the time they must be sent down again into the den and compelled to hold any military or other office which young men are qualified to hold: in this way they will get their experience of life, and there will be an opportunity of trying whether, when they are drawn all manner of ways by
540 temptation, they will stand firm or flinch.

And how long is this stage of their lives to last?

Fifteen years, I answered; and when they have reached fifty years of age, then let those who still survive and have distinguished

---

°See note 6 on 5.454a for the distinction between eristic and dialectic.

themselves in every action of their lives, and in every branch of knowledge, come at last to their consummation: the time has now arrived at which they must raise the eye of the soul to the universal light which lightens all things, and behold the absolute good; for that is the pattern according to which they are to order the State and the lives of individuals, and the remainder of their own lives also; making philosophy their chief pursuit, but, when their turn comes, toiling also at politics and ruling for the public good, doing this not as if it were something fine but as a necessary task;[*] and when they have brought up in each generation others like themselves and left them in their place to be governors of the State, then they will depart to the Islands of the Blessed and dwell there; and the city will give them public memorials and sacrifices and honor them, if the Pythian oracle[†] consent, as demigods, but if not, as in any case blessed and divine.

You are a sculptor, Socrates, and have made statues of our governors faultless in beauty.

Yes, I said, Glaucon, and of our governesses too;[‡] for you must not suppose that what I have been saying applies to men only and not to women as far as their natures can go.

There you are right, he said, since we have made them to share in all things like the men.

Well, I said, and you would agree (would you not?) that what has been said about the State and the government is not a mere dream, and although difficult, not impossible;[§] but only possible in the way which has been supposed; that is to say, when the true philosopher-kings are born in a State, one or more of them, despising the honors of this present world which they deem mean and worthless, esteeming above all things right and the honor that springs from right, and regarding justice as the greatest and most necessary of all things, whose ministers they are, and whose principles will be exalted by them when they set in order their own city?

How will they proceed?

---

[*]Compare 1.347c.
[†]The oracle of Apollo at Delphi. See 5.461e and 4.427b.
[‡]Compare 5.455b–457b.
[§]Compare 6.501a.

They will begin by sending out into the country all the inhabitants of the city who are more than ten years old, and will take 541 possession of their children, who will be unaffected by the habits of their parents; these they will train in their own habits and laws, I mean in the laws which we have given them: and in this way the State and constitution of which we were speaking will soonest and most easily attain happiness, and the nation which has such a constitution will gain most.

Yes, that will be the best way. And I think, Socrates, that you have very well described how, if ever, such a constitution might b come into being.

Enough, then, of the perfect State, and of the man who bears its image—there is no difficulty in seeing how we shall describe him.

There is no difficulty, he replied; and I agree with you in thinking that nothing more need be said.

BOOK 8

AND SO, GLAUCON, WE have arrived at the conclusion that in the
perfect State wives and children are to be in common; and that all
education and the pursuits of war and peace are also to be common, and the best philosophers and the bravest warriors are to be
their kings?

That, replied Glaucon, has been acknowledged.

Yes, I said; and we have further acknowledged that the governors, when appointed themselves, will take their soldiers and place
them in houses such as we were describing, which are common to
all, and contain nothing private, or individual; and about their property, you remember what we agreed?

Yes, I remember that no one was to have any of the ordinary possessions of mankind; they were to be warrior athletes and guardians,
receiving from the other citizens, in lieu of annual payment, only
their maintenance, and they were to take care of themselves and of
the whole State.

True, I said; and now that this division of our task is concluded,
let us find the point at which we digressed, that we may return
into the old path.*

There is no difficulty in returning; you implied, then as now, that
you had finished the description of the State: you said that such a
State was good, and that the man was good who answered to it, although, as now appears, you had more excellent things to relate
both of State and man. And you said further, that if this was the
true form, then the others were false; and of the false forms, you
said, as I remember, that there were four principal ones, and that
their defects, and the defects of the individuals corresponding to
them, were worth examining. When we had seen all the individuals,
and finally agreed as to who was the best and who was the worst of

---

*That is, 4.445c–e.

them, we were to consider whether the best was not also the happiest, and the worst the most miserable. I asked you what were the four forms of government of which you spoke, and then Polemarchus and Adeimantus put in their word; and you began again, and have found your way to the point at which we have now arrived.

Your recollection, I said, is most exact.

Then, like a wrestler,* he replied, you must put yourself again in the same position; and let me ask the same questions, and do you give me the same answer which you were about to give me then.

Yes, if I can, I will, I said.

I shall particularly wish to hear what were the four constitutions of which you were speaking.

That question, I said, is easily answered: the four governments of which I spoke, so far as they have distinct names, are first, those of Crete and Sparta, which are generally applauded;[1] what is termed oligarchy comes next; this is not equally approved, and is a form of government which teems with evils: thirdly, democracy, which naturally follows oligarchy, although very different: and lastly comes tyranny, great and famous, which differs from them all, and is the fourth and worst disorder of a State. I do not know, do you? of any other constitution which can be said to have a distinct character. There are lordships and principalities which are bought and sold, and some other intermediate forms of government. But these are nondescripts and may be found equally among Hellenes and among barbarians.

Yes, he replied, we certainly hear of many curious forms of government which exist among them.

Do you know, I said, that governments vary as the dispositions of men vary, and that there must be as many of the one as there are of the other? For we cannot suppose that States are made of "oak and rock,"† and not out of the human natures which are in them, and which in a figure turn the scale and draw other things after them?

---

*According to an ancient commentator, the reference is to the way in which wrestlers, after being thrown, rose and resumed their positions.

†Compare *Odyssey* 19.162. For the assumption that the characters of individuals determine the characters of states, see 4.435e.

Yes, he said, the States are as the men are; they grow out of human characters.

Then if the constitutions of States are five, the dispositions of individual minds will also be five?

Certainly.

Him who answers to aristocracy, and whom we rightly call just and good, we have already described.

We have.

Then let us now proceed to describe the inferior sort of na-   545
tures, being the contentious and ambitious, who answer to the Spartan polity; also the oligarchical, democratical, and tyrannical. Let us place the most just by the side of the most unjust, and when we see them we shall be able to compare the relative happiness or unhappiness of him who leads a life of pure justice or pure injustice. The inquiry will then be completed. And we shall know whether we ought to pursue injustice, as Thrasymachus advises,*   b
or in accordance with the conclusions of the argument to prefer justice.

Certainly, he replied, we must do as you say.

Shall we follow our old plan, which we adopted with a view to clearness, of taking the State first and then proceeding to the individual, and begin with the government of honor?—I know of no name for such a government other than timocracy or perhaps timarchy.† We will compare with this the like character in the individual; and, after that, consider oligarchy and the oligarchical man; and then again we will turn our attention to democracy and   c
the democratical man; and lastly, we will go and view the city of tyranny, and once more take a look into the tyrant's soul, and try to arrive at a satisfactory decision.

That way of viewing and judging of the matter will be very suitable.

---

*At 1.344c.

†*Timê* in Greek means "honor"; *timokratia* and *timarchia* are Platonic neologisms for the *philotimos politeia* ("honor-loving constitution" or, as Jowett translates, "government of honor") in which the ambitious silver class dominates. See 8.548c–e.

First, then, I said, let us inquire how timocracy (the government of honor) arises out of aristocracy (the government of the best).*

d Clearly, all political changes originate in divisions of the actual governing power; a government which is united, however small, cannot be moved.[2]

Very true, he said.

In what way, then, will our city be moved, and in what manner will the two classes of auxiliaries and rulers disagree among themselves or with one another? Shall we, after the manner of Homer, pray the muses to tell us "how discord first arose"?† Shall we imag-

e ine them in solemn mockery, to play and jest with us as if we were children, and to address us in a lofty tragic vein, making believe to be in earnest?[3]

How would they address us?

546 After this manner: A city which is thus constituted can hardly be shaken; but, seeing that everything which has a beginning has also an end, even a constitution such as yours will not last forever, but will in time be dissolved. And this is the dissolution: In plants that grow in the earth, as well as in animals that move on the earth's surface, fertility and sterility of soul and body occur when the circumferences of the circles of each are completed, which in short-lived existences pass over a short space, and in long-lived

b ones over a long space.[4] But to the knowledge of human fecundity and sterility all the wisdom and education of your rulers will not attain; the laws which regulate them will not be discovered by an intelligence which is alloyed with sense, but will escape them, and they will bring children into the world when they ought not. Now that which is of divine birth‡ has a period which is contained in a perfect number,§ but the period of human birth is comprehended

---

*Throughout books 8 and 9, Socrates uses the term "aristocracy" to refer to the government of "the best" that is only possible, he argues, in the ideal state.
†Adapted from *Iliad* 16.112.
‡"That which is of divine birth" is perhaps meant to signify the world as a whole; compare *Timaeus* 30a.
§That is, a period of gestation. The "perfect number" that describes the period of gestation of "that which is divinely born" is left unspecified.

in a number[5] in which first increments by involution and evolution
(or squared and cubed)* obtaining three intervals and four terms[†]
of like and unlike, waxing and waning numbers,[‡] make all the terms
commensurable and agreeable to one another. The base of these
with a third added, when combined with five and raised to the third   c
power, furnishes two harmonies,[§] the first a square which is 100
times as great,[||] and the other a figure having one side equal to the
former, but oblong, consisting of 100 numbers squared upon rational diameters of a square (*i.e.*, omitting fractions), the side of
which is five, each of them being less by one[#] or less by two perfect

---

*That is, by squaring a number and then multiplying it again by its square (cubing).

†More literally, "comprehending three distances and four limits." "Three distances" refers perhaps to the height, width, and depth of a square or rectangular
cube. "Four limits" may signify the four corner points on a cube that define its
height, width, and depth.

‡Alternatively, "of elements that make things like and unlike and cause increase
and decrease. . . ." These "elements" are perhaps the numbers 3, 4, and 5, which
are the lengths of the sides of the Pythagorean triangle. It may be significant that
the combined cubes of these numbers (that is, $3^3 + 4^3 + 5^3$) yield 216, which some
ancient theorists (for example, the Pythagoreans) identified as the minimum
number of days for human gestation.

§Literally, "the base 'thirded,' yoked to 5, yields two harmonies when thrice in-
creased." The base is 3, which is first multiplied by one and one-third times itself
(that is, $3 \times 4/3$, equaling 4); this figure (that is, 3×4, or 12) is then multiplied by
5, yielding 60. 60 is then multiplied by itself raised to the third power (that is,
60×60^3); this yields 12,960,000, which can also be expressed as $(3 \times 4 \times 5)^4$. The
number 12,960,000 "comprehends" two geometric figures representing "two har-
monies." The first figure is a square with sides measuring 3600 units ($3600 \times
3600 = 12,960,000$); the second is a rectangle with sides measuring 4800 and 2700
units ($4800 \times 2700 = 12,960,000$). Readers should note that, in the original text, the
number 12,960,000 is reached through a series of multiplications; Jowett's translation, "the base of these with a third *added*," misrepresents Socrates' mathematical
logic.

||The side of the square in question is 36 "100 times as great"—that is, 36×100,
which equals 3600.

#Alternatively, "a figure having one side equal to the other, but oblong [that is, in
a rectangle; two sides instead of four have the same measurement], having one
side that is 100 squares of the rational diameter of 5, minus 100." The rational diameter of 5 is 7, because the diameter of a square with sides of 5 units is the
square root of 50, and the closest rational number (that is, integer) to the square
root of 50 is 7, since $7 \times 7 = 49$. "100 squares of the rational diameter of 5," then,
is $100 \times 7 \times 7$, or 4900. Subtracting 100 from 4900 yields 4800.

squares of irrational diameters;° and 100 cubes of three.† Now this number represents a geometrical figure which has control over the good and evil of births.[6] For when your guardians are ignorant of the law of births, and unite bride and bridegroom out

d of season, the children will not be goodly or fortunate. And though only the best of them will be appointed by their predecessor, still they will be unworthy to hold their father's places, and when they come into power as guardians they will soon be found to fail in taking care of us, the muses, first by undervaluing music;‡ which neglect will soon extend to gymnastics; and hence the young men of your State will be less cultivated. In the succeeding generation rulers will be appointed who have lost the guardian power of test-

e ing the metal of your different races, which, like Hesiod's, are of
547 gold and silver and brass and iron.§ And so iron will be mingled with silver, and brass with gold, and hence there will arise dissimilarity and inequality and irregularity, which always and in all places are causes of hatred and war. This the Muses affirm to be the stock from which discord has sprung, wherever arising; and this is their answer to us.

Yes, and we may assume that they answer truly.

Why, yes, I said, of course they answer truly; how can the Muses speak falsely?

b And what do the Muses say next?

When discord arose, then the two races were drawn different ways: the iron and brass fell to acquiring money, and land, and houses, and gold, and silver; but the gold and silver races, not wanting money, but having the true riches in their own nature, inclined toward virtue and the ancient order of things. There was a battle between them, and at last they agreed to distribute their

c land and houses among individual owners; and they enslaved their

---

°This is shorthand for "or of 100 squares of irrational diameters, wanting 2 each," which presents an alternative way of arriving at the number 4800: that is, $(50-2) \times 100$. The irrational diameter is the square root of 50; the square of this number is 50; "wanting 2 each" means that 2 must be subtracted from 50, yielding 48.

†That is, $100 \times 3^3 = 2700$.

‡Compare 4.423e.

§Compare 3.415a–c.

friends and maintainers, whom they had formerly protected in the condition of freemen, and made of them subjects and servants; and they themselves were engaged in war and in keeping a watch against them.[7]

I believe that you have rightly conceived the origin of the change.

And the new government which thus arises will be of a form intermediate between oligarchy and aristocracy?

Very true.

Such will be the change, and after the change has been made, how will they proceed? Clearly, the new State, being in a mean   d
between oligarchy and the perfect State, will partly follow one and partly the other, and will also have some peculiarities.

True, he said.

In the honor given to rulers, in the abstinence of the warrior-class from agriculture, handicrafts, and trade in general, in the institution of common meals, and in the attention paid to gymnastics and military training—in all these respects this State will resemble the former.[8]

True.

But in the fear of admitting philosophers to power, because   e
they are no longer to be had simple and earnest, but are made up of mixed elements; and in turning from them to passionate and less complex characters, who are by nature fitted for war rather than peace; and in the value set by them upon military stratagems and contrivances, and in the waging of everlasting wars—this   548
State will be for the most part peculiar.

Yes.

Yes, I said; and men of this stamp will be covetous of money, like those who live in oligarchies; they will have a fierce secret longing after gold and silver, which they will hoard in dark places, having magazines and treasuries of their own for the deposit and concealment of them; also castles which are just nests for their eggs, and in which they will spend large sums on their wives, or on   b
any others whom they please.

That is most true, he said.

And they are miserly because they have no means of openly acquiring the money which they prize; they will spend that which is

another man's on the gratification of their desires, stealing their
pleasures and running away like children from the law, their father:
they have been schooled not by gentle influences but by force, for
they have neglected her who is the true muse, the companion of
c   reason and philosophy, and have honored gymnastics more than
music.

Undoubtedly, he said, the form of government which you describe is a mixture of good and evil.

Why, there is a mixture, I said; but one thing, and one thing only,
is predominantly seen—the spirit of contention and ambition; and
these are due to the prevalence of the passionate or spirited element.

Assuredly, he said.

Such is the origin and such the character of this State, which
has been described in outline only; the more perfect execution
d   was not required, for a sketch is enough to show the type of the
most perfectly just and most perfectly unjust; and to go through
all the States and all the characters of men, omitting none of
them, would be an interminable labor.

Very true, he replied.

Now what man answers to this form of government—how did
he come into being, and what is he like?

I think, said Adeimantus, that in the spirit of contention which
characterizes him, he is not unlike our friend Glaucon.

e   Perhaps, I said, he may be like him in that one point; but there
are other respects in which he is very different.

In what respects?

He should have more of self-assertion and be less cultivated
and yet a friend of culture; and he should be a good listener but
549   no speaker. Such a person is apt to be rough with slaves, unlike the
educated man, who is too proud for that; and he will also be cour-
teous to freemen, and remarkably obedient to authority; he is a
lover of power and a lover of honor; claiming to be a ruler, not because he is eloquent, or on any ground of that sort, but because he
is a soldier and has performed feats of arms; he is also a lover of
gymnastic exercises and of the chase.

Yes, that is the type of character that answers to timocracy.

Such a one will despise riches only when he is young; but as he

gets older he will be more and more attracted to them, because he ⟨b⟩
has a piece of the avaricious nature in him, and is not single-
minded toward virtue, having lost his best guardian.[9]

Who was that? said Adeimantus.

Philosophy, I said, tempered with music, who comes and takes
up her abode in a man, and is the only saviour of his virtue throughout life.

Good, he said.

Such, I said, is the timocratical youth, and he is like the timocratical State.

Exactly.

His origin is as follows:[10] He is often the young son of a brave ⟨c⟩
father, who dwells in an ill-governed city, of which he declines the
honors and offices, and will not go to law, or exert himself in any
way, but is ready to waive his rights in order that he may escape
trouble.

And how does the son come into being?

The character of the son begins to develop when he hears his
mother complaining that her husband has no place in the government, of which the consequence is that she has no precedence
among other women. Further, when she sees her husband not ⟨d⟩
very eager about money, and instead of battling and railing in the
law courts or assembly, taking whatever happens to him quietly;
and when she observes that his thoughts always centre in himself,
while he treats her with very considerable indifference, she is an-
noyed, and says to her son that his father is only half a man and far
too easy-going: adding all the other complaints about her own ill-
treatment which women are so fond of rehearsing. ⟨e⟩

Yes, said Adeimantus, they give us plenty of them, and their
complaints are so like themselves.

And you know, I said, that the old servants also, who are supposed to be attached to the family, from time to time talk privately
in the same strain to the son; and if they see anyone who owes
money to his father, or is wronging him in any way, and he fails to
prosecute them, they tell the youth that when he grows up he must
retaliate upon people of this sort, and be more of a man than his
father. He has only to walk abroad and he hears and sees the same ⟨550⟩
sort of thing: those who do their own business in the city are called

simpletons, and held in no esteem, while the busy-bodies are honored and applauded. The result is that the young man, hearing and
seeing all these things—hearing, too, the words of his father, and
having a nearer view of his way of life, and making comparisons of
him and others—is drawn opposite ways: while his father is water-
b ing and nourishing the rational principle in his soul, the others are
encouraging the passionate and appetitive; and he being not originally of a bad nature, but having kept bad company, is at last
brought by their joint influence to a middle point, and gives up
the kingdom which is within him to the middle principle of con-
tentiousness and passion, and becomes arrogant and ambitious.

You seem to me to have described his origin perfectly.

c Then we have now, I said, the second form of government and
the second type of character?

We have.

Next, let us look at another man who, as Æschylus says,

"Is set over against another State;"*

or rather, as our plan requires, begin with the State.

By all means.

I believe that oligarchy follows next in order.

And what manner of government do you term oligarchy?

A government resting on a valuation of property, in which the
d rich have power and the poor man is deprived of it.

I understand, he replied.

Ought I not to begin by describing how the change from timocracy to oligarchy arises?

Yes.

Well, I said, no eyes are required in order to see how the one
passes into the other.

How?

The accumulation of gold in the treasury of private individuals
is the ruin of timocracy; they invent illegal modes of expenditure;
for what do they or their wives care about the law?

---

*Adapted from Aeschylus, *Seven Against Thebes* 451 and 570.

Yes, indeed.

And then one, seeing another grow rich, seeks to rival him, and thus the great mass of the citizens become lovers of money.

e

Likely enough.

And so they grow richer and richer, and the more they think of making a fortune the less they think of virtue; for when riches and virtue are placed together in the scales of the balance the one always rises as the other falls.[11]

True.

And in proportion as riches and rich men are honored in the State, virtue and the virtuous are dishonored.

551

Clearly.

And what is honored is cultivated, and that which has no honor is neglected.

That is obvious.

And so at last, instead of loving contention and glory, men become lovers of trade and money; they honor and look up to the rich man, and make a ruler of him, and dishonor the poor man.

They do so.

They next proceed to make a law which fixes a sum of money as the qualification of citizenship;[12] the sum is higher in one place and lower in another, as the oligarchy is more or less exclusive; and they allow no one whose property falls below the amount fixed to have any share in the government. These changes in the constitution they effect by force of arms, if intimidation has not already done their work.

b

Very true.

And this, speaking generally, is the way in which oligarchy is established.

Yes, he said; but what are the characteristics of this form of government, and what are the defects of which we were speaking?[*]

c

First of all, I said, consider the nature of the qualification. Just think what would happen if pilots were to be chosen according to their property, and a poor man were refused permission to steer, even though he were a better pilot?

---

*See 8.544c.

You mean that they would shipwreck?

Yes; and is not this true of the government of anything?

I should imagine so.

Except a city?—or would you include a city?

Nay, he said, the case of a city is the strongest of all, inasmuch as the rule of a city is the greatest and most difficult of all.

d   This, then, will be the first great defect of oligarchy?

Clearly.

And here is another defect which is quite as bad.

What defect?

The inevitable division: such a State is not one, but two States, the one of poor, the other of rich men; and they are living on the same spot and always conspiring against one another.[13]

That, surely, is at least as bad.

Another discreditable feature is, that, for a like reason, they are incapable of carrying on any war. Either they arm the multitude, and then they are more afraid of them than of the enemy; or, if they do not call them out in the hour of battle, they are oligarchs indeed, few to fight as they are few to rule. And at the same time their fondness for money makes them unwilling to pay taxes.

How discreditable!

And, as we said before, under such a constitution the same persons have too many callings—they are husbandmen, tradesmen, warriors, all in one. Does that look well?

Anything but well.

There is another evil which is, perhaps, the greatest of all, and to which this State first begins to be liable.

What evil?

A man may sell all that he has, and another may acquire his property; yet after the sale he may dwell in the city of which he is no longer a part, being neither trader, nor artisan, nor horseman, nor hoplite,[14] but only a poor, helpless creature.

b   Yes, that is an evil which also first begins in this State.

The evil is certainly not prevented there; for oligarchies have both the extremes of great wealth and utter poverty.

True.

But think again: In his wealthy days, while he was spending his money, was a man of this sort a whit more good to the State for the purposes of citizenship? Or did he only seem to be a member of the ruling body, although in truth he was neither ruler nor subject, but just a spendthrift?

As you say, he seemed to be a ruler, but was only a spendthrift.   c

May we not say that this is the drone in the house who is like the drone in the honeycomb, and that the one is the plague of the city as the other is of the hive?[15]

Just so, Socrates.

And God has made the flying drones, Adeimantus, all without stings, whereas of the walking drones he has made some without stings, but others have dreadful stings; of the stingless class are those who in their old age end as paupers; of the stingers come all the criminal class, as they are termed.   d

Most true, he said.

Clearly then, whenever you see paupers in a State, somewhere in that neighborhood there are hidden away thieves and cutpurses and robbers of temples, and all sorts of malefactors.

Clearly.

Well, I said, and in oligarchical States do you not find paupers?

Yes, he said; nearly everybody is a pauper who is not a ruler.

And may we be so bold as to affirm that there are also many   e
criminals to be found in them, rogues who have stings, and whom the authorities are careful to restrain by force?

Certainly, we may be so bold.

The existence of such persons is to be attributed to want of education, ill-training, and an evil constitution of the State?

True.

Such, then, is the form and such are the evils of oligarchy; and there may be many other evils.

Very likely.

Then oligarchy, or the form of government in which the rulers   553
are elected for their wealth, may now be dismissed. Let us next proceed to consider the nature and origin of the individual who answers to this State.

By all means.

Does not the timocratical man change into the oligarchical on this wise?

How?

A time arrives when the representative of timocracy has a son: at first he begins by emulating his father and walking in his foot-steps, but presently he sees him of a sudden foundering against the State as upon a sunken reef, and he and all that he has are lost; he may have been a general or some other high officer who is brought to trial under a prejudice raised by informers, and either put to death or exiled or deprived of the privileges of a citizen, and all his property taken from him.

Nothing more likely.

And the son has seen and known all this—he is a ruined man, and his fear has taught him to knock ambition and passion head-foremost from his bosom's throne; humbled by poverty he takes to money-making, and by mean and miserly savings and hard work gets a fortune together. Is not such a one likely to seat the concu-piscent and covetous element on the vacant throne and to suffer it to play the great king within him, girt with tiara and chain and scimitar?

Most true, he replied.

And when he has made reason and spirit sit down on the ground obediently on either side of their sovereign, and taught them to know their place, he compels the one to think only of how lesser sums may be turned into larger ones, and will not allow the other to worship and admire anything but riches and rich men, or to be ambitious of anything so much as the acquisition of wealth and the means of acquiring it.

There is no swifter nor surer way of changing an ambitious youth into an avaricious one.

And the avaricious, I said, is the oligarchical youth?

Yes, he said; at any rate the individual out of whom he came is like the State out of which oligarchy came.

Let us then consider whether there is any likeness between them.

Very good.

First, then, they resemble one another in the value which they set upon wealth?

Certainly.

Also in their penurious, laborious character; the individual only satisfies his necessary appetites,* and confines his expenditure to them; his other desires he subdues, under the idea that they are unprofitable.

True.

He is a shabby fellow, who saves something out of everything and makes a purse for himself; and this is the sort of man whom the vulgar applaud. Is he not a true image of the State which he represents?   b

He appears to me to be so; at any rate money is highly valued by him as well as by the State.

You see that he is not a man of cultivation, I said.

I imagine not, he said; had he been educated he would never have made a blind god† director of his chorus, or given him chief honor.

Excellent! I said. Yet consider: Must we not further admit that owing to this want of cultivation there will be found in him drone-like desires as of pauper and rogue, which are forcibly kept down   c
by his general habit of life?

True.

Do you know where you will have to look if you want to discover his rogueries?

Where must I look?

You should see him where he has some great opportunity of acting dishonestly, as in the guardianship of an orphan.

Aye.

It will be clear enough then that in his ordinary dealings which give him a reputation for honesty, he coerces his bad passions by an enforced virtue; not making them see that they are wrong, or   d
taming them by reason, but by necessity and fear constraining them, and because he trembles for his possessions.

To be sure.

Yes, indeed, my dear friend, but you will find that the natural desires of the drone commonly exist in him all the same whenever he has to spend what is not his own.

---

*The distinction between necessary and unnecessary appetites (and pleasures) is fleshed out at 8.558d–559d.
†That is, Ploutos, the god of wealth.

Yes, and they will be strong in him, too.

The man, then, will be at war with himself; he will be two men, and not one;[16] but, in general, his better desires will be found to prevail over his inferior ones.

e

True.

For these reasons such a one will be more respectable than most people; yet the true virtue of a unanimous and harmonious soul will flee far away and never come near him.

I should expect so.

And surely the miser individually will be an ignoble competitor in a State for any prize of victory, or other object of honorable ambition; he will not spend his money in the contest for glory; so afraid is he of awakening his expensive appetites and inviting them to help and join in the struggle; in true oligarchical fashion he fights with a small part only of his resources, and the result commonly is that he loses the prize and saves his money.

555

Very true.

Can we any longer doubt, then, that the miser and money-maker answers to the oligarchical State?

b

There can be no doubt.

Next comes democracy; of this the origin and nature have still to be considered by us; and then we will inquire into the ways of the democratic man, and bring him up for judgment.

That, he said, is our method.

Well, I said, and how does the change from oligarchy into democracy arise? Is it not on this wise: the good at which such a State aims is to become as rich as possible, a desire which is insatiable?

What then?

The rulers being aware that their power rests upon their wealth, refuse to curtail by law the extravagance of the spendthrift youth because they gain by their ruin; they take interest from them and buy up their estates and thus increase their own wealth and importance?

c

To be sure.

There can be no doubt that the love of wealth and the spirit of moderation cannot exist together in citizens of the same State to any considerable extent; one or the other will be disregarded.

d

That is tolerably clear.

And in oligarchical States, from the general spread of careless-
ness and extravagance, men of good family have often been reduced to beggary?

Yes, often.

And still they remain in the city; there they are, ready to sting
and fully armed, and some of them owe money, some have for-
feited their citizenship; a third class are in both predicaments; and
they hate and conspire against those who have got their property,
and against everybody else, and are eager for revolution.   e

That is true.

On the other hand, the men of business, stooping as they walk,
and pretending not even to see those whom they have already ruined, insert their sting—that is, their money—into someone else
who is not on his guard against them, and recover the parent sum*
many times over multiplied into a family of children: and so they
make drone and pauper to abound in the State.   556

Yes, he said, there are plenty of them—that is certain.

The evil blazes up like a fire; and they will not extinguish it either by restricting a man's use of his own property, or by another
remedy.[17]

What other?

One which is the next best, and has the advantage of compelling the citizens to look to their characters: Let there be a general rule that everyone shall enter into voluntary contracts at his
own risk, and there will be less of this scandalous money-making,   b
and the evils of which we were speaking will be greatly lessened
in the State.

Yes, they will be greatly lessened.

At present the governors, induced by the motives which I have
named, treat their subjects badly; while they and their adherents,
especially the young men of the governing class, are habituated to
lead a life of luxury and idleness both of body and mind; they do
nothing, and are incapable of resisting either pleasure or pain.   c

Very true.

---

*Another pun on the word *tokos*, which means both "offspring" and "interest (on
a loan)"; compare 6.507a.

They themselves care only for making money, and are as indifferent as the pauper to the cultivation of virtue.

Yes, quite as indifferent.

Such is the state of affairs which prevails among them. And often rulers and their subjects may come in one another's way, whether on a journey or on some other occasion of meeting, on a pilgrimage or a march, as fellow-soldiers or fellow-sailors; aye, and they may observe the behavior of each other in the very moment of danger—for where danger is, there is no fear that the poor will be despised by the rich—and very likely the wiry, sunburnt poor man may be placed in battle at the side of a wealthy one who has never spoilt his complexion and has plenty of superfluous flesh—when he sees such a one puffing and at his wits'-end, how can he avoid drawing the conclusion that men like him are only rich because no one has the courage to despoil them? And when they meet in private will not people be saying to one another, "Our warriors are not good for much"?

Yes, he said, I am quite aware that this is their way of talking.

And, as in a body which is diseased the addition of a touch from without may bring on illness, and sometimes even when there is no external provocation, a commotion may arise within—in the same way wherever there is weakness in the State there is also likely to be illness, of which the occasion may be very slight, the one party introducing from without their oligarchical, the other their democratical allies, and then the State falls sick, and is at war with herself; and may be at times distracted, even when there is no external cause.

Yes, surely.

And then democracy comes into being after the poor have conquered their opponents, slaughtering some and banishing some,[18] while to the remainder they give an equal share of freedom and power; and this is the form of government in which the magistrates are commonly elected by lot.

Yes, he said, that is the nature of democracy, whether the revolution has been effected by arms, or whether fear has caused the opposite party to withdraw.

And now what is their manner of life, and what sort of a government have they? for as the government is, such will be the man.

Clearly, he said.

In the first place, are they not free;[19] and is not the city full of freedom and frankness—a man may say and do what he likes?

'Tis said so, he replied.

And where freedom is, the individual is clearly able to order for himself his own life as he pleases?

Clearly.

Then in this kind of State there will be the greatest variety of   c human natures?

There will.

This, then, seems likely to be the fairest of States, being like an embroidered robe which is spangled with every sort of flower. And just as women and children think a variety of colors to be of all things most charming, so there are many men to whom this State, which is spangled with the manners and characters of mankind, will appear to be the fairest of States.

Yes.

Yes, my good sir, and there will be no better in which to look for   d a government.

Why?

Because of the liberty which reigns there—they have a complete assortment of constitutions; and he who has a mind to establish a State, as we have been doing, must go to a democracy as he would to a bazaar at which they sell them, and pick out the one that suits him; then, when he has made his choice, he may found his State.

He will be sure to have patterns enough.   e

And there being no necessity, I said, for you to govern in this State, even if you have the capacity, or to be governed, unless you like, or to go to war when the rest go to war, or to be at peace when others are at peace, unless you are so disposed—there being no necessity also, because some law forbids you to hold office or be a dicast, that you should not hold office or be a dicast, if you have a fancy—is not this a way of life which for the moment is   558 supremely delightful?

For the moment, yes.

And is not their humanity to the condemned in some cases quite charming?[20] Have you not observed how, in a democracy,

many persons, although they have been sentenced to death or exile, just stay where they are and walk about the world—the gentleman parades like a hero, and nobody sees or cares?

Yes, he replied, many and many a one.

b   See, too, I said, the "considerateness" of democracy, and the
"don't care" about trifles, and the disregard which she shows of all
the fine principles which we solemnly laid down at the foundation
of the city—as when we said that, except in the case of some rarely
gifted nature,* there never will be a good man who has not from
his childhood been used to play amid things of beauty and make of
them a joy and a study—how grandly does she trample all these
fine notions of ours under her feet, never giving a thought to the
c   pursuits which make a statesman, and promoting to honor anyone
who professes to be the people's friend.

Yes, she is of a noble spirit.

These and other kindred characteristics are proper to democracy, which is a charming form of government, full of variety and
disorder and dispensing a sort of equality to equals and unequals
alike.[21]

We know her well.

Consider now, I said, what manner of man the individual is, or
rather consider, as in the case of the State, how he comes into
being.

Very good, he said.

Is not this the way—he is the son of the miserly and oligarchi-
d   cal father who has trained him in his own habits?

Exactly.

And, like his father, he keeps under by force the pleasures
which are of the spending and not of the getting sort, being those
which are called unnecessary?

Obviously.

Would you like, for the sake of clearness, to distinguish which
are the necessary and which are the unnecessary pleasures?

I should.

e   Are not necessary pleasures those of which we cannot get rid,

---

*Compare 6.492a and 6.496a–b.

and of which the satisfaction is a benefit to us? And they are rightly called so, because we are framed by nature to desire both what is beneficial and what is necessary, and cannot help it.

True.

We are not wrong therefore in calling them necessary? 559

We are not.

And the desires of which a man may get rid, if he takes pains from his youth upward—of which the presence, moreover, does no good, and in some cases the reverse of good—shall we not be right in saying that all these are unnecessary?

Yes, certainly.

Suppose we select an example of either kind, in order that we may have a general notion of them?

Very good.

Will not the desire of eating, that is, of simple food and condiments, in so far as they are required for health and strength, be of the necessary class? b

That is what I should suppose.

The pleasure of eating is necessary in two ways; it does us good and it is essential to the continuance of life?

Yes.

But the condiments are only necessary in so far as they are good for health?

Certainly.

And the desire which goes beyond this, of more delicate food, or other luxuries, which might generally be got rid of, if controlled and trained in youth, and is hurtful to the body, and hurtful to the soul in the pursuit of wisdom and virtue, may be rightly c
called unnecessary?

Very true.

May we not say that these desires spend, and that the others make money because they conduce to production?

Certainly.

And of the pleasures of love, and all other pleasures, the same holds good?

True.

And the drone of whom we spoke was he who was surfeited in pleasures and desires of this sort, and was the slave of the d   unnecessary desires, whereas he who was subject to the necessary only was miserly and oligarchical?

Very true.

Again, let us see how the democratical man goes out of the oligarchical: the following, as I suspect, is commonly the process.

What is the process?

When a young man who has been brought up as we were just now describing, in a vulgar and miserly way, has tasted drones' honey and has come to associate with fierce and crafty natures who are able to provide for him all sorts of refinements and varieties of pleasure—then, as you may imagine, the change will be-

e   gin of the oligarchical principle within him into the democratical?

Inevitably.

And as in the city like was helping like, and the change was effected by an alliance from without assisting one division of the citizens, so too the young man is changed by a class of desires coming from without to assist the desires within him, that which is akin and alike again helping that which is akin and alike?

Certainly.

And if there be any ally which aids the oligarchical principle within him, whether the influence of a father or of kindred, advis-

560   ing or rebuking him, then there arise in his soul a faction and an opposite faction, and he goes to war with himself.[22]

It must be so.

And there are times when the democratical principle gives way to the oligarchical, and some of his desires die, and others are banished; a spirit of reverence enters into the young man's soul, and order is restored.

Yes, he said, that sometimes happens.

And then, again, after the old desires have been driven out,

b   fresh ones spring up, which are akin to them, and because his father does not know how to educate him, wax fierce and numerous.

Yes, he said, that is apt to be the way.

They draw him to his old associates, and holding secret intercourse with them, breed and multiply in him.

Very true.

At length they seize upon the citadel of the young man's soul, which they perceive to be void of all accomplishments and fair

pursuits and true words, which make their abode in the minds of
men who are dear to the gods, and are their best guardians and
sentinels.

None better.   c

False and boastful conceits and phrases mount upward and
take their place.

They are certain to do so.

And so the young man returns into the country of the lotus-
eaters,* and takes up his dwelling there, in the face of all men;
and if any help be sent by his friends to the oligarchical part of
him, the aforesaid vain conceits shut the gate of the King's fastness;[23] and they will neither allow the embassy itself to enter, nor
if private advisers offer the fatherly counsel of the aged will they
listen to them or receive them. There is a battle and they gain the   d
day, and then modesty, which they call silliness, is ignominiously
thrust into exile by them, and temperance, which they nick-name
unmanliness, is trampled in the mire and cast forth; they persuade
men that moderation and orderly expenditure are vulgarity and
meanness, and so, by the help of a rabble of evil appetites, they
drive them beyond the border.[24]

Yes, with a will.

And when they have emptied and swept clean the soul of him
who is now in their power and who is being initiated by them in   e
great mysteries, the next thing is to bring back to their house insolence and anarchy and waste and impudence in bright array, having
garlands on their heads, and a great company with them, hymning
their praises and calling them by sweet names; insolence they term
"breeding," and anarchy "liberty," and waste "magnificence," and
impudence "courage." And so the young man passes out of his orig-   561
inal nature, which was trained in the school of necessity, into the
freedom and libertinism of useless and unnecessary pleasures.

Yes, he said, the change in him is visible enough.

After this he lives on, spending his money and labor and time
on unnecessary pleasures quite as much as on necessary ones; but

---

*Compare *Odyssey* 9.82–104. The reference here is to the "drone desires" mentioned at 8.559d.

if he be fortunate, and is not too much disordered in his wits, when years have elapsed, and the heyday of passion is over—supposing

b that he then readmits into the city some part of the exiled virtues, and does not wholly give himself up to their successors—in that case he balances his pleasures and lives in a sort of equilibrium, putting the government of himself into the hands of the one which comes first and wins the turn; and when he has had enough of that, then into the hands of another; he despises none of them, but encourages them all equally.

Very true, he said.

Neither does he receive or let pass into the fortress any true word of advice;[25] if anyone says to him that some pleasures are the

c satisfactions of good and noble desires, and others of evil desires, and that he ought to use and honor some, and chastise and master the others—whenever this is repeated to him he shakes his head and says that they are all alike, and that one is as good as another.

Yes, he said; that is the way with him.

Yes, I said, he lives from day to day indulging the appetite of the hour; and sometimes he is lapped in drink and strains of the flute; then he becomes a water-drinker, and tries to get thin; then

d he takes a turn at gymnastics; sometimes idling and neglecting everything, then once more living the life of a philosopher; often he is busy with politics, and starts to his feet and says and does whatever comes into his head; and, if he is emulous of anyone who is a warrior, off he is in that direction, or of men of business, once more in that. His life has neither law nor order; and this distracted existence he terms joy and bliss and freedom; and so he goes on.

e Yes, he replied, he is all liberty and equality.

Yes, I said; his life is motley and manifold and an epitome of the lives of many; he answers to the State which we described as fair and spangled. And many a man and many a woman will take him for their pattern, and many a constitution and many an example of manners are contained in him.

Just so.

562 Let him then be set over against democracy; he may truly be called the democratic man.

Let that be his place, he said.

Last of all comes the most beautiful of all, man and State alike, tyranny and the tyrant; these we have now to consider.

Quite true, he said.

Say then, my friend, in what manner does tyranny arise?—that it has a democratic origin is evident.

Clearly.

And does not tyranny spring from democracy in the same manner as democracy from oligarchy—I mean, after a sort?[26]

How?

The good which oligarchy proposed to itself and the means by which it was maintained was excess of wealth—am I not right? b

Yes.

And the insatiable desire of wealth and the neglect of all other things for the sake of money-getting were also the ruin of oligarchy?

True.

And democracy has her own good, of which the insatiable desire brings her to dissolution?

What good?

Freedom, I replied; which, as they tell you in a democracy, is the glory of the State—and that therefore in a democracy alone c will the freeman of nature deign to dwell.

Yes; the saying is in everybody's mouth.

I was going to observe, that the insatiable desire of this and the neglect of other things introduce the change in democracy, which occasions a demand for tyranny.

How so?

When a democracy which is thirsting for freedom has evil cupbearers presiding over the feast, and has drunk too deeply of the d strong wine of freedom,* then, unless her rulers are very amenable and give a plentiful draught, she calls them to account and punishes them, and says that they are cursed oligarchs.

Yes, he replied, a very common occurrence.

Yes, I said; and loyal citizens are insultingly termed by her "slaves" who hug their chains, and men of naught; she would have

---

*Literally, unmixed wine. Greeks typically drank wine mixed with water.

subjects who are like rulers, and rulers who are like subjects: these are men after her own heart, whom she praises and honors both in private and public. Now, in such a State, can liberty have any limit?

Certainly not.

By degrees the anarchy finds a way into private houses, and ends by getting among the animals and infecting them.[27]

How do you mean?

I mean that the father grows accustomed to descend to the level of his sons and to fear them, and the son is on a level with his father, he having no respect or reverence for either of his parents; and this is his freedom; and the metic is equal with the citizen, and the citizen with the metic, and the stranger is quite as good as either.

Yes, he said, that is the way.

And these are not the only evils, I said—there are several lesser ones: In such a state of society the master fears and flatters his students, and the students despise their masters and tutors; young and old are all alike; and the young man is on a level with the old, and is ready to compete with him in word or deed; and old men condescend to the young and are full of pleasantry and gayety; they are loth to be thought morose and authoritative, and therefore they adopt the manners of the young.

Quite true, he said.

The last extreme of popular liberty is when the slave bought with money, whether male or female, is just as free as his or her purchaser; nor must I forget to tell of the liberty and equality of the two sexes in relation to each other.

Why not, as Æschylus says, utter the word which rises to our lips?*

That is what I am doing, I replied; and I must add that no one who does not know would believe how much greater is the liberty which the animals who are under the dominion of man have in a democracy than in any other State: for, truly, the she-dogs, as the proverb says, are as good as their she-mistresses,† and the horses

---

*Adapted from a lost play.
†The proverb in question is "Like mistress, like her dog"; it refers to the imitation by female slaves of their mistresses' ways.

and asses have a way of marching along with all the rights and dig-
nities of freemen; and they will run at anybody who comes in their
way if he does not leave the road clear for them: and all things are
just ready to burst with liberty.   d

When I take a country walk, he said, I often experience what
you describe. You and I have dreamed the same thing.

And above all, I said, and as the result of all, see how sensitive
the citizens become; they chafe impatiently at the least touch of
authority, and at length, as you know, they cease to care even for
the laws, written or unwritten; they will have no one over them.   e

Yes, he said, I know it too well.

Such, my friend, I said, is the fair and glorious beginning out of
which springs tyranny.

Glorious indeed, he said. But what is the next step?

The ruin of oligarchy is the ruin of democracy; the same disease
magnified and intensified by liberty overmasters democracy—the
truth being that the excessive increase of anything often causes a
reaction in the opposite direction; and this is the case not only in
the seasons and in vegetable and animal life, but above all in forms
of government.   564

True.

The excess of liberty, whether in States or individuals, seems
only to pass into excess of slavery.

Yes, the natural order.

And so tyranny naturally arises out of democracy, and the most
aggravated form of tyranny and slavery out of the most extreme
form of liberty?

As we might expect.

That, however, was not, as I believe, your question—you rather
desired to know what is that disorder which is generated alike in
oligarchy and democracy, and is the ruin of both?   b

Just so, he replied.

Well, I said, I meant to refer to the class of idle spendthrifts, of
whom the more courageous are the leaders and the more timid
the followers, the same whom we were comparing to drones,
some stingless, and others having stings.

A very just comparison.

These two classes are the plagues of every city in which they are generated, being what phlegm and bile are to the body. And the good physician and lawgiver of the State ought, like the wise bee-master, to keep them at a distance and prevent, if possible, their ever coming in; and if they have anyhow found a way in, then he should have them and their cells cut out as speedily as possible.

Yes, by all means, he said.

Then, in order that we may see clearly what we are doing, let us imagine democracy to be divided, as indeed it is, into three classes; for in the first place freedom creates rather more drones in the democratic than there were in the oligarchical State.

That is true.

And in the democracy they are certainly more intensified.

How so?

Because in the oligarchical State they are disqualified and driven from office, and therefore they cannot train or gather strength; whereas in a democracy they are almost the entire ruling power, and while the keener sort speak and act, the rest keep buzzing about the bema* and do not suffer a word to be said on the other side; hence in democracies almost everything is managed by the drones.

Very true, he said.

Then there is another class which is always being severed from the mass.

What is that?

They are the orderly class, which in a nation of traders is sure to be the richest.

Naturally so.

They are the most squeezable persons and yield the largest amount of honey to the drones.

Why, he said, there is little to be squeezed out of people who have little.

And this is called the wealthy class, and the drones feed upon them.

That is pretty much the case, he said.

---

*The speaker's platform in, for example, the Assembly.

The people are a third class, consisting of those who work with   565
their own hands; they are not politicians, and have not much to
live upon. This, when assembled, is the largest and most powerful
class in a democracy.

True, he said; but then the multitude is seldom willing to con-
gregate unless they get a little honey.

And do they not share? I said. Do not their leaders deprive the
rich of their estates and distribute them among the people; at the
same time taking care to reserve the larger part for themselves?

Why, yes, he said, to that extent the people do share.   b

And the persons whose property is taken from them are compelled to defend themselves before the people as they best can?

What else can they do?

And then, although they may have no desire of change, the
others charge them with plotting against the people and being
friends of oligarchy?

True.

And the end is that when they see the people, not of their own
accord, but through ignorance, and because they are deceived by
informers, seeking to do them wrong, then at last they are forced
to become oligarchs in reality; they do not wish to be, but the   c
sting of the drones torments them and breeds revolution in
them.[28]

That is exactly the truth.

Then come impeachments and judgments and trials of one another.

True.

The people have always some champion* whom they set over
them and nurse into greatness.

Yes, that is their way.

This, and no other, is the root from which a tyrant springs;   d
when he first appears above ground he is a protector.

Yes, that is quite clear.

How, then, does a protector begin to change into a tyrant?

---

*"Demagogic" politicians (such as Cleon, who died in 422 B.C.E.) styled them-
selves as "champions [*prostatai*] of the people."

Clearly when he does what the man is said to do in the tale of the Arcadian temple of Lycæan Zeus.*

What tale?

The tale is that he who has tasted the entrails of a single human victim minced up with the entrails of other victims is destined to become a wolf. Did you never hear it?

Oh, yes.

And the protector of the people is like him; having a mob entirely at his disposal, he is not restrained from shedding the blood of kinsmen; by the favorite method of false accusation he brings them into court and murders them, making the life of man to disappear, and with unholy tongue and lips tasting the blood of his fellow-citizens; some he kills and others he banishes, at the same time hinting at the abolition of debts and partition of lands: and after this, what will be his destiny? Must he not either perish at the hands of his enemies, or from being a man become a wolf—that is, a tyrant?

Inevitably.

This, I said, is he who begins to make a party against the rich?

The same.

After a while he is driven out, but comes back, in spite of his enemies, a tyrant full grown.[29]

That is clear.

And if they are unable to expel him, or to get him condemned to death by a public accusation, they conspire to assassinate him.

Yes, he said, that is their usual way.

Then comes the famous request for a body-guard,[30] which is the device of all those who have got thus far in their tyrannical career—"Let not the people's friend," as they say, "be lost to them."

Exactly.

The people readily assent; all their fears are for him—they have none for themselves.

Very true.

And when a man who is wealthy and is also accused of being an enemy of the people sees this, then, my friend, as the oracle said to Crœsus,

---

*That is, Zeus the wolf-god. Tales about werewolves were popular in antiquity.

"By pebbly Hermus's shore he flees and rests not, and is not ashamed to be a coward."[31]

And quite right too, said he, for if he were, he would never be ashamed again.

But if he is caught he dies.

Of course.

And he, the protector of whom we spoke, is to be seen, not "larding the plain" with his bulk, but himself the overthrower of many, standing up in the chariot of State with the reins in his hand, no longer protector, but tyrant absolute.

No doubt, he said.

And now let us consider the happiness of the man, and also of the State in which a creature like him is generated.

Yes, he said, let us consider that.

At first, in the early days of his power, he is full of smiles, and he salutes everyone whom he meets; he to be called a tyrant, who is making promises in public and also in private! liberating debtors, and distributing land to the people and his followers, and wanting to be so kind and good to everyone!

Of course, he said.

But when he has disposed of foreign enemies by conquest or treaty, and there is nothing to fear from them, then he is always stirring up some war or other, in order that the people may require a leader.

To be sure.

Has he not also another object, which is that they may be impoverished by payment of taxes, and thus compelled to devote themselves to their daily wants and therefore less likely to conspire against him?

Clearly.

And if any of them are suspected by him of having notions of freedom, and of resistance to his authority, he will have a good pretext for destroying them by placing them at the mercy of the enemy; and for all these reasons the tyrant must be always getting up a war.

He must.

Now he begins to grow unpopular.

b   A necessary result.

Then some of those who joined in setting him up, and who are in power, speak their minds to him and to one another, and the more courageous of them cast in his teeth what is being done.

Yes, that may be expected.

And the tyrant, if he means to rule, must get rid of them; he cannot stop while he has a friend or an enemy who is good for anything.

He cannot.

And therefore he must look about him and see who is valiant, c who is high-minded, who is wise, who is wealthy; happy man, he is the enemy of them all, and must seek occasion against them whether he will or no, until he has made a purgation of the State.[32]

Yes, he said, and a rare purgation.

Yes, I said, not the sort of purgation which the physicians make of the body; for they take away the worse and leave the better part, but he does the reverse.

If he is to rule, I suppose that he cannot help himself.

d   What a blessed alternative, I said: to be compelled to dwell only with the many bad, and to be by them hated, or not to live at all!

Yes, that is the alternative.

And the more detestable his actions are to the citizens the more satellites and the greater devotion in them will he require?

Certainly.

And who are the devoted band, and where will he procure them?

They will flock to him, he said, of their own accord, if he pays them.

e   By the dog! I said, here are more drones, of every sort and from every land.

Yes, he said, there are.

But will he not desire to get them on the spot?

How do you mean?

He will rob the citizens of their slaves; he will then set them free and enrol them in his body-guard.

To be sure, he said; and he will be able to trust them best of all.

What a blessed creature, I said, must this tyrant be; he has put 568 to death the others and has these for his trusted friends.

Yes, he said; they are quite of his sort.

Yes, I said, and these are the new citizens whom he has called into existence, who admire him and are his companions, while the good hate and avoid him.

Of course.

Verily, then, tragedy is a wise thing and Euripides a great tragedian.

Why so?

Why, because he is the author of the pregnant saying,

"Tyrants are wise by living with the wise;"[33]   b

and he clearly meant to say that they are the wise whom the tyrant makes his companions.

Yes, he said, and he also praises tyranny as godlike; and many other things of the same kind are said by him and by the other poets.

And therefore, I said, the tragic poets being wise men will forgive us and any others who live after our manner, if we do not receive them into our State, because they are the eulogists of tyranny.

Yes, he said, those who have the wit will doubtless forgive us.   c

But they will continue to go to other cities and attract mobs, and hire voices fair and loud and persuasive, and draw the cities over to tyrannies and democracies.[34]

Very true.

Moreover, they are paid for this and receive honor—the greatest honor, as might be expected, from tyrants, and the next greatest from democracies; but the higher they ascend our constitution hill, the more their reputation fails, and seems unable from short-   d
ness of breath to proceed farther.

True.

But we are wandering from the subject: Let us therefore return and inquire how the tyrant will maintain that fair, and numerous, and various, and ever-changing army of his.

If, he said, there are sacred treasures in the city, he will confiscate and spend them; and in so far as the fortunes of attainted persons may suffice, he will be able to diminish the taxes which he would otherwise have to impose upon the people.

e   And when these fail?

Why, clearly, he said, then he and his boon companions, whether male or female, will be maintained out of his father's estate.[35]

You mean to say that the people, from whom he has derived his being, will maintain him and his companions?

Yes, he said; they cannot help themselves.

But what if the people fly into a passion, and aver that a grown-up son ought not to be supported by his father, but that the father should be supported by the son? The father did not bring him 569   into being, or settle him in life, in order that when his son became a man he should himself be the servant of his own servants and should support him and his rabble of slaves and companions; but that his son should protect him, and that by his help he might be emancipated from the government of the rich and aristocratic, as they are termed. And so he bids him and his companions depart, just as any other father might drive out of the house a riotous son and his undesirable associates.

By heaven, he said, then the parent will discover what a mon-
b   ster he has been fostering in his bosom; and, when he wants to drive him out, he will find that he is weak and his son strong.

Why, you do not mean to say that the tyrant will use violence? What! beat his father if he opposes him?

Yes, he will, having first disarmed him.

Then he is a parricide, and a cruel guardian of an aged parent; and this is real tyranny, about which there can be no longer a mis-take: as the saying is, the people who would escape the smoke
c   which is the slavery of freemen, has fallen into the fire which is the tyranny of slaves. Thus liberty, getting out of all order and rea-son, passes into the harshest and bitterest form of slavery.

True, he said.

Very well; and may we not rightly say that we have sufficiently discussed the nature of tyranny, and the manner of the transition from democracy to tyranny?

Yes, quite enough, he said.

BOOK 9

LAST OF ALL COMES the tyrannical man; about whom we have 571 once more to ask, how is he formed out of the democratical? and how does he live, in happiness or in misery?

Yes, he said, he is the only one remaining.

There is, however, I said, a previous question which remains unanswered.

What question?

I do not think that we have adequately determined the nature and number of the appetites, and until this is accomplished the inquiry will always be confused. b

Well, he said, it is not too late to supply the omission.

Very true, I said; and observe the point which I want to understand: Certain of the unnecessary pleasures and appetites I conceive to be unlawful; everyone appears to have them, but in some persons they are controlled by the laws and by reason, and the better desires prevail over them—either they are wholly banished or they become few and weak; while in the case of others they are stronger, and there are more of them. c

Which appetites do you mean?

I mean those which are awake when the reasoning and human and ruling power is asleep; then the wild beast within us, gorged with meat or drink, starts up and, having shaken off sleep, goes forth to satisfy his desires; and there is no conceivable folly or crime—not excepting incest or any other unnatural union, or par- d ricide, or the eating of forbidden food—which at such a time, when he has parted company with all shame and sense, a man may not be ready to commit.

Most true, he said.

But when a man's pulse is healthy and temperate, and when before going to sleep he has awakened his rational powers, and fed them on noble thoughts and inquiries, collecting himself in meditation; after having first indulged his appetites neither too much e   nor too little, but just enough to lay them to sleep, and prevent them and their enjoyments and pains from interfering with the higher principle°—which he leaves in the solitude of pure abstraction, free to contemplate and aspire to the knowledge of the

572   unknown, whether in past, present, or future: when again he has allayed the passionate element, if he has a quarrel against anyone— I say, when, after pacifying the two irrational principles, he rouses up the third, which is reason, before he takes his rest, then, as you know, he attains truth most nearly, and is least likely to be the

b   sport of fantastic and lawless visions.

    I quite agree.

    In saying this I have been running into a digression; but the point which I desire to note is that in all of us, even in good men, there is a lawless wild-beast nature, which peers out in sleep.[1] Pray, consider whether I am right, and you agree with me.

    Yes, I agree.

    And now remember the character which we attributed to the

c   democratic man. He was supposed from his youth upward to have been trained under a miserly parent, who encouraged the saving appetites in him, but discountenanced the unnecessary, which aim only at amusement and ornament?

    True.

    And then he got into the company of a more refined, licentious sort of people, and taking to all their wanton ways rushed into the opposite extreme from an abhorrence of his father's meanness. At

d   last, being a better man than his corruptors, he was drawn in both directions until he halted midway and led a life, not of vulgar and slavish passion, but of what he deemed moderate indulgence in various pleasures. After this manner the democrat was generated out of the oligarch?

    Yes, he said; that was our view of him, and is so still.

    And now, I said, years will have passed away, and you must conceive this man, such as he is, to have a son, who is brought up in his father's principles.

    I can imagine him.

°That is, the rational part of the soul.

Then you must further imagine the same thing to happen to the son which has already happened to the father: he is drawn into a perfectly lawless life, which by his seducers is termed perfect liberty; and his father and friends take part with his moderate desires, and the opposite party assist the opposite ones. As soon as these dire magicians and tyrant-makers find that they are losing their hold on him, they contrive to implant in him a master-passion, to be lord over his idle and spendthrift lusts—a sort of monstrous winged drone—that is the only image which will adequately describe him.

Yes, he said, that is the only adequate image of him.

And when his other lusts, amid clouds of incense and perfumes and garlands and wines, and all the pleasures of a dissolute life, now let loose, come buzzing around him, nourishing to the utmost the sting of desire which they implant in his drone-like nature, then at last this lord of the soul, having Madness for the captain of his guard, breaks out into a frenzy; and if he finds in himself any good opinions or appetites in process of formation, and there is in him any sense of shame remaining, to these better principles he puts an end, and casts them forth until he has purged away temperance and brought in madness to the full.

Yes, he said, that is the way in which the tyrannical man is generated.

And is not this the reason why, of old, love has been called a tyrant?[2]

I should not wonder.

Further, I said, has not a drunken man also the spirit of a tyrant? He has.

And you know that a man who is deranged, and not right in his mind, will fancy that he is able to rule, not only over men, but also over the gods?

That he will.

And the tyrannical man in the true sense of the word comes into being when, either under the influence of nature or habit, or both, he becomes drunken, lustful, passionate? O my friend, is not that so?

Assuredly.

Such is the man and such is his origin. And next, how does he live?

d   Suppose, as people facetiously say, you were to tell me.

I imagine, I said, at the next step in his progress, that there will be feasts and carousals and revellings and courtesans, and all that sort of thing; Love is the lord of the house within him, and orders all the concerns of his soul.[3]

That is certain.

Yes; and every day and every night desires grow up many and formidable, and their demands are many.

They are indeed, he said.

His revenues, if he has any, are soon spent.

True.

e   Then come debt and the cutting down of his property.

Of course.

When he has nothing left, must not his desires, crowding in the nest like young ravens, be crying aloud for food; and he, goaded on by them, and especially by love himself, who is in a manner the captain of them, is in a frenzy, and would fain discover whom he can defraud or despoil of his property, in order that he may grat-

574   ify them?

Yes, that is sure to be the case.

He must have money, no matter how, if he is to escape horrid pains and pangs.

He must.

And as in himself there was a succession of pleasures, and the new got the better of the old and took away their rights, so he being younger will claim to have more than his father and his mother, and if he has spent his own share of the property, he will take a slice of theirs.

No doubt he will.

b   And if his parents will not give way, then he will try first of all to cheat and deceive them.

Very true.

And if he fails, then he will use force and plunder them.

Yes, probably.

And if the old man and woman fight for their own, what then, my friend? Will the creature feel any compunction at tyrannizing over them?

Nay, he said, I should not feel at all comfortable about his parents.

But, O heavens! Adeimantus, on account of some newfangled love of a harlot, who is anything but a necessary connection, can you believe that he would strike the mother who is his ancient friend and necessary to his very existence, and would place her under the authority of the other, when she is brought under the same roof with her; or that, under like circumstances, he would do   c the same to his withered old father, first and most indispensable of friends, for the sake of some newly found blooming youth who is the reverse of indispensable?

Yes, indeed, he said; I believe that he would.

Truly, then, I said, a tyrannical son is a blessing to his father and mother.

He is indeed, he replied.

He first takes their property, and when that fails, and pleasures   d are beginning to swarm in the hive of his soul, then he breaks into a house, or steals the garments of some nightly wayfarer; next he proceeds to clear a temple.[4] Meanwhile the old opinions which he had when a child, and which gave judgment about good and evil, are overthrown by those others which have just been emancipated, and are now the body-guard of love* and share his empire. These in his democratic days, when he was still subject to the laws and to his fa-   e ther, were only let loose in the dreams of sleep. But now that he is under the dominion of Love, he becomes always and in waking reality what he was then very rarely and in a dream only; he will commit the foulest murder, or eat forbidden food, or be guilty of any other horrid act. Love is his tyrant, and lives lordly in him and lawlessly, and being himself a king, leads him on, as a tyrant leads a State, to   575 the performance of any reckless deed by which he can maintain himself and the rabble of his associates, whether those whom evil communications have brought in from without, or those whom he himself has allowed to break loose within him by reason of a similar evil nature in himself. Have we not here a picture of his way of life?

---

*For the reliance of tyrants on bodyguards, see 8.566b.

Yes, indeed, he said.

And if there are only a few of them in the State, and the rest of
b   the people are well disposed, they go away and become the body-
guard of mercenary soldiers of some other tyrant who may probably want them for a war; and if there is no war, they stay at home
and do many little pieces of mischief in the city.

What sort of mischief?

For example, they are the thieves, burglars, cut-purses, footpads,
robbers of temples, man-stealers of the community; or if they are
able to speak, they turn informers and bear false witness and take
bribes.

c   You describe a small catalogue of evils, if the perpetrators of
them are few in number.

Yes, I said; but small and great are comparative terms, and all
these things, in the misery and evil which they inflict upon a State,
do not come within a thousand miles of the tyrant; when this noxious class and their followers grow numerous and become conscious of their strength, assisted by the infatuation of the people,
they choose from among themselves the one who has most of the
d   tyrant in his own soul, and him they create their tyrant.

Yes, he said, and he will be the most fit to be a tyrant.

If the people yield, well and good; but if they resist him, as he
began by beating his own father and mother, so now, if he has the
power, he beats them, and will keep his dear old fatherland or
motherland, as the Cretans say,° in subjection to his young retain-
ers whom he has introduced to be their rulers and masters. This is
the end of his passions and desires.

e   Exactly.

When such men are only private individuals and before they
get power, this is their character; they associate entirely with their
own flatterers or ready tools; or if they want anything from anybody, they in their turn are equally ready to bow down before
576 them: they profess every sort of affection for them; but when they
have gained their point they know them no more.

°"Motherland" (*metris*), as opposed to the more typical "fatherland" (*patris*), was
apparently the favored expression on Crete.

Yes, truly.

They are always either the masters or servants and never the friends of anybody; the tyrant never tastes of true freedom or friendship.

Certainly not.

And may we not rightly call such men treacherous?

No question.

Also they are utterly unjust, if we were right in our notion of justice?   b

Yes, he said, and we were perfectly right.

Let us, then, sum up in a word, I said, the character of the worst man: he is the waking reality of what we dreamed.

Most true.

And this is he who being by nature most of a tyrant bears rule, and the longer he lives the more of a tyrant he becomes.

That is certain, said Glaucon, taking his turn to answer.

And will not he who has been shown to be the wickedest, be also the most miserable? and he who has tyrannized longest and   c
most, most continually and truly miserable; although this may not be the opinion of men in general?*

Yes, he said, inevitably.

And must not the tyrannical man be like the tyrannical State, and the democratical man like the democratical State; and the same of the others?

Certainly.

And as State is to State in virtue and happiness, so is man in relation to man?

To be sure.   d

Then comparing our original city, which was under a king, and the city which is under a tyrant, how do they stand as to virtue?†

They are the opposite extremes, he said, for one is the very best and the other is the very worst.

There can be no mistake, I said, as to which is which, and therefore I will at once inquire whether you would arrive at a similar

---

*Compare 9.580a and 1.344c–d.
†That is, *aretê*; see note 6 on 1.335b.

decision about their relative happiness and misery.[5] And let us not be astounded as we look upon the tyrant, who is only one man, not even if there are some few around him who seem content; but let us go as we ought into every corner of the city and look all about, and then we will give our opinion.

A fair invitation, he replied; and I see, as everyone must, that a tyranny is the wretchedest form of government, and the rule of a king the happiest.

And in estimating the men, too, may I not fairly make a like request, that I should have a judge whose mind can enter into and see through human nature? he must not be like a child who looks at the outside and is dazzled at the pompous aspect which the tyrannical nature assumes to the beholder, but let him be one who has a clear insight.[6] May I suppose that the judgment is given in the hearing of us all by one who is able to judge, and has dwelt in the same place with him, and been present at his daily life and known him in his family relations, where he may be seen stripped of his tragedy attire,[7] and again in the hour of public danger—he shall tell us about the happiness and misery of the tyrant when compared with other men?

That again, he said, is a very fair proposal.

Shall I assume that we ourselves are able and experienced judges and have before now met with such a person? We shall then have someone who will answer our inquiries.

By all means.

Let me ask you not to forget the parallel of the individual and the State; bearing this in mind, and glancing in turn from one to the other of them, will you tell me their respective conditions?

What do you mean? he asked.

Beginning with the State, I replied, would you say that a city which is governed by a tyrant is free or enslaved?

No city, he said, can be more completely enslaved.

And yet, as you see, there are freemen as well as masters in such a State?

Yes, he said, I see that there are—a few; but the people, speaking generally, and the best of them are miserably degraded and enslaved.

Then if the man is like the State, I said, must not the same rule prevail? His soul is full of meanness and vulgarity—the best elements in him are enslaved; and there is a small ruling part, which is also the worst and maddest.

Inevitably.

And would you say that the soul of such a one is the soul of a freeman or of a slave?

He has the soul of a slave, in my opinion.

And the State which is enslaved under a tyrant is utterly incapable of acting voluntarily?

Utterly incapable.

And also the soul which is under a tyrant (I am speaking of the soul taken as a whole) is least capable of doing what she desires; there is a gadfly which goads her, and she is full of trouble and remorse?

Certainly.

And is the city which is under a tyrant rich or poor?

Poor.

And the tyrannical soul must be always poor and insatiable?

True.

And must not such a State and such a man be always full of fear?

Yes, indeed.

Is there any State in which you will find more of lamentation and sorrow and groaning and pain?

Certainly not.

And is there any man in whom you will find more of this sort of misery than in the tyrannical man, who is in a fury of passions and desires?

Impossible.

Reflecting upon these and similar evils, you held the tyrannical State to be the most miserable of States?

And I was right, he said.

Certainly, I said. And when you see the same evils in the tyrannical man, what do you say of him?

I say that he is by far the most miserable of all men.

There, I said, I think that you are beginning to go wrong.

What do you mean?

I do not think that he has as yet reached the utmost extreme of misery.

Then who is more miserable?

One of whom I am about to speak.

Who is that?

c He who is of a tyrannical nature, and instead of leading a private life has been cursed with the further misfortune of being a public tyrant.

From what has been said, I gather that you are right.

Yes, I replied, but in this high argument you should be a little more certain, and should not conjecture only; for of all questions, this respecting good and evil is the greatest.

Very true, he said.

d Let me then offer you an illustration, which may, I think, throw a light upon this subject.

What is your illustration?

The case of rich individuals in cities who possess many slaves: from them you may form an idea of the tyrant's condition, for they both have slaves; the only difference is that he has more slaves.

Yes, that is the difference.

You know that they live securely and have nothing to apprehend from their servants?

What should they fear?

Nothing. But do you observe the reason of this?

Yes; the reason is, that the whole city is leagued together for the protection of each individual.

e Very true, I said. But imagine one of these owners, the master say of some fifty slaves, together with his family and property and slaves, carried off by a god into the wilderness, where there are no freemen to help him—will he not be in an agony of fear lest he and his wife and children should be put to death by his slaves?

Yes, he said, he will be in the utmost fear.

579 The time has arrived when he will be compelled to flatter several of his slaves, and make many promises to them of freedom and other things, much against his will—he will have to cajole his own servants.

Yes, he said, that will be the only way of saving himself.

And suppose the same god, who carried him away, to surround him with neighbors who will not suffer one man to be the master of another, and who, if they could catch the offender, would take his life?

His case will be still worse, if you suppose him to be every- b
where surrounded and watched by enemies.

And is not this the sort of prison in which the tyrant will be bound—he who being by nature such as we have described, is full of all sorts of fears and lusts? His soul is dainty and greedy, and yet alone, of all men in the city, he is never allowed to go on a journey, or to see the things which other freemen desire to see, but he lives in his hole like a woman hidden in the house,[8] and is jealous of any other citizen who goes into foreign parts and sees anything of interest. c

Very true, he said.

And by virtue of evils such as these, will not he who is ill-governed in his own person—the tyrannical man, I mean—whom you just now decided to be the most miserable of all—will not he be yet more miserable when, instead of leading a private life, he is constrained by fortune to be a public tyrant? He has to be master of others when he is not master of himself: he is like a diseased or paralytic man who is compelled to pass his life, not in retirement, but fighting and combating with other men. d

Yes, he said, the similitude is most exact.

Is not his case utterly miserable? and does not the actual tyrant lead a worse life than he whose life you determined to be the worst?

Certainly.

He who is the real tyrant, whatever men may think, is the real slave, and is obliged to practise the greatest adulation and servility, and to be the flatterer of the vilest of mankind. He has desires which he is utterly unable to satisfy, and has more wants than any- e
one, and is truly poor, if you know how to inspect the whole soul of him: all his life long he is beset with fear and is full of convulsions and distractions, even as the State which he resembles: and surely the resemblance holds?

Very true, he said.

Moreover, as we were saying before, he grows worse from hav- 580
ing power: he becomes and is of necessity more jealous, more faithless, more unjust, more friendless, more impious, than he

was at first; he is the purveyor and cherisher of every sort of vice, and the consequence is that he is supremely miserable, and that he makes everybody else as miserable as himself.

No man of any sense will dispute your words.

Come, then, I said, and as the general umpire in theatrical con-
b   tests proclaims the result,[9] do you also decide who in your opinion is first in the scale of happiness, and who second, and in what order the others follow: there are five of them in all—they are the royal,[10] timocratical, oligarchical, democratical, tyrannical.

The decision will be easily given, he replied; they shall be cho-
ruses coming on the stage, and I must judge them in the order in which they enter, by the criterion of virtue and vice, happiness and misery.

Need we hire a herald, or shall I announce that the son of Ariston (the best)* has decided that the best and justest is also the
c   happiest, and that this is he who is the most royal man and king over himself; and that the worst and most unjust man is also the most miserable, and that this is he who being the greatest tyrant of himself is also the greatest tyrant of his State?

Make the proclamation yourself, he said.

And shall I add, "whether seen or unseen by gods and men"?

Let the words be added.

Then this, I said, will be our first proof; and there is another,
d   which may also have some weight.[11]

What is that?

The second proof is derived from the nature of the soul: seeing that the individual soul, like the State, has been divided by us into three principles, the division may, I think, furnish a new demonstration.

Of what nature?

It seems to me that to these three principles three pleasures correspond; also three desires and governing powers.

How do you mean? he said.

There is one principle with which, as we were saying, a man

---

*Ariston's name is derived from the adjective *aristos* ("best"); see 2.368a and also note 6 on 1.335b.

learns, another with which he is angry; the third, having many forms, has no special name, but is denoted by the general term appetitive, from the extraordinary strength and vehemence of the desires of eating and drinking and the other sensual appetites which are the main elements of it; also money-loving, because such desires are generally satisfied by the help of money.

That is true, he said.

If we were to say that the loves and pleasures of this third part were concerned with gain, we should then be able to fall back on a single notion; and might truly and intelligibly describe this part of the soul as loving gain or money.

I agree with you.

Again, is not the passionate element° wholly set on ruling and conquering and getting fame?

True.

Suppose we call it the contentious or ambitious—would the term be suitable?

Extremely suitable.

On the other hand, everyone sees that the principle of knowledge is wholly directed to the truth, and cares less than either of the others for gain or fame.

Far less.

"Lover of wisdom," "lover of knowledge," are titles which we may fitly apply to that part of the soul?

Certainly.

One principle prevails in the souls of one class of men, another in others, as may happen?

Yes.

Then we say that the three primary classes of men are the wisdom-loving, the honor-loving, and the profit-loving?

Exactly.

And there are three kinds of pleasure, which are their several objects?

Very true.

Now, if you examine the three classes of men, and ask of them in

---

°That is, the "spirit" (*thumos*).

turn which of their lives is pleasantest, each will be found praising his own and depreciating that of others: the money-maker will con-

d   trast the vanity of honor or of learning if they bring no money with the solid advantages of gold and silver?

True, he said.

And the lover of honor—what will be his opinion? Will he not think that the pleasure of riches is vulgar, while the pleasure of learning, if it brings no distinction, is all smoke and nonsense to him?

Very true.

And how, may we suppose, will the philosopher estimate the

e   value of the other pleasures in comparison to the pleasure of knowing how the truth stands and of always being in such a happy state while he learns? Will he not estimate that they are very far away from true pleasure? Does he not call the other pleasures necessary, under the idea that if there were no necessity for them, he would rather not have them?

There can be no doubt of that, he replied.

Since, then, the pleasures of each class and the life of each are in

582   dispute, and the question is not which life is more or less honorable, or better or worse, but which is the more pleasant or painless—how shall we know who speaks truly?

I cannot myself tell, he said.

Well, but what ought to be the criterion? Is any better than ex-perience, and wisdom, and reason?

There cannot be a better, he said.

Then, I said, reflect. Of the three individuals, which has the greatest experience of all the pleasures which we enumerated? Has the lover of gain, in learning the nature of essential truth, greater experience of the pleasure of knowledge than the philoso-

b   pher has of the pleasure of gain?

The philosopher, he replied, has greatly the advantage; for he has of necessity always known the taste of the other pleasures from his childhood upward: but the lover of gain in all his experi-ence has not of necessity tasted—or, I should rather say, even had he desired, could hardly have tasted—the sweetness of learning and knowing truth.

Then the lover of wisdom has a great advantage over the lover of gain, for he has a double experience?

Yes, very great.

c

Again, has he greater experience of the pleasures of honor, or the lover of honor of the pleasures of wisdom?

Nay, he said, all three are honored in proportion as they attain their object; for the rich man and the brave man and the wise man alike have their crowd of admirers, and as they all receive honor they all have experience of the pleasures of honor; but the delight which is to be found in the knowledge of true being is known to the philosopher only.

His experience, then, will enable him to judge better than anyone?[12]

d

Far better.

And he is the only one who has wisdom as well as experience?

Certainly.

Further, the very faculty which is the instrument of judgment is not possessed by the covetous or ambitious man, but only by the philosopher?

What faculty?

Reason, with whom, as we were saying, the decision ought to rest.

Yes.

And reasoning is peculiarly his instrument?

Certainly.

If wealth and gain were the criterion, then the praise or blame of the lover of gain would surely be the most trustworthy?

e

Assuredly.

Or if honor, or victory, or courage, in that case the judgment of the ambitious or pugnacious would be the truest?

Clearly.

But since experience and wisdom and reason are the judges—

The only inference possible, he replied, is that pleasures which are approved by the lover of wisdom and reason are the truest.

And so we arrive at the result, that the pleasure of the intelligent part of the soul is the pleasantest of the three, and that he of us in whom this is the ruling principle has the pleasantest life.

583

Unquestionably, he said, the wise man speaks with authority when he approves of his own life.

And what does the judge affirm to be the life which is next, and the pleasure which is next?

Clearly that of the soldier and lover of honor; who is nearer to himself than the money-maker.

Last comes the lover of gain?

Very true, he said.

b   Twice in succession, then, has the just man overthrown the unjust in this conflict;[13] and now comes the third trial, which is dedicated to Olympian Zeus the saviour:* a sage whispers in my ear that no pleasure except that of the wise is quite true and pure—all others are a shadow only; and surely this will prove the greatest and most decisive of falls?

Yes, the greatest; but will you explain yourself?

c   I will work out the subject and you shall answer my questions.

Proceed.

Say, then, is not pleasure opposed to pain?

True.

And there is a neutral state which is neither pleasure nor pain?

There is.

A state which is intermediate, and a sort of repose of the soul about either—that is what you mean?

Yes.

You remember what people say when they are sick?

What do they say?

That after all nothing is pleasanter than health. But then they
d   never knew this to be the greatest of pleasures until they were ill.

Yes, I know, he said.

And when persons are suffering from acute pain, you must have heard them say that there is nothing pleasanter than to get rid of their pain?

I have.

And there are many other cases of suffering in which the mere

---

*The temple of Zeus at Olympia was an important pan-Hellenic site; dedication to Olympian Zeus marks the significance of an object or deed.

rest and cessation of pain, and not any positive enjoyment, are extolled by them as the greatest pleasure?

Yes, he said; at the time they are pleased and well content to be at rest.

Again, when pleasure ceases, that sort of rest or cessation will   e be painful?

Doubtless, he said.

Then the intermediate state of rest will be pleasure and will also be pain?

So it would seem.

But can that which is neither become both?

I should say not.

And both pleasure and pain are motions of the soul, are they not?

Yes.

But that which is neither was just now shown to be rest and not   584 motion, and in a mean between them?

Yes.

How, then, can we be right in supposing that the absence of pain is pleasure, or that the absence of pleasure is pain?

Impossible.

This, then, is an appearance only, and not a reality; that is to say, the rest is pleasure at the moment and in comparison of what is painful, and painful in comparison of what is pleasant; but all these representations, when tried by the test of true pleasure, are not real, but a sort of imposition?

That is the inference.

Look at the other class of pleasures which have no antecedent   b pains and you will no longer suppose, as you perhaps may at present, that pleasure is only the cessation of pain, or pain of pleasure.

What are they, he said, and where shall I find them?

There are many of them: take as an example, the pleasures of smell, which are very great and have no antecedent pains; they come in a moment, and when they depart leave no pain behind them.

Most true, he said.

Let us not, then, be induced to believe that pure pleasure is the   c cessation of pain, or pain of pleasure.

No.

Still, the more numerous and violent pleasures which reach the soul through the body are generally of this sort—they are reliefs of pain.

That is true.

And the anticipations of future pleasures and pains are of a like nature?

Yes.

d   Shall I give you an illustration of them?

Let me hear.

You would allow, I said, that there is in nature an upper and lower and middle region?

I should.

And if a person were to go from the lower to the middle region, would he not imagine that he is going up; and he who is standing in the middle and sees whence he has come, would imagine that he is already in the upper region, if he has never seen the true upper world?

To be sure, he said; how can he think otherwise?

e   But if he were taken back again he would imagine, and truly imagine, that he was descending?

No doubt.

All that would arise out of his ignorance of the true upper and middle and lower regions?

Yes.

Then can you wonder that persons who are inexperienced in the truth, as they have wrong ideas about many other things, should also have wrong ideas about pleasure and pain and the intermediate state;[14] so that when they are only being drawn toward
585   the painful they feel pain and think the pain which they experience to be real, and in like manner, when drawn away from pain to the neutral or intermediate state, they firmly believe that they have reached the goal of satiety and pleasure; they, not knowing pleasure, err in contrasting pain with the absence of pain, which is like contrasting black with gray instead of white—can you wonder, I say, at this?

No, indeed; I should be much more disposed to wonder at the opposite.

Look at the matter thus: Hunger, thirst, and the like, are priva-
tions* of the bodily state? b

Yes.

And ignorance and folly are inanitions of the soul?

True.

And food and wisdom are the corresponding satisfactions of
either?

Certainly.

And is the satisfaction derived from that which has less or from
that which has more existence the truer?

Clearly, from that which has more.

What classes of things have a greater share of pure existence,
in your judgment—those of which food and drink and condiments and all kinds of sustenance are examples, or the class
which contains true opinion and knowledge and mind and all the
different kinds of virtue? Put the question in this way: Which c
has a more pure being—that which is concerned with the invariable, the immortal, and the true, and is of such a nature, and
is found in such natures; or that which is concerned with and
found in the variable and mortal, and is itself variable and mortal?

Far purer, he replied, is the being of that which is concerned
with the invariable.

And does the essence of the invariable partake of knowledge
in the same degree as of essence?

Yes, of knowledge in the same degree.

And of truth in the same degree?

Yes.

And, conversely, that which has less of truth will also have less
of essence?

Necessarily.

Then, in general, those kinds of things which are in the service d
of the body have less of truth and essence than those which are in
the service of the soul?

Far less.

---

*That is, "deprivations." The Greek word *kenosis* literally means an "emptying."

And has not the body itself less of truth and essence than the soul?

Yes.

What is filled with more real existence, and actually has a more real existence, is more really filled than that which is filled with less real existence and is less real?

Of course.

And if there be a pleasure in being filled with that which is according to nature, that which is more really filled with more real being will more really and truly enjoy true pleasure; whereas that which participates in less real being will be less truly and surely satisfied, and will participate in an illusory and less real pleasure?

Unquestionably.

Those, then, who know not wisdom and virtue, and are always busy with gluttony and sensuality, go down and up again as far as the mean; and in this region they move at random throughout life, but they never pass into the true upper world; thither they neither look, nor do they ever find their way, neither are they truly filled with true being, nor do they taste of pure and abiding pleasure. Like cattle, with their eyes always looking down and their heads stooping to the earth, that is, to the dining-table, they fatten and feed and breed,[15] and, in their excessive love of these delights, they kick and butt at one another with horns and hoofs which are made of iron; and they kill one another by reason of their insatiable lust. For they fill themselves with that which is not substantial, and the part of themselves which they fill is also unsubstantial and incontinent.

Verily, Socrates, said Glaucon, you describe the life of the many like an oracle.

Their pleasures are mixed with pains—how can they be otherwise? For they are mere shadows and pictures of the true, and are colored by contrast, which exaggerates both light and shade, and so they implant in the minds of fools insane desires of themselves; and they are fought about as Stesichorus says that the Greeks fought about the shadow of Helen at Troy, in ignorance of the truth.[16]

Something of that sort must inevitably happen.

And must not the like happen with the spirited or passionate element of the soul? Will not the passionate man who carries his passion into action, be in the like case, whether he is envious and ambitious, or violent and contentious, or angry and discontented, if he be seeking to attain honor and victory and the satisfaction of   d his anger without reason or sense?

Yes, he said, the same will happen with the spirited element also.

Then may we not confidently assert that the lovers of money and honor, when they seek their pleasures under the guidance and in the company of reason and knowledge, and pursue after and win the pleasures which wisdom shows them, will also have the truest pleasures in the highest degree which is attainable to them, inasmuch as they follow truth; and they will have the pleasures   e which are natural to them, if that which is best for each one is also most natural to him? [17]

Yes, certainly; the best is the most natural.

And when the whole soul follows the philosophical principle, and there is no division, the several parts are just, and do each of them their own business, and enjoy severally the best and truest   587 pleasures of which they are capable?

Exactly.

But when either of the two other principles prevails, it fails in attaining its own pleasure, and compels the rest to pursue after a pleasure which is a shadow only and which is not their own?

True.

And the greater the interval which separates them from philosophy and reason, the more strange and illusive will be the pleasure?

Yes.

And is not that farthest from reason which is at the greatest distance from law and order?

Clearly.

And the lustful and tyrannical desires are, as we saw, at the greatest distance?   b

Yes.

And the royal and orderly desires are nearest?

Yes.

Then the tyrant will live at the greatest distance from true or natural pleasure, and the king at the least?

Certainly.

But if so, the tyrant will live most unpleasantly, and the king most pleasantly?

Inevitably.

Would you know the measure of the interval which separates them?

Will you tell me?

There appear to be three pleasures, one genuine and two spurious: now the transgression of the tyrant reaches a point beyond the spurious; he has run away from the region of law and reason, and taken up his abode with certain slave pleasures which are his satellites, and the measure of his inferiority can only be expressed in a figure. [18]

How do you mean?

I assume, I said, that the tyrant is in the third place from the oligarch;° the democrat was in the middle?

Yes.

And if there is truth in what has preceded, he will be wedded to an image of pleasure which is thrice removed as to truth from the pleasure of the oligarch?

He will.

And the oligarch is third from the royal;† since we count as one royal and aristocratical?

Yes, he is third.

Then the tyrant is removed from true pleasure by the space of a number which is three times three?

Manifestly.

The shadow, then, of tyrannical pleasure determined by the number of length will be a plane figure.

Certainly.

And if you raise the power and make the plane a solid, there is no difficulty in seeing how vast is the interval by which the tyrant is parted from the king.

Yes; the arithmetician will easily do the sum.

°The tyrannical man is "three times removed" from his oligarchical counterpart if one counts inclusively, as the Greeks regularly did; compare 10.597e.
†That is, since the "timarchic" man is between them. Once again, Socrates counts inclusively.

Or if some person begins at the other end and measures the interval by which the king is parted from the tyrant in truth of pleasure, he will find him, when the multiplication is completed, living 729 times more pleasantly, and the tyrant more painfully by this same interval.* e

What a wonderful calculation! And how enormous is the distance which separates the just from the unjust in regard to pleasure and pain! 588

Yet a true calculation, I said, and a number which nearly concerns human life, if human beings are concerned with days and nights and months and years.

Yes, he said, human life is certainly concerned with them.

Then if the good and just man be thus superior in pleasure to the evil and unjust, his superiority will be infinitely greater in propriety of life and in beauty and virtue?

Immeasurably greater.

Well, I said, and now having arrived at this stage of the argument, we may revert to the words which brought us hither: Was not someone saying that injustice was a gain to the perfectly unjust who was reputed to be just? b

Yes, that was said.

Now, then, having determined the power and quality of justice and injustice, let us have a little conversation with him.

What shall we say to him?

Let us make an image of the soul that he may have his own words presented before his eyes. [19]

Of what sort? c

An ideal image of the soul, like the composite creations of ancient mythology, such as the Chimera, or Scylla, or Cerberus,† and there are many others in which two or more different natures are said to grow into one.

---

*The tyrant is 3×3 (that is, 9) times removed from the "kingly" man; the kingly man's pleasure—which Socrates envisions in a "solid" figure—is therefore 9^3 (that is, 729) times greater than the tyrant's.

†Mythological monsters: The Chimera was envisioned as a conflation of a lion, a goat, and a serpent. The sea-dwelling Scylla had six heads and twelve feet. Cerberus was the triple-headed dog that guarded the underworld.

There are said to have been such unions.

Then do you now model the form of a multitudinous, many-headed monster, having a ring of heads of all manner of beasts, tame and wild, which he is able to generate and metamorphose at will.

d   You suppose marvellous powers in the artist; but, as language is more pliable than wax or any similar substance, let there be such a model as you propose.

Suppose now that you make a second form as of a lion, and a third of a man, the second smaller than the first, and the third smaller than the second.

That, he said, is an easier task; and I have made them as you say.

And now join them, and let the three grow into one.

That has been accomplished.

Next fashion the outside of them into a single image, as of a man, so that he who is not able to look within, and sees only the
e   outer hull, may believe the beast to be a single human creature.

I have done so, he said.

And now, to him who maintains that it is profitable for the human creature to be unjust, and unprofitable to be just, let us reply that, if he be right, it is profitable for this creature to feast the multitudinous monster and strengthen the lion and the lion-like
589   qualities, but to starve and weaken the man, who is consequently liable to be dragged about at the mercy of either of the other two; and he is not to attempt to familiarize or harmonize them with one another—he ought rather to suffer them to fight, and bite and devour one another.

Certainly, he said; that is what the approver of injustice says.

To him the supporter of justice makes answer that he should ever so speak and act as to give the man within him in some way or
b   other the most complete mastery over the entire human creature. He should watch over the many-headed monster like a good husbandman, fostering and cultivating the gentle qualities, and preventing the wild ones from growing; he should be making the lion-heart his ally, and in common care of them all should be uniting the several parts with one another and with himself.

Yes, he said, that is quite what the maintainer of justice will say.

And so from every point of view, whether of pleasure, honor, or advantage, the approver of justice is right and speaks the truth, and the disapprover is wrong and false and ignorant?

Yes, from every point of view.

Come, now, and let us gently reason with the unjust, who is not intentionally in error. [20] "Sweet sir," we will say to him, "what think you of things esteemed noble and ignoble? Is not the noble that which subjects the beast to the man, or rather to the god in man? and the ignoble that which subjects the man to the beast?" He can hardly avoid saying, Yes—can he, now?

Not if he has any regard for my opinion.

But, if he agree so far, we may ask him to answer another question: "Then how would a man profit if he received gold and silver on the condition that he was to enslave the noblest part of him to the worst? Who can imagine that a man who sold his son or daughter into slavery for money, especially if he sold them into the hands of fierce and evil men, would be the gainer, however large might be the sum which he received? [21] And will anyone say that he is not a miserable caitiff who remorselessly sells his own divine being to that which is most godless and detestable? Eriphyle took the necklace as the price of her husband's life,* but he is taking a bribe in order to compass a worse ruin."

Yes, said Glaucon, far worse—I will answer for him.

Has not the intemperate been censured of old, because in him the huge multiform monster is allowed to be too much at large?

Clearly.

And men are blamed for pride and bad temper when the lion and serpent element in them disproportionately grows and gains strength?

Yes.

And luxury and softness are blamed, because they relax and weaken this same creature, and make a coward of him?

Very true.

---

*Oedipus's son Polyneices, exiled from Thebes by his brother Eteocles, sought to restore himself to power with the help of King Amphiareus of Argos; to secure the reluctant King's cooperation, he bribed Amphiareus' wife, Eriphyle, with a necklace.

And is not a man reproached for flattery and meanness who subordinates the spirited animal to the unruly monster, and, for the sake of money, of which he can never have enough, habituates him in the days of his youth to be trampled in the mire, and from being a lion to become a monkey?

c   True, he said.

And why are mean employments and manual arts a reproach?[22] Only because they imply a natural weakness of the higher principle; the individual is unable to control the creatures within him, but has to court them, and his great study is how to flatter them.

Such appears to be the reason.

And therefore, being desirous of placing him under a rule like that of the best, we say that he ought to be the servant of the best,
d   in whom the Divine rules; not, as Thrasymachus supposed, to the injury of the servant, but because everyone had better be ruled by divine wisdom dwelling within him; or, if this be impossible, then by an external authority, in order that we may be all, as far as possible, under the same government, friends and equals.

True, he said.

e   And this is clearly seen to be the intention of the law, which is the ally of the whole city; and is seen also in the authority which we exercise over children, and the refusal to let them be free until
591   we have established in them a principle analogous to the constitution of a State, and by cultivation of this higher element have set up in their hearts a guardian and ruler like our own, and when this is done they may go their ways.

Yes, he said, the purpose of the law is manifest.

From what point of view, then, and on what ground can we say that a man is profited by injustice or intemperance or other baseness, which will make him a worse man, even though he acquire money or power by his wickedness?

From no point of view at all.

What shall he profit, if his injustice be undetected and unpunished?
b   He who is undetected only gets worse,[23] whereas he who is detected and punished has the brutal part of his nature silenced and humanized; the gentler element in him is liberated, and his whole soul is perfected and ennobled by the acquirement of justice and temperance and wisdom, more than the body ever is by

receiving gifts of beauty, strength, and health, in proportion as the soul is more honorable than the body.

Certainly, he said.

To this nobler purpose the man of understanding will devote   c the energies of his life. And in the first place, he will honor studies which impress these qualities on his soul, and will disregard others?

Clearly, he said.

In the next place, he will regulate his bodily habit and training, and so far will he be from yielding to brutal and irrational pleasures, that he will regard even health as quite a secondary matter; his first object will be not that he may be fair or strong or well, unless he is likely thereby to gain temperance, but he will always de-   d sire so to attemper the body as to preserve the harmony of the soul?

Certainly he will, if he has true music in him.

And in the acquisition of wealth there is a principle of order and harmony which he will also observe; he will not allow himself to be dazzled by the foolish applause of the world, and heap up riches to his own infinite harm?

Certainly not, he said.

He will look at the city which is within him, and take heed that   e no disorder occur in it, such as might arise either from superfluity or from want; and upon this principle he will regulate his property and gain or spend according to his means.

Very true.

And, for the same reason, he will gladly accept and enjoy such   592 honors as he deems likely to make him a better man; but those, whether private or public, which are likely to disorder his life, he will avoid?

Then, if that is his motive, he will not be a statesman.

By the dog of Egypt,* he will! In the city which is his own he certainly will, though in the land of his birth perhaps not, unless he have a divine call.

I understand; you mean that he will be a ruler in the city of

---

*Compare 3.399e.

which we are the founders, and which exists in idea only; for I do
not believe that there is such a one anywhere on earth?

In heaven, I replied, there is laid up a pattern of it, methinks,
which he who desires may behold, and beholding, may set his own
house in order. But whether such a one exists, or ever will exist in
fact, is no matter;* for he will live after the manner of that city,
having nothing to do with any other.

I think so, he said.

BOOK 10

OF THE MANY EXCELLENCES which I perceive in the order of our State, there is none which upon reflection pleases me better than the rule about poetry.

To what do you refer?

To the rejection of imitative poetry, which certainly ought not to be received; as I see far more clearly now that the parts of the soul have been distinguished.[1]

What do you mean?

Speaking in confidence, for I should not like to have my words repeated to the tragedians and the rest of the imitative tribe—but I do not mind saying to you, that all poetical imitations are ruinous to the understanding of the hearers, and that the knowledge of their true nature is the only antidote to them.

Explain the purport of your remark.

Well, I will tell you, although I have always from my earliest youth had an awe and love of Homer, which even now makes the words falter on my lips, for he is the great captain and teacher of the whole of that charming tragic company;[2] but a man is not to be reverenced more than the truth, and therefore I will speak out.

Very good, he said.

Listen to me, then, or, rather, answer me.

Put your question.

Can you tell me what imitation is? for I really do not know.[3]

A likely thing, then, that I should know.

Why not? for the duller eye may often see a thing sooner than the keener.

Very true, he said; but in your presence, even if I had any faint notion, I could not muster courage to utter it. Will you inquire yourself?

Well, then, shall we begin the inquiry in our usual manner: Whenever a number of individuals have a common name, we assume them to have also a corresponding idea or form; do you understand me?

I do.

b   Let us take any common instance; there are beds and tables in the world—plenty of them, are there not?

Yes.

But there are only two ideas or forms of them—one the idea of a bed, the other of a table.[4]

True.

And the maker of either of them makes a bed or he makes a table for our use, in accordance with the idea—that is our way of speaking in this and similar instances—but no artificer makes the ideas themselves: how could he?

Impossible.

And there is another artist—I should like to know what you would say of him.

c   Who is he?

One who is the maker of all the works of all other workmen.

What an extraordinary man!

Wait a little, and there will be more reason for your saying so. For this is he who is able to make not only vessels of every kind, but plants and animals, himself and all other things—the earth and heaven, and the things which are in heaven or under the earth; he makes the gods also.

d   He must be a wizard and no mistake.

Oh! you are incredulous, are you? Do you mean that there is no such maker or creator, or that in one sense there might be a maker of all these things, but in another not? Do you see that there is a way in which you could make them all yourself?

What way?

An easy way enough; or rather, there are many ways in which the feat might be quickly and easily accomplished, none quicker

e   than that of turning a mirror round and round—you would soon enough make the sun and the heavens, and the earth and yourself, and other animals and plants, and all the other things of which we were just now speaking, in the mirror.

Yes, he said; but they would be appearances only.

Very good, I said, you are coming to the point now. And the

painter, too, is, as I conceive, just such another—a creator of appearances, is he not?

Of course.

But then I suppose you will say that what he creates is untrue. And yet there is a sense in which the painter also creates a bed?

Yes, he said, but not a real bed.

And what of the maker of the bed? were you not saying that he too makes, not the idea which, according to our view, is the essence of the bed, but only a particular bed? 597

Yes, I did.

Then if he does not make that which exists he cannot make true existence, but only some semblance of existence; and if anyone were to say that the work of the maker of the bed, or of any other workman, has real existence, he could hardly be supposed to be speaking the truth.

At any rate, he replied, philosophers would say that he was not speaking the truth.[5]

No wonder, then, that his work, too, is an indistinct expression of truth.

No wonder. b

Suppose now that by the light of the examples just offered we inquire who this imitator is?

If you please.

Well, then, here are three beds: one existing in nature, which is made by God,* as I think that we may say—for no one else can be the maker?

No.

There is another which is the work of the carpenter?

Yes.

And the work of the painter is a third?

Yes.

Beds, then, are of three kinds, and there are three artists who superintend them: God, the maker of the bed, and the painter?

Yes, there are three of them.

God, whether from choice or from necessity, made one bed in c

---

*See note 24 on 2.379a.

nature and one only; two or more such ideal beds neither ever have been nor ever will be made by God.

Why is that?

Because even if He had made but two, a third would still appear behind them which both of them would have for their idea, and that would be the ideal bed and not the two others.

Very true, he said.

God knew this, and he desired to be the real maker of a real bed, not a particular maker of a particular bed, and therefore he created a bed which is essentially and by nature one only.

So we believe.

Shall we, then, speak of him as the natural author or maker of the bed?

Yes, he replied; inasmuch as by the natural process of creation he is the author of this and of all other things.

And what shall we say of the carpenter—is not he also the maker of the bed?

Yes.

But would you call the painter a creator and maker?

Certainly not.

Yet if he is not the maker, what is he in relation to the bed?

I think, he said, that we may fairly designate him as the imitator of that which the others make.

Good, I said; then you call him who is third in the descent from nature an imitator?

Certainly, he said.

And the tragic poet is an imitator, and, therefore, like all other imitators, he is thrice removed from the king and from the truth?[6]

That appears to be so.

Then about the imitator we are agreed. And what about the painter? I would like to know whether he may be thought to imitate that which originally exists in nature, or only the creations of artists?

The latter.

As they are or as they appear? you have still to determine this.

What do you mean?

I mean, that you may look at a bed from different points of view, obliquely or directly or from any other point of view, and the bed will appear different, but there is no difference in reality. And the same of all things.

Yes, he said, the difference is only apparent.

Now let me ask you another question: Which is the art of painting designed to be—an imitation of things as they are, or as they appear—of appearance or of reality?

Of appearance.

Then the imitator, I said, is a long way off the truth, and can do all things because he lightly touches on a small part of them, and that part an image. For example: A painter will paint a cobbler, carpenter, or any other artist, though he knows nothing of their arts; and, if he is a good artist, he may deceive children or simple persons, when he shows them his picture of a carpenter from a distance, and they will fancy that they are looking at a real carpenter.

Certainly.

And whenever anyone informs us that he has found a man who knows all the arts, and all things else that anybody knows, and every single thing with a higher degree of accuracy than any other man—whoever tells us this, I think that we can only imagine him to be a simple creature who is likely to have been deceived by some wizard or actor whom he met, and whom he thought allknowing, because he himself was unable to analyze the nature of knowledge and ignorance and imitation.

Most true.

And so, when we hear persons saying that the tragedians, and Homer, who is at their head, know all the arts and all things human, virtue as well as vice, and divine things too, for that the good poet cannot compose well unless he knows his subject, and that he who has not this knowledge can never be a poet, we ought to consider whether here also there may not be a similar illusion.[7] Perhaps they may have come across imitators and been deceived by them; they may not have remembered when they saw their works that these were but imitations thrice removed from the truth, and could easily be made without any knowledge of the truth, because they are appearances only and not realities? Or, after all, they may be in the right, and poets do really know the things about which they seem to the many to speak so well?

The question, he said, should by all means be considered.

Now do you suppose that if a person were able to make the original as well as the image, he would seriously devote himself to the image-making branch? Would he allow imitation to be the ruling principle of his life, as if he had nothing higher in him?

b

I should say not.

The real artist, who knew what he was imitating, would be interested in realities and not in imitations; and would desire to leave as memorials of himself works many and fair; and, instead of being the author of encomiums, he would prefer to be the theme of them.

Yes, he said, that would be to him a source of much greater honor and profit.

Then, I said, we must put a question to Homer;[8] not about medicine, or any of the arts to which his poems only incidentally refer: we are not going to ask him, or any other poet, whether he has cured patients like Asclepius,° or left behind him a school of medicine such as the Asclepiads were, or whether he only talks about medicine and other arts at second-hand; but we have a right to know respecting military tactics, politics, education, which are the chiefest and noblest subjects of his poems, and we may fairly ask him about them. "Friend Homer," then we say to him, "if you are only in the second remove from truth in what you say of virtue, and not in the third—not an image maker or imitator— and if you are able to discern what pursuits make men better or worse in private or public life, tell us what State was ever better governed by your help? The good order of Lacedæmon is due to Lycurgus,† and many other cities, great and small, have been similarly benefited by others; but who says that you have been a good legislator to them and have done them any good? Italy and Sicily boast of Charondas,‡ and there is Solon who is renowned among us; but what city has anything to say about you?" Is there any city which he might name?

c

d

e

°On Asclepius and the Asclepiadae, see 3.405d-406c.

†The traditional founder of the Spartan (Lacedaemonian) constitution and way of life (perhaps early eighth century B.C.E.).

‡Lawgiver in the city-state Catana (on Sicily) and Rhegium (in southern Italy) who was active in the sixth century B.C.E.

I think not, said Glaucon; not even the Homerids° themselves pretend that he was a legislator.

Well, but is there any war on record which was carried on successfully by him, or aided by his counsels, when he was alive?

There is not.

Or is there any invention of his applicable to the arts or to human life, such as Thales the Milesian† or Anacharsis the Scythian,‡ and other ingenious men have conceived, which is attributed to him?

There is absolutely nothing of the kind.

But, if Homer never did any public service, was he privately a guide or teacher of any?[9] Had he in his lifetime friends who loved to associate with him, and who handed down to posterity a Homeric way of life, such as was established by Pythagoras,§ who was so greatly beloved for his wisdom, and whose followers are to this day quite celebrated for the order which was named after him?

Nothing of the kind is recorded of him. For, surely, Socrates, Creophylus, the companion of Homer,[10] that child of flesh, whose name always makes us laugh, might be more justly ridiculed for his stupidity, if, as is said, Homer was greatly neglected by him and others in his own day when he was alive?

Yes, I replied, that is the tradition. But can you imagine, Glaucon, that if Homer had really been able to educate and improve mankind—if he had possessed knowledge, and not been a mere imitator—can you imagine, I say, that he would not have had many followers, and been honored and loved by them?[11] Protagoras of Abdera and Prodicus of Ceos[12] and a host of others have

---

°By the classical period, the Homeridae (literally, "sons of Homer") established themselves as authoritative interpreters of the works attributed in antiquity to Homer.

†Thales (late seventh to early sixth century B.C.E.) of Miletus was credited in antiquity with predicting the occurrence of a solar eclipse that took place in 585 B.C.E.; he is often cited as one of the "seven sages" and is credited with bringing Egyptian techniques of "land measurement" (that is, geometry) to the Greek world.

‡Anacharsis apparently traveled widely in Greece in the early sixth century B.C.E.; he was credited by some with the invention of the anchor and the potter's wheel.

§The Pythagoreans were known for their asceticism.

only to whisper to their contemporaries: "You will never be able to manage either your own house or your own State until you ap-
d point us to be your ministers of education"—and this ingenious device of theirs has such an effect in making men love them that their companions all but carry them about on their shoulders. And is it conceivable that the contemporaries of Homer, or again of Hesiod, would have allowed either of them to go about as rhap-sodists,* if they had really been able to make mankind virtuous? Would they not have been as unwilling to part with them as with gold, and have compelled them to stay at home with them? Or, if
e the master would not stay, then the disciples would have followed him about everywhere, until they had got education enough?

Yes, Socrates, that, I think, is quite true.

Then must we not infer that all these poetical individuals, be-ginning with Homer, are only imitators; they copy images of virtue and the like, but the truth they never reach? The poet is like a painter who, as we have already observed, will make a like-
601 ness of a cobbler though he understands nothing of cobbling; and his picture is good enough for those who know no more than he does, and judge only by colors and figures.

Quite so.

In like manner the poet with his words and phrases may be said to lay on the colors of the several arts, himself understanding their nature only enough to imitate them; and other people, who are as ignorant as he is, and judge only from his words, imagine that if he speaks of cobbling, or of military tactics, or of anything else, in metre and harmony and rhythm, he speaks very well— such is the sweet influence which melody and rhythm by nature
b have. And I think that you must have observed again and again what a poor appearance the tales of poets make when stripped of the colors which music puts upon them, and recited in simple prose.

Yes, he said.

They are like faces which were never really beautiful, but only

---

*Rhapsodes were professional (often itinerant) performers of epic poetry; see note 5 on 1.334a.

blooming; and now the bloom of youth has passed away from them?

Exactly.

Here is another point: The imitator or maker of the image knows nothing of true existence; he knows appearances only. Am I not right?   c

Yes.

Then let us have a clear understanding, and not be satisfied with half an explanation.

Proceed.

Of the painter we say that he will paint reins, and he will paint a bit?

Yes.

And the worker in leather and brass will make them?

Certainly.

But does the painter know the right form of the bit and reins? Nay, hardly even the workers in brass and leather who make them; only the horseman who knows how to use them—he knows their right form.[13]

Most true.

And may we not say the same of all things?

What?

That there are three arts which are concerned with all things: d one which uses, another which makes, a third which imitates them?

Yes.

And the excellence or beauty or truth of every structure, animate or inanimate, and of every action of man, is relative to the use for which nature or the artist has intended them.

True.

Then the user of them must have the greatest experience of them, and he must indicate to the maker the good or bad qualities which develop themselves in use; for example, the flute-player will tell the flute-maker which of his flutes is satisfactory to the performer; he will tell him how he ought to make them, and the   e other will attend to his instructions?

Of course.

The one knows and therefore speaks with authority about the

goodness and badness of flutes, while the other, confiding in him, will do what he is told by him?

True.

The instrument is the same, but about the excellence or badness of it the maker will only attain to a correct belief; and this he will gain from him who knows, by talking to him and being compelled to hear what he has to say, whereas the user will have knowledge?

True.

But will the imitator have either? Will he know from use whether or no his drawing is correct or beautiful? or will he have right opinion from being compelled to associate with another who knows and gives him instructions about what he should draw?

Neither.

Then he will no more have true opinion than he will have knowledge about the goodness or badness of his imitations?

I suppose not.

The imitative artist will be in a brilliant state of intelligence about his own creations?

Nay, very much the reverse.

And still he will go on imitating without knowing what makes a thing good or bad, and may be expected therefore to imitate only that which appears to be good to the ignorant multitude?

Just so.

Thus far, then, we are pretty well agreed that the imitator has no knowledge worth mentioning of what he imitates. Imitation is only a kind of play or sport,[14] and the tragic poets, whether they write in iambic or in heroic verse, are imitators in the highest degree?

Very true.

And now tell me, I conjure you, has not imitation been shown by us to be concerned with that which is thrice removed from the truth?

Certainly.

And what is the faculty in man to which imitation is addressed?

What do you mean?

I will explain: The body which is large when seen near, appears small when seen at a distance?

True.

And the same objects appear straight when looked at out of the water, and crooked when in the water; and the concave becomes convex, owing to the illusion about colors to which the sight is liable. Thus every sort of confusion is revealed within us; and this is that weakness of the human mind on which the art of conjuring   d
and of deceiving by light and shadow and other ingenious devices imposes, having an effect upon us like magic.

True.

And the arts of measuring and numbering and weighing come to the rescue of the human understanding—there is the beauty of them—and the apparent greater or less, or more or heavier, no longer have the mastery over us, but give way before calculation and measure and weight?[15]

Most true.

And this, surely, must be the work of the calculating and rational principle in the soul?   e

To be sure.

And when this principle measures and certifies that some things are equal, or that some are greater or less than others, there occurs an apparent contradiction?

True.

But were we not saying that such a contradiction is impossible—the same faculty cannot have contrary opinions at the same time about the same thing?

Very true.

Then that part of the soul which has an opinion contrary to   603
measure is not the same with that which has an opinion in accordance with measure?

True.

And the better part of the soul is likely to be that which trusts to measure and calculation?

Certainly.

And that which is opposed to them is one of the inferior principles of the soul?

No doubt.

This was the conclusion at which I was seeking to arrive when I said that painting or drawing, and imitation in general, when doing their own proper work, are far removed from truth, and the

companions and friends and associates of a principle within us
which is equally removed from reason, and that they have no true
or healthy aim.

Exactly.

The imitative art is an inferior who marries an inferior, and has
inferior offspring.

Very true.

And is this confined to the sight only, or does it extend to the
hearing also, relating in fact to what we term poetry?

Probably the same would be true of poetry.

Do not rely, I said, on a probability derived from the analogy of
painting; but let us examine further and see whether the faculty
with which poetical imitation is concerned is good or bad.

By all means.

We may state the question thus: Imitation imitates the actions
of men, whether voluntary or involuntary, on which, as they imagine, a good or bad result has ensued, and they rejoice or sorrow
accordingly. Is there anything more?

No, there is nothing else.

But in all this variety of circumstances is the man at unity with
himself—or, rather, as in the instance of sight there were confusion and opposition in his opinions about the same things, so here
also are there not strife and inconsistency in his life? though I need
hardly raise the question again, for I remember that all this has
been already admitted; and the soul has been acknowledged by us
to be full of these and ten thousand similar oppositions occurring
at the same moment?[*]

And we were right, he said.

Yes, I said, thus far we were right; but there was an omission
which must now be supplied.

What was the omission?

Were we not saying that a good man, who has the misfortune to
lose his son or anything else which is most dear to him, will bear
the loss with more equanimity than another?[†]

---

[*]Compare 4.439c–441c.
[†]Compare 3.387d–e.

Yes.

But will he have no sorrow, or shall we say that although he cannot help sorrowing, he will moderate his sorrow?

The latter, he said, is the truer statement.

Tell me: will he be more likely to struggle and hold out against his sorrow when he is seen by his equals, or when he is alone? 604

It will make a great difference whether he is seen or not.

When he is by himself he will not mind saying or doing many things which he would be ashamed of anyone hearing or seeing him do?

True.

There is a principle of law and reason in him which bids him resist, as well as a feeling of his misfortune which is forcing him to indulge his sorrow? b

True.

But when a man is drawn in two opposite directions, to and from the same object, this, as we affirm, necessarily implies two distinct principles in him?

Certainly.

One of them is ready to follow the guidance of the law?

How do you mean?

The law would say that to be patient under suffering is best, and that we should not give way to impatience, as there is no knowing whether such things are good or evil; and nothing is gained by impatience; also, because no human thing is of serious importance, and grief stands in the way of that which at the moment is most required. c

What is most required? he asked.

That we should take counsel about what has happened, and when the dice have been thrown order our affairs in the way which reason deems best; not, like children* who have had a fall, keeping hold of the part struck and wasting time in setting up a howl, but always accustoming the soul forthwith to apply a remedy, raising up that which is sickly and fallen, banishing the cry of sorrow by the healing art. d

---

*Compare 10.608a and also 9.577a.

Yes, he said, that is the true way of meeting the attacks of fortune.

Yes, I said; and the higher principle is ready to follow this suggestion of reason?

Clearly.

And the other principle, which inclines us to recollection of our troubles and to lamentation, and can never have enough of them, we may call irrational, useless, and cowardly?

Indeed, we may.

e   And does not the latter—I mean the rebellious principle—furnish a great variety of materials for imitation? Whereas the wise and calm temperament, being always nearly equable, is not easy to imitate or to appreciate when imitated, especially at a public festival when a promiscuous crowd is assembled in a theatre. For the feeling represented is one to which they are strangers.[16]

605   Certainly.

Then the imitative poet who aims at being popular is not by nature made, nor is his art intended, to please or to affect the rational principle in the soul; but he will prefer the passionate and fitful temper, which is easily imitated?

Clearly.

And now we may fairly take him and place him by the side of the painter, for he is like him in two ways: first, inasmuch as his creations have an inferior degree of truth—in this, I say, he is like

b   him; and he is also like him in being concerned with an inferior part of the soul; and therefore we shall be right in refusing to admit him into a well-ordered State, because he awakens and nourishes and strengthens the feelings and impairs the reason. As in a city when the evil are permitted to have authority and the good are put out of the way, so in the soul of man, as we maintain, the imitative poet implants an evil constitution, for he indulges the irrational nature which has no discernment of greater and less, but

c   thinks the same thing at one time great and at another small—he is a manufacturer of images and is very far removed from the truth.

Exactly.

But we have not yet brought forward the heaviest count in our accusation: the power which poetry has of harming even the good (and there are very few who are not harmed), is surely an awful thing?

Yes, certainly, if the effect is what you say.

Hear and judge: The best of us, as I conceive, when we listen to a passage of Homer or one of the tragedians, in which he represents some pitiful hero who is drawling out his sorrows in a long   d
oration, or weeping, and smiting his breast—the best of us, you know, delight in giving way to sympathy, and are in raptures at the excellence of the poet who stirs our feelings most.[17]

Yes, of course, I know.

But when any sorrow of our own happens to us, then you may observe that we pride ourselves on the opposite quality—we would fain be quiet and patient; this is the manly part, and the other which delighted us in the recitation is now deemed to be the part   e
of a woman.

Very true, he said.

Now can we be right in praising and admiring another who is doing that which any one of us would abominate and be ashamed of in his own person?

No, he said, that is certainly not reasonable.

Nay, I said, quite reasonable from one point of view.   606

What point of view?

If you consider, I said, that when in misfortune we feel a natural hunger and desire to relieve our sorrow by weeping and lamentation, and that this feeling which is kept under control in our own calamities is satisfied and delighted by the poets; the better nature in each of us, not having been sufficiently trained by reason or habit, allows the sympathetic element to break loose because the sorrow is another's; and the spectator fancies that there can be no   b
disgrace to himself in praising and pitying anyone who comes telling him what a good man he is, and making a fuss about his troubles; he thinks that the pleasure is a gain, and why should he be supercilious and lose this and the poem too? Few persons ever reflect, as I should imagine, that from the evil of other men something of evil is communicated to themselves. And so the feeling of sorrow which has gathered strength at the sight of the misfortunes of others is with difficulty repressed in our own.

How very true!   c

And does not the same hold also of the ridiculous? There are jests which you would be ashamed to make yourself, and yet on the comic stage, or indeed in private, when you hear them, you are greatly amused by them, and are not at all disgusted at their unseemliness; the case of pity is repeated; there is a principle in human nature which is disposed to raise a laugh, and this which you once restrained by reason, because you were afraid of being thought a buffoon, is now let out again; and having stimulated the risible faculty at the theatre, you are betrayed unconsciously to yourself into playing the comic poet at home.

Quite true, he said.

d   And the same may be said of lust and anger and all the other affections, of desire, and pain, and pleasure, which are held to be inseparable from every action—in all of them poetry feeds and waters the passions instead of drying them up; she lets them rule, although they ought to be controlled, if mankind are ever to increase in happiness and virtue.

I cannot deny it.

e   Therefore, Glaucon, I said, whenever you meet with any of the eulogists of Homer declaring that he has been the educator of Hellas, and that he is profitable for education and for the ordering of human things, and that you should take him up again and again and get to know him and regulate your whole life according to him,
607 we may love and honor those who say these things—they are excellent people, as far as their lights extend; and we are ready to acknowledge that Homer is the greatest of poets and first of tragedy writers; but we must remain firm in our conviction that hymns to the gods and praises of famous men are the only poetry which ought to be admitted into our State. For if you go beyond this and allow the honeyed muse to enter, either in epic or lyric verse, pleasure and pain will be kings in your state, and not law and the rational principle that is always judged best for the common interest.[18]

That is most true, he said.

b   And now since we have reverted to the subject of poetry, let this our defence serve to show the reasonableness of our former judgment in sending away out of our State an art having the tendencies which we have described; for reason constrained us. But that she* may not impute to us any harshness or want of politeness, let us tell her that there is an ancient quarrel between philosophy and poetry; of which there are many proofs,[19] such as the saying of "the yelping hound howling at her lord," or of one "mighty in the vain talk of fools," and "the mob of sages circumventing c Zeus," and the "subtle thinkers who are beggars after all";† and there are innumerable other signs of ancient enmity between them. Notwithstanding this, let us assure our sweet friend and the sister art of imitation, that if she will only prove her title to exist in a well-ordered State we shall be delighted to receive her—we are very conscious of her charms; but we may not on that account betray the truth. I dare say, Glaucon, that you are as much charmed by her as I am, especially when she appears in Homer? d

Yes, indeed, I am greatly charmed.

Shall I propose, then, that she be allowed to return from exile, but upon this condition only—that she make a defence of herself in lyrical or some other metre?

Certainly.

And we may further grant to those of her defenders who are lovers of poetry and yet not poets the permission to speak in prose on her behalf: let them show not only that she is pleasant, but also useful to States and to human life, and we will listen in a kindly spirit; for if this can be proved we shall surely be the gainers—I e mean, if there is a use in poetry as well as a delight?

Certainly, he said, we shall be the gainers.

If her defence fails, then, my dear friend, like other persons who are enamoured of something, but put a restraint upon themselves when they think their desires are opposed to their interests, so, too, must we after the manner of lovers give her up, though not without a struggle. We, too, are inspired by that love of poetry which the education of noble States has implanted in us, and 608 therefore we would have her appear at her best and truest; but so long as she is unable to make good her defence, this argument of

---

*That is, poetry, which is referred to by feminine pronouns through Jowett's translation of this passage. In subsequent pages, Jowett also uses feminine pronouns when referring to the soul (*psychê* in Greek) and justice (*dikaiosynê*).
†The sources of these sayings are unknown.

ours shall be a charm to us, which we will repeat to ourselves while we listen to her strains; that we may not fall away into the childish love of her which captivates the many. At all events we are well aware that poetry being such as we have described is not to be regarded seriously as attaining to the truth; and he who listens to her, fearing for the safety of the city which is within him, should be on his guard against her seductions and make our words his law.

b

Yes, he said, I quite agree with you.

Yes, I said, my dear Glaucon, for great is the issue at stake, greater than appears, whether a man is to be good or bad.[20] And what will anyone be profited if under the influence of honor or money or power, aye, or under the excitement of poetry, he neglect justice and virtue?

Yes, he said; I have been convinced by the argument, as I believe that anyone else would have been.

c

And yet no mention has been made of the greatest prizes and rewards which await virtue.[21]

What, are there any greater still? If there are, they must be of an inconceivable greatness.

Why, I said, what was ever great in a short time? The whole period of threescore years and ten° is surely but a little thing in comparison with eternity?

Say rather 'nothing,' he replied.

And should an immortal being seriously think of this little space rather than of the whole?

d

Of the whole, certainly. But why do you ask?

Are you not aware, I said, that the soul of man is immortal and imperishable?[22]

He looked at me in astonishment, and said: No, by heaven: And are you really prepared to maintain this?[23]

Yes, I said, I ought to be, and you too—there is no difficulty in proving it.

I see a great difficulty; but I should like to hear you state this argument of which you make so light.

°Jowett's translation is less than literal; literally translated, the Greek reads, "This entire time, from childhood to old age, would be something slight compared to everything [that is, the whole of time]."

Listen, then.

I am attending.

There is a thing which you call good and another which you call evil?

Yes, he replied.

Would you agree with me in thinking that the corrupting and destroying element is the evil, and the saving and improving element the good?

Yes.

And you admit that everything has a good and also an evil; as ophthalmia° is the evil of the eyes and disease of the whole body; as mildew is of corn, and rot of timber, or rust of copper and iron: in everything, or in almost everything, there is an inherent evil and disease?

Yes, he said.

And anything which is infected by any of these evils is made evil, and at last wholly dissolves and dies?

True.

The vice and evil which are inherent in each are the destruction of each; and if these do not destroy them there is nothing else that will; for good certainly will not destroy them, nor, again, that which is neither good nor evil.

Certainly not.

If, then, we find any nature which having this inherent corruption cannot be dissolved or destroyed, we may be certain that of such a nature there is no destruction?

That may be assumed.

Well, I said, and is there no evil which corrupts the soul?

Yes, he said, there are all the evils which we were just now passing in review: unrighteousness, intemperance, cowardice, ignorance.

But does any of these dissolve or destroy her?—and here do not let us fall into the error of supposing that the unjust and foolish man, when he is detected, perishes through his own injustice, which is an evil of the soul. Take the analogy of the body: The evil

---

°Eye inflammation.

of the body is a disease which wastes and reduces and annihilates the body; and all the things of which we were just now speaking come to annihilation through their own corruption attaching to d   them and inhering in them and so destroying them. Is not this true?

Yes.

Consider the soul in like manner. Does the injustice or other evil which exists in the soul waste and consume her? Do they by attaching to the soul and inhering in her at last bring her to death, and so separate her from the body?

Certainly not.

And yet, I said, it is unreasonable to suppose that anything can perish from without through affection of external evil which could not be destroyed from within by a corruption of its own?

It is, he replied.

e   Consider, I said, Glaucon, that even the badness of food, whether staleness, decomposition, or any other bad quality, when confined to the actual food, is not supposed to destroy the body; although, if the badness of food communicates corruption to the body, then we should say that the body has been destroyed by a corruption of itself, which is disease, brought on by this; but that 610   the body, being one thing, can be destroyed by the badness of the food, which is another, and which does not engender any natural infection—this we shall absolutely deny?

Very true.

And, on the same principle, unless some bodily evil can produce an evil of the soul, we must not suppose that the soul, which is one thing, can be dissolved by any merely external evil which belongs to another?

Yes, he said, there is reason in that.

Either, then, let us refute this conclusion, or, while it remains b   unrefuted, let us never say that fever, or any other disease, or the knife put to the throat, or even the cutting up of the whole body into the minutest pieces, can destroy the soul, until she herself is proved to become more unholy or unrighteous in consequence of these things being done to the body; but that the soul, or anything else if not destroyed by an internal evil, can be destroyed by an ex- c   ternal one, is not to be affirmed by any man.

And surely, he replied, no one will ever prove that the souls of men become more unjust in consequence of death.

But if someone who would rather not admit the immortality of the soul boldly denies this, and says that the dying do really become more evil and unrighteous, then, if the speaker is right, I suppose that injustice, like disease, must be assumed to be fatal to the unjust, and that those who take this disorder die by the natural inherent power of destruction which evil has, and which kills them sooner or later, but in quite another way from that in which, at present, the wicked receive death at the hands of others as the penalty of their deeds?

Nay, he said, in that case injustice, if fatal to the unjust, will not be so very terrible to him, for he will be delivered from evil. But I rather suspect the opposite to be the truth, and that injustice which, if it have the power, will murder others, keeps the murderer alive—aye, and well awake, too; so far removed is her dwelling-place from being a house of death.

True, I said; if the inherent natural vice or evil of the soul is unable to kill or destroy her, hardly will that which is appointed to be the destruction of some other body, destroy a soul or anything else except that of which it was appointed to be the destruction.

Yes, that can hardly be.

But the soul which cannot be destroyed by an evil, whether inherent or external, must exist forever, and, if existing forever, must be immortal?

Certainly.

That is the conclusion, I said; and, if a true conclusion, then the souls must always be the same, for if none be destroyed they will not diminish in number. Neither will they increase, for the increase of the immortal natures must come from something mortal, and all things would thus end in immortality.

Very true.

But this we cannot believe—reason will not allow us—any more than we can believe the soul, in her truest nature, to be full of variety and difference and dissimilarity.[24]

What do you mean? he said.

It is not easy, I said, for something to be immortal that is compounded out of many elements and not compounded in the finest way, as now seemed to us to be the case with the soul.

Certainly not.

Her immortality is demonstrated by the previous argument, and there are many other proofs; but to see her as she really is, not as we now behold her, marred by communion with the body and other miseries, you must contemplate her with the eye of reason, in her original purity; and then her beauty will be revealed, and justice and injustice and all the things which we have described will be manifested more clearly. Thus far, we have spoken the truth concerning her as she appears at present, but we must remember also that we have seen her only in a condition which may be compared to that of the sea-god Glaucus,* whose original image can hardly be discerned because his natural members are broken off and crushed and damaged by the waves in all sorts of ways, and incrustations have grown over them of sea-weed and shells and stones, so that he is more like some monster than he is to his own natural form. And the soul which we behold is in a similar condition, disfigured by ten thousand ills. But not there, Glaucon, not there must we look.

Where, then?

At her love of wisdom.† Let us see whom she affects, and what society and converse she seeks in virtue of her near kindred with the immortal and eternal and divine; also how different she would become if, wholly following this superior principle, and borne by a divine impulse out of the ocean in which she now is, and disengaged from the stones and shells and things of earth and rock which in wild variety spring up around her because she feeds upon earth, and is overgrown by the good things in this life as they are termed:‡ then you would see her as she is, and know whether she have one shape only or many, or what her nature is. Of her affections and of the forms which she takes in this present life I think that we have now said enough.

True, he replied.

---

*Fisherman who was transformed into a sea-god.
†That is, at the soul's "philosophy."
‡That is, material goods, including wealth, fame, and prestige.

And thus, I said, we have fulfilled the conditions of the argument; we have not introduced the rewards and glories of justice, which, as you were saying, are to be found in Homer and Hesiod; but justice in her own nature has been shown to be the best for the soul in her own nature. Let a man do what is just, whether he have the ring of Gyges or not, and even if in addition to the ring of Gyges he put on the helmet of Hades.*   b

Very true.

And now, Glaucon, there will be no harm in further enumerating how many and how great are the rewards which justice and the other virtues procure to the soul from gods and men, both in life and after death.   c

Certainly not, he said.

Will you repay me, then, what you borrowed in the argument?[25]

What did I borrow?

The assumption that the just man should appear unjust and the unjust just: for you were of opinion that even if the true state of the case could not possibly escape the eyes of gods and men, still this admission ought to be made for the sake of the argument, in order that pure justice might be weighed against pure injustice. Do you remember?   d

I should be much to blame if I had forgotten.

Then, as the cause is decided, I demand on behalf of justice that the estimation in which she is held by gods and men and which we acknowledge to be her due should now be restored to her by us; since she has been shown to confer reality, and not to deceive those who truly possess her, let what has been taken from her be given back, that so she may win that palm of appearance which is hers also, and which she gives to her own.†

Th. demand, he said, is just.   e

In the first place, I said—and this is the first thing which you

---

*The dog-skin "cap of Hades," which provides invisibility, is mentioned in *Iliad* 5.844.

†Literally, "the prizes of victory which it [that is, justice] acquires through reputation and confers on those who possess it [that is, individuals who are just]"; compare "the palms of victory which the gods give the just," at 10.613b.

will have to give back—the nature both of the just and unjust is truly known to the gods.

Granted.

And if they are both known to them, one must be the friend and the other the enemy of the gods, as we admitted from the beginning?°

True.

And the friend of the gods may be supposed to receive from them all things at their best, excepting only such evil as is the necessary consequence of former sins?

Certainly.

Then this must be our notion of the just man, that even when he is in poverty or sickness, or any other seeming misfortune, all things will in the end work together for good to him in life and death: for the gods have a care of anyone whose desire is to become just and to be like God, as far as man can attain the divine likeness, by the pursuit of virtue?

Yes, he said; if he is like God he will surely not be neglected by him.

And of the unjust may not the opposite be supposed?

Certainly.

Such, then, are the palms of victory which the gods give the just?

That is my conviction.

And what do they receive of men? Look at things as they really are, and you will see that the clever unjust are in the case of runners, who run well from the starting-place to the goal, but not back again from the goal:† they go off at a great pace, but in the end only look foolish, slinking away with their ears draggling on their shoulders, and without a crown; but the true runner comes to the finish and receives the prize and is crowned. And this is the way with the just; he who endures to the end of every action and occasion of his entire life has a good report and carries off the prize which men have to bestow.

°See 1.352b.

†The "goal" is in the mid-course turning point. Both foot and chariot races were typically run in two segments, the first going to and the second returning from a turning point (or post).

True.

And now you must allow me to repeat of the just the blessings which you were attributing to the fortunate unjust.[26] I shall say of them, what you were saying of the others, that as they grow older, they become rulers in their own city if they care to be; they marry whom they like and give in marriage to whom they will; all that you said of the others I now say of these. And, on the other hand, of the unjust I say that the greater number, even though they escape in their youth, are found out at last and look foolish at the end of their course, and when they come to be old and miserable are flouted alike by stranger and citizen; they are beaten, and then come those things unfit for ears polite, as you truly term them; they will be racked and have their eyes burned out, as you were saying. And you may suppose that I have repeated the remainder of your tale of horrors. But will you let me assume, without reciting them, that these things are true?

Certainly, he said, what you say is true.

These, then, are the prizes and rewards and gifts which are bestowed upon the just by gods and men in this present life, in addition to the other good things which justice of herself provides.

Yes, he said; and they are fair and lasting.

And yet, I said, all these are as nothing either in number or greatness in comparison with those other recompenses which await both just and unjust after death.* And you ought to hear them, and then both just and unjust will have received from us a full payment of the debt which the argument owes to them.

Speak, he said; there are few things which I would more gladly hear.

Well, I said, I will tell you a tale;[27] not one of the tales which Odysseus tells to the hero Alcinoüs, yet this, too, is a tale of a hero, Er the son of Armonius, a Pamphylian by birth.[28] He was slain in battle, and ten days afterward, when the bodies of the dead were taken up already in a state of corruption, his body was found unaffected by decay, and carried away home to be buried. And on the twelfth day, as he was lying on the funeral pyre, he returned to

d

e

614

b

---

*Compare 10.608c.

life and told them what he had seen in the other world. He said
c   that when his soul left the body he went on a journey with a great
company, and that they came to a mysterious place at which there
were two openings in the earth; they were near together, and over
against them were two other openings in the heaven above. In the
intermediate space there were judges seated, who commanded the
just, after they had given judgment on them and had bound their
sentences in front of them, to ascend by the heavenly way on the
right hand; and in like manner the unjust were bidden by them to
descend by the lower way on the left hand; these also bore the
symbols of their deeds, but fastened on their backs. He drew near,
d   and they told him that he was to be the messenger who would
carry the report of the other world to them, and they bade him
hear and see all that was to be heard and seen in that place. Then
he beheld and saw on one side the souls departing at either opening of heaven and earth when sentence had been given on them;
and at the two other openings other souls, some ascending out of
the earth dusty and worn with travel, some descending out of
e   heaven clean and bright. And arriving ever and anon they seemed
to have come from a long journey, and they went forth with glad-
ness into the meadow, where they encamped as at a festival; and
those who knew one another embraced and conversed, the souls
which came from earth curiously inquiring about the things
above, and the souls which came from heaven about the things
beneath. And they told one another of what had happened by
the way, those from below weeping and sorrowing at the remem-
615   brance of the things which they had endured and seen in their
journey beneath the earth (now the journey lasted a thousand
years),* while those from above were describing heavenly delights
and visions of inconceivable beauty. The story, Glaucon, would
take too long to tell; but the sum was this: He said that for every
wrong which they had done to anyone they suffered tenfold; or
b   once in a hundred years—such being reckoned to be the length of
man's life, and the penalty being thus paid ten times in a thousand
years. If, for example, there were any who had been the cause of

---

*Compare *Phaedrus* 249b.

many deaths, or had betrayed or enslaved cities or armies, or been guilty of any other evil behavior, for each and all of their offences they received punishment ten times over, and the rewards of beneficence and justice and holiness were in the same proportion. I need hardly repeat what he said concerning young children dying almost as soon as they were born. Of piety and impiety to gods and parents, and of murderers, there were retributions other and greater far which he described. He mentioned that he was present when one of the spirits asked another, "Where is Ardiæus the Great?"° (Now this Ardiæus lived a thousand years before the time of Er: he had been the tyrant of some city of Pamphylia, and had murdered his aged father and his elder brother, and was said to have committed many other abominable crimes.) The answer of the other spirit was: "He comes not hither, and will never come."† And this, said he, was one of the dreadful sights which we ourselves witnessed. We were at the mouth of the cavern, and, having completed all our experiences, were about to reascend, when of a sudden Ardiæus appeared and several others, most of whom were tyrants; and there were also, besides the tyrants, private individuals who had been great criminals: they were just, as they fancied, about to return into the upper world, but the mouth, instead of admitting them, gave a roar, whenever any of these incurable sinners or someone who had not been sufficiently punished tried to ascend; and then wild men of fiery aspect, who were standing by and heard the sound, seized and carried them off; and Ardiæus and others they bound head and foot and hand, and threw them down and flayed them with scourges, and dragged them along the road at the side, carding them on thorns like wool, and declaring to the passers-by what were their crimes and that they were being taken away to be cast into hell.‡ And of all the many torments which they had endured, he said that there was none like the terror which each of them felt at that moment, lest they should hear the voice; and when there was silence, one by one

c

d

e

616

°A fictional figure.
†Compare *Gorgias* 525c–d.
‡That is, Tartarus, the lowest place in the underworld. Compare *Gorgias* 523b and *Phaedo* 112a–b.[p. 000]

they ascended with exceeding joy. These, said Er, were the penal-
b ties and retributions, and there were blessings as great.

Now when the spirits which were in the meadow had tarried
seven days, on the eighth they were obliged to proceed on their
journey, and, on the fourth day after, he said that they came to a
place where they could see from above a line of light, straight as a
column, extending right through the whole heaven and through
the earth, in color resembling the rainbow, only brighter and
purer; another day's journey brought them to the place, and there,
in the midst of the light, they saw the ends of the chains of heaven
c let down from above:[29] for this light is the belt of heaven, and
holds together the circle of the universe,[30] like the under-girders
of a trireme.° From these ends is extended the spindle of Necessity,† on which all the revolutions turn. The shaft and hook of this
spindle are made of steel, and the whorl‡ is made partly of steel
and also partly of other materials.[31] Now the whorl is in form like
d the whorl used on earth; and the description of it implied that there
is one large hollow whorl which is quite scooped out, and into this
is fitted another lesser one, and another, and another, and four
e others, making eight in all, like vessels which fit into one another;
the whorls show their edges on the upper side, and on their lower
side all together form one continuous whorl. This is pierced by the
spindle, which is driven home through the centre of the eighth.
The first and outermost whorl has the rim broadest, and the seven
inner whorls are narrower, in the following proportions—the sixth
is next to the first in size, the fourth next to the sixth; then comes
the eighth; the seventh is fifth, the fifth is sixth, the third is seventh, last and eighth comes the second. The largest (or fixed stars)
is spangled, and the seventh (or sun) is brightest; the eighth (or
617 moon) colored by the reflected light of the seventh; the second
and fifth (Saturn and Mercury) are in color like one another, and
yellower than the preceding; the third (Venus) has the whitest

---

°Warship with three banks of oars.
†Various "pre-Socratic philosophers," such as Empedocles and Parmenides, conceived of "Necessity" as a cosmic principle. The personification of Necessity in
this passage is in keeping with traditional poetic practices.
‡That is, the weight on the end of a spindle that keeps it twirling.

light; the fourth (Mars) is reddish; the sixth (Jupiter) is in white-
ness second. Now the whole spindle has the same motion; but, as
the whole revolves in one direction, the seven inner circles move
slowly in the other, and of these the swiftest is the eighth; next in
swiftness are the seventh, sixth, and fifth, which move together;
third in swiftness appeared to move according to the law of this   b
reversed motion, the fourth; the third appeared fourth, and the
second fifth. The spindle turns on the knees of Necessity; and on
the upper surface of each circle is a siren,* who goes round with
them, hymning a single tone or note.[32] The eight together form
one harmony;[33] and round about, at equal intervals, there is another band, three in number, each sitting upon her throne: these   c
are the Fates,† daughters of Necessity, who are clothed in white
robes and have chaplets upon their heads, Lachesis and Clotho
and Atropos, who accompany with their voices the harmony of
the sirens—Lachesis singing of the past, Clotho of the present,
Atropos of the future; Clotho from time to time assisting with a
touch of her right hand the revolution of the outer circle of the
whorl or spindle, and Atropos with her left hand touching and
guiding the inner ones, and Lachesis laying hold of either in turn,
first with one hand and then with the other.   d

When Er and the spirits arrived, their duty was to go at once to
Lachesis; but first of all there came a prophet who arranged them
in order; then he took from the knees of Lachesis lots and samples
of lives, and having mounted a high pulpit, spoke as follows: "Hear
the word of Lachesis, the daughter of Necessity. Mortal souls, behold a new cycle of life and mortality. Your genius‡ will not be al-
lotted to you, but you will choose your genius; and let him who
draws the first lot have the first choice, and the life which he   e
chooses shall be his destiny. Virtue is free, and as a man honors or

---

*The sirens in *Odyssey* 12 are singers whose alluring song dangerously distracts
passing seafarers. In contrast, Socrates envisions them simply as immortal singers.
†In sources dating to the archaic period, the Fates (*Moirai*, or "Apportioners") are
identified as daughters of the goddess Night, or of Zeus and Themis; they are traditionally conceived of as spinners who spin and cut threads that determine the
courses of individual human lives. Clotho means "Spinner"; Lachesis, "Getting-
by-Lot"; and Atropos, "Irresistible."
‡That is, "guardian spirit" (*daimon*).

dishonors her he will have more or less of her; the responsibility is
with the chooser—God is justified."[34] When the Interpreter had
thus spoken he scattered lots indifferently among them all, and
each of them took up the lot which fell near him, all but Er himself (he was not allowed), and each as he took his lot perceived the
number which he had obtained. Then the Interpreter placed on
618 the ground before them the samples of lives; and there were
many more lives than the souls present, and they were of all sorts.
There were lives of every animal and of man in every condition.
And there were tyrannies among them, some lasting out the tyrant's
life, others which broke off in the middle and came to an end in
poverty and exile and beggary; and there were lives of famous
b   men, some who were famous for their form and beauty as well as
for their strength and success in games, or, again, for their birth
and the qualities of their ancestors; and some who were the reverse of famous for the opposite qualities. And of women likewise; there was not, however, any definite character in them,
because the soul, when choosing a new life, must of necessity become different. But there was every other quality, and they all
mingled with one another, and also with elements of wealth and
poverty, and disease and health; and there were mean states also.
And here, my dear Glaucon, is the supreme peril of our human
state; and therefore the utmost care should be taken. Let each one
c   of us leave every other kind of knowledge and seek and follow
one thing only, if peradventure he may be able to learn and may
find someone who will make him able to learn and discern between good and evil, and so to choose always and everywhere the
better life as he has opportunity. He should consider the bearing
of all these things which have been mentioned severally and collectively upon virtue; he should know what the effect of beauty is
d   when combined with poverty or wealth in a particular soul, and
what are the good and evil consequences of noble and humble
birth, of private and public station, of strength and weakness, of
cleverness and dulness, and of all the natural and acquired gifts of
the soul, and the operation of them when conjoined; he will then
look at the nature of the soul, and from the consideration of all
these qualities he will be able to determine which is the better and
which is the worse; and so he will choose, giving the name of evil

to the life which will make his soul more unjust, and good to the ‎ e
life which will make his soul more just; all else he will disregard.
For we have seen and know that this is the best choice both in life
and after death. A man must take with him into the world below
an adamantine faith in truth and right, that there too he may be ‎ 619
undazzled by the desire of wealth or the other allurements of evil,
lest, coming upon tyrannies and similar villainies, he do irremedi-
able wrongs to others and suffer yet worse himself; but let him
know how to choose the mean and avoid the extremes on either
side, as far as possible, not only in this life but in all that which is
to come. For this is the way of happiness. ‎ b

And according to the report of the messenger from the other
world this was what the prophet said at the time: "Even for the
last comer, if he chooses wisely and will live diligently, there is appointed a happy and not undesirable existence. Let not him who
chooses first be careless, and let not the last despair." And when
he had spoken, he who had the first choice came forward and in a
moment chose the greatest tyranny; his mind having been dark-
ened by folly and sensuality, he had not thought out the whole
matter before he chose, and did not at first sight perceive that he
was fated, among other evils, to devour his own children. But when
he had time to reflect, and saw what was in the lot, he began to ‎ c
beat his breast and lament over his choice, forgetting the proclamation of the prophet; for, instead of throwing the blame of his
misfortune on himself, he accused chance and the gods, and everything rather than himself. Now he was one of those who came
from heaven, and in a former life had dwelt in a well-ordered
State, but his virtue was a matter of habit only, and he had no phi- ‎ d
losophy. And it was true of others who were similarly overtaken,
that the greater number of them came from heaven and therefore
they had never been schooled by trial, whereas the pilgrims who
came from earth, having themselves suffered and seen others suffer, were not in a hurry to choose. And owing to this inexperience
of theirs, and also because the lot was a chance, many of the souls
exchanged a good destiny for an evil or an evil for a good. For if a
man had always on his arrival in this world dedicated himself from
the first to sound philosophy, and had been moderately fortunate
in the number of the lot, he might, as the messenger reported, be ‎ e

happy here, and also his journey to another life and return to this, instead of being rough and underground, would be smooth and heavenly. Most curious, he said, was the spectacle—sad and laughable and strange; for the choice of the souls was in most cases based on their experience of a previous life. There he saw the soul which had once been Orpheus choosing the life of a swan out of enmity to the race of women, hating to be born of a woman because they had been his murderers;* he beheld also the soul of Thamyras choosing the life of a nightingale;† birds, on the other hand, like the swans and other musicians, wanting to be men. The soul which obtained the twentieth lot chose the life of a lion, and this was the soul of Ajax the son of Telamon,‡ who would not be a man, remembering the injustice which was done him in the judgment about the arms. The next was Agamemnon, who took the life of an eagle, because, like Ajax, he hated human nature by reason of his sufferings. About the middle came the lot of Atalanta;§ she, seeing the great fame of an athlete, was unable to resist the temptation: and after her there followed the soul of Epeus the son of Panopeus‖ passing into the nature of a woman cunning in the arts; and far away among the last who chose, the soul of the jester Thersites# was putting on the form of a monkey. There came also the soul of Odysseus having yet to make a choice, and his lot happened to be the last of them all. Now the recollection of former toils had disenchanted him of ambition, and he went about for a considerable time in search of the life of a private man who had

620

b

c

---

*Swans were thought to sing when they were about to die; Orpheus was supposed to have been killed by Maenads (female worshipers of Dionysus).

†Thamyras was a legendary Thracian singer who was punished for challenging the Muses to a contest; the songs of nightingales were considered sweet but mournful.

‡Ajax (in Greek, Aias) was a Greek chieftain (from the island Salamis) at Troy who figures prominently in *Iliad*. According to various traditions, Ajax committed suicide after the armor of the dead Achilles was awarded to Odysseus.

§Legendary Arcadian maiden and huntress who, since she was unwilling to marry, challenged all her suitors to footraces.

‖Epeus (also spelled Epeius) was the architect of the Trojan horse; see *Odyssey* 8.493.

#A commoner in the Greek army at Troy who dares to criticize Agamemnon and is beaten by Odysseus; compare *Iliad* 2.211–277.

no cares; he had some difficulty in finding this, which was lying about and had been neglected by everybody else; and when he saw it, he said that he would have done the same had his lot been first instead of last, and that he was delighted to have it. And not only did men pass into animals, but I must also mention that there were animals tame and wild who changed into one another and into corresponding human natures—the good into the gentle and the evil into the savage, in all sorts of combinations.

All the souls had now chosen their lives, and they went in the order of their choice to Lachesis, who sent with them the genius whom they had severally chosen, to be the guardian of their lives and the fulfiller of the choice: this genius led the souls first to Clotho, and drew them within the revolution of the spindle impelled by her hand, thus ratifying the destiny of each; and then, when they were fastened to this, carried them to Atropos, who spun the threads and made them irreversible, whence without turning round they passed beneath the throne of Necessity; and when they had all passed, they marched on in a scorching heat to the plain of Forgetfulness,* which was a barren waste destitute of trees and verdure; and then toward evening they encamped by the river of Unmindfulness, whose water no vessel can hold; of this they were all obliged to drink a certain quantity, and those who were not saved by wisdom drank more than was necessary; and each one as he drank forgot all things. Now after they had gone to rest, about the middle of the night there were a thunderstorm and earthquake, and then in an instant they were driven upward in all manner of ways to their birth, like stars shooting. He himself was hindered from drinking the water. But in what manner or by what means he returned to the body he could not say; only, in the morning, awaking suddenly, he found himself lying on the pyre.

And thus, Glaucon, the tale has been saved and has not perished, and will save us if we are obedient to the word spoken; and we shall pass safely over the river of Forgetfulness, and our soul will not be defiled. Wherefore my counsel is that we hold fast ever

---

*Also mentioned as a feature of the underworld in Aristophanes, *Frogs* 186 (produced in 405 B.C.E.).

to the heavenly way and follow after justice and virtue always, considering that the soul is immortal and able to endure every sort of good and every sort of evil. Thus shall we live dear to one another and to the gods, both while remaining here and when, like conquerors in the games who go round to gather gifts, we receive our reward. And it shall be well with us both in this life and in the pilgrimage of a thousand years which we have been describing.[35]

ENDNOTES

Book 1

1. (1.331d) *if Simonides is to be believed:* Like his father, Cephalus, who quotes Pindar to support his views (1.331), Polemarchus cites a saying of Simonides as justification for his understanding of justice. Both poets are quoted again in book 2 along with several others (namely Homer, Hesiod, Aeschylus), as Glaucon and Adeimantus detail how poetry helps perpetuate the commonly accepted view of justice as an unprofitable inconvenience (see especially 2.363a–366a). These early indications of poetry's influence on basic ethical attitudes and beliefs prepare for Socrates' focus, in books 2 and beyond, on poetic "imitation" (*mimesis*) and on poetry's role in education and acculturation.

2. (1.332b) *And are enemies also to receive what we owe to them?:* The notion that it is proper to help friends and harm enemies is asserted in a variety of poetic texts from the archaic and classical periods. The poem composed by the Athenian statesman Solon (late seventh to early sixth centuries B.C.E.), which begins with an invocation to the Muses, is exemplary; in its first few verses, the author prays, "Grant me prosperity from the blessed gods and let me have respect from all men; may I be sweet to my friends and bitter to my enemies."

3. (1.332b) *an enemy . . . owes to an enemy that which is due or proper to him—that is to say, evil:* In *Crito* and other dialogues, Plato represents Socrates vigorously contesting the notion that it is acceptable (and just) to harm one's enemies and retaliate against those who have caused injury.

4. (1.332c) *if we asked him what due or proper thing is given by medicine, and to whom, what answer do you think that he would make to us?:* Analogies comparing justice—whether in everyday moral choices made by individuals, as here, or in the authority exercised by political leaders, as at 1.340d ff.—to various arts and skills (*techni* in Greek—for example, of the doctor, helmsman, and musician) are central to *Republic*'s analysis of justice. The implications of these analogies are considerable, as are the effects. One important effect is to suggest a link between "justice" and knowledge, or expertise, which enables one to distinguish between appearance (seeming) and reality (being), as at 1.334c–335b and 1.339d–341a. These suggestions set the stage for Socrates' subsequent arguments that "justice" in the individual results from the rule of the soul's rational (that is, knowledgeable) principle over

"spirit" and "appetites" (book 4), and that justice in the state can be realized only when the rulers are "philosophers" (books 5–7).

5. (1.334a) *a lesson which I suspect you must have learnt out of Homer:* Several epic poems composed in dactylic hexameter, including *Iliad* and *Odyssey*, were attributed to "Homer" in antiquity. *Iliad* is set at and around Troy (a non-Greek city in Asia Minor) in the tenth year of the legendary war between the Greeks and the Trojans; *Odyssey* relates the homecoming of Odysseus to the island of Ithaca in the tenth year after the Greek victory at Troy. Unlike Plato's interlocutors, modern scholars (with a few exceptions) tend to view *Iliad* and *Odyssey* as products of centuries of oral story-telling and poetic improvisation, rather than creations of a single individual (that is, "Homer"). *Iliad* and *Odyssey*, in more or less the forms that they now have, became widely known throughout Greece during the latter half (650–500 B.C.E.) of the archaic period, and Athenians in the fifth and fourth centuries B.C.E. revered them as key cultural landmarks. Several Platonic dialogues, including *Republic* and *Ion*, attest to the contemporary popularity of the Homeric epics, which were widely performed by "rhapsodes" and subjected to analysis and interpretation by professional critics. It is worth noting how Plato has his interlocutors speak of Homer (and other poets) in the present tense, as if they were still alive.

6. (1.335b) *in the good qualities of horses, not of dogs?:* The Greek literally reads "in regard to the excellence (*aretê*) of dogs, or of horses. . . ." *Aretê*, from which the adjective *aristos* ("best") is derived, is the condition or quality that makes a given thing or individual "good." When used in general terms of human beings, it commonly refers to moral excellence as well as other qualities or factors (such as intelligence, courage in battle, self-restraint, piety, physical attractiveness, birth, wealth) that would make a man stand out among—and be "better" than—his fellow citizens. *Aretê*, then, is sometimes translated as "virtue" (see below at 1.348c), but in typical usage its range of meaning is generally broader than that of the English word "virtue."

7. (1.336a) *Periander or Perdiccas or Xerxes or Ismenias the Theban:* Periander was tyrant of Corinth (c.625–585 B.C.E.). The Macedonian king named Perdiccas to whom Socrates refers here is probably Perdiccas II (c.450–413 B.C.E.). Xerxes was the king of Persia (d.465 B.C.E.) who led the invasion of Greece in the late 480s B.C.E. Ismenias the Theban is possibly the Ismenias who, in 395 B.C.E., took gold from the Persians in exchange for his help in fomenting war between the Thebans and the Spartans. Since the "dramatic date" of *Republic* is necessarily earlier than 395, Socrates' reference to this Ismenias constitutes a (presumably deliberate) anachronism.

8. (1.338c) *justice is nothing else than the interest of the stronger:* Thrasymachus' definition relies on a term (that is, *to sumpheron*—"interest" or "advantage") that he expressly precluded Socrates from using at 1.336c–d. Nonetheless, that justice is advantageous to the just person is a concept that Socrates, along with Glaucon and Adeimantus, will develop, although along lines wholly different from those in Thrasymachus' mind.

9. (1.338d) *have you never heard that forms of government differ—there are tyrannies, and there are democracies, and there are aristocracies?:* As he draws attention to the ways in which the ruling authority of a community is responsible for determining what constitutes acceptable (that is, "just") behavior on the part of its inhabitants, Thrasymachus shifts the focus of the conversation from the "just" behavior of ordinary individuals to the "just" exercise of political power. From this point on, the investigation moves back and forth between the two points of focus. It can be argued that these two kinds of "justice" are fundamentally different. Yet Socrates will eventually define justice as a condition of the soul that is responsible for all kinds of "just" behavior, whether in private dealings or in the exercise of political power (4.442d–443e), and the conflation that begins here anticipates his formulation.

10. (1.341d) *every art has an interest?:* The way in which Socrates, here and elsewhere, conflates the practitioner of a given skill or craft (for example, a doctor) with the *technê* itself (for example, medicine) is noteworthy.

11. (1.343b) *and you further imagine that the rulers of States, if they are true rulers, never think of their subjects as sheep, and that they are not studying their own advantage day and night:* Thrasymachus' contemptuous dismissal of Socrates' view of leadership looks ahead to the metaphor developed in books 2–5 that likens the guardians of the ideal city-state, as leaders and protectors, to shepherds and their dogs—see, for example, 5.451c.

12. (1.343d) *the unjust man has always more and the just less:* The phrase *pleon echein*—in Greek, literally "to have more"—recurs throughout the first two books of *Republic* to describe (1) the self-aggrandizing behavior of the unjust man, who feels no scruple about competing with others (and harming them, if need be) in order to get all that he wants, and (2) the advantages that such aggressively self-seeking behavior is thought to bring. Compare 1.349b: "Does the just man try to gain any advantage [*pleon echein*] over the just?," 2.359c: "then we shall discover . . . the just and unjust man to be proceeding along the same road, following their interest [*dia pleonexian*]," and 2.362b: "and at every contest, whether in public or private, [the unjust man] gets the better [*pleonektein*] of his antagonists." Thrasymachus' glamorization of the pursuit of personal advantage and power (*pleonexia*) has much in common with Callicles' argument concerning the "law of nature" in *Gorgias* 482c–486d as well as with the argument of Antiphon's "On Truth." Although Thrasymachus' praise of injustice is surely meant to seem at first blush outrageous and "sophistic" in character, Plato's interlocutors invite us to believe that his ideas, for all the arresting frankness of their expression, are really in accordance with mainstream values. See Glaucon at 2.358c: "I hear the voices of Thrasymachus and myriads of others dinning in my ears," Adeimantus at 2.367: "I dare say that Thrasymachus and others . . . ," and, more generally,

Socrates at 6.493a: "all those mercenary individuals, whom the many call Sophists . . . do, in fact, teach nothing but the opinion of the many." Compare *Gorgias* 492d.

13. (1.344a) *the happiest of men:* Compare "happy and blessed" at the end of 1.344b just below. "Happy" and "blessed" are both translations for the adjective *eudaimon*; "happiness" and "blessedness" are interchangeably used to translate the noun *eudaimonia*, which literally refers to the state of having a favorable guardian spirit (*daimon*) presiding over one's life. The "happiness" that is *Republic*'s focus is thus not mere temporary joy or delight; it is, rather, long-term (that is, lifelong) fulfillment and contentment.

14. (1.344e) *Is the attempt to determine the way of man's life so small a matter in your eyes—to determine how life may be passed by each one of us to the greatest advantage?:* This is the first of several passages in *Republic* in which Socrates or another speaker accentuates the profound significance of the issues under discussion. Compare, for example, 1.347e, 2.367c–d, 5.450b, and 10.608b.

15. (1.345a) *even if uncontrolled and allowed to have free play:* The Greek literally reads "even if one lets it [that is, injustice] go and does not prevent it from doing what it wants." This sentence marks the beginning of Socrates' effort, which he sustains throughout *Republic*, to disassociate "happiness" and personal "profit" from the satisfaction of appetites and desires—that is, "doing what one *wants*."

16. (1.347a) *no one is willing to govern . . . without remuneration:* This important idea is developed in book 7, especially at 7.519c–521b and 7.540b.

17. (1.348c–d) *And would you call justice vice? No, I would rather say sublime simplicity. Then would you call injustice malignity?:* For the broad range of meaning of *aretê* (translated in the text surrounding this passage as "virtue"), see note 6 on 1.335b. The word translated here as "vice," *kakia*, has a similarly broad range of meaning and refers to the condition or quality that makes a given thing or individual "base" (*kakos*), including (for human beings) ugliness, poverty, and lowliness in social station, as well as moral defect. When Thrasymachus identifies injustice with *aretê* in the exchange that immediately follows, he asserts in essence that the self-aggrandizement he has associated with injustice makes one stand out and be "better." The assertion is bold, since justice is typically conceived of as one of the chief "virtues" (*aretai*), but hardly nonsensical, given Thrasymachus' view of the material advantages of injustice.

18. (1.352a) *And is not injustice equally fatal when existing in a single person . . . making him an enemy to himself and the just?:* This statement and the discussion leading up to it look ahead to the analysis in books 4, 8, and 9 of injustice and its effects on the individual's soul.

19. (1.352d) *Would you not say that a horse has some end?:* The word *ergon* in Greek, rendered here as "end," is perhaps better translated as "function."

This question and the analysis it introduces reinforce a concept already introduced at 1.346a–b, that every thing (or person) has a single function (*ergon*). Both passages anticipate the crucial organizational principle of the ideal city-state—that is, the mandate that every citizen should have one and only one occupation (2.370a–b)—which becomes the foundation for the conceptions of justice in the individual as well as the community that are advanced in books 4, 8, and 9.

20. (1.353b) *And has not the eye an excellence?:* Once again, "excellence" is *aretê* in Greek; see note 6 on 1.335b.

21. (1.353d) *and has not the soul an end which nothing else can fulfil?:* The notions that the human soul (*psychê* in Greek) has a function—that is, to live—and that it fulfills that function well, producing a "good" and "happy" life by virtue of its excellence (*aretê*), are fundamental to *Republic*. Although we are not meant to be satisfied with the case Socrates makes in this passage for justice as the "excellence" that enables the soul to fulfill its function (see 1.354a–c, below), the formulations he develops in this passage preview the argument he will make at length, especially in books 4, 8, and 9.

22. (1.354b) *Nevertheless, I have not been well entertained; but that was my own fault and not yours:* Socrates' observation about the unsatisfactory nature of the discussion so far (his ironic comment at 2.368b notwithstanding) directs attention to the problem of definition. The advantages of and happiness brought by justice (or injustice) cannot be properly assessed before justice and injustice are defined. Compare the end of *Protagoras* (361c).

Book 2

1. (2.357a–b) *do you wish really to persuade us, or only to seem to have persuaded us, that to be just is always better than to be unjust?:* The differences between seeming and being, appearance and reality, are central to *Republic* (especially books 6 and 7), and Plato does not miss an opportunity to draw attention to them. Compare Glaucon's question here with 1.334c–335b and 1.339d–341a.

2. (2.358e) *They say that to do injustice is, by nature, good; to suffer injustice, evil; but that the evil is greater than the good:* Glaucon's summary of the (popular will) common understanding of justice and injustice, especially the sentiment that suffering injustice is far worse than doing injustice, parallels in several aspects the views that Plato attributes to Polus and Callicles in *Gorgias*. Although Glaucon and later Adeimantus raise many important points concerning the ambiguities of popular moral values, their representations of "what most people think"—and of the moral messages of poetic works—are tendentious, and they provide the basis for Socrates' claim in book 6 that it is "the many" who are in fact responsible for the corruption of young people. See 6.492d–494a and 1.344c.

3. (2.360c) *a man is just, not willingly or because he thinks that justice is any good to him individually, but of necessity, for wherever anyone thinks that he can safely be unjust, there he is unjust:* Glaucon here inverts the maxim commonly attributed to Socrates that "no one does wrong willingly." Compare Socrates at 3.413a and also Adeimantus at 2.366c–d, who adds that even someone who appreciates that justice is best will not be "angry with the unjust . . . because he also knows that men are not just of their own free will."

4. (2.362c) *and out of his gains he can benefit his friends, and harm his enemies:* By identifying the gain over antagonists (that is, *pleonexia*) as the phenomenon that enables one to "help friends and hurt enemies," Glaucon makes an explicit connection between Thrasymachus' boldly expressed defense of injustice (as *pleonexia*) and the traditional conception of justice as "helping friends and hurting enemies" that Polemarchus articulates at the beginning of book 1. See note 12 on 1.343d.

5. (2.365d) *secret brotherhoods and political clubs:* Brotherhoods (literally, "conspiracies") and political clubs flourished in Athens in the late fifth century B.C.E.; their members typically included men from aristocratic families who were disenchanted with the institutions and practices of democracy.

6. (2.365d) *professors of rhetoric:* Several dialogues by Plato, notably *Gorgias*, *Phaedrus*, and *Protagoras*, are concerned with the teaching of rhetoric by professional (and at times highly paid) instructors. Plato sometimes distinguishes such "professors of rhetoric" from "sophists"; sometimes he does not (for example, in *Protagoras*).

7. (2.366c) *men are not just of their own free will:* See note 3 on 2.360c.

8. (2.367a) *but everyone would have been his own watchman:* The word for "watchman" in Greek is *phylax*, also translated as "guardian." Adeimantus' use of the word here anticipates the attention that will be given in books 2–7 to the "guardians" in the ideal state. Compare the equally pointed use of *phylax* at 8.549b and 3.413e.

9. (2.367e) *I had always admired the natural ability of Glaucon and Adeimantus:* The Greek word *physis*, when used in reference to human beings, describes their natural and innate abilities, dispositions, and talents. Throughout the rest of *Republic*, Socrates will repeatedly emphasize the importance of *physis*, which, he asserts, varies considerably from individual to individual. (See, for example, 2.370b, where he and Adeimantus agree that "we are not all alike; there are diversities of natures among us which are adapted to different occupations.") This view of *physis*, which has its roots in traditional aristocratic ideology and its assumptions about the innate superiority of the "well-born," has enormous implications for the political philosophy advanced in *Republic*.

10. (2.369a) *I propose . . . that we inquire into the nature of justice and injustice, first as they appear in the State, and secondly in the individual, proceeding*

from the greater to the lesser and comparing them: The assumptions that
the same conditions give rise to "justice" in the community and in the individual and that, as a consequence, the "justice" of an individual is completely comparable to that of a city-state, are crucial to Socrates' argument,
and they are never challenged by his interlocutors. Compare 4.442d for another reassertion that "justice" in community is identical to that in the individual, and also 4.435d–e and 8.544d for the assumption that the traits
of a given community or people are determined by the characters of its individual members.

11. (2.369b) *Can any other origin of a State be imagined?:* Theories about the
origins of human society abounded in the fifth and fourth centuries B.C.E.;
compare, for example, *Protagoras* 320c–323a.

12. (2.370b) *we are not all alike; there are diversities of natures among us which
are adapted to different occupations:* This is a crucial assumption and formulation in *Republic*; see note 9 on 2.367e.

13. (2.370c) *when one man does one thing which is natural to him and does it at
the right time, and leaves other things:* This is another crucial formulation,
which is anticipated by the argument at 1.353b–d concerning the unique
functions of eyes, ears, etc.

14. (2.371c) *In well-ordered States [salesmen] are commonly those who are the
weakest in bodily strength, and therefore of little use for any other purpose:*
Plato has Socrates reflect typical Athenian prejudices about the inferior
character and abilities of merchants and laborers. Compare 6.495d–e and
9.590c.

15. (2.372a) *Probably in the dealings of these citizens with one another:*
Adeimantus' inference about where to "locate" justice in the ideal community is borne out in the discussion at 4.432d–434a.

16. (2.372e) *But if you wish also to see a State at fever-heat, I have no objection:*
Despite Socrates' reservations concerning the "fevered" and "unhealthy"
condition of a city that provides for more than its citizens' most basic needs,
the refinements Glaucon asks for are in fact crucial to Socrates' conceptual-
izations of the ideal city-state and thus of justice itself, since they enable him
to posit the need in the "fevered" city for a force of specialized warriors—
that is, the guardians (2.374d), whose education and way of life become a
principal focus of the *Republic*.

17. (2.374c) *But is war an art so easily acquired that a man may be a warrior
who is also a husbandman [that is, a farmer], or shoemaker, or other artisan[?]:* Greek city-states, including Athens, did not have professional standing armies during the archaic and classical periods. Rather, citizens were
called up for service at times of need, and even the elite warriors of Sparta
had interests aside from their military duties, insofar as they were landown-
ers and therefore "farmers." Although the Peloponnesian War brought about
a marked increase in the number of mercenary soldiers and began a trend

toward military professionalism, relatively few men in Plato's day were full-time professional soldiers. The army of "guardians" that Socrates envisions would have been unprecedented.

18. (2.375c) *how shall we find a gentle nature which has also a great spirit, for the one is the contradiction of the other?:* This is one of several places in which Socrates acknowledges that the combination of natural qualities required for guardians (and later for the "true" philosophers who are to govern the ideal state) is rare and difficult to nurture properly. See note 9 on 2.367e, and compare also 6.485a–486e and 6.503b–c. There is surely some humor in Socrates' ensuing comparison of the ideal state's guardians to dogs and in his assertions concerning the dog's "philosophical nature" (2.375a–376c). None-theless, the comparison pointedly looks back at the discussion in book 1, during which leadership in human communities is likened to the supervision of flocks by shepherds and their dogs (see note 11 on 1.343b). Moreover, the dog's "philosophical" gift for distinguishing "familiars" from "strangers" harks back to the problem of recognition faced by those who define justice as "helping friends and hurting enemies" (1.334c–335b).

19. (2.376c) *Then we have found the desired natures; and now that we have found them, how are they to be reared and educated?:* Socrates asserts throughout *Republic* that the best "natures," rare as they are, will amount to nothing (or, worse yet, become corrupted) unless they are carefully nurtured and trained from early childhood. Compare this long section on the early education and training of the ideal city-state's future warriors, which continues through most of book 3 (to 3.412b), with the equally long section describing the education of future philosopher-rulers (6.502c–7.540c). Compare also passages at 4.423e and 4.429e–430b, 6.494a–495b, 8.546d, and 8.549b, where Socrates emphasizes the importance of education (*paideia*), nurture (*trophê*), and "music" (*mousikê*—see the next note).

20. (2.376e) *[education] has two divisions: gymnastics for the body, and music for the soul:* The word translated as "music" is *mousikê* in Greek, derived from *Mousai*, the generic name of the patron goddesses of music, poetry, dance, etc. *Mousikê* has a far broader range of meaning than its English derivative "music." It refers to education in poetry, drama, and literature, and thus to general cultural cultivation; hence Socrates' description of *mousikê* as "education for the soul." Yet, since most of Greek poetry (including drama) was sung and performed with the accompaniment of instruments such as pipes (*auloi*) and various types of lyres, it was inherently musical in our modern sense of the word. See 3.401d–402a and 8.549b for the importance of *mousikê*.

21. (2.377c) *You may find a model of the lesser in the greater . . . :* This statement launches a critique of the content and form of poetic (that is, "mimetic") texts that extends well into book 3. Socrates' comparison of Homer's and Hesiod's works to children's stories, though somewhat dismissive, reflects

the important fact that memorization of passages from *Iliad*, *Odyssey*, *Theogony*, *Works and Days*, and other well-known texts, was a basic component in the education of young boys throughout the classical period and beyond. Glaucon's and Adeimantus' detailed descriptions of the popular view of justice, with its many quotations from "the poets," are plainly designed to leave the impression that these texts exert considerable (and dangerous) moral influence on adults as well as children, as they convey problematic views of justice and its rewards. See, for example, 2.365e: "If the poets speak truly, why, then, we had better be unjust . . ."; see also note 1 on 1.331d.

Socrates' critique begins with the content of poetic works: their representations of the gods (2.379e–383c) and their presentations of heroic figures such as Achilles in *Iliad* (3.386a–391e). Discussion of depictions of mortal men (3.392a–c) is deemed premature, since Socrates and his companions have yet to determine what kind of behavior—that is, "just" or "unjust"—merits imitation. The style and manner of representation are next considered, with special attention to the psychological dangers of direct imitation (*mimesis*), as opposed to simple narrative in which performers never assume characters' identities (3.392d–398c). Further formal considerations involve the modes (harmonies) used in musical accompaniment as well as the choice of instruments (3.398d–399e) and rhythms (3.399e–400e). Socrates' basic complaints against poetic texts such as *Iliad* are that (1) they set forth inappropriate conceptions of the essence and activities of the gods, and (2) they provide unwholesome models of conduct to young, uncritical, and easily influenced minds. As emerges at 3.410b–412b, the overall goal of the "musical" and gymnastic curricula proposed for young guardians is to cultivate, in an appropriate balance, the qualities of courage (ferocity) and temperance (gentleness); see note 18 on 2.375c.

Socrates' criticisms of the harmful moral messages conveyed by poetic texts may justifiably strike some readers as simplistic, insofar as they overlook the complexity and sophistication of the perspectives offered in works such as *Iliad* and *Odyssey* on the workings of society and the social responsibilities of individuals. Yet texts such as *Frogs*, a comedy by Aristophanes that was first performed in 405 B.C.E., suggest that the concerns raised in this section of *Republic* about the form and content of poetic texts were influenced by a broader cultural debate. Although he takes his censorship (especially of the content of poems) to an extreme, Plato's Socrates is by no means alone in voicing anxieties about the psychological and ethical effects of poetry and music. Indeed, musical innovations first in narrative poetry (that is, dithyrambs) and then in the lyric portions of tragedy caused a stir in the late fifth century, and they seem to have been what fomented a concern about poetic propriety that preoccupied certain segments of Athenian society into the fourth century. It is worth noting how adamantly Socrates insists in *Republic* that innovations in music and poetry cannot be tolerated; such proscriptions are reminiscent of the views attributed to the archly conservative "Aeschylus" in *Frogs*.

22. (2.378b) *the young man should not be told that in committing the worst of crimes he is far from doing anything outrageous:* In *Clouds* (produced 423 B.C.E.), Aristophanes has a young man, who has been educated in Socrates' "Think-Factory" (*phrontisterion*), justify his abuse of his own father with a reference to Zeus' mistreatment of Cronus. *Clouds* represents Socrates as an unscrupulous sophist, and in *Apology*, Plato has Socrates blame the comedy for fomenting harmful misconceptions about him. This passage of *Republic*, in which Socrates vehemently condemns the myths about Uranus, Cronus, and Zeus and the "lessons" they convey, is perhaps meant to counter further Aristophanes' unflattering representation of Socrates.

23. (2.378d) *these tales must not be admitted into our State, whether they are supposed to have an allegorical meaning or not. For a young person cannot judge what is allegorical and what is literal:* Several individuals during the fifth and fourth centuries proposed allegorical readings of passages in *Iliad* and *Odyssey* that, for example, identified the gods with various elements (fire, air, water, earth) and interpreted stories such as the one about Hephaestus' efforts to protect Hera in the light of theories about the interactions of elements. At 10.605c–608a, Socrates expresses deep reservations about the discriminatory abilities of (most) adults as well as children.

24. (2.379a) *God is always to be represented as he truly is:* Although Socrates does refer here to "god" (*theos* in Greek) in the singular, Jowett's use of the capital G is misleading. The god of whom Socrates speaks here and elsewhere should not be identified with the God of today's monotheistic religions, even though many of the qualities he attributes to god (perfection, immutability, beneficence, truthfulness) are in accordance with the conceptions of monotheistic systems of belief. Overall, Socrates' conceptions of divinity (as Plato represents them) seem very flexible, at least in terms of number. At times he is content to speak of the traditional pantheon of gods (Zeus, Hera, Apollo, et al.), and at times he speaks of "god" in the singular. This is not unprecedented, however, and Greeks regularly spoke of god in the singular if they did not have a particular deity in mind, or if they wanted to refer to divine power in some general way. Socrates, it is true, was charged in 399 B.C.E. with "impiety" because of his failure to recognize the gods recognized by the Athenian polis, but the verb "to recognize" (*nomizein*) in this context can refer to ritual practice as well as "belief." It is not clear that a flirtation with monotheism, of the sort that Plato represents here, would have supplied Socrates' opponents with sufficient grounds for leveling the charge of impiety.

25. (2.380a) *neither will we allow our young men to hear the words of Aeschylus:* It is difficult to imagine that Plato (or Socrates) seriously believed that excision of objectionable material from *Iliad*, *Odyssey*, and other major poetic works was a practical undertaking. Rather, Socrates' method of citing passage after passage that "we will not allow our young men to hear" seems intended to point out the pervasive problems in the contents and "messages" of even the most revered works.

26. (2.380a) *the house of Pelops:* Pelops was the son of Tantalus and the father of Atreus and Thyestes, and thus the grandfather (via Atreus) of Agamemnon and Menelaus. The troubles of the many generations in Pelops' family were popular subjects of tragic drama (for example, the extant *Oresteia* trilogy by Aeschylus). The southern region of Greece in which Sparta and Epidaurus are situated is called the Peloponnese (literally, Pelops' island) after Pelops.

27. (2.382c) *Whereas the lie in words is in certain cases useful and not hateful:* These reflections on the usefulness of lies in certain limited circumstances anticipates the provision made at 3.414b–415d for "needful falsehoods" in the ideal city-state. Compare 3.387c and 3.389b, and also 1.331c.

Book 3

1. (3.389d) *he will punish him for introducing a practice which is equally subversive and destructive of ship or State:* The metaphorical comparison of the polis to a ship at sea is common in classical literature. "Justice" has already been compared to the piloting of ships at 1.332e, and the affinities of political communities to ships will be underscored again, in a powerful and suggestive image, at 6.488a–489a.

2. (3.391a) *Loving Homer as I do, I hardly like to say:* The Greek literally reads, "I hesitate, indeed, on account of Homer, to say. . . .": Here and again at 10.595b and 10.607a–608a (compare 2.383a), Plato has Socrates acknowledge the powerful charm and appeal of the poems attributed to Homer and of poetry in general. This does not mean, however, that these works are beneficial to their listeners, or useful to communities; their great charm, according to Socrates, is what renders them dangerous insofar as it makes them so appealing. The seductive power of pleasant things, which makes most people incapable of distinguishing what is truly good from what is immediately pleasurable and gratifying, is a recurrent concern in *Republic* and several other Platonic dialogues, notably *Philebus*.

3. (3.392c) *we cannot determine until we have discovered what justice is, and how naturally advantageous to the possessor, whether he seem to be just or not:* Socrates provides some indirect indications at 10.603e–605c as to how mortal men and women are to be represented.

4. (3.392d) *And narration may be either simple narration or imitation, or a union of the two?:* Socrates' division of poetry into three formal categories—(1) simple narration, in which performers never assume the identities of characters, (2) simple imitation, in which performers always assume the identities of characters, as in dramatic performances, and (3) a mixed, or "double," form—collapses the established distinctions between genres, such as epic poetry (a "mixed" form) and tragic drama (pure imitation), thus paving the way for his characterizations of Homer as "first of the tragedians" (10.595b and 10.607a). It also provides him with additional means for criticizing poetic works such as *Iliad* on the grounds that their imitative element violates the ideal state's foundational "one person, one job" rule (3.394d–396b; compare 2.370b).

5. (3.397d) *but the mixed style is also very charming: and indeed the pantomimic . . . is the most popular style with children and their attendants, and with the world in general:* See note 2 on 3.391a.

6. (3.398e) *The harmonies which you mean are the mixed or tenor Lydian, and the full-toned or bass Lydian, and such like: Harmoniai*, translated by the terms "modes" and also "harmonies," differ in their arrangements of intervals between notes and also in pitch. Socrates' judgments about the ethos and ethical effects of different *harmoniai*, especially his high regard for the popular Dorian mode, largely accords with assessments in other sources, except for the fact that he chooses to ignore the Phrygian mode's secondary association with orgiastic frenzy (compare Aristotle, *Politics* 8.1342a32–b12).

7. (3.399c–d) *we shall not want multiplicity of notes or a panharmonic scale? . . . Then we shall not maintain the artificers of lyres with three corners and complex scales, or the makers of any other many-stringed, curiously harmonized instruments?:* Musical innovators in late-fifth-century Athens transformed traditional modes by changing the tunings on and adding extra strings to instruments such as lyres. Another contemporary innovation was the more frequent use of instruments such as the triangular harp (*trigonos*), which Jowett misleadingly translates by the phrase "lyre with three corners." The high-pitched *trigonos* had many strings, and, like the pipe (*aulos*), it was associated with intense emotion, sensuality, and licentiousness.

Music was generally thought in antiquity to have strong ethical effects. Conservative segments of Athenian society accordingly took a dim view of the sorts of innovations described above (as well as experiments with rhythm, described below), on the grounds that they had undesirable effects on conduct and were conducive to "loose behavior" as well as general disregard for traditional norms and standards of decorum. On the topic of music's ethical influence and the dangers of innovation, Socrates in *Republic* heartily concurs with the traditionalists; "musical training," he states at 3.401d–402a, "is a more potent instrument than any other, because rhythm and harmony find their way into the inward places of the soul, on which they mightily fasten. . . ." His repeated insistence that, to preserve the ideal state, rulers must guard "above all" against innovations in music and poetry (4.424b–e; compare 8.546d), is hardly surprising.

8. (3.399e) *The preferring of Apollo and his instruments to Marsyas and his instruments is not at all strange, I said:* Apollo's instruments are the cithara and other lyres; the instruments of the satyr Marsyas, who lost a musical contest with Apollo and was flayed for his impudence in challenging the god, are pipes (*auloi*). The music of the *aulos* was generally linked to ecstasy, frenzy, and sensuality, whereas the music of stringed instruments was considered more restrained and dignified. In endorsing the Phrygian mode (3.399a–c), Socrates ignores its association with *auloi*; see note 6 above on 3.398e.

9. (3.399e) *complex systems of metre, or metres of every kind:* The rhythms of Greek poetry were quantitative, based on combinations of long and short syllables (in *metra* or longer *cola*) according to fixed patterns that permitted some limited variations. (Long syllables were generally "held" for twice as long as short syllables.) Experiments with rhythmic variation (and hence complexity) comprised another set of innovations in the late fifth century that met with disapproval from conservative critics.

10. (3.400a) *there are some three principles of rhythm out of which metrical systems are framed:* Theorists classified the basic rhythms (that is, iambic, trochaic, anapestic, dactylic, paeonic, cretic) into three groups, depending on the proportion of long and short syllables in their *metra*. Iambic and trochaic, which alternate short and long syllables, were grouped together; anapestic and dactylic, which alternate a long syllable with two short syllables, were likewise grouped together. The paeonic, which featured a long syllable followed by three short syllables, was grouped with its variant, "cretic."

11. (3.400a) *four notes out of which all the harmonies are composed:* This is perhaps a reference to the systems of four notes (that is, tetrachords) that were the bases of scales and therefore of *harmoniai*, or modes.

12. (3.400d) *our principle is that rhythm and harmony are regulated by the words, and not the words by them:* Greek music traditionally featured no vocal flourishes such as coloratura, although in the late fifth century singers experimented with stretching out a single syllable over more than one note. This practice (*epektasis*) was yet another innovation that met with disapproval from those with conservative tastes.

13. (3.400d–e) *The beauty of style and harmony and grace and good rhythm depend on simplicity:* Eschewing complexity and variety in favor of simplicity (in the positive sense of the word) is the unifying principle of Socrates' educational program for future guardians; see Socrates' assertion at 3.404e that complexity engenders "license" in the soul and "disease" in the body, whereas simplicity guards against both, and also 3.398a–b, 3.399c–e, 3.404b, and 3.410a. For the negative association of "simplicity" with foolishness, see Thrasymachus' ironic comment on "sublime simplicity" at 1.348c.

14. (3.401c) *then will our youth dwell in a land of health:* Socrates' description of the young guardians' healthy spiritual condition anticipates his definition of

justice (in the individual) as the healthy, balanced, and harmonious state of the soul at 4.444c–d.

15. (3.402c) *neither we nor our guardians . . . can ever become musical until we and they know the essential forms of temperance, courage, liberality, magnificence, and their kindred, as well as the contrary forms, . . . and can recognize them and their images wherever they are found. . . . :* Scholars vigorously debate whether readers are meant to assume that Socrates is referring at this point to the metaphysical "ideas" (that is, of good-in-itself, beauty-in-itself, etc.) that are identified in books 6 and 7 as the ultimate objects of philosophical inquiry. Although the term used here (*ta eidê*) is the one used later in *Republic* and in other Platonic dialogues to designate the ideas, it is perhaps wise to assume that, since the ideas have not yet come up in *Republic*'s conversation, Socrates is currently using the term in a less specialized sense, simply to indicate that all who aim to be properly educated should be exposed, via *mousikê*, to examples of temperance, courage, and other worthy qualities (compare 3.396d–e).

16. (3.402e) *But let me ask you another question: Has excess of pleasure any affinity to temperance?:* This question, which leads to a brief discussion of how intense homoerotic attachments must be banned in the ideal state, constitutes a striking transition between the discussions of the young guardians' training in *mousikê* and *gymnastikê*. Later in *Republic* (5.474d) Glaucon graciously accepts being characterized, for the sake of the argument, as a "man of pleasure" (literally, an "erotic man"—that is, someone who falls in love with handsome youths), and the verses quoted by Socrates at 2.368a reveal that, until recently, Glaucon has also been the object of an older man's attentions. Moreover, in *Symposium*, *Phaedrus*, and elsewhere, Plato has Socrates playfully confess his erotic attraction to handsome young men, such as Alcibiades and Agathon. It is always made plain, however, that Socratic *eros* is wholly spiritual. The point in this passage is that, although love of beauty is ennobling and worth cultivating, it does not legitimize intemperate lust for handsome young men or boys.

17. (3.404b) *My meaning may be learned from Homer:* Socrates' reliance upon "Homer" as an authority on diet, exercise, and medicine may come as a bit of a surprise after his extensive critical analysis of various elements in *Iliad* and *Odyssey*. It is perhaps best to take with some grains of salt Plato's references to the expertise of Homer and other poets on various practical matters.

18. (3.405b) *pride himself on his litigiousness:* Fifth- and fourth-century critics of democracy frequently alleged that the Athenians were overly fond of going to court, both as prosecutors and as jurors. The analogy developed in this passage between medicine, which cures the ailments of the body, and corrective justice, which seeks to "cure" the ills of the soul, is paralleled in some regards in *Gorgias*.

19. (3.407e) *Then, he said, you regard Asclepius as a statesman*: The parallels
between rulers who care for their subjects and doctors who care for their
patients have already been suggested in book 1 (for example, at 1.341c), and
they figure prominently in other Platonic dialogues concerned with political
leadership and management. *Statesman* 293c–d advances the notion that the
good ruler, like a doctor, will be obliged to make difficult decisions (such as
the life-and-death choices that Socrates attributes to Asclepius) and do
painful, unpleasant things.

20. (3.408c–d) *Ought there not to be good physicians in a State, and are not the
best those who have treated the greatest number of constitutions, good and
bad, and are not the best judges in like manner those who are acquainted
with all sorts of moral natures?*: Among Plato's dialogues, *Gorgias* is noteworthy for its extensive comparison of corrective justice, which metes out
(often painful) punishments in order to ameliorate defects of the soul, and
the art of medicine, which implements (often painful) treatments in order
to cure disease in the body. In this passage, however, Socrates (perhaps with
some irony) adduces an important difference between the expertise of doctors and that of people who sit in judgment of crimes—doctors benefit from
the experience of physical illness, but jurors/judges (*dikastai* in Greek) are
not profited by exposure to crime and moral defect.

21. (3.410e) *And in our opinion the guardians ought to have both these qualities?*:
The cultivation of courage (3.386a–389d) and temperance (3.389d–391e)
has been a preoccupation of Socrates' description of the guardians' early education and thus of his discussion of poetry's content and its musical accompaniment. For more on the importance of fostering these two qualities in
the citizenry, see Plato, *Statesman* 306a–311c and *Laws* 1.626d–636c.

22. (3.412b) *Very good, I said; then what is the next question?*: In the short section that follows this question (through 3.417b), Socrates introduces several
important provisions about the organization of the ideal city-state and, more
particularly, about the guardians' way of life. These provisions include: the
testing of the guardians so that they may be divided into two groups, rulers
(who are "guardians" in the limited sense of the word) and their helpers
("auxiliaries"); the devising of a "royal lie" designed to make citizens accept
their division into "classes" of gold (rulers), silver (auxiliaries) and bronze
and iron (craftsmen, farmers, et al.); the promotion and demotion of children born into each class according to their natural abilities (*physis*); and the
requirement that the guardians (both rulers and auxiliaries) have no private
property and "live together like soldiers in a camp" (3.416e). This last requirement, along with the provision that rulers and auxiliaries "possess"
their women and children in common (4.423e), receives fuller treatment in
book 5.

23. (3.413c) *we must inquire who are the best guardians of their own conviction
that what they think the interest of the State is to be the rule of their lives:*

Described here is the battery of tests and trials (of memory, physical endurance, and mental stability) that young guardians must undergo; those who are to be rulers will need to undergo, beginning at age twenty, yet another series of tests that measure their intellectual sophistication (7.537a–540c).

24. (3.413e) *good guardians of themselves and of the music which they have learned:* See note 8 on 2.367a.

25. (3.414c) *only an old Phoenician tale:* Cadmus, the legendary founder of Thebes in Boeotia, came to Greece from Phoenicia (on the eastern edge of the Mediterranean Sea). The tale is that Cadmus killed the dragon that dwelled at the site of his newly founded city and threw its teeth in the ground; from these teeth sprang fully armed men, called Spartoi (that is, "Sown Men"). This is one of several myths that describe how individuals, or an entire people, came to be born from the earth.

26. (3.415a) *Some of you have the power of command, and in the composition of these he has mingled gold . . . :* As Socrates indicates at 8.546e, the conception of people characterized by gold, silver, bronze, and iron is borrowed from Hesiod, *Works and Days* 109–201, which describes how the earth was successively peopled by a golden "race" (*genos*), a silver race, a bronze race, a race of "heroes," and the current race of "iron."

27. (3.415d) *Not in the present generation:* At 7.540e–541b Socrates acknowledges that it would be generally impossible to persuade adults to accept the beliefs and ideals necessary for the institution of the ideal state; compare 6.501a.

28. (3.416e–417a) *for that commoner metal has been the source of many unholy deeds, but their own is undefiled:* Socrates' assertion concerning the (inevitably) corrupting influence of wealth counters the original assumption of Cephalus, who claimed at 1.331a–b that his wealth is what has enabled him to be "just" throughout his life. Property-holding in the guardian classes violates the ideal state's foundational one-person-one-job rule, insofar as it would consequently lead rulers and auxiliaries to become "good housekeepers and husbandmen instead of guardians . . ." (3.417a). Compare Socrates' more general indication at 4.421d–422a that excessive wealth among the bronze/iron class (who are allowed to possess private property) would be "the parent of luxury and indolence."

Book 4

1. (4.423a–b) *Hellenes or barbarians:* Greeks (that is, Hellenes) saw themselves as ethnically and culturally distinct from other people, such as the local peoples of Asia Minor (for example, Lydians and Phrygians), as well as Egyptians, Persians, and Scythians. See also 4.435e–4.436a and 5.470c.

2. (4.424a) *the general principle that friends have all things in common:* Socrates casually mentions here another strikingly unusual aspect of the guardians' way of life: the absence of individual families and the common "possession" of women and children. Although Adeimantus does not question Socrates' provision about the guardians' wives and children at this point, it is examined in detail beginning at 5.449c.

3. (4.424c) *when modes of music change, the fundamental laws of the State always change with them:* The word translated here as "modes" is not *harmoniai* (see note 6 on 3.398e), but the more general term *tropoi* ("styles," "manners"). Damon's theory concerning the relationship between musical innovation and change in fundamental political laws naturally follows on what Socrates has set forth in book 3 concerning the ethical influence of music (compare *Laws* 2.673a). The underlying logic is that, if the character of people changes (because of their exposure to new types of music), this ethical transformation will inevitably lead to changes in basic customs and laws (compare *Laws* 3.700a–701d). Hence Socrates' insistence that the guardians must, above all, guard against innovation in music and education; compare 8.546e.

4. (4.424d) *in the form of amusement; and at first sight it appears harmless:* On the importance of children's games and play to the overall welfare and stability of the state, see also *Laws* 7.793d–794a and 7.797a–798e, which present more detailed arguments against permitting innovations in children's games.

5. (4.426b–c) *do not these States resemble the persons whom I was describing?:* The allusion is to 3.405a–410a. As in the earlier passage, this description of the "ill-ordered state" that forbids constitutional change but continually experiments with legislative tinkering plainly alludes to contemporary Athens. See note 18 on 3.405b.

6. (4.428a) *And is not a similar method to be pursued about the virtues, which are also four in number?:* Traditional conceptions of the virtues (*aretai*) admitted some variation. Here, the virtues are wisdom (*sophia*), courage (*andreia*), temperance or moderation (*sophrosynê*), and justice (*dikaiosynê*); in *Protagoras*, Plato has Socrates and Protagoras add piety (*hosiotês*) to these four. The process of elimination by which Socrates proposes to discover "justice" in the ideal state may, with good reason, strike some readers as simplistic and unconvincing, and it is perhaps wisest to assume that his argument in the following passage is meant to be merely suggestive. See 4.435c–d for the first of several passages in which Socrates and his interlocutors acknowledge the provisional and inadequate nature of their discussion.

7. (4.432d) *Why, my good sir, at the beginning of our inquiry, ages ago, there was Justice tumbling out at our feet, and we never saw her; nothing could be more ridiculous:* See 2.372a and also 2.370b. The definition of justice that emerges in this passage—that is, of doing one's own business—looks back to the formulation of justice introduced by Polemarchus at 1.332b as "giving what is due or proper," insofar as the role of leadership is "due" and "proper"

to the guardians in the ideal state, as it also is to the "rational principle" in the individual human being (4.441e).

8. (4.433a) *Justice was doing one's own business, and not being a busybody:* The verb "to be a busybody" (*polypragmonein*) and the related noun (*polypragmosynê*, "meddlesomeness") and adjective (*polypragmon*) were ideologically charged terms in fifth- and fourth-century Athens. They were typically used by critics of Athenian democracy to disparage its empowerment of average citizens who, as members of the Assembly and as jurors in courts, could "meddle" in affairs of state as well as in the lives of important men. The same terms were also used to critique the "meddling" of Athens in the affairs of the city-states that were its nominal allies in the Delian League. The association of injustice in the state with *polypragmosynê*, which is described at 4.434a–c as the "meddling" of the bronze/iron class in the business of rulers and auxiliaries, is an obvious criticism of the current institutions and practices of Athenian democracy. The earlier comparison at 3.389c of average individuals to the patients of a doctor or the crew on a ship anticipates this passage's emphasis on the dysfunction that occurs when such people attempt to give orders instead of taking them.

It is worth noting how Socrates and his interlocutors, here in book 4 and in the more detailed analysis of the four "degenerate" political constitutions in books 8 and 9, assume that the division of the ideal city-state's citizens into three groups (rulers, auxiliaries, all others) reflects the actual and natural categorization of people in all types of political communities. This assumption follows upon their agreement that in the ideal state people are grouped according to their *natural* abilities, and it furnishes them the grounds for assessing the defects of any political arrangement that fails to observe the ideal state's distinctions and prohibitions against "meddling."

9. (4.435b–c) *we may assume that he has the same three principles in his own soul which are found in the State; and he may be rightly described in the same terms, because he is affected in the same manner?:* This assumption, which Socrates strives to justify in the following pages, is a corollary of the major assumption that "justice" in the state is qualitatively identical to "justice" in the individual (2.368c–e; compare below at 4.442d). The understanding of human psychology that Socrates advances in this passage capitalizes on commonplace conceptions (for example, the opposition between "reason" and "appetites") but is nonetheless distinctive. In particular, his conception of the third and intermediate part of the soul ("spirit" or "passion" [*thumos*]), which he posits as reason's "ally" (4.440a–441c), requires special explanation. In *Phaedrus*, Plato has Socrates develop a similar (though not identical) image of the soul, which is likened to a chariot with a team of two horses. The charioteer (that is, "reason") drives; of the two horses, the one on the right side is fair and disciplined, corresponding to the "spirited" part

(*thumos*) of the soul in *Republic*, whereas his dark and unruly counterpart on the left corresponds to *Republic*'s appetitive part.

10. (4.435d) *I do not think that the method which we are employing is at all adequate to the accurate solution of this question:* This is the first of several important passages in *Republic* in which Socrates, Glaucon, and/or Adeimantus acknowledge the methodological inadequacies of their discussion and call attention to the fact that, in the current circumstances, they are not able to explore their concerns properly. Compare 5.450e–451a and 5.472b–c; 6.484a, 6.504b, 6.506c–d, and 6.509c; 7.517b, 7.532d–e, 7.536b–c; and 10.595c. The cumulative effect of these passages is to highlight the provisional and suggestive nature of the conversation dramatized in *Republic*.

11. (4.435e) *the Thracians, Scythians, and in general the Northern nations:* Thrace was located on the northern edge of the Aegean Sea; the Scythians were a nomadic people based, during the classical period, in the area north of the Black Sea. Phoenicia, mentioned below, was located on the eastern edge of the Mediterranean Sea. Socrates' statement reflects the standard cultural and ethnic prejudices that Greeks of his time entertained, and also the thinking of medical theorists such as Hippocrates, who argued that climate influenced the character of individuals and whole peoples. On Phoenician and Egyptian "character" and the importance of climate, compare *Laws* 5.747c–e.

12. (4.437d) *is not thirst the desire which the soul has of drink, and of drink only; not of drink qualified by anything else . . . ?:* That is, if one is thirsty for a *cold* drink, one is actually subject to two separate conditions: thirst (which makes one desire a drink) and heat (which makes one desire coldness). Appetite for *good* food is accordingly an appetite for food that is modified by some other force or factor.

13. (4.439e) *And what of passion, or spirit? Is it a third, or akin to one of the preceding?:* The Greek word translated here as "passion" and "spirit" is *thumos*, which the ensuing discussion identifies as the source of anger and indignation. This understanding basically accords with traditional conceptions of *thumos* as the wellspring of courage and daring, and also competitiveness (compare Euripides, *Medea* 1079–1080 and Aristophanes, *Acharnians* 480). Given the pains Socrates takes in the ensuing exchange to distinguish "spirit" from the appetitive part of the soul, it seems that Plato could not assume that his readers would automatically see *thumos* as something other than (an) appetite.

14. (4.442a) *the concupiscent, which in each of us is the largest part of the soul and by nature most insatiable of gain:* So, too, the bronze/iron group is the largest in the state—far larger than the classes of (gold) rulers and (silver) auxiliaries. In statements such as this, we can see the complete interdependence of the psychological theory that Socrates develops in *Republic* and the political philosophy that arises from his conception of the ideal state.

15. (4.443c–d) *But in reality justice was such as we were describing, being concerned, however, not with the outward man, but with the inward, which is the true self and concernment of man:* Socrates' striking conclusion, that the "justice" of an individual is not the product of his or her deeds and dealings with others but is rather the well-ordered "psychological" state that naturally gives rise to "just" actions, departs radically from traditional conceptions of "justice" and has far-reaching implications. Most notably, Socrates' formulation deemphasizes the political and social interactions that are the focal points of most considerations of "justice," since these are merely the results of the rule of reason in the soul over spirit and appetites. On the logic advanced in *Republic*, an individual can be "just" even if he or she has no social contact with other human beings.

16. (4.444b) *Must not injustice be a strife which arises among the three principles—a meddlesomeness, and interference . . . ?:* Stasis ("strife") typically refers to civil strife and factionalism within a polis. Many Greek city-states, including Athens, had considerable experience with *stasis* in the classical period; during the Peloponnesian War, factional strife within Athens brought about two oligarchic coups (411–410 and 404–403 B.C.E.). "Meddlesomeness" is Jowett's translation for the noun *polypragmosynê*, which is derived from the verb *polypragmonein*, translated above as "to be a busybody" (4.433a). "Interference" is his translation for *allotriopragmosynê*, a variation of *polypragmosynê*. For the political and ideological thrust of these last two terms, see note 8 on 4.433a.

    Socrates' leading question strikes yet another blow at Athenian democracy. By linking *polypragmosynê* ("meddlesomeness") to civil strife and factionalism (*stasis*), Socrates insinuates that there is inherent dysfunction in a political system (such as Athens') that encourages its citizens to become politically active. This formulation harks back to Socrates' identification of injustice as the source of "divisions and hatreds and fighting" at 1.351d.

17. (4.444c) *they are like disease and health; being in the soul just what disease and health are in the body:* The comparison of justice and injustice in the soul to bodily health and disease previews the arguments that Socrates will develop in books 8 and 9 about the psychological dysfunction brought about by "injustice" as it has just been defined in book 4.

Book 5

1. (5.449b) *when Polemarchus, who was sitting just a little way off, just beyond Adeimantus, began to whisper to him:* The personal interactions in this passage are noteworthy. Polemarchus, who was at the beginning of the dialogue an uncritical proponent of the commonplace view of justice, seems caught up in the spirit of the discussion among Socrates and the two brothers, and ventures to seek clarification (via Adeimantus) about two key proposals

concerning the guardians' way of life. Even Thrasymachus, who was openly hostile to Socrates in book 1, appears won over (5.450a–b); it is he who now emphasizes the importance of the conversation (compare Socrates at 1.344e) and urges Socrates to cooperate with the group's request for more details about the "community" of wives and children.

The lengthy digression that Polemarchus' request initiates postpones further consideration of the dialogue's main questions—that is, whether justice leads to "happiness" and is "profitable"—until book 8. At first Socrates and his interlocutors are concerned with considering the role to be undertaken by women of the guardian classes and the "community" of wives and children; Glaucon, however, insists that Socrates address the more general questions of whether the ideal city-state could ever be brought into being, and under what conditions it might be founded (5.471c–e; compare 5.466c). This prompts Socrates to make his famous claim that the ideal state will come into being only when "philosophers are kings, or the kings and princes of this world have the spirit and power of philosophy" (5.473d–e). Socrates' assertion leads in turn to efforts to (1) define "philosophy" and "philosophers" (5.474b–6.487a), (2) explain the unfavorable reputation of philosophers in contemporary Athens (6.487a–497a), (3) identify the ultimate goal of the philosopher's education (6.502c–7.521b), and (4) elucidate how future philosophers might be prepared to achieve that goal (7.521c–540c).

Though technically parts of a digression, these topics are clearly of central importance to *Republic*. The philosopher-ruler is the key figure upon whom the ideal (that is, just) state depends for its (hypothetical) existence, and he (or she) is also implicitly the exemplar of justice in the individual, since he (or she) is "orderly and divine, as far as the nature of man allows" (6.500c–d). It should be noted that Plato strives to create strong impressions in his readers' imaginations throughout this long section, in which he has Socrates convey some of his most vivid and memorable images—including the simile of the sun at 6.507a–509b and the allegory of the cave at 7.514a–518b; see also the metaphor of the ship of state at 6.488a–489a, and the image of philosophy as a bride abandoned by her true grooms and forced to "wed" unworthy suitors at 6.495b–496a.

2. (5.449d) *the right or wrong management of [domestic] matters will have a great and paramount influence on the State for good or for evil.* The notion that proper "household management" was intimately connected to the effective management of political affairs became widely accepted in Athens during the classical period; in *Protagoras* 318e–319a, for example, Plato has Protagoras claim to teach his students how they "might best arrange their household business and become most successful with respect to the affairs of the city." Socrates' outline in books 2 and 3 of the guardians' early education argues for a yet more intense connection between "domestic affairs" (that is, the education and training of children) and the successful management of the polis.

3. (5.451a) *the danger is not that I shall be laughed at . . . but that I shall miss the truth . . . and drag my friends after me in my fall:* Socrates was formally accused and convicted in 399 B.C.E. on charges of impiety and "corrupting the youth." It is in the light of the latter charge, perhaps, that Plato has Socrates express caution about speaking his mind and (potentially) misleading his young companions. Glaucon's reassurance that Socrates "shall not be held to be a deceiver" may be equally pointed.

4. (5.452a) *several of our proposals . . . being unusual, may appear ridiculous:* Socrates repeatedly draws attention to the possibility that his proposals concerning guardian women may strike many as "ridiculous"; compare 5.452c and 5.457a–b, and also 5.473d–e, where he introduces the concept of the philosopher-ruler. Utopian social models that empowered women (and also featured "communism" in wives and children) were satirized by comic playwrights, such as Aristophanes in *The Women at the Assembly* (*Ecclesiazusae*), which was produced in 392 B.C.E. Socrates' comments seem aimed at acknowledging—and discrediting—this kind of comic satire.

5. (5.452c–d) *when first the Cretans, and then the Lacedaemonians, introduced the custom:* "Lacedaemonian" and "Laconian" refer to the territory around the polis of Sparta and its inhabitants. Greek men in the classical period regularly stripped when they exercised and competed in athletic contests; in his *History of the Peloponnesian War* 1.6, Thucydides concurs that this practice was an innovation that the Spartans (that is, Lacedaemonians) introduced to Greece at some point in the distant past.

6. (5.454a) *glorious is the power of the art of contradiction!:* The "art of contradiction" is *antilogike technê* (literally, the "skill of antilogic"), a technique of argumentation whereby speakers cause their listeners to think of an object (or person or action) as first possessing one quality (or predicate) and then its opposite. "Antilogic" represents one of several techniques that someone seeking success in verbal debates could deploy and is therefore associated with the practice of "eristic." Socrates opposes eristic argumentation (aiming at persuasion and victory, no matter what the cost) to dialectic (aiming at the truth, no matter what the cost) just below at 5.454a, where he contrasts the "spirit of contention" with that "of fair discussion," and again at 7.539c. See also *Meno* 75c and *Philebus* 17a.

7. (5.454d) *a physician and one who is in mind a physician may be said to have the same nature:* The Greek text is difficult. Some editors prefer a reading that translates as "a male physician and a female physician may be said to have the same nature"; others prefer the reading "one physician and another may be said. . . ."

8. (5.454d–e) *but if the difference consists only in women bearing and men begetting children, this does not amount to a proof that a woman differs from a man in respect of the sort of education she should receive:* Socrates' assertion of the potential equality between men and women (which is perhaps at

odds with the remark at 5.455d about "the general inferiority of the female sex"), and his judgment that the current practice of not training women for war is "in reality a violation of nature" (5.456c) are striking. Women in Athens during the classical period had no political franchise and were generally not educated outside the home. Although several dramas dating to the fifth century (for example, Aeschylus' *Oresteia* trilogy [458 B.C.E.] and Aristophanes' *Lysistrata* [411 B.C.E.]) feature characters who debate the fairness and propriety of this kind of marginalization, there seems to have been little doubt in the minds of Athenian men that their wives, daughters, and sisters were meant to stay in the home. Mythical women warriors, such as Amazons, were universally represented as dangerous aberrations.

Modern scholars differ in their assessments of Plato's "feminism." On the one hand, he has Socrates assert that women as well as men are capable of becoming philosopher-rulers (7.540c); on the other, perhaps reflecting the cultural realities of his day, he never represents respectable Athenian women (that is, the relatives of citizen men) participating in philosophical conversations, and female figures in his dialogues (the probably fictional Diotima in *Symposium*, Pericles' mistress Aspasia in *Menexenus*) are few and far between.

9. (5.457c) *Yes, that was a mighty wave which you have escaped:* Waves were thought to come in groups of three, with the third as the largest (and potentially most dangerous). See below at 5.472a. The three "waves" are the challenges Socrates faces in (1) explaining how female guardians are to be trained and educated (5.451c–457c), (2) justifying the "community" of wives and children among the guardians (5.457c–471c), and (3) explaining how the ideal city-state might come into being. Socrates' effort to respond to this final challenge occupies the rest of book 5 and all of books 6 and 7.

10. (5.458d) *necessity, not geometrical, but another sort of necessity which lovers know, and which is far more convincing and constraining to the mass of mankind:* Socrates refers here to the "necessity" of sexual passion, which most people cannot resist, and which differs completely from the logical necessity of mathematical reasoning.

11. (5.458e) *the next thing will be to make matrimony sacred in the highest degree:* To Athenian ears, the phrase *hieros gamos* ("sacred marriage") would have signified, first and foremost, the marriage of Zeus and Hera, which was regularly celebrated at a special festival. The phrase underscores the solemnity of the "marriages" among guardians.

12. (5.459c–d) *our rulers will find a considerable dose of falsehood and deceit necessary for the good of their subjects: . . . the use of all these things regarded as medicines might be of advantage:* See note 27 on 2.382c, and also 3.414b–415d for "needful falsehoods" in the ideal city-state.

13. (5.460c) *but the offspring of the inferior, or of the better when they chance to be deformed, will be put away in some mysterious, unknown place, as they should be:* Sickly, deformed, or unwanted infants were regularly exposed and

left to die outside the city limits in Athens and elsewhere in Greece; the decision to expose an infant typically was made by the father or male head of household. Socrates' provision for the "putting away" of sickly and deformed children is wholly in keeping with this practice; the only difference is that the decision in the ideal city-state would be made by the polis' officials, not the father.

14. (5.460e) *A woman . . . at twenty years of age may begin to bear children to the State, and continue to bear them until forty:* In Athens, girls were generally married at puberty and began bearing children immediately; men did not marry until much later in life (that is, at approximately age thirty). Socrates' provision for the female guardians' late start in childbearing is noteworthy.

15. (5.462c) *And is not that the best-ordered State in which the greatest number of persons apply the terms "mine" and "not mine" in the same way to the same thing?:* Like the prohibition against private property (3.416e–417b), the creation of what is in essence a common family among the guardians is aimed at keeping them from developing private interests at odds with those of the community as a whole (5.463c–464b).

16. (5.465d) *The Olympic victor . . . is deemed happy in receiving a part only of the blessedness which is secured to our citizens, who have won a more glorious victory and have a more complete maintenance at the public cost:* Victors in the games at Olympia and other pan-Hellenic sites were rewarded in Athens with public honors and privileges, including meals (paid for out of the polis' treasury) in the Prytaneum. (Compare *Apology* 36d.) Socrates' pronouncement concerning the "victory" of the guardians and the rewards they receive answers the complaint Adeimantus lodges on behalf of the guardians at 4.419a.

17. (5.466d) *The inquiry . . . has yet to be made, whether such a community will be found possible . . . and if possible, in what way possible:* See note 9 on 5.457c and note 21 on 5.471c.

18. (5.469b) *Do you think it right that Hellenes should enslave Hellenic States, or allow others to enslave them, if they can help?:* See note 1 on 4.423a, and also 5.470c. Although Greeks rarely served as slaves in other Greek city-states, Greek armies could sell their Hellenic captives to non-Greek foreigners. What is said in these paragraphs raises the question: Do Socrates and his interlocutors assume that there will be slaves in the ideal city-state, although their role in the community is never discussed? Scholars disagree about the implications of this sentence and the following remarks. Slaves were universally present in all Greek communities, and although the ideal state differs radically in several regards from existing states (see, for example, 6.497a–c), it is perhaps reasonable to infer from this passage that it was not meant to differ as far as the practice of slavery was concerned.

19. (5.469d) *And is there not illiberality and avarice in robbing a corpse . . . ?:* Victorious armies regularly stripped weapons from corpses of the enemy dead; the armor subsequently would be dedicated to the gods and displayed in temples. Destroying crops and livestock and burning buildings (5.470a) were also standard practices in war.

20. (5.470c) *we shall say that Hellas is then in a state of disorder and discord:* Socrates' distinction between *stasis* ("civil strife") and *polemos* ("war") reflects standard usage; his redefinition of the term *stasis* to cover conflicts *between* city-states is, however, unusual.

21. (5.471c) *Is such an order of things possible, and how, if at all?:* See note 9 on 5.457c and note 17 on 5.466d. Socrates' reference to "the first and second waves" in the following paragraphs looks back to 5.457b–c.

22. (5.472e) *And is our theory a worse theory because we are unable to prove the possibility of a city being ordered in the manner described?:* Although Socrates eventually argues that the ideal state is in fact possible and is not "a mere dream" (7.540d), his assertion concerning the utility and importance of ideal models, even when they are unrealizable, is noteworthy.

23. (5.473c–d) *"Until philosophers are kings, or the kings and princes of this world have the spirit and power of philosophy . . . cities will never have rest from their evils . . . and then only will this our State have a possibility of life and behold the light of day":* This striking statement, which (as Glaucon imagines just below) most people would strenuously reject, dominates the discussion in books 5–7 and sets the stage for *Republic*'s analysis of justice's "profitability" in books 8–10, as well as its reconsideration of poetic mimesis in book 10. The immediate problem it raises is how the "philosopher" (literally, "lover of wisdom") is to be distinguished from other people who seem to be curious about the world around them and lovers of learning (5.474b–476c).

24. (5.476d) *But take the case of the other, who recognizes the existence of absolute beauty and is able to distinguish the idea from the objects which participate in the idea . . . is he a dreamer, or is he awake?:* Socrates' effort to separate philosophers, who are keen to perceive absolute beauty (as well as absolute justice, absolute good, and so forth), from mere lovers of sights (*philotheamones*), who perceive beautiful things but "have no sense of absolute beauty" (5.476c), introduces concepts, terminology, and analogies that are central to the theory of knowledge developed in *Republic* as well as its metaphysics (that is, the theory of the "ideas")

The notion that there is, for example, a single "idea" (*idea*, or *eidos*) of beauty, which is perfect, unalterable, and eternal and is also the source of the beauty in all "beautiful" phenomenal objects (including people, ideas, institutions, etc.) is familiar from other Platonic dialogues, notably *Symposium*, *Phaedo*, and *Phaedrus*. Phenomenal objects that are "beautiful" are said to "participate" temporarily and partially in the idea of beauty (also termed "absolute beauty," "beauty-in-itself"); the temporary and partial nature of their participation accounts for the facts (1) that phenomenal objects do not seem equally beautiful to all observers (5.479a–e), and (2) that the beauty—of a rose, for instance—is impermanent. Phenomenal objects capable of being apprehended by the senses are themselves impermanent; in the language of *Republic*, they belong to the class of objects that are "becoming" (that is, between absolute "being" and absolute "nonbeing"). The only objects in the realm of absolute being (and thus the only objects that are truly "real") are the ideas and mathematical objects, such as the circle, triangle, etc., that are wholly independent of anything that is physically and phenomenally manifest.

This theory of "ideas" is in part indebted to the formulations concerning "being" or "that which is" (*to on*) of Parmenides of Elea (late sixth–early fifth century B.C.E.), who similarly asserts that "being" can be apprehended only through reason (*logos*) and not via the senses, which are misleading. Complementing his conception of the metaphysical "ideas" and their relationship to phenomenal objects, Socrates begins to elaborate in this passage a theory of knowledge, to be refined at 6.509d–511e, that is in fact a theory about the different faculties of cognition (*dynameis*) that people exercise as they contemplate different types of objects (5.476d–480a). The ideas, which are not apprehensible by means of the senses, are perceived through the exercise of what Socrates in this passage alternatively calls *gnosis* or *epistemê* (translated as "knowledge" by Jowett); in contrast, everything in the realm of "becoming" is apprehensible by the separate faculty of *doxa* ("opinion"), which is intermediate between true knowledge and pure ignorance. Only the ideas, then, can be "known" in the absolute sense; about any phenomenal object, one can only "opine" (5.477a–b; compare 5.479e).

People who have "a sense of beautiful things" but "no sense of absolute beauty" are likened to dreamers who mistake their dreams for waking reality (5.476c); they will later be compared to the blind (6.484c–d; compare 6.506c) and, in the allegory of the cave, to prisoners in a cavern who erroneously believe that a parade of shadow-images is real (7.514a–518b). Only those few who are able and willing to contemplate "the very truth of each thing" (literally, "each thing that is"; 6.484d) are "awake" and truly sighted and "free"; these people are the genuine "philosophers" who ought to be entrusted with political governance (see 6.504d–506e). Through these potent images, Plato has Socrates stake out a rather limited definition of what, properly speaking, constitutes "philosophy," as well as a bold claim for philosophy's supreme relevance to the proper conduct of human affairs (for example, at 6.500c–501b and 6.506b). One particularly important assertion is that the philosopher's awareness of the relative meanness and insignificance of all things in the phenomenal realm will ineluctably lead him or her to despise wealth, honor, and other "material" goods (for example, 7.540d–e).

25. (5.476d) *But suppose that the latter should quarrel with us and dispute our statement:* Some scholars suggest that this is an allusion to Antisthenes

(450–c.360 B.C.E.), a member of Socrates' circle, who became a rival of Plato in the fourth century and, it seems, was skeptical of the theory of ideas that Plato has Socrates advance in this passage. On the other hand, "the latter" (literally, "this man") could refer generically to any hypothetical "lover" of sounds and sights "who opines only."

26. (5.476e) *Something that is or is not?:* The verb "to be" (*einai* in Greek) has a broad semantic range; it can refer to existence, essence or quality, or truthfulness. Socrates' question is therefore open to interpretation.

27. (5.477a) *for how can that which is not ever be known?:* Parmenides similarly asserts that "that which is not" cannot be "spoken or thought." In his "On Nature" (or "On What Is Not"), a treatise apparently aimed at challenging Parmenides' conception of "being," Gorgias argued (1) that nothing "is," (2) that, even if something "is," it cannot be comprehended, and (3) that, even if something could be comprehended by an individual, this comprehension could not be communicated to another. Socrates' insistence in this passage that there is something "that is" which is absolutely knowable seems aimed at valorizing Parmenides' conception of knowledge in the face of challenges such as Gorgias'.

28. (5.478d) *Then you would infer that opinion* [doxa] *is intermediate?:* Compare 6.506c, where Socrates claims "all mere opinions are bad, and the best of them blind."

29. (5.479c) *or the children's puzzle about the eunuch aiming at the bat:* According to an ancient commentator, the riddle is: "How did a man who isn't a man aim at (*ballei*) but not hit (*ou ballei*) a bird that isn't a bird, which he saw (that is, thought he saw) but didn't see (that is, didn't actually see) sitting on a tree that wasn't a tree, with a stone that wasn't a stone?" The eunuch is the man who isn't a man, and the bat is the bird that isn't a bird; the verb *ballein* means both "to aim at" and "to strike"; the word for "tree" (*xulon*) can also mean "reed" or "rafter," and a pumice stone both is and isn't a "stone."

Book 6

1. (6.484a) *if there were not many other questions awaiting us:* Socrates' reminder is yet another acknowledgment of the incomplete nature of *Republic*'s discussion of justice and its advantages; see note 8 on 4.435c.

2. (6.484c–d) *are not such persons, I ask, simply blind?:* Analogies comparing knowledge and wisdom to sight, and ignorance to blindness, are common in Greek poetry; for example, they figure prominently—and paradoxically—in Sophocles' *Oedipus the King* (produced c.430 B.C.E.). In *Republic*, Socrates uses the faculty of sight and the experience of seeing visible objects with the eyes as a metaphor for the faculty of "knowledge" (*epistemê*) and the experience of apprehending intelligible objects (that is, the ideas) with the mind (6.507b–509c); see also the allegory of the cave, 7.514a–518b). But he also contrasts intellectual apprehension of the ideas with the apprehension of visible and other phenomenal objects with the eyes and other senses, most notably in his description of the divided line (6.509d–511e).

3. (6.485a) *In the first place . . . the nature of the philosopher has to be ascertained:* See note 18 on 2.375c.

4. (6.486a) *There should be no secret corner of illiberality:* Aneleutheria ("illiberality") refers first and foremost to stinginess with property and resources; *megaloprepeia* ("high-mindedness," "magnanimity") denotes generosity with material goods. Socrates uses the terms more broadly to contrast general narrow-mindedness with breadth of spirit and "vision."

5. (6.487b) *They fancy that they are led astray a little at each step in the argument . . . all their former notions appear to be turned upside down:* Adeimantus' frank remarks about Socrates' method echo, in a friendly way, the complaints of interlocutors in other dialogues, such as Callicles in *Gorgias* 497a. By having Socrates take pains to satisfy Adeimantus' questions about the differences between the common estimations of philosophers (as being either useless or corrupt) and the claims that have just been made about their fitness for political rule, Plato further discredits the allegations that Socrates carelessly and unscrupulously "corrupted the youth" (see also note 12 on 6.494c and note 3 on 5.451a.)

6. (6.488a–b) *Imagine then a fleet or a ship in which there is a captain who is taller and stronger than any of the crew, but he is a little deaf and has a similar infirmity in sight, and his knowledge of navigation is not much better:* The image of the ship of state provides an unflattering image of contemporary Athenian politics. The captain/ship-owner, who is tall and strong but short-sighted and hard of hearing, represents the Athenian people; the unruly and ignorant sailors who compete to steer the ship stand in for politicians who vie for control of the government. The true pilot, who is dismissed as a useless stargazer because no one respects his expertise and abilities, is the philosopher.

7. (6.491d) *we know that all germs or seeds . . . when they fail to meet with proper nutriment, or climate, or soil . . . are all the more sensitive to the want of a suitable environment, for evil is a greater enemy to what is good than to what is not:* Compare Socrates' emphases throughout book 3 on the strict education of future guardians in the ideal state.

8. (6.492a) *he is like a plant which, . . . if sown and planted in an alien soil, becomes the most noxious of all weeds, unless he be preserved by some divine power:* Compare 6.493a, 6.496a–c, and 8.558b. It seems likely that Plato intends his readers to see Socrates as one such divinely protected individual.

9. (6.492a) *Are not the public who say these things the greatest of all Sophists?:* Compare 6.493a on how the sophists, whom the many "deem to be their adversaries, do, in fact, teach nothing but the opinion of the many"; see also note 12 on 1.343d.

10. (6.493d) *the so-called necessity of Diomede:* This is a proverbial expression (of uncertain origin) for unavoidable necessity. It perhaps refers to an incident (not related in *Iliad* or *Odyssey*) that occurred when Odysseus tried to kill Diomedes; on the way back to the Greek camp he in turn bound Odysseus and beat him with the flat of his sword blade.

11. (6.494a) *Then the world cannot possibly be a philosopher?:* Literally, the Greek reads "Then the many [or the majority] cannot be philosophic." This brief but crucial statement provides a succinct connection between the metaphysical and epistemological and political concerns of *Republic* and echoes Parmenides' disparagement of the "confusion in the breasts" of most mortals, who "know nothing."

12. (6.494c) *And what will a man such as he is be likely to do under such circumstances, especially if he be a citizen of a great city, rich and noble, and a tall, proper youth?:* Plato undoubtedly means his readers to think of the Athenian general and statesman Alcibiades (450–404 B.C.E.). Alcibiades, the ward of the famous statesman Pericles, was aristocratic, handsome, charismatic, successful, and also undisciplined and capricious. He is memorably represented in *Symposium* as being completely in love with Socrates. Suspicion that Socrates had unduly influenced Alcibiades, who defected to the Spartans during the Peloponnesian War, may have lent weight to the charge of "corrupting the youth" that was leveled against Socrates in 399 B.C.E. In this passage and elsewhere (for example, *Symposium* 215e–216b), Plato seems keen to clear Socrates of responsibility for Alcibiades' misdeeds. He may have had other young men in mind, as well, such as Dionysius II of Syracuse. As a young man, Dionysius was encouraged by his uncle Dion to study philosophy with Plato, but upon succeeding his father as tyrant of Syracuse, Dionysius fell out with both his uncle and his tutor.

13. (6.496d) *he holds his peace, and goes his own way:* Socrates' defense of the man who, in a dysfunctional political community, keeps to himself (that is, practices *apragmosynê,* or "lack of involvement") is in keeping with his criticism of "meddlesomeness" (*polypragmosynê*) that impairs city-states such as Athens; see note 8 on 4.433a.

14. (6.497c–d) *you may remember my saying before, that some living authority would always be required in the State having the same idea of the constitution which guided you when you were laying down the laws.* Compare 3.412a–c. *Statesman* 293c–297e offers a different perspective on the supreme importance of the "living authority" of the statesman.

15. (6.497e) *I declare that States should pursue philosophy, not as they do now, but in a different spirit:* In particular, Socrates objects to permitting young men to study philosophy; he elaborates his reasons at 7.537b–540c.

16. (6.498d) *against the day when they live again, and hold the like discourse in another state of existence:* The reference to reincarnation anticipates the myth of the afterlife that Socrates relates at 10.617b–621b.

17. (6.499b) *whether they will or not:* Compare 1.345e and book 7 in general, especially 7.519c–521b and 7.540b.

18. (6.499d) *There is no impossibility in all this; that there is a difficulty, we ac-knowledge ourselves:* Compare Adeimantus' query at 5.471e, and also 7.540d.

19. (6.499e) *do not attack the multitude: they will change their minds:* It is to be assumed that the people in the ideal state's bronze/iron class, though unable to be *philosophoi* themselves, would harbor no hostility to philosophy, since its practitioners would be their rulers and caretakers. If the ideal state is a possibility, however remote, so too is the widespread acceptance of philosophy that Socrates optimistically envisions in this passage.

20. (6.500d) *will he, think you, be an unskilful artificer of justice, temperance, and every civil virtue?:* Compare 7.540c, where Glaucon proclaims that Socrates is a "sculptor" who has "made statues of our governors faultless in beauty."

21. (6.501a) *They will begin by taking the State and the manners of men, from which, as from a tablet, they will rub out the picture, and leave a clean surface:* Compare 7.540e–541a. The assumption in both of these passages— that it is practically impossible to rehabilitate the attitudes and beliefs of adults (and even teenagers) who have been acculturated to a dysfunctional system of values—underlies the emphases in book 2 and 3 on the early education of the guardians. Plato arguably demonstrates the impossibility of such rehabilitation in his many "aporetic" dialogues (for example, *Protagoras, Gorgias, Laches, Ion, Euthyphro,* etc.), which feature Socrates in conversation with men who, though ultimately incapable of accounting for their beliefs and values, are nonetheless unable and unwilling to give up them up.

22. (6.502a) *Will anyone deny the other point, that there may be sons of kings or princes who are by nature philosophers?:* Some scholars see in this question a reference to Dionysius II of Syracuse. See note 12 on 6.494c.

23. (6.503b) *Yes, my friend, I said, and I then shrank from hazarding . . . that the perfect guardian must be a philosopher:* Socrates assimilates the reluctance experienced by the personified discussion, or *logos,* to the "fear and hesitation" he claimed to feel at 5.472a. From this point through the end of book 7, Socrates makes several disclaimers about the inexact and provisional nature of the concepts he advances; see note 10 on the remarks at 4.435d, about which Socrates reminds Adeimantus at 6.504b.

24. (6.503b) *And do not suppose that there will be many of them:* Compare 6.485a–486e and 2.375c.

25. (6.504b) *We were saying . . . that he who wanted to see them in their perfect beauty must take a longer and more circuitous way, at the end of which they would appear:* Compare 4.435c–d. In his or her investigations of justice, temperance, courage, etc., the philosopher who is a guardian in the ideal state would be able to take none of the "shortcuts" that Socrates and his companions have taken in *Republic.* Socrates' comments are perhaps intended to remind readers that they should not confuse the conversation represented in this dialogue with true "dialectic" practiced by philosophers (compare 7.531d–534e).

26. (6.505a) *for you have often been told that the idea of good is the highest knowledge, and that all other things become useful and advantageous only by their use of this:* According to the theory of the ideas, all "good" objects in the phenomenal realm are "good" by virtue of their participation in the form/idea of the good; therefore, the only sure way of knowing the "relative" goodness of something is to evaluate it in light of the form of the good. Since what is "good" is the ultimate object of every human pursuit (6.505d–e), knowledge of the idea of the good is supremely important. As he has Socrates tentatively express his ideas about what the form of the good is, Plato invites readers to imagine that Socrates, Adeimantus, and presumably Glaucon have often discussed it, and that Socrates' insistence that the idea of the good is the supreme object of learning is nothing new.

27. (6.505b) *You are further aware that most people affirm pleasure to be the good:* For Plato's recurrent concern that most people identify what is pleasing with what is good, see note 2 on 3.391a.

28. (6.507c) *But have you remarked that sight is by far the most costly and complex piece of workmanship which the artificer of the senses ever contrived?:* See *Phaedrus* 250d for another assertion concerning the qualities that distinguish sight from the other senses. The "artificer (*demiourgos*) of the senses" is presumably "god," but this is not made explicit.

29. (6.508b) *And the power which the eye possesses is a sort of effluence which is dispensed from the sun?:* There was considerable theoretical speculation in the classical period about the mechanics of sight and vision, to which Plato alludes in several passages—for example, *Phaedrus* 251c, *Timaeus* 45b–c, and *Meno* 76c–d.

30. (6.508b c) *And this is he whom I call the child of the good, whom the good begat in his own likeness, to be in the visible world . . . what the good is in the intellectual world in relation to mind and the things of mind:* The cosmology Socrates proposes, that the sun is the offspring of the good ("begat in his likeness") is idiosyncratic. Nonetheless, his description of the sun as the offspring of the good builds on established associations between knowledge and physical sight (compare 6.484c); it also capitalizes on the keen awareness of the sun's importance that would have been natural (and inevitable) in the pre-industrial society of classical Athens (compare 6.509b). On the logic of the analogy, just as the sun is responsible for the existence of all objects in the phenomenal realm, the idea of the good brings into being all objects in the intelligible realm. Moreover, just as the sun is the source of light in the phenomenal realm, which enables the eye to see physical objects (including the sun itself), the good is likewise the source of truth in the intelligible realm, which makes the soul (or mind) capable of apprehending intelligible objects (including the good itself). The power to exercise the faculty of sight, vis-à-vis

objects in the phenomenal realm, is thus comparable to the power to exercise the faculty of reason, or knowledge, vis-à-vis objects in the intelligible realm.

"The offspring of the good, which the good engendered as an analogue to itself" is a more literal translation of the words that Jowett translates as "the child of the good, whom the good begat in his own likeness." Jowett's translation is plainly inspired by—and it arguably intends to evoke—passages in the King James version of the Bible, particularly Genesis 1:26–27 and Matthew 1:1–16.

31. (6.509c) *Glaucon said, with a ludicrous earnestness: By the light of heaven, how amazing!:* The phrase translated by Jowett as "with a ludicrous earnestness" is in Greek the adverb *geloiôs* ("humorously" or "facetiously"). Compare 6.506d, where Socrates, though urged on by Glaucon, claims to be anxious about attempting to describe the idea of the good, fearing that his "indiscreet zeal will bring ridicule [*gelota*]" upon him. The "light" tone adopted by Socrates and Glaucon is yet another reminder that the ideas advanced here about the idea of the good, though suggestive and important, are not meant to stand as definitive "last words."

32. (6.509d–e) *Now take a line which has been cut into two unequal parts, and divide each of them again in the same proportion . . . and you will find that the first section in the sphere of the visible consists of images:* The figure of the divided line supplies key refinements to the theory of knowledge (that is, the theory about distinct cognitive faculties that are used to apprehend different types of objects) that is first advanced at 5.476d–480a.

Socrates' focus is initially on the objects of perception. In addition to the now familiar distinction between intelligible objects and objects in the phenomenal realm (here represented by "visible objects"), two new distinctions are introduced. Reflections, shadows, imitations, and the like are grouped together and differentiated from other objects in the phenomenal realm; within the intelligible realm, objects that the soul apprehends on the basis of untested hypotheses (that is, mathematical objects) are differentiated from those that are apprehended through dialectic, which tests hypotheses and "ascends to a first principle" (that is, the ideas).

Reflecting the fact that intelligible objects, which neither come into being nor can be destroyed, are more "real" than objects in the phenomenal realm, the line is unequally divided, with the larger portion given to the intelligible. The two main segments are also unequally divided in the same proportion as the whole line, and again the divisions reflect the relative "reality" of the different types of objects within, respectively, the intelligible and phenomenal realms. Thus the segment of the line representing reflections, shadows, and imitations is smallest of all. If each of the line's four segments is designated by a letter (for example, A for the segment representing the ideas, B for the other intelligible objects, C for phenomenal objects generally, and D for reflections, etc.), then the line's proportions can be expressed in the following terms: AB : CD :: A : B :: C : D.

33. (6.510b) *There are two subdivisions, in the lower of which the soul uses the figures given by the former division as images; the inquiry can only be hypothetical . . . ; in the higher of the two, the soul passes out of hypotheses . . . proceeding only in and through the ideas themselves:* Despite Socrates' initial emphasis on the differences among the *objects* represented by the divided line, his concern—beginning with this sentence—shifts to distinguishing the cognitive processes and faculties whereby mathematical objects and the ideas are apprehended. Mathematicians, as Socrates and Glaucon agree at 7.531e–532a, are not required "to give and take a reason" for the objects they study; they hypothesize, for example, a circle, and study its properties, but never question whether the circle they study actually exists or not. They rely, moreover, on visible images (for example, circles that are physically drawn) for their investigations. In contrast, dialecticians—that is, those who study the ideas—depend on no such physical models and, most importantly, test their hypotheses; they do not take for granted the existence of the ideas they investigate. Mathematical "objects" per se, then, do not differ substantively from the ideas, and they are capable of being apprehended by the faculty of "reason" (*noesis*) as well as that of "understanding" (*dianoia*); see 6.511d. It is, rather, the exercise of *noesis* that differs radically from the exercise of *dianoia*. The distinction here between *noesis* and *dianoia* looks ahead to the description of the philosopher's education at 7.521c–540a, in which training in mathematical subjects—that is, "number science" (*arithmetikê*), plane and solid geometry, astronomy, and harmonics—constitutes a mere "prelude" that prepares the future philosopher for his or her study of dialectic (7.531d).

34. (6.511b) *that other sort of knowledge which reason itself attains by the power of dialectic:* Dialectic and its use are described in more detailed, albeit still tentative, terms at 7.531d–539d.

35. (6.511d–e) *let there be four faculties in the soul . . . and let us suppose that the several faculties have clearness in the same degree that their objects have truth:* The terms Socrates now uses for the four cognitive faculties, which are rendered differently by different translators, are *noesis* ("reason"), *dianoia* ("understanding"), *pistis* ("faith or conviction"), and *eikasia* ("perception of shadows" in Jowett, but often translated elsewhere as "imagination"). *Noesis* and *dianoia* fall under the rubric of *epistemê* (*gnosis, gnome*), the terms used in book 5 to describe the general cognitive faculty that enables one to apprehend objects in the "higher" intelligible realm, whereas *pistis* and *eikasia* are different species of *doxa*, the general faculty by which phenomenal objects are perceived. See note 33 on 6.510b and note 24 on 5.476d.

Book 7

1. (7.514a) *Behold! human beings living in an underground den:* Socrates' allegory of the cave builds on the image of the divided line as well as the analogy established in the simile of the sun comparing the eye's ability to
apprehend the objects in the physical realm to the mind's ability to apprehend intelligible objects. Likening the prisoners to "ourselves" (7.515a) and
the world of daily experience to mere shadows and echoes, it vividly reinforces Socrates' contention that most people are mistaken in their belief that
the phenomenal world is real and knowable (see 7.517a–c). In contrast to
the simile, the allegory accentuates the difficulties of apprehending the idea
of the good, which is once again represented by the sun, and consequently
of developing the cognitive faculty that enables this apprehension. It emphasizes the emotional as well as physical distress of the prisoner (that is, future philosopher) who, upon being released from his bonds, is disabused of
his assumptions about "reality" as he makes the arduous upward journey out
of the cave into the bright light of day (7.515c–d). The released prisoner,
once accustomed to looking at the sunlit world and the sun itself, will also
have difficulties when he is forced to reenter the dark and shadowy cave; the
description of his tense dealings with his former fellow-prisoners at 7.517a–e
harks back to Socrates' explanation of the philosopher's apparent uselessness
in 6.488a–489a, and it resonates as well with what is suggested in *Republic*
and other dialogues (for example, *Phaedo, Gorgias*) about the philosopher's
disdain for material goods and "prizes."

    Not all the details in the allegory stand up to logical analysis. For exam-
ple, the identity of the individuals responsible for the parade of shadow-
casting objects and for the releasing of the prisoner (7.514c–515d) is not
accounted for, nor is it clear how the released prisoner could be "compelled
to fight in courts of law . . . about the images or the shadows of images of
justice" once he returns to the cave (7.517d). Moreover, whereas the divided
line's differentiation of cognitive faculties is clearly important to the allegory's distinctions among stages of cognitive development, it does not seem
necessary to insist on precise correspondence between the stages of the released prisoner's upward progress and the line's four segments. The allegory's purpose, however, is to be powerfully suggestive, and logic is not its
primary concern. Its point is simply, as Socrates intimates in 7.516e–519a,
that the situation of the prisoners in the cave represents the lot of most people. Just as the prisoners (except for the fortunate few who are released) are
unable to conceive of a world outside the dim cave, so most people are incapable of apprehending anything other than the phenomenal world (the
world of "becoming"—see 518c, and also note 24 on 5.476d). Moreover, just
as only a few prisoners are released, only a few people are permitted (by a
lucky and rare combination of circumstances) to develop the higher cognitive

faculties of *dianoia* and *noesis* and thus the ability to apprehend the intellectual world (the world of "being").

2. (7.515e) *And suppose once more, that he is reluctantly dragged up a steep and rugged ascent:* Socrates' description of the released prisoner's upward journey evokes the mythological motif of *anabasis*—that is, an upward journey out of the underworld. Compare 7.521c.

3. (7.517b) *and you will not misapprehend me if you interpret the journey upward to be the ascent of the soul into the intellectual world, in my view, at least, which, at your desire, I have expressed—whether rightly or wrongly, God knows:* Compare Socrates' reluctance to describe the idea of the good at 6.504b and 6.509c.

4. (7.518b) *certain professors of education:* Some sophists and professional teachers of rhetoric claimed to be able to instill knowledge (*epistemê*) in their students. According to Socrates' argument, however, the faculty of *epistemê* is already in the soul; as the discussion of books 6 and 7 makes plain, cultivating this faculty is a challenging and difficult process that few are capable of undertaking since, as he states in the immediately following paragraph, it involves the reorientation of the whole soul away from "becoming" and toward "being."

5. (7.520c) *Wherefore each of you, when his turn comes, must go down to the general underground abode, and get the habit of seeing in the dark:* The verb "go down" (or "descend") in Greek is *katabainein*. *Katabasis* (the opposite of *anabasis*; see note 2 on 7.515e) typically refers to a journey to the underworld undertaken by a heroic figure such as Heracles, Theseus, or Orpheus.

6. (7.521c) *as some are said to have ascended from the world below to the gods?:* The reference may be to individuals like Asclepius, who was apotheosized after being killed by Zeus, and Semele, the Theban princess who was pregnant with Dionysus when she was killed by Zeus' thunderbolt.

7. (7.521c) *the turning over of an oyster-shell: Ostrakon* in Greek actually means "potsherd" (pottery fragment), not "oyster-shell." For the purposes of the game to which Socrates alludes, a potsherd was painted black on one side and white on the other; when it was flipped in the air, the players called "night" or "day," just as people today call "heads" and "tails" when coins are flipped. Socrates' meaning is that education is a serious affair that cannot be left to chance.

8. (7.521d) *Usefulness in war:* Arithmetic, plane and solid geometry, and astronomy, which constitute four of the five preparatory disciplines that future philosophers should study as they train their souls to move from "becoming to being," all had obvious military applications. Nonetheless, when discussing geometry and astronomy, Socrates insists that utility in war is not the most important determinant of these disciplines' value to guardians in training (7.526a and 7.528d–529a). Rather, they are useful primarily because they "make more easy the vision of the idea of good" (7.526d–e).

   9. (7.522c) *The little matter of distinguishing one, two, and three—in a word,
   number and calculation: do not all arts and sciences necessarily partake of
   them?:* "Number" (*arithmos*) and "calculation" (*logismos*) lead "the soul toward being" (7.523a) because they help people make sense of confusing appearances and thus lead them to look beyond mere appearances (7.523b).
   All of the mathematical disciplines that Socrates goes on to describe, beginning with *arithmetikê* (the "science of number"), are essential to the philosopher's training since it helps him (or her) "rise out of the sea of change and
   lay hold of true being" (7.525b).

  10. (7.523a) *It appears to me to be a study of the kind which we are seeking, and
   which leads naturally to reflection, but never to have been rightly used; for
   the true use of it is simply to draw the soul toward being:* Compare 7.527a–b
   and 7.529a–531c for critiques of the methods and emphases of those who
   currently study geometry, astronomy, and harmonics.

  11. (7.524d) *And to which class do unity and number belong?:* That is, do "unity
   and number" belong to the class of impressions that are not innately confusing and require no "calculation" or to the class that requires abstract reasoning to be properly understood? The phrase "unity and number" reflects the
   fact that Plato did not consider "one" a number.

  12. (7.524e) *"What is absolute unity?":* Any single object in the phenomenal
   world (that is, a visible "one") is actually both "one" and "many"; for example, one flower has many petals, one piece of fruit has many seeds. The realization that every visible "one" is in fact both "one" and "many" accordingly
   leads one to wonder about the "absolute unity" that is not also "many," and
   to realize eventually that this "absolute unity" is not to be found in the phenomenal world.

  13. (7.525d–e) *absolute unity:* That is, the unit that is adopted for the purpose of
   a given calculation and which is, for the purpose of that calculation, indivisible. Such a unit is, strictly speaking, hypothetical.

  14. (7.527a–b) *They have in view practice only, and are always speaking . . . of
   squaring and extending and applying and the like—they confuse the necessities of geometry with those of daily life; whereas knowledge is the real object
   of the whole science:* In the fifth century B.C.E., some geometers tried their
   hand at town planning; for example, Hippodamus of Miletus designed the
   grid-iron layouts of streets in Piraeus and the Athenian colony of Thurii (in
   Italy). Such undertakings seem to have struck many people as "ridiculous";
   in Aristophanes' *Birds* (produced in 414 B.C.E.), the geometer Meton is
   comically represented as a pompous would-be town planner.

  15. (7.527d) *I am amused, I said, at your fear of the world, which makes you
   guard against the appearance of insisting upon useless studies:* Socrates'
   gentle admonition resonates with what has been established about the "unphilosophic" nature of the many and their current prejudice against philosophy; see, for example, 6.488e–489a and 6.494a.

16. (7.528a) *Then take a step backward, for we have gone wrong in the order of the sciences:* Solid geometry, which Socrates proposes as the logical follow-up for the study of plane geometry, is less complex and abstract than astronomy, which is the study of "solid objects in revolution [that is, motion]." The subjects of the entire preparatory curriculum (that is, *arithmetikê*, plane geometry, solid geometry or stereometry, astronomy, harmonics) are increasingly complex and abstract, and they are organized so as to make future philosophers ready for the supremely difficult and wholly abstract operations of dialectic.

17. (7.528b) *but so little seems to be known as yet about these subjects:* Problems of solid geometry had concerned several theoreticians (for example, Anaxagoras, Democritus, some in the Pythagorean school) in the fifth century. What Glaucon apparently means here is that solutions to complex stereometrical problems (that is, beyond simple problems such as the doubling of a cube) had not yet been discovered.

18. (7.529b) *whether a man gapes at the heavens or blinks on the ground, seeking to learn some particular of sense, I would deny that he can learn, for nothing of that sort is matter of science:* As in the case of geometry (7.527a), Socrates argues that astronomy ought not be pursued for the sake of understanding physical phenomena (that is, the movements of heavenly bodies), but rather as abstract geometry in four dimensions that is concerned with "true motions of absolute slowness and absolute swiftness." So too "harmonics," which is concerned with the motion of sounds (7.530d), is to be studied for the sake of understanding abstract "harmonies" of number as opposed to those that can be physically heard (7.531c).

   Plato perhaps has Socrates specifically disavow interest in problems dealing with "some particular of sense" in order to distance him further from the figure of "Socrates" in Aristophanes' *Clouds*, whose "Think-Factory" sponsors ridiculous research in "astronomy" and other fields. See note 22 on 2.378b and note 10 on 7.523a.

19. (7.530d) *There is a second, I said, which is the counterpart of the one already named:* Astronomy, which has been "already named," is the study of the motion of solid bodies in space; its "sister science" is harmonics, the study of the motion of sound. For the comparison of the functions of the ear and eye, see 6.5076–d.

20. (7.530d) *as the Pythagoreans say:* The reference is to the followers of Pythagoras, the religious thinker and theorist who settled in Croton in southern Italy during the sixth century B.C.E. Pythagoreans were known in the classical period for their ascetic way of life, their belief in the reincarnation of the soul, and their mathematically based study of music and harmonics.

21. (7.531a) *The teachers of harmony compare the sounds and consonances which are heard only, and their labor, like that of the astronomers, is in vain:* This is most likely a reference to the Pythagoreans.

22. (7.531a) *condensed notes, as they call them: Pyknomata* in Greek is a technical term that apparently refers to combinations of two quarter-tone (or semitone) intervals.

23. (7.531b) *one set of them declaring that they distinguish an intermediate note and have found the least interval which should be the unit of measurement:* For example, the quarter-tone. Other theorists (perhaps including Plato himself) posited the semi-tone as "the least interval," with a view not only to simplifying the analysis of music, but also encouraging simplicity in musical composition.

24. (7.531b) *plectrum:* The plectrum was the pick by which the strings of an instrument were plucked. The metaphor developed in the first sentence of this paragraph plainly alludes to the torturing and beating of slaves.

25. (7.531d) *the prelude, or what?: Prooimion* in Greek refers broadly to the introductory section of a song (or poem or speech). The musical metaphor is continued in the following paragraphs, where Socrates refers to the *nomos*, or "song," that dialectic performs.

26. (7.531d–e) *For you surely would not regard the skilled mathematician as a dialectician?:* Compare 6.510b–511d. Unlike the mathematician who, for example, assumes the existence of "absolute unity" (7.525d–526a,) the dialectician's study of "the idea of one" would not be complete until he had "ascended to first principles" (6.511a–b) and showed by argument that such a concept is essential to the rational understanding of both the intelligible and phenomenal worlds.

27. (7.532d) *This, however, is not a theme to be treated of in passing only. . . . And so, whether our conclusion be true or false, let us assume all this, and proceed at once from the prelude or preamble to the chief strain, and describe that in like manner:* Socrates' reticence in describing dialectic mirrors the reserve he displays when discussing the idea of the good, which is the ultimate object of dialectic. Compare 7.517b. The word translated here as "chief strain" is *nomos*, which also means "law" and/or "custom."

28. (7.533d) *Custom terms them sciences:* That is, *epistemai* (the plural of *epistemê*). Whereas the term *epistemai* is "customarily" used to refer to disciplines, or fields of study, Socrates has earlier used *epistemê* to designate the cognitive faculty by which objects in the intelligible world are apprehended.

29. (7.534d) *you would not allow the future rulers to be like posts, having no reason in them, and yet to be set in authority over the highest matters?:* Jowett's interpretation, that *grammai* in this context refers to the lines at the start of racecourses (hence his translation "posts"), is disputable. The reference is more likely to *alogoi grammai*—that is, "irrational quantities" such as the square root of negative one. If so, there would be a witty play on the adjective *alogos* ("irrational," "having no reason") since those who are unable to approach the idea of the good through dialectic are unable to give an account (*logon dounai*) of it. Compare 7.531e, where Socrates and Glaucon

agree that mathematicians are incapable of reasoning (literally, unable to *logon dounai*).

30. *(7.536c) Certainly not, I said; and yet perhaps, in thus turning jest into earnest I am equally ridiculous. . . . I had forgotten . . . that we were not serious, and spoke with too much excitement. For when I saw philosophy so undeservedly trampled under foot of men. . . . :* Socrates painted a vivid (and somewhat playful) picture of philosophy bereft of legitimate "suitors" and forced to "marry . . . a bald little tinker" at 6.495c–496a. His statement that he and his interlocutors "are not serious" may come as a surprise, given the stress repeatedly laid on the importance of the issues raised in *Republic*; see note 14 on 1.344e. Nonetheless, it is in keeping with the many advertisements concerning the provisional nature of the conversation, and it perhaps should stand as a reminder that Plato did not hope to accomplish anything truly "serious" in this or any other dialogue. For the fundamentally "playful" nature of writing, see *Phaedrus* 274c–278e.

31. *(7.537e) Do you not remark, I said, how great is the evil which dialectic has introduced?:* Socrates' acknowledgment that dialectic is potently destabilizing, since it inevitably causes one to devalue that which one prized in the past (and which others may still prize) and to develop "a questioning spirit" that "asks what is fair and honorable" (7.538d), paves the way for his distinction between dialectic, as practiced for socially constructive ends by the true philosopher, and "antilogic" and "eristic," as pursued by those who carelessly engage in arguments simply for the sake of winning (7.539b–d; see note 6 on 5.454a). It also reinforces his point that philosophy (that is, dialectic) is not suitable for young, restless people, no matter how gifted (7.539a–b; compare 6.498b–c).

Book 8

1. *(8.544c) the four governments of which I spoke . . . are first, those of Crete and Sparta, which are generally applauded:* In contrast to Athens' democracy, the governments of Crete and Sparta strictly limited political franchise. Critics of Athenian democracy praised the Spartan constitution in particular, and Plato is careful to have Socrates associate it with "timarchy," which is characterized by "love of honor" (see 545b), and not with the more degenerate "oligarchy," in which wealth alone determines qualification for political franchise and leadership.

2. *(8.545d) Clearly, all political changes originate in divisions of the actual governing power; a government which is united, however small, cannot be moved:* Compare the concern for *stasis* (factionalism and civil strife) at 4.444b.

3. *(8.545e) Shall we imagine them in solemn mockery, to play and jest with us as if we were children, and to address us in a lofty tragic vein, making believe to be in earnest?:* As above at 7.536b–c, Plato has Socrates call attention

to the fundamentally "playful" nature of the discussion, and he seems to invite his readers not to take what is claimed in 8.546a–c too literally.

4. (8.546a) *In plants that grow in the earth, as well as in animals that move on the earth's surface, fertility and sterility of soul and body occur when the circumferences of the circles of each are completed, which in short-lived existences pass over a short space, and in long-lived ones over a long space:* Socrates envisions the "cycle" of fertility for each species of living thing as represented by a circle; for a short-lived species, the representative circle is small and so is its circumference, whereas the circle is larger for the longer-lived. The notion advanced here—that the cycles of fertility and sterility in individual species are mathematically comprehensible—anticipates what is suggested in 8.546b–c about the existence of a rational, mathematically comprehensible order governing the cosmos as a whole.

5. (8.546b) *but the period of human birth is comprehended in a number . . . :* Adopting the voice of the Muses, Socrates presents a calculation for the number that comprehends, or governs, human births. The number (12,960,000) is in fact a "master number" that comprehends the area of two great figures, one of which is a square with sides of 3600 units, and the other a rectangle with sides of 4800 and 2700 units.

The "number of Plato" is a notoriously difficult passage that has garnered a great deal of scholarly attention. Critics have offered a number of interpretations of its significance. It is possible that the number and its calculation are indebted to Pythagorean mathematical theories, and it is also possible that the two figures comprehended in the master number 12,960,000 represent two periods in the "lifetime" of the cosmos with which human births, if they are to be "goodly and fortunate" (8.546c), must somehow be in accord. All such interpretations are speculative, however. As suggested in note 3 on 8.545e, the fact that Socrates ascribes the calculation of the number to the Muses (who, he imagines, "play and jest with us as if we were children") should make us cautious about attempting to interpret the number and its calculation in an overly precise manner. Nonetheless, it seems reasonable to suppose that the passage in 8.546a–c is intended to convey, in general and suggestive terms, two facts: (1) that there is a rational order governing the cosmos, which can be expressed in mathematical terms, and (2) that this order is extremely difficult to comprehend. However its philosophical significance is interpreted, the passage puts Plato's mathematical sophistication on full display.

6. (8.546c) *Now this number represents a geometrical figure which has control over the good and evil of births:* More literally, "this entire geometric number has authority over this sort of thing, [that is] better and inferior births." Jowett's translation is somewhat misleading, since the entire "geometric number" comprehends the *two* geometric *figures* described in the immediately preceding passage. The apparent meaning of this sentence is that, to be appropriate and "good," human births must somehow be in accordance with the cosmic order that the figures suggest; precisely how this accordance is to be accomplished is left unspecified.

7. (8.547b–c) *There was a battle between them, and at last they agreed to distribute their land and houses among individual owners; and they enslaved their friends and maintainers . . . and they themselves were engaged in war and in keeping a watch against them:* Compare 3.416d–417b and 5.462b–464d, where Socrates links private property to the development of private interests that differ from those of the community as a whole and are thus detrimental, as is reasserted at 8.550d. Socrates' assumption seems to be that the possession of private property goes hand in hand with the establishment of individual families and households; see, for example, the reference to "wives" at 8.548a–b.

8. (8.547d) *In the honor given to rulers, in the abstinence of the warrior-class from agriculture, handicrafts, and trade in general, in the institution of common meals, and in the attention paid to gymnastics and military training—in all these respects this State will resemble the former:* Plato surely intends Socrates' description of the practices of the ruling class in the timarchic state to remind his readers of the Spartans. See note 1 on 8.544c.

9. (8.549b) *having lost his best guardian:* The language used in this passage, which identifies *logos* ("reason," which Jowett translates as "philosophy") mixed with *mousikê* ("music") as the best guardian (*aristos phylax*) and savior of virtue, is pointed; compare 2.367a.

10. (8.549c) *His origin is as follows. . . . :* The vivid vignette describing the origin of the timarchic man, who is seduced into straying from the ways of his virtuous father by the nagging of his malcontent mother and household slaves, seems designed to reinforce the argument that individual families—and the private interests and loyalties they inevitably cause to develop—are detrimental to the development of "virtue" in both individuals and communities. Dysfunction in the family similarly accounts for the development of other "degenerate" personalities; compare 8.553a–d, 8.558c–560e, and 9.572d–575a.

11. (8.550e) *And so they grow richer and richer, and the more they think of making a fortune the less they think of virtue; for when riches and virtue are placed together in the scales of the balance the one always rises as the other falls:* This directly counters Cephalus' assertion at 1.331b that wealth facilitates virtue; compare 3.416d–417b.

12. (8.551a–b) *They next proceed to make a law which fixes a sum of money as the qualification for citizenship:* The ownership of property (often land), as well as birth from citizen parents, were the typical qualifications for citizenship in Greek city-states.

13. (8.551d) *The inevitable division: such a State is not one, but two States, the one of poor, the other of rich men; and they are living on the same spot and*

always conspiring against one another: Compare 4.422e; see also 4.422a on the corrosive social effects of wealth and poverty, and 8.555c on the incompatibility of wealth and self-restraint.

14. (8.552a) *nor horseman, nor hoplite:* Hoplites were heavily armed infantrymen. Since Greek men typically supplied their own armor (and their own horses, if in the cavalry), and since the hoplite's armor was expensive (as was the upkeep of horses), only men from wealthier classes served as hoplites and cavalrymen.

15. (8.552c) *May we not say that this is the drone in the house who is like the drone in the honeycomb, and that the one is the plague of the city as the other is of the hive?:* The images of the beehive and its drones (both "stingless" and "with stingers") remain central throughout the rest of book 8 and in book 9's discussion of the "tyrannical" personality. Within the individual soul, "drones" are desires and appetites that interfere with reason's rule. In the state, "drones" are the criminals (who have "stings") and paupers (who are "stingless") created by extremes of wealth and poverty; it is the "drones with stingers" who, in Socrates' account, exercise increasingly greater power in the increasingly degenerate constitutions.

16. (8.554d–e) *The man, then, will be at war with himself; he will be two men, and not one:* The oligarchic city is similarly described as being two cities "conspiring against one another" at 8.551d.

17. (8.556a) *The evil blazes up like a fire; and they will not extinguish it either by restricting a man's use of his own property, or by another remedy:* This critique of what had become, by Plato's day, common money-lending practices reflects the prejudices of upper-class Athenians against traders and bankers (many of whom were non-Athenian), as well as more general anxieties about the monetarized economy that had been rapidly developing from the mid-fifth century B.C.E. in Athens and other Greek city-states.

18. (8.557a) *And then democracy comes into being after the poor have conquered their opponents, slaughtering some and banishing some:* Socrates' account of democracy's development from oligarchy, while incorporating elements that reflect how democratic governments arose in some Greek city-states (including Athens) during the fifth century, is nonetheless not aimed first and foremost at historical accuracy. His subsequent account of democracy's degeneration into tyranny (8.562a–569c) likewise incorporates reflections of actual events and phenomena into an essentially fictional framework. Nonetheless, many magistrates in classical Athens were elected by lot, and the following description of the democratic city, with its love of "freedom and frankness," is plainly designed to evoke the political institutions and social arrangements of Athens.

19. (8.557b) *In the first place, are they not free[?]:* The emphasis on democracy's love of freedom (compare 8.562b–c) recalls the popular identification of happiness with the freedom "to do what one wants," which Socrates challenges at the beginning of the dialogue (1.345a).

20. (8.558a) *And is not their humanity to the condemned in some cases quite charming?:* The wording in Greek is ambiguous and variously interpreted. It may refer to the relaxed behavior of people who have been condemned for crimes, or conversely to the insouciant attitudes of those who have sat in judgment.

21. (8.558c) *These and other kindred characteristics are proper to democracy, which is a charming form of government . . . dispensing a sort of equality to equals and unequals alike:* Socrates' acknowledgment that democracy is "charming" (literally, *hedeia*, or "pleasant"), insofar as it affords the greatest number of people the greatest amount of freedom, should be interpreted in the light of *Republic*'s sustained interest in disassociating what is pleasant from what is good and beneficial. See 8.561c, as well as note 2 on 3.391a. The "equality" of Athens and democracy in general is opposed to the ideal state's recognition of inequality; compare 2.370a.

22. (8.560a) *and he goes to war with himself:* That is, he falls into *stasis* (civil war) with himself; compare 4.444b.

23. (8.560c) *the aforesaid vain conceits shut the gate of the King's fastness:* The language continues the image of the rational part of the soul (which is the soul's king) as being seated—and besieged—in an acropolis, or citadel; compare 8.561b.

24. (8.560d) *modesty, which they call silliness, is ignominiously thrust into exile by them, and temperance, which they nick-name unmanliness, is trampled in the mire and cast forth; . . . they drive them beyond the border:* Compare Thrasymachus' attempt to redefine virtue (*aretê*) and baseness (*kakia*) at 1.348c–d. In his account of the *stasis* on Corcyra in 427 B.C.E. (*History of the Peloponnesian War* 3.82–84), Thucydides describes a convolution of basic moral terminology very much like the one outlined in these paragraphs.

25. (8.561b) *any true word of advice:* That is, *logos*. Socrates describes *logos* (that is, "reason," "rational accounting") as the guardian (*phylax*) and "saviour" of virtue at 8.549b.

26. (8.562a) *And does not tyranny spring from democracy in the same manner as democracy from oligarchy—I mean, after a sort?:* That is, each degenerate constitution is destroyed by what it erroneously values in the place of true virtue (*aretê*). Just as democracy, in Socrates' logic, is destroyed by its desire for freedom (*eleutheria*), so democracy and oligarchy are brought to ruin because of the premiums they place, either covertly or overtly, on wealth.

27. (8.562e) *By degrees the anarchy finds a way into private houses, and ends by getting among the animals and infecting them:* A similar point is made in a treatise dating to approximately 430 B.C.E., titled "The Constitution of the Athenians" (alternatively, "The Old Oligarch"), which was erroneously attributed in antiquity to Plato's contemporary (and fellow Socratic) Xenophon.

28. (8.565b–c) *And the end is that when they see the people . . . seeking to do them wrong, then at last they are forced to become oligarchs in reality; they* *do not wish to be, but the sting of the drones torments them and breeds revolution in them:* Socrates' representation of how wealthy men are forced against their will to oppose democratic governments involves some special pleading and seems tailored to support the political biases of *Republic*.

29. (8.566a) *After a while he is driven out, but comes back, in spite of his enemies, a tyrant full grown:* Plato probably intends his readers to think of the Athenian tyrant Peisistratus (mid-sixth century B.C.E.), whose rise to power is described in Herodotus, *Histories* 1.59–64.

30. (8.566b) *Then comes the famous request for a body-guard:* A corps of armed bodyguards was the hallmark of tyrants in ancient Greek city-states. Readers are probably meant to think of figures like Dionysius I of Syracuse and others, as well as Peisistratus. Some of the details Socrates gives concerning the tyrant's brutal techniques for maintaining power also recall the strategies of the so-called Thirty Tyrants who seized control of Athens in 404 at the end of the Peloponnesian War. Plato's original readers would have surely appreciated the irony in the fact that the word for "bodyguards" is *phylakes*, the very term that Socrates and his companions have used throughout *Republic* to designate the guardians of the ideal state.

31. (8.566c) *"By pebbly Hermus's shore he flees and rests not, and is not ashamed to be a coward":* This is a quotation from Herodotus, *Histories* 1.55. The Lydian king Croesus was a descendant of Gyges, who is mentioned in *Republic* at 2.359c–360a; he was counseled by the oracle at Delphi to flee when a "mule" (that is, Cyrus, who had ethnically mixed parentage) sat on the throne of Persia.

32. (8.567c) *happy man, he is the enemy of them all, and must seek occasion against them whether he will or no, until he has made a purgation of the State:* The emphasis on the ways in which the budding tyrant is compelled against his will (in this case, to kill all worthy rivals and allies) marks an important point in Socrates' effort to discredit Thrasymachus' assertion that the tyrant enjoys the maximum amount of "freedom." Compare 1.344c and 9.578c–579c.

33. (8.568b) *"Tyrants are wise by living with the wise":* The verse, which is also attributed to Euripides in *Theages* 125b, is in fact from Sophocles' lost *Ajax of Locris*. Socrates' ironic praise of tragedy's "wisdom" resonates with the concerns raised earlier about the problematic moral messages conveyed by poetic texts.

34. (8.568c) *But they will continue to go to other cities and attract mobs, and hire voices fair and loud and persuasive, and draw the cities over to tyrannies and democracies:* The insinuation that democracy is one step away from tyranny would have surely affronted most Athenians, who considered democracy, with its respect for law and guarantee of freedom, the opposite of tyranny.

35. (8.568e) *Why, clearly, he said, then he and his boon companions, whether male or female, will be maintained out of his father's estate:* Athenians viewed

the abuse and neglect of elderly parents with abhorrence, and the image
of the tyrant as an ungrateful "son" who brutally abuses his aged parent (that
is, the people, or *demos*) is viscerally jolting. See also 7.537e–538c, where the
immature dialectician is compared to an ungrateful adopted son. In Aristophanes' *Clouds*, Socrates is represented as indirectly responsible for a son's
beating of his aged and indulgent father. The strong aversion to such violence
that is attributed to Socrates in this passage is perhaps another step in Plato's
effort to counter Aristophanes' unflattering portrayal. See note 22 on 2.378b.

Book 9

1. (9.572b) *even in good men, there is a lawless wild-beast nature, which peers
   out in sleep:* Compare 9.588b–e, where Socrates suggests that the soul is like
   a hybrid creature that is part human, part lion, and part chimerical beast.
   These vivid formulations pave the way for Socrates' conclusion concerning
   the value of justice in the individual—that is, that it is what strengthens the
   truly human element of the soul and is thus what "humanizes" human beings (9.588e–589c). As the agent of "humanization," justice is thus the "excellence" (*aretê*) that enables human beings to fulfill their unique function
   (*ergon*) and so attain happiness (*eudaimonia*); compare 1.352e–354b. It is
   doubtless no accident that Thrasymachus, the proponent of injustice and
   self-aggrandizement, is initially represented as beast-like (1.336b).
2. (9.573b) *And is not this the reason why, of old, love has been called a
   tyrant?:* The overwhelming, "tyrannical" power of *eros* ("lust," "sexual passion") is a familiar poetic topic. Compare the description at 9.575a of the
   domination of the tyrant's soul by sexual desire.
3. (9.573d) *Love is the lord of the house within him, and orders all the concerns of his soul:* The image of the tyrannical man as dominated by sexual
   appetite (*eros*) stands in contrast to the characterization developed in *Republic* and other dialogues of the philosopher who, though a "lover," directs
   his erotic energy toward spiritual rather than physical pursuits and always
   prefers what is beneficial over what is gratifying. See note 16 on 3.402e.
   Socrates' characterization of the tyrant/tyrannical man as a slave of *eros* also
   capitalizes on the fact that *eros* was metaphorically associated (especially in
   classical Athens) with "lust" for political power and prominence.
4. (9.574d) *He first takes their property, and . . . then he breaks into a
   house . . . ; next he proceeds to clear a temple:* The modus operandi of the
   tyrannical man, which includes the abuse of his parents and his reliance on
   an ever more powerful "bodyguard" (that is, of unruly appetites), mirrors
   that of the actual tyrant. See 8.566b and 8.568e–569c; also 9.575d.
5. (9.576d) *There can be no mistake . . . as to which is which, and therefore I
   will at once inquire whether you would arrive at a similar decision about
   their relative happiness and misery:* Socrates' assessment of the misery of

the city-state ruled by a tyrant would have been very much in keeping with the judgment of most Athenians. It is his judgment of the tyrant's *personal* misery that goes against the "common view," as set forth by Thrasymachus in book 1 and again by Glaucon and Adeimantus in book 2.

6. (9.577a) *I should have a judge whose mind can enter into and see through human nature? he must not be like a child who looks at the outside and is dazzled . . . but let him be one who has a clear insight:* Socrates similarly warns in book 10 against being "like children" and indulging in "childish love," as he reminds Glaucon that emotions like grief ought to be restrained (10.604c), and that the poetry of Homer and "other tragedians" must be excluded from the ideal city-state (10.608a). Compare his insistence at 5.466b that the judgment of the best life ought not be clouded by "some youthful conceit of happiness." Concerns about the "childishness" of (most) adults, who are readily taken in by appearances and more eager to obtain what is immediately gratifying than what is of lasting benefit, deeply inform *Republic's* examination of justice and its formulations concerning the ideal state, and they go hand in hand with its concerns about the premium that most people put on pleasure. See note 2 on 3.391a; also *Gorgias* 521e–522a and *Crito* 49b.

7. (9.577b) *where he may be seen stripped of his tragedy attire:* See 8.568a–b for Socrates' ironic commendation of tragedy's glamorization of tyranny and tyrants.

8. (9.579b) *he lives in his hole like a woman hidden in the house:* The comparison of the tyrant to a woman "hidden in the house" aims to discredit in the most devastating terms the claims to freedom, "excellence," and, by extension, manliness that Thrasymachus had made on behalf of the tyrant at 1.344a–c. In contrast to the "feminine" tyrant, the philosopher, whom many people might consider "unmanly" because of his failure to concern himself with material success (compare 8.549d), emerges as the true epitome of masculinity, in control of both himself and his life.

9. (9.580a–b) *as the general umpire in theatrical contests proclaims the result:* Participants in the dramatic competitions held in the Theater of Dionysus at Athens were awarded prizes by a panel of ten judges, one of whom was chosen to announce the results. The references in this passage to the judgment of and awarding of prizes to dramas in theatrical competitions, a process that presumably took into account public reactions to the performances, underscore how Glaucon's assessments are influenced by neither showy exteriors nor the need to cater to popular sentiments. Compare, for example, 9.577b; also 7.527d–528a.

10. (9.580b) *they are the royal:* The word *basilikon* can also be translated as "kingly." Socrates also calls the constitution of the ideal state and its corresponding individual "aristocratic" (for example, at 8.544e), since that which is "best" (*aristos*) rules in both. Compare 9.587c–d.

11. (9.580c–d) *Then this, I said, will be our first proof; and there is another, which may also have some weight:* Socrates actually offers three "proofs" of the tyrant's misery and, conversely, of the happiness of the just man and philosopher. The second proof (9.580d–583a) argues that the pleasures experienced by "lovers of wisdom" are far superior to those of "lovers of gain," and the third (9.583b–587c) argues that the "pleasures" valued by "lovers of gain" and "lovers of honor" are in fact not pleasures at all, but mere efforts to void pain.

The number three, which signified completeness in a variety of situations and phenomena (for example, the number of rounds in wrestling matches and other competitions, the number of libations poured at religious rituals, etc.), figures prominently in *Republic*. There are three "proofs" of the philosopher and just man's happiness in book 9, and there are three arguments discrediting poetry's claims to political and practical utility in book 10. The final calculation of the tyrant's misery and the philosopher's happiness is based on squaring and cubing the number 3 because, as it is decided, the tyrant is three times removed from the oligarchical man, who is in turn three times removed from the just "aristocratic" man (9.587c–588a); at 10.597e and 10.601d–602a, poetic imitation is determined to be three times removed from the truth. At 5.472a, Socrates likens Glaucon's and Adeimantus' challenges to his conception of the ideal state to three great waves. Most fundamentally, there are three classes in the ideal city-state and three corresponding parts of the soul.

Just as the definition of justice in book 4 harks back to Polemarchus' initial effort to define justice as "giving what is due" (4.433a; compare 1.332a–c), the three proofs offered in book 9 of justice's benefits return to but also reconfigure Thrasymachus' definition of justice as "the advantage of the stronger" (or superior) (1.338c). Reason is the "strongest" (that is, best) element; the advantage that it pursues is for the benefit of the entire soul.

12. (9.582d) *His experience, then, will enable him to judge better than anyone?:* Socrates' contention that the philosopher is the best judge of the relative merits of all pleasures may merit more scrutiny than Glaucon gives. It is consistent, nonetheless, with the presumptions about the philosopher's competence that have been made throughout *Republic*. Compare also 9.577b, where Socrates and Glaucon assume that they are "able and experienced judges."

13. (9.583b) *Twice in succession, then, has the just man overthrown the unjust in this conflict:* The metaphor is from wrestling (compare 8.544b). To win a match, the victor had to throw and pin his opponent three times.

14. (9.584e) *Then can you wonder that persons who are inexperienced in the truth, as they have wrong ideas about many other things, should also have wrong ideas about pleasure and pain and the intermediate state[?]:* The "unphilosophic" nature of most people has already been asserted at 6.494a, and the commonplace yet problematic identification of pleasure with "the good" is discussed at 6.505c; see also note 2 on 3.391a. This passage's analysis of pleasure and pain as "motions" of the soul (9.583e) is ultimately aimed at discrediting the common identification of pleasure with bodily and emotional gratification. On Socrates' argument, the apparent "pleasures" of eating, drinking, etc., are merely cessations of pain (that is, hunger, thirst, etc.) and are thus "states of rest" that, by definition, are not truly pleasant (9.583e). Moreover, the distinctions made by means of the divided line between phenomenal objects, which have a low "degree of truth" insofar as they are impermanent and subject to change, and intellectual objects that are permanent and unchanging (6.510a), permit Socrates to argue here that food, drink, and other "substances" provide satisfaction only in temporary and incomplete ways, since they are not in contact with "pure being," whereas the substance of philosophical contemplation, "which is concerned with the invariable, the immortal" (9.585b–c), is able to supply something akin to genuine pleasure (9.587b). Compare *Gorgias* 491e–497a.

15. (9.586a) *Like cattle, with their eyes always looking down and their heads stooping to the earth, that is, to the dining-table, they fatten and feed and breed:* This powerful (and powerfully unflattering) image of the behavior of most people, who conduct themselves like animals, anticipates Socrates' identification of justice as the *aretê* that humanizes human beings (9.588e–589c).

16. (9.586c) *as Stesichorus says that the Greeks fought about the shadow of Helen at Troy, in ignorance of the truth:* The lyric poet Stesichorus (sixth century B.C.E.) composed a poem, often called his "palinode," in which he asserted that the gods sent a phantom image of Helen to Troy, while Helen herself went to Egypt. Plato has Socrates quote the opening lines of the palinode at *Phaedrus* 243a–b.

17. (9.586d–e) *Then may we not confidently assert that the lovers of money and honor, when they seek their pleasures under the guidance . . . of reason and knowledge . . . will also have the truest pleasures in the highest degree which is attainable to them . . . ?:* Socrates' statement seems to suggest that non-philosophers can, within limits, achieve some pleasure and satisfaction in life. His argument concerning justice as a whole, however, raises fascinating questions about whether he would admit that non-philosophers are truly capable of being "just" and therefore happy. Compare, for example, 10.619c–d.

18. (9.587c) *and the measure of his inferiority can only be expressed in a figure:* As in the calculation at 8.546b–c of the number governing human births, there may be Pythagorean influences in this geometric expression of the distance between the philosopher's happiness and the tyrant's misery. The figure ultimately arrived at is a square-sided cube of 729 units that symbolizes the completeness of the philosopher's happiness on two levels; first, it is the cube of the square of 3. (See note 11 on 9.580c for the significance of the number 3 in *Republic*). Since, as Jowett notes, it is also (nearly) the number of days and nights in a year, it suggests that the philosopher has more pleasure than the tyrant every day and every night of every year.

19. (9.588b) *Let us make an image of the soul, that he may have his own words presented before his eyes:* By envisioning the soul as a composite creature, part human but mostly animal, Socrates develops another powerful image that enables him to discredit injustice's claim to conferring benefit. On the bestializing effect of injustice (9.588e–589c), see also 9.571c.

20. (9.589c) *Come, now, and let us gently reason with the unjust, who is not intentionally in error:* For the Socratic "maxim" that no one does wrong willingly, see 2.360c, 2.366c, and 3.413a; also 1.336e.

21. (9.589e) *Who can imagine that a man who sold his son or daughter into slavery for money . . . would be the gainer, however large might be the sum which he received?:* Children, especially sons, represented continuity for the family; to sell one's children into slavery constituted a violation of kinship ties and was also tantamount to destroying one's family. Socrates' analogy comparing the person who marginalizes his or her rational element to one who sells his children into slavery highlights how such marginalization leads only to short-term, inconsequential "gains" and long-term, permanent damage.

22. (9.590c) *And why are mean employments and manual arts a reproach?:* See note 14 on 2.371c.

23. (9.591a–b) *What shall he profit, if his unjustice be undetected and unpunished? He who is undetected only gets worse:* Socrates makes an almost identical point in *Gorgias* 473b–479e.

Book 10

1. (10.595a–b) *To the rejection of imitative poetry, which certainly ought not be received; as I see far more clearly now that the parts of the soul have been distinguished:* As Socrates eventually argues (10.602c–606d), poetic mimesis appeals to and strengthens the appetitive part of the soul; it "feeds and waters the passions instead of drying them up; [and] lets them rule, although they ought to be controlled" (10.606d). In addition, poetic mimesis and all other forms of imitation strengthen the faculty of *eikasia*, which the divided line distinguishes as the least important cognitive faculty (6.509d–511e). Poetry is thus the opposite of the mathematical disciplines discussed at length in book 7, which strengthen the soul's rational element by drawing "the mind to the contemplation of true being" (7.525a) and spurring the development of the faculties of *dianoia* and, ultimately, *noesis*. This analysis of poetry's deleterious psychological effects, which complements what has already been asserted in books 2 and 3 about the problematic behavioral models provided in poetic texts such as *Iliad*, is preceded by two examinations of its distance from "the truth." The first examination relies upon the divided line's distinctions among objects of perception (10.596a–598d). Imitators such as painters and poets, who create reflections of phenomenal objects that are themselves mere "copies" of intelligible objects, work with no knowledge

of or concern for "what is" and therefore impart no useful information (10.598b–e). Their work as creators of objects in the least significant segment of the divided line is contrasted with the work of real craftsmen, who create phenomenal objects such as beds and tables, and with the work of the maker of the ideas, who is simply identified as god (*theos*) in 10.597b–d, and they are ultimately characterized as ignorant men who appeal to others who are equally ignorant (10.601a–b). The second examination contrasts the knowledge that an imitator has of a given object with that of its user and its maker (10.601b–602c). It reaches the same conclusions as the first: that is, that imitators such as poets have no useful information to impart, and that their imitations are three times removed from what is true and real (10.602b; compare 10.597e). In the first examination particularly, Socrates uses the visual medium of painting to criticize the "truth-value" of poetry, and he rather crudely exploits the obvious differences between a bed in a painting and a bed that one actually sleeps on to suggest that artistic imitations are generally not "useful." However we may judge his arguments, his narrowly utilitarian criteria put him in a position to challenge long-standing assumptions about the ethical value of poetic texts such as *Iliad* and *Odyssey* and, as well, reverential conceptions of Homer and his fellow poets as knowledgeable teachers of "virtue" (10.598d–601b). Book 10's critique of poetry, then, takes readers back not only to the arguments for censorship in books 2 and 3, but also to the very beginning of book 1, where Polemarchus cites the poet Simonides as an authority on justice (1.331d).

2. (10.595c) *for he is the great captain and teacher of the whole of that charming tragic company:* The conception of Homer as a "tragedian," reiterated below at 10.598d, 10.605c, and 10.607a, is novel but it is anticipated by the discussion of the different forms of poetic *mimesis* (that is, simple narration, direct imitation, and the mixture of narration and direct imitation) at 3.392d. Epic poems fall into the "mixed" category because they directly present speeches by figures such as Achilles and Agamemnon, and thus they can be considered kindred to tragedy, which is purely imitative. Socrates' characterization of Homer as a tragedian may also be intended to draw attention to the general influence of epic poetry on Athenian drama in the classical period.

3. (10.595c) *Can you tell me what imitation is? for I really do not know:* Socrates' disavowal of knowledge about the nature of "imitation" is noteworthy, given the detailed discussion of poetic mimesis in book 3. Nonetheless, it is consistent with his cautious professions of ignorance about the idea of the good and dialectic in books 6 and 7, and it is perhaps well motivated at this moment, since the theory of the ideas is about to become the basis for his argument against poetry's ability to convey useful, "truthful" information.

4. (10.596b) *But there are only two ideas or forms of them—one the idea of a bed, the other of a table:* If all phenomenal objects owe their existence in the world of "becoming" to their "participation" in the ideas, which exist in the world of "being," the positing of "ideas" of "bed" and "table" makes sense, and it plainly suits Socrates' purposes at this point. It is debatable, however, whether Plato would have considered these ideas worthy of extended investigation, especially when compared with such ideas as those of justice, moderation, courage, and beauty, as well as the idea of the good.

5. *(10.597a) At any rate, he replied, philosophers would say that he was not speaking the truth:* Literally, "he would not seem [to say true things] to those who occupy themselves with arguments such as these." Socrates apparently means that people who investigate "being" (that is, philosophers) would not admit that a physical bed made by a craftsman "exists," since it is only part of the world of "becoming."

6. *(10.597e) And the tragic poet is an imitator, and, therefore, like all other imitators, he is thrice removed from the king and from the truth?:* As at 9.587c–d, Socrates counts inclusively. "The king" in this sentence is god, the maker of the ideal bed. Compare 6.509d, where the idea of the good is said to be a "ruling power" (literally, "to be king") over the realm of intelligible objects. Despite this coincidence in language, it is not safe to assume that the idea of the good is identifiable with "god."

7. *(10.598d–e) And so, when we hear persons saying that the tragedians, and Homer . . . know all the arts and all things human, virtue as well as vice . . . we ought to consider whether here also there may not be a similar illusion:* Such knowledge of "all things human" is, in effect, what Polemarchus claims for Simonides at 1.331d. Compare Adeimantus' liberal quotations from poetry at 2.363a–366a, and the purported claims of the "eulogists of Homer" at 10.606e.

8. *(10.599b) Then . . . we must put a question to Homer:* The point that poets have no true knowledge of their subject matter is made, in somewhat different terms, in *Ion* 533e–535a, where Socrates suggests to the rhapsode Ion that divine inspiration, and not expert knowledge (*technê*), is what enables artists like Homer to create poetry.

9. *(10.600a) But, if Homer never did any public service, was he privately a guide or teacher of any?:* In *Gorgias* 515a–b, Socrates poses an analogous question to the ambitious politician Callicles.

10. *(10.600b) Creophylus, the companion of Homer:* Some sources call Creophylus Homer's *hetairos* (that is, "friend, companion, also disciple"), while others claim that he was a son-in-law. The name Creophylus "makes us laugh" because, as it is apparently derived from the words for "meat" (*kreas*) and "race" or "tribe" (*phylon*), it can be interpreted as meaning something like "made from meat" (hence Jowett's interpolation, "that child of flesh"). The story about Creophylus' disregard for Homer does not appear in other sources.

11. *(10.600c) can you imagine . . . that he would not have had many followers, and been honored and loved by them?:* In *Gorgias* 519c–d, Socrates similarly

asserts that, if students mistreat their instructor (that is, a Sophist or rhetorician like Gorgias), the fault lies with the instructor and exposes his failure as an educator.

12. (10.600c) *Protagoras of Abdera and Prodicus of Ceos:* Protagoras, from Abdera in Thrace, was one of the most prominent and successful "sophists" in Athens in the mid-fifth century B.C.E. See note 2 on 5.449d for the educational claim that Plato puts in Protagoras' mouth in *Protagoras* 318e–319a. If the "dramatic date" of *Republic* is meant to be 411 or 410 B.C.E., the reference to Protagoras in the present tense would be anachronistic. Prodicus, from the island Ceos, was another prominent and successful Sophist who was active in Athens during Socrates' lifetime; in *Protagoras*, he and Protagoras are represented as staying in the home of the wealthy Athenian Callias.

13. (10.601c) *only the horseman who knows how to use them—he knows their right form:* The superior "knowledge" attributed in this passage to the person who uses a given object is not to be confused with the philosopher's knowledge (*epistemê*) of the ideas.

14. (10.602b) *Imitation is only a kind of play or sport:* Compare *Phaedrus* 274c–278e; also *Laws* 3.685a, 4.712b, and 7.817a–d; *Republic* 7.536b–c. As these and other passages suggest, Plato would have readily acknowledged that his own dialogues, qua "imitations," are in the final analysis "play," albeit an especially constructive type of "play."

15. (10.602d) *And the arts of measuring and numbering and weighing come to the rescue of the human understanding . . . and the apparent greater or less . . . give way before calculation and measure and weight?:* Compare 7.522c–526c, especially 7.522e–524d.

16. (10.604e) *And does not . . . the rebellious principle . . . furnish a great variety of materials for imitation? Whereas the wise and calm temperament . . . is not easy to imitate or to appreciate when imitated, especially . . . when a promiscuous crowd is assembled in a theatre. . . . :* This concession that the sober behavior of upright, self-restrained figures does not make for "good theater" figures into a broad critique of the dynamics of public performance, whether in theatrical competitions or political assemblies or law courts, that takes shape in several Platonic dialogues. *Gorgias* 501d–511a, for example, highlights how dramatists and politicians alike, as they compete for public favor, are obliged to "flatter" their audiences and cater to their tastes; compare what Socrates says about sophists in *Republic* 6.493a–d. Plato's dialogues themselves, we might imagine, offer alternatives to the unwholesome yet exciting exhibitions on the tragic stage, and they arguably live up to the standards Socrates establishes in this passage for imitations of "the wise and calm temperament." Yet they were hardly intended for popular consumption by the "promiscuous crowd" and would thus bear out Socrates' point that the "imitative poet who aims at being popular" is bound to prefer the easily imitated "passionate and fitful temper."

17. (10.605c–d) *the best of us . . . delight in giving way to sympathy, and are in raptures at the excellence of the poet who stirs our feelings most:* Socrates' acknowledgment of the powerful appeal of "moving" passages in poetry resonates with his repeated professions of affection for Homer, and also looks ahead to his conclusion that "hymns to the gods and praises of famous men are the only poetry which ought to be admitted into our State" (10.607a). This is a far stricter provision for "censorship" than what was argued for, vis-à-vis the education of children in the guardian classes, in books 2 and 3, and reflects the emerging concern in *Republic*'s later books that adults, even when intelligent and well disciplined, can readily become "childish."

18. (10.607a) *For if you go beyond this and allow the honeyed muse to enter, either in epic or lyric verse, not law and the reason of mankind, which by common consent have ever been deemed best, but pleasure and pain will be the rulers in our State:* See note 2 on 3.391a and note 6 on 9.577a; also 6.505c.

19. (10.607b) *let us tell her that there is an ancient quarrel between philosophy and poetry; of which there are many proofs:* As far back as the archaic period, individuals such as Xenophanes criticized the representations of the gods in Homer. These men were themselves poets, but it is perhaps fair to identify in their works the beginnings of a "quarrel" between poetry and philosophy. On the other hand, it may be wise to take Socrates' claim about the antiquity of the quarrel with a few grains of salt—since Xenophanes and his kind were not "philosophers" according to the standards developed in books 6 and 7 of *Republic*—and to construe what is said here as an effort to promote and justify the systematic critique of poetry and its cultural impact that Plato undertakes in his dialogues.

20. (10.608b) *for great is the issue at stake, greater than appears, whether a man is to be good or bad:* Literally, "for great is the contest. . . ." See note 14 on 1.344e.

21. (10.608c) *And yet no mention has been made of the greatest prizes and rewards which await virtue:* The challenge that Glaucon and Adeimantus set up for Socrates in book 2 (culminating at 2.367a–e) was to demonstrate that justice is intrinsically "profitable" and injustice "unprofitable," regardless of external circumstances such as rewards or penalties. At this point, which marks the beginning of *Republic*'s final section, Socrates argues that his companions should return to him what was "borrowed in the argument" (10.612c)—that is, the recognition of and rewards given for justice by both human beings and gods, in this life and the next. The consideration of the rewards for justice and penalties for injustice in the hereafter, which are of far longer duration and far greater consequence than what is received while one is alive, motivate the discussion of the soul's immortality that begins just below.

22. (10.608d) *Are you not aware, I said, that the soul of man is immortal and imperishable?:* In *Phaedo* and *Phaedrus*, Plato has Socrates contend that the soul is immortal, and that the death or destruction of the body does not entail the death or destruction of the soul. Whereas Socrates simply assumes that the soul is immortal in *Gorgias* 523a–b, he offers explanations, or "proofs," of its immortality here and also in *Phaedo* 64a–107d and *Phaedrus* 245c–246a. The argument made below in 10.608d–611a—that is, that things can be destroyed only by their own particular "evil" (*kakon* in Greek) and that, since the soul is not destroyed by its evil (that is, injustice), it cannot be destroyed at all and is therefore immortal—differs from what is adduced in *Phaedo* and *Phaedrus*, and these differences suggest that Plato did not intend Socrates' arguments to be construed as offering definitive answers. Rather, the reasoning presented here about everything having a particular "evil" seems to hark back to and reinforce the crucial assumptions introduced at 1.352d–354a that each thing, whether living or inanimate, has a single function, and that there is a unique "excellence" that enables this function to be performed well.

23. (10.608d) *He looked at me in astonishment, and said: No, by heaven: And are you really prepared to maintain this?:* The notion that souls (*psychai*) somehow survived the body and were taken to the underworld (or, in special instances, to the Islands of the Blessed) was widely accepted, and it was central to both the Orphic and Pythagorean systems of belief. Socrates has already introduced the concept of the soul's reincarnation at 6.498d. What surprises Glaucon at this moment is, perhaps, Socrates' readiness to make a *rational* case for the immortality of the soul.

24. (10.611a–b) *But this we cannot believe . . . any more than we can believe the soul . . . to be full of variety and difference and dissimilarity:* In *Phaedo* 72b, Plato has Socrates use similar reasoning to establish that the living "come from the dead"—that is, by the process of reincarnation. The contention immediately below that the soul "cannot be compounded of many elements" also corresponds with *Phaedo* 79d–80b, and the image of the soul as marred by communion with the body and other miseries resembles what Socrates asserts in *Phaedo* 67a and 82e. For the need to contemplate the soul "in her original purity" (that is, apart from the body), see also *Gorgias* 524d–525a.

25. (10.612c) *Will you repay me, then, what you borrowed in the argument?:* See book 2, especially 2.361c and 2.367c–e, as well as note 21 on 10.608c. Socrates' language may deliberately echo the terms in which he, Cephalus, and Polemarchus initially discussed justice at 1.331a–332c—that is, as the repayment of debts and the giving of what is "due."

26. (10.613c) *And now you must allow me to repeat of the just the blessings which you were attributing to the fortunate unjust:* At 2.360e–362c, Glaucon imagines the lot of the "happy" unjust man, who literally gets away with murder, and that of the wrongly tormented "unhappy" just man; here Socrates reverses their situations.

27. (10.614b) *I will tell you a tale:* Like *Republic*, *Gorgias* and *Phaedo* conclude with tales about the afterlife, which describe the experiences of the soul when separated from the body; in *Phaedrus* 246a–256e, Socrates presents another, quite lengthy eschatological myth. Like the myth of Er in *Republic*, these stories describe the rewards received after death by those who have been virtuous in life and, conversely, the punishments of those who have been unjust, but their details and emphases differ considerably. Glaucon prefaces the myth in *Republic* by claiming that nothing would be "more pleasant" (*hedion* in Greek—Jowett's translation of Glaucon's statement "there are few things which I would more gladly hear" is less than literal). Although the myth's concerns are very serious, Glaucon's words suggest that Plato did not mean his readers to take it as literal truth. As with the different arguments for the soul's existence in *Republic* and other dialogues, it is worth considering how the details and emphases in this and the other eschatological myths may be determined by the particular concerns of their dialogues.

28. (10.614b) *not one of the tales which Odysseus tells to the hero Alcinoüs, yet this, too, is a tale of a hero, Er the son of Armenius, a Pamphylian by birth:* Books 9–12 of *Odyssey*, in which Odysseus tells Alcinoüs, king of the Phaeacians, about his wanderings after the fall of Troy, were traditionally called "the tales to Alcinoüs" (*apologoi Alcinou*). The phrase rendered by Jowett as "a tale of a hero" (*apologon alkimou andros*) is plainly meant to be a pun on *apologos Alcinou*. There has been a good deal of speculation since antiquity on Plato's source(s) for the story of Er, son of Armenius. Pamphylia was a territory in southern Asia Minor, and the names "Er" and "Armenius" also suggest that the story has an origin in the Near East. Some scholars have also interpreted "Pamphylia" as meaning "from every tribe" (that is, *pan + phylon*), thus suggesting that Er is a figure universally representative of humanity.

29. (10.616b–c) *another day's journey brought them to the place, and there, in the midst of the light, they saw the ends of the chains of heaven let down from above:* It is difficult to determine where exactly Er and his fellow travelers are standing; what kind of place could afford this comprehensive view of the cosmos, in all its enormity? Other elements in the description are equally challenging; how, for example, does the spindle of Necessity hang from the ends of the light shaft that binds heaven and earth together but also turn on Necessity's knees? There is much scholarly debate over the significance of various details in the description that follows, and it seems wisest to approach the whole picture with a flexible imagination. However its details are construed, the overall purpose of Er's vision of the light binding the universe together and of the spindle of Necessity is to convey the sense of cosmic order. All that happens in human life, including and especially the judgment of one's past life and one's choice of the next life (10.617d–620d), occurs in accordance with this order, and thus "justice" is shown to be a fundamental cosmic principle.

There is also disagreement about the sources of inspiration for the cosmic vision revealed to Er. The geocentric conception of the cosmos seems to reflect contemporary astronomical theories, as does the conception of the heavenly bodies, whose movements in the sky are contained (or reflected?) in the eight concentric hemispheres that comprise the whorl of Necessity's spindle. Several scholars argue that these conceptions reflect Pythagorean speculation, at least in part. At 7.529a–530b, however, Socrates draws a distinction between the true astronomy practiced by philosophers, which is concerned with abstract problems of movement, and the pedestrian concerns of the Pythagoreans and others, who (so Socrates claims) content themselves with studying the motions of mere physical entities. The image of the concentric hemispheres of the heavens presented in the figure of Necessity's whorl is plainly an ideal model concerned with elucidating cosmic order *in toto*, and as such it seems to accord with the aims and goals of what Socrates has defined as "true" astronomy. If the image draws on Pythagorean thinking, it perhaps also offers a critique of and corrective to it. Nonetheless, the placement of the image within a myth that has been characterized as "pleasant" (see note 27 on 10.614b) ought make us wary of believing that Plato intended his readers to take its details literally.

30. (10.616c) *for this light is the belt of heaven, and holds together the circle of the universe:* The "line of light, straight as a column" mentioned just above is envisioned as penetrating the center of both the heavens and the earth, which is itself at the center of the heavens. Some scholars interpret the reference to "under-girders of a trireme" to mean that bands of light must also wrap around the outside of the heavens. The term "under-girders" (*hypozomata*), however, can refer to cables that pass from bow to stern within a ship's hull and hold it together lengthwise. If these kinds of cables are what Plato had in mind, then it seems likely that we are meant to envision heaven and earth held together by only a single, central shaft of light.

31. (10.616c) *the whorl is made partly of steel and also partly of other materials:* The whorl of Necessity's spindle differs from ordinary whorls in that it is perfectly hemispherical and composed of eight hollow hemispheres of different thicknesses and materials and colors, which fit together, one inside the other. Each hemisphere contains or represents—it is not entirely clear which is the more proper conception—a heavenly body and its placement in the heavens, except for the outermost one, which contains or represents "the fixed stars" and so has several heavenly bodies. The "movements" of the heavenly bodies and the appearances of their different rates of speed are accounted for by the rotations (at different speeds) of the hemispheres, which are counter to the rotation of the spindle as a whole.

32. (10.617b) *a siren, who goes round with them, hymning a single tone or note:* The notion of "astral music" is clearly Pythagorean; compare 7.530d, where the studies of astronomy and harmonics are said, following the Pythagoreans, to be "sister sciences."

33. (10.617b) *The eight together form one harmony: Harmonia*, literally "tuning," usually refers to notes that are sequentially rather than simultaneously sung or played. Although it may be that the sirens emit their single notes simultaneously, it is perhaps more reasonable to assume that they sing in sequence, and that the notes they emit make up two tetrachords.

34. (10.617e) *"the responsibility is with the chooser—God is justified":* The prophet's pronouncement begins *Republic's* final argument for the utility of philosophy. Not only does the person who practices philosophy choose wisely and so become "happy" while he or she is alive on earth, but the ability that he or she gains to "learn and discern between good and evil," and to determine (literally, "reason out") which qualities of the soul are better and worse, is the only thing that will enable him or her to choose the next life wisely, "undazzled by the desire of wealth or the other allurements of evil . . ." (10.618b–619b). Without philosophy, one lacks the reasoning ability (*logos*) to make the best decisions, as is borne out by the example of the man whose *aretê* in his former life "was a matter of habit only," and who has no *logos* to keep him from choosing the greatest tyranny as his next life (10.619b–d). So, too, it is only the saving grace of philosophic *logos* that keeps souls from drinking too much from the river of Unmindfulness (10.621a). The fact that the myth is offered as a fanciful and "pleasant" construction does not detract from the overall seriousness and significance of what it conveys. This passage, which accentuates the responsibility that individuals have for shaping their lives, is very much in keeping with the major concerns of *Republic*. That there is a lottery determining the order in which one may choose one's future life is a concession to the fact that control over circumstances is not complete; nonetheless, as the prophet insists, "Even for the last comer, if he chooses wisely . . . there is appointed a happy and not undesirable existence" (10.619b).

35. (10.621c) *And it shall be well with us both in this life and in the pilgrimage of a thousand years which we have been describing:* Literally rendered, the last words of *Republic* are, "and as we receive the rewards of justice, just like victors in games collecting prizes, both here and in the thousand-year journey that we have described, let us do well." The phrase "let us do well" (*eu prattômen*) is in the subjunctive mood and is therefore hortatory, not declarative. In Greek the expression "to do well" has some of the same ambiguities that it can have in English, since it means both "to act well" and "to do good things, and also to fare well." *Eu prattômen* is a favorite phrase of salutation and farewell in the letters attributed to Plato, and it may reflect his personal usage. They are fitting closing words for *Republic*, which has been concerned all along with "doing" and "faring" well.

INSPIRED BY PLATO AND *REPUBLIC*

"The safest general characterization of the European philosophical tradition is that it consists of a series of footnotes to Plato." Alfred North Whitehead's wry assessment of Plato's importance to the philosophical tradition of Europe is something of an exaggeration. Yet it is not wholly inaccurate. Beginning with Aristotle (384–322 B.C.E.), who spent twenty years as Plato's student at the Academy, virtually all philosophers and philosophical schools active in lands exposed to Hellenic culture owe significant debts of inspiration to Plato. As is abundantly evident from Aristotle's extant works, the efforts of later philosophers to respond to key Platonic texts such as *Republic* have necessarily entailed the interpretation and transformation and (at times) misrepresentation of Plato's thought. Thus, as we consider the legacy of Plato both in and beyond the field of philosophy, we will do well to keep in mind that, at times, the relationship between what Plato may have intended to convey and what he inspired can be tenuous.

Aristotle expected his readers and students to be familiar with the Platonic dialogues, and it is fair to say that some of his best-known works—*Nicomachean Ethics, Politics, Poetics,* and *Metaphysics*—are fundamentally "inspired by" *Republic*, insofar as they seek to refine and (in places) contest what Plato has Socrates suggest about the relationship between moral excellence and happiness in the individual, the proper organization of a functional political community, the need to censor poetry (especially tragedy), and the theory of the ideas. The Academy ceased to be the chief institution for the study and transmission of Plato's thought in the third century B.C.E., but, by this time, Plato's works were widely read in the Hellenic world, and they became popular in the elite philhellenic circles of Roman society during the second and first centuries B.C.E. The Roman politician, orator, and philosopher Marcus Tullius Cicero (106–43 B.C.E.) was profoundly influenced by Plato, and he modeled several of his philosophical treatises on

Platonic dialogues, including his *De republica* (*On the Common-wealth*), which was intended as a Romanized version of *Republic*. A few centuries later Plotinus (205–270 C.E.), after settling in Rome to teach philosophy, developed a comprehensive system of philosophical thought and religious belief that was founded on key concepts derived from Plato's works—most notably, the idea of the good in books 6–7 of *Republic*—which Plotinus identified with "the One." This system came to be known as "Platonism," or "Neo-Platonism"; its principal tenets are expounded in six collections of Plotinus' writings, which Plotinus' student Porphyry (c.234–c.305 C.E.) published at the beginning of the fourth century, and which came to be called *Enneads*. It is through *Enneads* and the writings of Porphyry that Saint Augustine (354–430 C.E.) was exposed to Platonism, ensuring that Plato's thought had a lasting (albeit indirect) influence upon the philosophical direction of Christianity for the next thousand years. In 529 C.E., on the order of the emperor Justinian, the Academy (along with all other philosophical schools in Athens) was forced to close. Before this happened, the Neo-Platonist philosopher Proclus (c.410–485) brought the study of Plato back to the Academy. Proclus served as the Academy's head for several years and wrote commentaries on *Republic*, *Timaeus*, and *Parmenides*, which are still extant today.

The writings of Saint Thomas Aquinas (c.1225–1274), particularly the *Summa Theologica* (1266–1273), established Aristotle as the most important ancient philosopher in the late Middle Ages and early Renaissance. "Platonism," however, enjoyed a second flowering in the fifteenth and sixteenth centuries thanks to the efforts of the Florentine scholar Marsilio Ficino (1433–1499), whose effort to forge a fresh integration of Platonic thought and Christianity—an effort that found its most complete expression in *Platonic Theology* (1482)—was deeply influenced by Plotinus and Proclus. By the end of the sixteenth century, literate people in Europe had access to printed texts of Plato's dialogues, both in Greek and in translations into various modern languages. It is accordingly no surprise to find that, during the modern period, Plato's words and thoughts have been quoted and referred to—and reaffirmed and disputed and praised and condemned—by numerous important philosophers in Europe and Great Britain: among them, Michel de Montaigne

(1533–1592), François Marie Arouet ("Voltaire," 1694–1778), Friedrich Schleiermacher (1768–1834), Georg Hegel (1770–1831), John Stuart Mill (1806–1873), Friedrich Nietzsche (1844–1900), Martin Heidegger (1889–1976), and Karl Popper (1902–1994). Meriting special mention here is the famous group of "Cambridge Platonists," led by Benjamin Whichcote (1609–1683), who sought at the beginning of the scientific age—in a particularly difficult period of British history—to reconcile Christian beliefs with the Platonic conception of a rationally ordered universe.

The practical influence of *Republic* is more difficult to gauge than its impact on the theorizing of later thinkers. Nonetheless, over the centuries, individuals have discovered in Plato's works the inspiration for undertaking political or social or educational reform. The following two examples are illustrative. First, as is discussed in the introduction, Plato and his friend Dion (c.408–354 B.C.E.) evidently planned to educate the young Dionysius II of Syracuse in the hopes that, upon succeeding his father as the city's ruler, he would put into practice the political ideals they cherished, which may have been something like the proposals for the ideal state and the government of philosopher-rulers that Plato has Socrates advance in *Republic*. More recently—and more modestly—Benjamin Jowett (1818–1893), the translator of this edition of *Republic*, placed Plato's dialogues at the center of the humanities curriculum as part of his program of educational reform at Oxford University. It is interesting to note that Jowett seems to have met with more success than Dion. Whereas Dion was eventually assassinated for his zealous efforts to bring political and social reform to Syracuse and other Greek cities on Sicily, Jowett's Plato-inspired campaign helped modernize Oxford and transform it into one of the world's leading educational institutions.

Lastly, we may note that *Republic* has inspired not only much expository analysis, but also countless creative presentations, literary and otherwise. Many depictions of both utopian societies and their dystopian counterparts, ranging from Thomas More's *Utopia* (1516) to Jonathan Swift's *Gulliver's Travels* (1726) to Aldous Huxley's *Brave New World* (1932) to George Orwell's *1984* (1949), have their roots in the ideal city brought to life by Socrates, Glaucon, and

Adeimantus. Contemporary films such as *Gattaca* (1997) and *The Matrix* (1999) may not owe direct inspiration to *Republic*, but they participate in a long tradition of artistic works that ultimately trace their concerns back to the political, social, and metaphysical issues raised in *Republic*. Robert Pirsig's *Zen and the Art of Motorcycle Maintenance* (1974) represents a different type of inventively constructed narrative that looks critically at the formulations of Platonic philosophy and the influence that Plato has had on subsequent ages.

The field of philosophy has greatly changed since Plato began to teach near the shrine of Academus on the outskirts of Athens. It has evolved into a complex and sophisticated discipline that deals with issues and problems that Plato and his contemporaries would have been unable to conceive of, much less address. Nonetheless, as Alfred North Whitehead has suggested, the philosophical studies pursued today in Europe, Britain, and the United States are (still) deeply indebted to Plato. Most basically, Plato seems to deserve much credit for establishing that it is appropriate and meaningful for "philosophers"—in the name of the "love of wisdom" (*philosophia*)—to pursue a variety of interests, from ethics to political theory to metaphysics to epistemology to theology to logic, and to discover for themselves the modes of expression that best permit them to convey their ideas.

COMMENTS & QUESTIONS

In this section, we aim to provide the reader with an array of per-spectives on the text, as well as questions which challenge those perspectives. The commentary has been culled from sources as di-verse as reviews contemporaneous with the work, letters written by the author, literary criticism of later generations, and apprecia-tions written throughout the work's history. Following the com-mentary, a series of questions seeks to filter Plato's Republic *through a variety of voices and bring about a richer understanding of this enduring work.*

Comments

ARISTOTLE (384–322 B.C.E.)

The members of a state must either have (1) all things or (2) nothing in common, or (3) some things in common and some not. That they should have nothing in common is clearly impossible, for the consti-tution is a community, and must at any rate have a common place—one city will be in one place, and the citizens are those who share in that one city. But should a well-ordered state have all things, as far as may be, in common, or some only and not others? For the citizens might conceivably have wives and children and property in com-mon, as Socrates proposes in the *Republic* of Plato. Which is better, our present condition, or the proposed new order of society?

There are many difficulties in the community of women. And the principle on which Socrates rests the necessity of such an in-stitution evidently is not established by his arguments. . . .

We ought to reckon, not only the evils from which the citizens will be saved, but also the advantages which they will lose. The life which they are to lead appears quite impracticable. The error of Socrates must be attributed to the false notion of unity from which he starts. Unity there should be, both of the family and of the state, but in some respects only. For there is a point at which a state may attain such a degree of unity as to be no longer a state, or at which, without actually ceasing to exist, it will become an inferior state.

—from book II, 1260b27–61a12, and 1263b29–34 in *Politics*, translated by Benjamin Jowett, Oxford: Clarendon Press (1905)

PLUTARCH (C.50–120 C.E.)

It is unlikely that either the Romans or the Greeks will find fault with the Academy, since in this book, which presents the *Lives* of Dion and Brutus, each nation receives very similar treatment. Dion was a disciple of Plato who knew the philosopher personally, while Brutus was nurtured on his doctrines, so that both men were trained in the same wrestling school, one might say, to take part in the struggle for supreme power. There is a remarkable similarity in many of their actions, and so we should not be surprised that they often illustrate a particular conviction of their teacher of virtue, namely that power and good fortune must be accompanied by wisdom and justice if a man's political actions are to be seen as noble as well as great.

—from "Dion," chapter 1, in *The Age of Alexander: Nine Greek Lives by Plutarch*, translated by Ian Scott-Kilvert, Harmondsworth, UK: Penguin Books, 1973

DESIDERIUS ERASMUS (C.1466–1536)

Surely you don't believe that there is any difference between those who sit in Plato's cave gazing in wonder at the images and likenesses of various things—as long as they desire nothing more and are no less pleased—and that wiseman who left the cave and sees things as they really are?

—from *The Praise of Folly* (1509), translated by Clarence H. Miller, New Haven, CT: Yale University Press, 1979

GEORG WILHELM FRIEDRICH HEGEL (1770–1831)

Plato's *Republic*, which passes proverbially as an empty ideal, is in essence nothing but an interpretation of the nature of Greek ethical life. Plato was conscious that there was breaking into that life in his own time a deeper principle which could appear in it directly only as a longing still unsatisfied, and so only as something corruptive. To combat it, he needs must have sought aid from that very longing itself. But this aid had to come from on High and all that Plato could do was to seek it in the first place in a particular external form of that same Greek ethical life. By that means he thought to master this corruptive invader, and thereby he did fatal injury to the deeper impulse which underlay it, namely free infinite personality. Still, his genius is proved by the fact that the principle on which the distinctive character of his Idea of the state turns is precisely the pivot on which the impending world revolution turned at that time.

—from the preface to *Hegel's Philosophy of Right* (1821),
translated by T. M. Knox,
Oxford: Clarendon Press, 1942

FRIEDRICH VON SCHLEGEL (1772–1829)
Plato's philosophy is a dignified preface to future religion.

—from "Selected Ideas," in *Dialogue on Poetry and
Literary Aphorisms* (1797–1800),
translated by Ernst Behler and Roman Struc,
University Park: Pennsylvania State University Press, 1968

RALPH WALDO EMERSON (1803–1882)
Out of Plato come all things that are still written and debated among men of thought. Great havoc makes he among our originalities. We have reached the mountain from which all these boulders were detached. The Bible of the learned for twenty-two hundred years, every brisk young man who says in succession fine things to each reluctant generation,—Boethius, Rabelais, Erasmus, Bruno, Locke, Rousseau, Alfieri, Coleridge,—is some reader of Plato, translating into the vernacular, wittily, his best things. Even the men of grander proportion suffer some deduction from the misfortune (shall I say?) of coming after this exhausting generalizer. St. Augustine, Copernicus, Newton, Behmen, Swedenborg, Goethe, are likewise his debtors and must say after him. For it is fair to credit the broadest generalizer with all the particulars deducible from his thesis. Plato is philosophy, and philosophy, Plato.

—from "Plato; or The Philosopher,"
in *Representative Men* (1850),
J. M. Dent & Sons, 1908

SØREN KIERKEGAARD (1813–1855)

What Socrates really meant by wanting to have "the poets" expelled from the state was that by writing in the medium of the imagination instead of precipitating men into ethical realization in actuality, the poets spoiled them and weaned them or kept them from it. One could be tempted by and large to make the same charge against "pastors" today. Yes, compared to Socrates Plato himself is a misunderstanding. Only Socrates managed to hold his uncompromising position of continually expressing the existential, constantly remaining in the present—thus he had no doctrine, no system and the like, but had one in action. Plato took his time—with the help of this enormous illusion there came to be a doctrine. By degrees the existential disappeared from view and the doctrine grew dogmatically broader and broader.

> —from "Socrates," vol. 4, entry 4275,
> in *Søren Kierkegaard's Journals and Papers*,
> edited and translated by Howard V. Hong and
> Edna H. Hong, Bloomington:
> Indiana University Press, 1975

KARL MARX (1818–1883)

Plato's Republic, in so far as division of labour is treated in it, as the formative principle of the State, is merely the Athenian idealisation of the Egyptian system of castes, Egypt having served as the model of an industrial country to many of his contemporaries also, amongst others to Isocrates, and it continued to have this importance to the Greeks of the Roman Empire.

> —from part 4, chapter 14, section 5, in *Capital:*
> *A Critique of Political Economy* (1867–1894),
> translated by Samuel Moore and Edward Aveling and
> edited by Frederick Engels,
> New York: Modern Library, 1906

FRIEDRICH NIETZSCHE (1844–1900)

It was *modesty* that in Greece coined the word "philosopher" and left the extraordinary insolence of calling oneself wise to the actors of the spirit—the modesty of such monsters of pride and conceit as Pythagoras, as Plato.

—from book 5, number 351, in *The Gay Science* (1882),
edited by Bernard Williams and
translated by Josefine Nauckhoff, Cambridge and
New York: Cambridge University Press, 2001

RICHARD GARNETT (1835–1906)

In estimating the *Republic*'s place in the history of thought we must take into account the circumstances under which it was composed. The exact date is uncertain, but whether it existed in the form of a book by 393 B.C. or not, its ideals certainly then existed in Plato's mind and were known to his fellow-citizens, for the community of goods and the community of women are ridiculed in the *Ecclesiazusae* of Aristophanes, acted in that year. As a young man Plato had passed through terrible experiences, the complete shipwreck of the vessel of State by the disastrous termination of the Peloponnesian War, the atrocities of the oligarchical party who thereupon gained dominion in Athens, and the unjust execution of his own adored master by an ignorant and misguided democracy. Such events were well calculated to engender in Plato's mind a distrust of all existing political systems, and to set him upon seriously projecting something to replace them. Ever since, the creation of ideal communities has been the frequent amusement of superior minds, and although every such endeavour has but strengthened the conviction that, as a matter of fact, the development of society must proceed upon the lines marked out for it from the beginning, in these, nevertheless, the aspiration after something

> Too bright and good
> For human nature's daily food

is no unimportant factor. The winged genius which in ancient works of art accompanies the chariot of hero or demi-god adds nothing to the power or the speed, but stimulates the ardour of the charioteer.

Plato is broadly distinguished from his successors, More, Campanella, Bacon, Brockden Brown, etc., and his later self in his

Critias, in this respect, that whereas these represent their ideal communities as already existing and only needing to be described, his Republic exists merely in thought, and not even there until it has been provided with a sound basis by a preliminary discussion of the abstract principles of justice. "Nothing actually existing in the world," says [translator Benjamin] Jowett, "at all resembles Plato's ideal State, nor does he himself imagine that such a state is possible."

—from "Plato's 'Republic,'" in *Modern English Essays*, vol. 2,
London and Toronto: J. M. Dent and Sons, 1922

T. HERBERT WARREN (1853–1930)

The *Republic* [is] the greatest of Plato's dialogues, because it is the most Platonic, because it exhibits best the peculiar merit of Plato, adequacy of style to subject, of manner to matter; because, while the matter is profoundly difficult and varied, the artistic handling, both as a whole and in detail, does not sink under this difficulty and variety, is not overlaid or embarrassed by it, but rises to it, is equal to it, and expresses and conveys it with the grace and ease of complete mastery.

The matter of the *Republic* is great. Its scope is nothing less than the whole of life and its surroundings in the world, aye, and in the other, beginning before the cradle, and extending beyond the grave.

How, placed as we are, shall we live best? How are we to make the best of one or of both worlds? What is right to do? What is the most perfect state of human society and life we can imagine if our dreams could come true?

This, under its many forms, and with all that it involves, is the grand question that is asked in the *Republic* as a practical question, and answered as a practical question, or if partly in dreaming, then with such dreams as are the inspiration of waking moments, when

> "Tasks in hours of insight willed
> Can be through hours of gloom fulfilled."

For this is the secret of Plato, that he is a dreamer, but a dreamer who is also a man of the world who has known men and cities, kings and councils, and peoples.

—from his introduction to *Republic*,
London: Macmillan, 1888

ALFRED NORTH WHITEHEAD (1861–1947)
The safest general characterization of the European philosophical tradition is that it consists of a series of footnotes to Plato.

—from part 2, chapter 1, section 1,
in *Process and Reality*, New York:
Macmillan, 1929

WILLIAM BUTLER YEATS (1865–1939)
It is terrible to desire and not possess, and terrible to possess and not desire. Because of these we long for an age which has that unity which Plato somewhere defined as sorrowing and rejoicing over the same things.

—from a letter to Olivia Shakespear (May 25, 1933),
in *Collected Letters of William Butler Yeats*,
vol. 3 edited by John Kelly,
Oxford: Clarendon Press, 1997

ERICH KAHLER (1885–1970)
Plato's was essentially a dualistic theory. To him, the divine ideas, the universals, the general qualities, the genera, were the only real beings, that, like the deities, had an absolute, independent existence. God himself was the supreme idea. The man, the animal, the beautiful, the good, the brave, and so on, represented realities, the archetypes of life of which the individuals, the earthly forms of those general qualities, as they appeared in daily life, were mere shadows and faint replicas.

—from "Reason and Science,"
in *Man the Measure: A New Approach to History*,
New York: Pantheon Books, 1943

HANNAH ARENDT (1906–1975)
Our tradition of political thought had its definite beginning in the teachings of Plato and Aristotle. I believe it came to a no less definite end in the theories of Karl Marx.

—from "Tradition and the Modern Age,"
in *Between Past and Future*,
New York: Penguin Books, 1954

Questions

1. What perspectives on justice and its relationship to happiness emerge from *Republic*? Do you think that Socrates and his companions make a convincing case for understanding justice as something that is concerned "not with the outward man, but with the inward, which is the true self and concernment of man" (4.443c–d)? How would you respond to the claim that the just man is someone who "does not permit the several elements within him to interfere with one another, or any of them to do the work of others" and who "sets in order his own inner life" (4.443d)?

2. Are you convinced that justice, as Socrates and his companions define it, is something intrinsically valuable? Are you convinced that the just man can be "happy" even if he does not enjoy a reputation for justice, nor any other material benefit?

3. Have Socrates and his companions persuaded you that the ideal city-state they describe in *Republic* is truly the best political community possible? Why or why not? If you are not convinced, how would you respond to their arguments?

4. Do Socrates' arguments for the censorship of poetry and music still hold water? Is he correct in asserting that "when modes of music change, the fundamental laws of the State always change with them," and does he seem to have a point in claiming that artistic innovation "is full of danger to the whole State" (4.424c)? Why or why not? If you are not convinced by his arguments for censoring and controlling artistic expression, how would you counter them?

5. Is there anything of value in the critique of democracy that emerges in *Republic*, especially in 8.555b–558c? How do you respond to Socrates' estimation that the "democratic constitution" is second only to tyranny in its dysfunction?

FOR FURTHER READING

Editions (with Greek Texts and English Commentaries)

Readers who do not know Greek may find the introductions and commentaries in these editions useful. Those by Halliwell and Murray are accessible and interesting.

Adam, James, ed. *The* Republic *of Plato.* Second edition. Introduction by D. A. Rees. Cambridge: Cambridge University Press, 1963.

Halliwell, Stephen, ed. *Plato:* Republic *10.* Warminster, UK: Aris and Philips, 1988.

————. *Plato:* Republic *5.* Warminster, UK: Aris and Philips, 1993.

Jowett, Benjamin, and Lewis Campbell, eds. *Plato's* Republic. 3 vols. Oxford: Clarendon Press, 1894. Reprinted New York and London: Garland Publishing, 1987.

Murray, Penelope, ed. *Plato on Poetry:* Ion; Republic *376e–398b9;* Republic *595–608b10.* Cambridge: Cambridge University Press, 1996.

Translations

Bloom, Allan, trans. *The* Republic *of Plato.* New York: Basic Books, 1991.

Cooper, John M., trans. *Plato: Complete Works.* D. S. Hutchinson, associate editor. Indianapolis. Hackett Publishing Company, 1997.

Grube, G. M. A., trans. *Plato:* Republic. Revised by C. D. C. Reeve. Indianapolis: Hackett Publishing Company, 1992. Also in John M. Cooper, trans., *Plato: Complete Works* (see above), pp. 971–1223.

Lee, Desmond, trans. *Plato:* The Republic. New York and London:

Penguin Books, 2003. Reissue of 1955 edition with updated bibliography.

Shorey, Paul, trans. *Plato:* Republic. 2 vols. London, New York, and Cambridge, MA: W. Heinemann, G. P. Putnam's Sons, and Harvard University Press (Loeb Classical Library), 1930–1935.

Interpretative Guides to the Republic

Annas, Julia. *An Introduction to Plato's* Republic. Oxford: Clarendon Press, 1981.

Baracchi, Claudia. *Of Myth, Life, and War in Plato's* Republic. Bloomington: Indiana University Press, 2002.

Howland, Jacob. The Republic: *The Odyssey of Philosophy.* New York: Twayne Publishers, 1993.

Pappas, Nickolas. *Routledge Philosophy Guidebook to Plato and the* Republic. Second edition. New York and London: Routledge, 2003.

White, Nicholas. *A Companion to Plato's Republic.* Oxford: Blackwell Press, 1979.

Critical Works on Plato

Annas, Julia, and Christopher Rowe, eds. *New Perspectives on Plato, Modern and Ancient.* Cambridge, MA: Harvard University Press, 2002.

Blondell, Ruby. *The Play of Character in Plato's Dialogues.* Cambridge: Cambridge University Press, 2002.

Guthrie, W. K. C. *A History of Greek Philosophy* (Vol. 4: *Plato*). Cambridge and New York: Cambridge University Press, 1969.

Hobbs, Angela. *Plato and the Hero: Courage, Manliness, and the Impersonal Good.* Cambridge and New York: Cambridge University Press, 2000.

Irwin, Terence. *Plato's Ethics.* New York and Oxford: Oxford University Press, 1995.

Kahn, Charles H. *Plato and the Socratic Dialogue: The Philosophical Use of a Literary Form.* Cambridge: Cambridge University Press, 1996.

Morgan, Kathryn A. *Myth and Philosophy from the Pre-Socratics to Plato*. Cambridge: Cambridge University Press, 2000.

Nails, Debra. *Agora, Academy, and the Conduct of Philosophy* (Philosophical Studies Series, 63). Dordrecht, Netherlands, Boston, and London: Kluwer Academic Publishers, 1995.

———. *The People of Plato: A Prosopography of Plato and Other Socratics*. Indianapolis: Hackett Publishing Company, 2002.

Nightingale, Andrea Wilson. *Genres in Dialogue: Plato and the Construct of Philosophy*. Cambridge: Cambridge University Press, 1995.

———. "On Wandering and Wondering: *Theôria* in Greek Philosophy and Culture." *Arion* 9.2 (third series; Fall 2001), pp. 23–58.

Philosophy Before Plato

Guthrie, W. K. C. *A History of Greek Philosophy* (Vol. 3: *The Sophists and Socrates*). Cambridge: Cambridge University Press, 1969.

Kerferd, G. *The Sophistic Movement*. Cambridge: Cambridge University Press, 1981.

McKirahan, Richard D., Jr. *Philosophy Before Socrates: An Introduction with Text and Commentary*. Indianapolis: Hackett Publishing Company, 1994.

Background on Greek and Athenian Culture

Davies, J. K. *Democracy and Classical Greece*. Cambridge, MA: Harvard University Press, 1993.

Ober, Josiah. *Political Dissent in Democratic Athens: Intellectual Critics of Popular Rule*. Princeton, NJ: Princeton University Press, 1998.

Pomeroy, Sarah, and Stanley M. Burstein, Walter Donlan, Jennifer Tolbert Roberts. *Ancient Greece: A Political, Social, and Cultural History*. Oxford, and New York: Oxford University Press, 1999.

West, M. L. *Ancient Greek Music*. Oxford: Oxford University Press, 1992.

INDEX

O

P

R